Food Cultures of the World Encyclopedia

Food Cultures of the World Encyclopedia

ASIA AND OCEANIA

Volume 3

KEN ALBALA, EDITOR

 GREENWOOD

AN IMPRINT OF ABC-CLIO, LLC
Santa Barbara, California • Denver, Colorado • Oxford, England

Library of Congress Cataloging-in-Publication Data

Food cultures of the world encyclopedia / Ken Albala, editor.
    v. cm.
   Includes bibliographical references and index.
   ISBN 978-0-313-37626-9 (hard copy : alk. paper) — ISBN 978-0-313-37627-6 (ebook) 1. Food habits—Encyclopedias. 2. Food preferences—Encyclopedias. I. Albala, Ken, 1964–
   GT2850.F666 2011
   394.1'2003—dc22   2010042700

ISBN: 978-0-313-37626-9
EISBN: 978-0-313-37627-6

15 14 13 12 11   1 2 3 4 5

This book is also available on the World Wide Web as an eBook.
Visit www.abc-clio.com for details.

Greenwood
An Imprint of ABC-CLIO, LLC

ABC-CLIO, LLC
130 Cremona Drive, P.O. Box 1911
Santa Barbara, California 93116-1911

This book is printed on acid-free paper ∞

Manufactured in the United States of America

The publisher has done its best to make sure the instructions and/or recipes in this book are correct. However, users should apply judgment and experience when preparing recipes, especially parents and teachers working with young people. The publisher accepts no responsibility for the outcome of any recipe included in this volume.

Contents

List of Abbreviations

c = cup

fl oz = fluid ounce

gal = gallon

in. = inch

lb = pound

mL = milliliter

oz = ounce

pt = pint

qt = quart

tbsp = tablespoon

tsp = teaspoon

Preface

This encyclopedia is the culmination of nearly a decade's work on the *Food Culture around the World* series. As that project expanded to 20 volumes, we realized that many peoples and places, fascinating and important in their own right, had not been covered. Considering that the cultural study of food has become more sophisticated and comprehensive over the past decade, that food has become a legitimate academic topic in curricula at every level of education, and that we seem to become more obsessed with food every day, we recognized that we simply could not leave out much of the planet. The only way to satisfy this growing demand is the set you see before you, which includes material covered in the series plus new articles that span the globe. We have gathered food scholars from around the world—people whose passion and expertise have given them deep insight into the ingredients, cooking methods, and ways of eating and thinking about food in their respective countries.

A number of questions regarding breadth and depth naturally arose in planning this work, particularly about the level of analysis for each article. Could we do justice to the vast array of distinct cuisines on earth? Could we include regional coverage for well-recognized food cultures? That is, rather than the nation-state as the criterion for inclusion, why not add Alsace, Provence, and Burgundy with France, or Sichuan, Hunan, and Canton with China? It became apparent that we would need another 20 volumes or risk very brisk, superficial coverage and that as arbitrary as the construction of nation-states has been historically, in particular the way minority cultures have tended to be obscured, the best way to organize this encyclopedia was by nation. Regional variations and minority groups can, of course, be discussed within the framework of nation-based articles. On the other hand, some groups frankly demanded separate entries—those who stood out as unique and distinct from the majority culture in which they happen politically to be included, or in some cases those people who either transcend national boundaries or even those very small places, whose great diversity demanded separate coverage as truly different from the culture around them. Thus we include the Basques separate from Spain and France, and the Hmong. We have not, however, included every single people merely on the basis of national status. This should not be taken to suggest that these cultures are unimportant but merely that many places share a common culture with those around them, though divided by national borders. In such cases we have provided cross-references. This seemed a preferable solution to suffering repetitiveness or unmanageable size.

The format for each entry also raised many questions. "Eating Out," for example, is simply not relevant in some places on earth. Would forcing each article into a common structure ultimately do injustice to the uniqueness of each culture? In the end it seemed that the ability to conduct cross-cultural analysis proved one of the most valuable assets of this set, so that one could easily compare what's for lunch in Brazil or Brunei. Moreover, tracing the various global currents of influence has been made possible since a shared set of parameters places each article on a common footing. We can trace, for example, the culinary influence of various peoples as they spread around the world. In this respect this work is unique. There are several excellent food encyclopedias on the market, all of which cover individual ingredients, topical themes, cooking methods, and sometimes recipes. None, however, treats individual food cultures as discrete units of analysis, and for students hoping to find an in-depth but succinct description of places, or for those hoping to compare a single food topic across cultures, this is the only source to which they can turn. We anticipate that this work will be invaluable for students, scholars, food writers, as well as that indomitable horde popularly known as foodies.

The other major question in designing this encyclopedia was how to define what exactly constitutes a *food culture*. This term should be distinguished from *cuisine,* which refers only to the cooking, serving, and appreciation of food. Naturally we include this within each entry and in doing so have taken the broadest possible definition of the term *cuisine.* That is, if a people cooks and recognizes a common set of recipes and discusses them with a common vocabulary, then it should be deemed a cuisine. Thus there is no place on earth without a cuisine. A nation, continent, region, and even a small group may share a common cuisine. This encyclopedia, however, covers much more. It explores the social context of consumption, the shared values and symbolic meanings that inform food choices, and the rituals and daily routine—indeed everything that constitutes a food culture. Thus we include religion, health, mealtimes, and special occasions, as well as the way certain foods confer status or have meanings beyond simple sensory gratification. Nor have we neglected the gastronomic angle, as recipes are an essential expression of what people think is good to eat, and their popularity is the outcome of decisions made at every level of society, from the farmer who grows food, and the environment and material resources that make it possible, to the government policy that promotes certain ingredients, to the retailers who market them, to the technologies by which they are transformed, and to the individual preference of family members at the level of the household. To this end we have added food culture snapshots to each entry, which puts a human face on the broader topics under discussion.

As with the series that preceded this encyclopedia, our aim is to present the panoply of human experience through the lens of food in an effort to better understand and appreciate our differences. We will find remarkably common experiences among us, especially as the world increasingly falls under the sway of corporate multinational food industries, but we will also find deep, profound, and persistent distinctions, ones that should and must be preserved because they are essential to who were are and how we define ourselves. These are differences that should not be effaced nor lost as our tastes become increasingly cosmopolitan. I hope that in reading these articles you find, like me, that the world is a marvelously diverse place and what people eat tells us about them in such an immediate and palpable way that in a certain sense you feel you know the people at some level. This, of course, is the first step toward understanding, appreciating, and living with each other peacefully on this small lump of turf we call earth.

Ken Albala
University of the Pacific

Aboriginal Australians

Overview

The Commonwealth of Australia is an island country located between the Indian and South Pacific Oceans. It is comprised of the continental mainland, the island of Tasmania, and several smaller surrounding islands. Consisting of six states, Australia is the world's sixth-largest country, just slightly smaller than the continental United States. The continent was inhabited by Aboriginal settlers from Southeast Asia up to 60,000 years ago. The British took possession of the country in the late 18th century and turned it into a prison colony for their criminals, and Australia officially became a country in 1901.

The majority of the country's population is concentrated along the southeastern and eastern coasts. The central region is sparsely populated because of its dry, desert environment. As a whole, the country receives very little rainfall and struggles to manage its limited freshwater resources. The country boasts more than 21 million citizens, with indigenous Australians making up only 1 percent of the population, just over 500,000 people.

Indigenous Australians are defined as those whose ancestors lived on the continent and its neighboring islands before British colonists began to arrive in the 17th century. The Northern Territory has the highest proportion of Aboriginal Australians among its population, and the state of Victoria has the lowest. The percentage of Aboriginal Australians living in remote areas of Australia is just slightly lower than for Aboriginal Australians who dwell in or near urban settings.

Aboriginal Australians' diets vary by location. Generally, the closer a family lives to an urban center, the more processed, Western-style foods they consume. The farther a family lives from a city, the more likely they are to supplement the processed, Western foods they consume with traditional foods and cooking methods.

Food Culture Snapshot

Jack and Ann Smith are Aboriginal Australians who live with their two children, Nicole and Jonah, and Jack's unemployed brother, Mark, in a modest neighborhood in Walkerville, South Australia, a suburb northeast of the city of Adelaide. A few years back, Jack and Ann moved their family closer to the city from the bush, or the desert region where the nomadic Aboriginal populations traditionally lived. In Walkerville, Jack works as a mechanic, and Ann has a job as a housekeeper. Still, they struggle to pay the bills and buy groceries every month because they make nearly 50 percent less than the average nonindigenous Australian family does. This lower-class lifestyle affects their diet, which incorporates many processed, fatty Western foods and very few traditional foods and cooking methods. However, processed foods are not new to the Aboriginal Australian diet; since the late 18th century, in the bush, nearly everyone has relied on government rations of processed food to survive as European settlement killed off more and more natural food sources. The only difference now is that there is a much larger selection to choose from.

For daily breakfasts, Ann makes sure to stock up on plenty of fresh fruit for a family favorite, fruit salad with cream and sugar, which Jack eats before heading to work at 6 A.M. She also stocks up on cream, as the rest of the family loves it on top of cereal with fruit juice when they wake up at 7 A.M. for school. Mark, Jack's brother, typically gets the children ready for school so Ann can leave for work at 6:30 A.M. He spends the rest of his day doing chores around the house for the family to help contribute.

Most of the family eats lunch out during the day. Jack and Ann often buy meat pies from convenience stores during work around noon, and the children purchase chicken nuggets and toasted cheese sandwiches from their school cafeteria. The children also drink off-brand sodas with fruit flavors like passion fruit and mango or their favorite juice, Ribena, which is made from black currants. Mark is the only one who eats lunch at home, and he typically makes himself a *snag on the dag,* which is a pork sausage that is quickly grilled and served in a piece of white sandwich bread with barbecue sauce.

At dinnertime, Nicole and Jonah beg their mother to cook frozen French fries sprinkled with chicken salt, which is chicken-flavored salt. Ann gets out pre-formed frozen hamburger patties that she throws on the family grill and a bag of frozen mixed vegetables that she heats in the microwave. For a treat, especially on the weekends, Ann uses all-purpose flour and butter to make *quandong* crumble from the country's wild native peach.

Quandong Crumble

Filling

1 c dried quandongs, rehydrated in water overnight

1 c peeled, chopped apple

½ c water

¾ c sugar

1 tbsp fresh lemon juice

1 tbsp cornstarch or arrowroot

Crumble Topping

½ stick cold butter (2 oz), chopped into cubes

1⅓ c flour

¼ c rolled oats

3 tbsp sugar

½ tsp ground cinnamon

Preheat oven to 400°F. To make the crumble topping, put all of the crumble ingredients in a bowl and work them with your fingers until pea-sized bits of butter are integrated with the rest of the ingredients. Place quandong, apple, water, sugar, lemon juice, and cornstarch in a baking pan and toss to thoroughly combine. Sprinkle crumble on top of filling and bake for 45 minutes, or until filling is bubbling and thickened and crumble is browned.

Since leaving the bush three years ago, the Smith family has experienced many changes in their eating habits and cooking methods. While he was growing up in the outback, Jack's mother would grab one of the chooks (chickens) they raised in their backyard and slaughter it before dinner. When Jack brought home a live chook recently, both of his children cried for hours after the slaughter. The older Smiths miss the days when a few hours of hunting would yield a kangaroo; these days, money is the only currency that will buy them meat. A special meal used to mean freshly caught echidna (porcupine) cooked in a ground oven and johnnycakes (a campfire flatbread) shared with several other families, but today, a special monthly treat is an intimate meal with the immediate family at the local Mackas (McDonald's) for burgers, fries, and Happy Meals.

Major Foodstuffs

Aboriginal Australians have the oldest living culinary tradition in the world. They are believed to have entered northern Australia 40,000–60,000 years ago. From there, Aboriginal families and clans spread across the country, each adapting to wildly different climates and environments, from humid rain forests to achingly dry deserts, from sunny coastlines to snowy mountaintops. Due to such an assortment of climates and settings, it is difficult to generalize about early Aboriginal cuisine.

However, a few commonalities were shared by almost all Aboriginal clans before the Europeans settled in Australia in the year 1788. Early Aboriginal clans were hunter-gatherers who moved frequently based on food supplies. Their diet consisted of over 1,000 different plants and a variety of wild animals. It was largely vegetarian with the occasional infusion of meat and had a heavy focus on grains. Women and children gathered plants (nuts, tubers, seeds, and fruit), caught small animals, and fished, which accounted for a majority of the clan's diet. Men were responsible for hunting large and small animals, including kangaroos, emus, wild birds, bandicoots (mouse-sized marsupials), and turtles.

Variations existed based on region, with desert clans dining on *witchetty* grubs (moth larvae) and flying foxes (bats) and coastal clans serving shellfish, stingrays, and oysters. To catch their meals, they would use spears, sharpened animal bones, nets, or whatever they could fashion or use from their surroundings. Almost all Aboriginal communities made some form of flatbread on their campfires, commonly known as damper. To make most dampers, they would gather seeds, dry them, and then grind them when they needed flour. The result was much heartier than the wheat-flour damper of today and was also very nourishing.

After European settlement, foodstuffs available to Aboriginal Australians changed drastically, altering their basic diet. As land was cleared for more settlement, crops, and livestock, more wild Australian plant and animal foods were destroyed or displaced, affecting the availability of traditional Aboriginal food sources. To account for this gap in their natural diet, the government assisted Aboriginals with rations of processed, Western, high-fat foods, which still account for a majority of their food today. Traditional foods and cooking methods are still used but only by those families living remotely and only as a supplement to the high-calorie, low-nutrient processed food they regularly eat.

Cooking

Traditional Aboriginal Australian cooking was viewed by Europeans as simple, but it was very time- and labor-intensive and required many skills from the clan cook. These abilities included adapting to different weather and environments, getting creative when tools or new cooking methods were needed, knowing which kind of wood works with which sort of food, and so on. Some plants and fruits were edible in their raw state, but several required cooking in hot ashes or soaking in water to improve digestibility or to leach out toxins in the food. For instance, *munja* seeds, or kernels from the cycad palm, were great for drying and grinding into flour, but fresh munja contains a poisonous acid. Aboriginals would cut the seed into thin slices with a sharpened kangaroo-bone blade and dry the pieces. When they needed flour, they would soak the pieces in water until the acid was released and then grind them into flour for bread making. This and other traditional cooking methods were passed down to their children through songs, along with an oral history of their culture.

Their cooking equipment and methods were quite rudimentary and yet sophisticated; they could steam and smoke food in an earth oven or char it in an ash oven, grill it over hot ashes, bake it in hot ashes (parching), or roast it on hot coals (mainly reserved for small animals and seafood). For example, to cook damper or other flatbreads, a cook would build a large fire, scrape aside the hot coals, set the dough in the center of the fire, and then top the dough with hot coals and ashes to bake.

To cook a kangaroo, they would build a ground oven by digging a shallow hole and starting a wood fire in it. Stones would be placed on top of the fire, and when the fire burned down and the stones were hot, soaked branches were placed on top. The branches would start steaming, and then the meat would be placed on top and covered with more hot stones, wet leaves, and paper bark to make an airtight seal until the meat was cooked. Cooking equipment had to be light, portable, and made from the land, like *coolamons* (vessels) made from bark or tree gnarls.

For the modern, remote-living Aboriginal family, some aspects of their modern cookery reflect traditional as well as Western cooking methods, like using the Western methods of boiling and frying over a traditional open fire. How remote a particular

Aboriginal community is will determine what sort of cooking equipment is available. Many remote areas have no running water or electricity. If a family is lucky enough to have a kerosene-run refrigerator, it breaks often, or funds are too short to run it all the time. A camp might have a small propane cooktop, but typically Aboriginals rely on cooking over an open campfire or use ready-made convenience foods that require little to no cooking, purchased from a station store or a monthly mail truck. After European settlement, certain cooking equipment was introduced into remote Aboriginal communities to make open-fire cooking easier, like shovels for handling fires and making damper and cast iron or steel camp ovens (a three-legged pot with a lid that acts as an oven when placed into hot coals).

Damper Bread

Ingredients

1 c self-rising flour

Dash of salt

1 tbsp sugar

½ tsp baking soda

½ tbsp butter

½ c milk

Mix the flour with the salt, sugar, and baking soda, then rub the butter into the flour until you get pea-sized bits. Stir in milk until the mix forms into a dough. Shape into small biscuits, and bake in a 400°F oven for 15 minutes, or until bread is fully browned.

Billy cans are pots used to boil water or brew tea over open fires, and nearly every family has a coveted billy can. Aboriginals supplement processed foods by hunting and gathering native foods whenever possible, and adapting native cooking to Western cooking equipment and methods. A common sight that blends the Western and Aboriginal worlds is a campfire pot boiling a leg of kangaroo with the paw curled over the edge of the pot.

Several organizations and individuals are striving to preserve Aboriginal Australian culinary heritage. Professional chef and Aboriginal Australian Mark Olive works in remote indigenous communities, organizing workshops to reclaim traditional Aboriginal cooking methods and educating kids about these traditions as well as nutrition. Modern, non-remote-living Aboriginal families use even fewer traditional cooking methods and recipes than their remote-living brothers. The most common cooking methods involve using a microwave, a stovetop or basic oven, and the occasional barbecue grill. Since these families have easier access to a wide range of processed food and tend to own a refrigerator or freezer, frozen or premade foods like fish sticks and sausage rolls are popular. This means that instead of cooking food, only reheating is needed. While this average family tends to have better living conditions than those living in more remote locations (electricity and running water are much more common), housing and cooking equipment tend to be modest and are often in need of repair.

If a traditional Aboriginal recipe is made, the main ingredients are almost always replaced with available Western ingredients, and Western cooking methods are used; it is often for celebration or reminiscence, rather than a daily or religious sustenance. For example, a traditional Aboriginal stew might contain kangaroo or emu meat and be cooked on an open fire, but today, they might use corned beef, a preserved meat that was served at the station camps because it required no refrigeration, and a stovetop. Many modern Aboriginal families still rely on corned beef for a large quantity of their meat supply, not because of poor refrigeration but rather because these are the traditions they remember.

Typical Meals

For remote-living Aboriginal Australians, breakfast starts with leftover food from the day before. During mid- to late afternoon, they eat dinner, which consists of vegetables, grains, and occasionally meat or fish depending on the community's location and is typically prepared at the main camp. Throughout the day, they also consume snacks au naturel, eaten fresh while hunting and gathering, typically berries, nuts, insects, and plants.

Traditional Aboriginal eating habits are still factored into some modern, remote-living Aboriginal communities, which include taboos and eating order. Meat is a rare treat and carefully split up among the community based on rank. Men are favored, with the hunter giving away choice bits to his relatives, who might pass some down to the women. Offal, which is really prized, goes to the elders. The hunter may invoke a traditional law called "The Vow," where he is allowed to lay claim to a choice piece of offal, and if anyone else in the tribe eats it, they will have broken the law. Other taboos include various foods that are forbidden to be eaten based on circumstances, particularly around menstruating women and girls, and boys around the age of initiation. For example, young boys about to undergo initiation are forbidden to eat wallaby (a small relative of the kangaroo) and two kinds of bandicoot because they have been known to turn black beards brown, an unfavorable color.

Urban-living Aboriginal Australians' typical meals are most similar to a Western diet. Breakfast is often cereal with cream or whole milk, toast with Vegemite (a yeast-based spread), or a bigger fried English breakfast of sausage, tomatoes, mushrooms, fried eggs, and toast. Lunch can be fast food or something convenient and prepackaged, like meat pies and sausage rolls with tomato sauce that can be bought at gas stations and convenience stores.

Dinner is made up of cheap meats (pork, lamb, beef, and chicken are common), cooked simply—either grilled, fried (breaded meat cutlets is a popular dish), boiled, or baked—or it can consist of frozen, premade food like a frozen pizza or shepherd's pie. A few times a month, a typical family treats themselves to a meal at a fast-food restaurant.

Eating Out

Regardless of where they live, many Aboriginal Australians are classified as lower class or impoverished, so the opportunity to dine out does not come often. For remote-living Aboriginals, restaurants are few and far between in the bush, so dining out often involves picking up premade food from a local store.

For urban-dwelling Aboriginal Australians, there are certainly more opportunities to dine out, as proximity to an urban center typically means there are more restaurants, and fast-food restaurants are a popular choice. McDonald's is widely popular across Australia, as are other U.S. fast-food companies like KFC, Subway, and Burger King. Even so, an outing to a fast-food restaurant is a special occasion, because families are often large and money is scarce.

Restaurants that serve traditional Aboriginal Australian food do not really exist in Australia, and if they do, they often go out of business because the general population does not dine on native Australian ingredients or traditional Aboriginal Australian cuisine. For example, professional Aboriginal chef Mark Olive opened an indigenous Australian restaurant called The Midden in Sydney in 1996, but the restaurant lasted for only 18 months as there was not enough interest in it. Plenty of non-Aboriginal Australian chefs are using native ingredients in their cuisine but not to create Aboriginal Australian food. A lamb meat pie flavored with native lemon verbena and wattleseed (an Australian acacia) would be a good example of how chefs are utilizing native ingredients within popular European dishes. The use of native foods in restaurants is currently a trend, and often these restaurants charge far beyond an average Aboriginal's dining budget and the native population is not able to enjoy the food.

Special Occasions

Special occasions like cultural ceremonies traditionally drew together a large group of Aboriginals, so there was a great need to hold such occasions near an abundant source of food. This means many ceremonial foods were linked with seasonal abundance. For instance, spring and summer in the mountains in the states of Victoria and New South Wales yield large quantities of *bogong* moths, so ceremonies that take place during that time often occurred in the mountains so there would be a plentiful food source for the group. The moths were simply roasted and eaten whole.

Although they do not perform ceremonies nearly as frequently as their ancestors did, modern remote-living Aboriginal Australians still perform ceremonies whenever possible and try to use traditional recipes and ingredients whenever possible. For example, for the Kunapipi (Fertility Mother) ceremonies, a hearty damper is made from munja seeds; it can be stored for months before the ceremony to save time and energy. Urban Aboriginal Australians do participate in such ceremonies and foods but not nearly as often.

Diet and Health

The diet of the average Aboriginal Australian family has been modified drastically over the past 200 years; a brief history of this change is warranted to understand the modern Aboriginal Australian diet. Traditional Aboriginal Australian cuisine was based on the belief that people should live in harmony with their environment instead of damaging it, as well as a practice of seasonal eating. As hunter-gatherers, they would travel around based on the season and available food supply, and as a result, they often ate fresher food, which is healthier than processed food. This also helped prevent them from completely depleting a food supply in a single area, as they constantly moved to find new food sources. Through trial and error, they discovered foods that hurt their bodies and foods that increased their health, and they passed this knowledge down to younger generations through songs and stories.

The Europeans settled in the country in the late 18th century and took ownership of the land because they assumed it was *terra nullius,* a legal term that means "owned by no one." Aboriginal Australian clans were displaced or killed as Europeans spread out for settlements and to raise herds and grow crops. Life as hunter-gatherers taught Aboriginals to adapt to new environments, and they coped by hunting the herds and cooking them using traditional methods, as well as hunting newly introduced vermin like rabbits that were killing off native animals.

Shortly after European settlement, the newly formed government started handing out rations of Western food to displaced Aboriginal Australians, and they quickly became dependent on the handouts. Other Aboriginals were sent to work at pastoral stations where they received similar rations in exchange for work—foods they had never tried such as corned beef, flour, sugar, and tea. At this point, Aboriginal diets depended largely on how well the station stores were stocked. If the station store manager wasn't empathetic to the Aboriginals, the store would lack healthy, nutritious food, which negatively affected Aboriginal health, as the foods available were low in calcium and vitamins. They shifted from a mainly vegetarian diet to a meat-focused diet because rations rarely had fruit, vegetables, and dairy, due to poor transportation methods and a lack of refrigeration.

Families were separated, and from the late 18th through the late 19th century, Australian federal and state governments removed Aboriginal children from their homes and placed them into European Australian households, which made it difficult to pass on the oral culture and culinary traditions of their people. However, this did not eliminate Aboriginal Australian culinary culture completely; some remote-living Aboriginals adapted by finding time to hunt and gather traditional *bush tucker* (Aboriginal food) on the weekends, and when work on the stations would slow down, many would go on a walkabout, or a spiritual walk into the bush to live off the land, rebuild their health and strength, and share Aboriginal traditions.

In the late 1960s Aboriginal civil rights were finally recognized, and government control over where they lived and moved was taken away. Many Aboriginal Australian workers were let go from their station jobs and forced to live in fringe camps and be on welfare, which only further cemented their dependence on processed foods that were cheap and easily available in local stores. There was also a decline in gathering bush tucker, which was exacerbated by the ongoing clearing of land for more settlement areas.

From the 1960s until the present, Aboriginal clans and families have taken various paths that have ultimately led them to one of two destinations: living in a rural, remote Aboriginal community, often close to the outback, or moving closer to cities and towns and attempting to assimilate even more into Western society. Those who created their own remote Aboriginal communities still rely on station stores or monthly mail trucks for their food supplies. Canned fruit, powdered milk, rice, and canned meat are staples in a modern remote Aboriginal diet. But ever-adaptive, remote-living Aboriginals have combined parts of Western culture with their traditional culture, supplementing processed foods with Aboriginal foods and cooking methods whenever possible. Many families adapt popular recipes from other ethnic cuisines to their native food supply and cooking methods, and curried *gulah,* or spaghetti and kangaroo meatballs, is commonly found in modern Aboriginal campsites. Bush plum pudding is another common recipe found in campsites during the holidays, an Aboriginal take on the popular British Christmas dish.

Those Aboriginal families who chose to live closer to Western society had better exposure to food sources in the form of grocery stores, which meant direct access to fresh fruit, vegetables, and dairy. But meat and sugar still play a significant role in their diet, just as they did at the pastoral stations. Even though Aboriginals living in a nonremote area can now self-select their diet for the first time in 100 years, they still cling to their learned pastoral station diets because that is what they know. Fast-food outlets are also finding their way into the average modern nonremote Aboriginal diet. Almost all of these communities (remote and nonremote) are lower class or impoverished, so food supplies vary based on the money a family or community can generate at any given time.

An interesting twist in the history of Aboriginal Australian cuisine is the native-foods industry of Australia. Created in the 1970s, the native-foods industry comprises indigenous Australian foods such as fruits, spices, nuts, and herbs, commercially manufactured for restaurants and gourmet stores. A positive side of the Australian native-foods industry is that it utilizes Aboriginal cultural heritage and provides Aboriginals with jobs. However, most native foods are so high priced that neither remote nor nonremote Aboriginal families can afford to work them into their regular diets.

Due to the westernization of their diets to varying degrees, both remote-living and urban-dwelling Aboriginal Australians have a number of serious health concerns, including obesity, diabetes, cardiovascular disease, and alcohol and drug abuse. As of 2005, 57 percent of Aboriginal Australians were overweight or obese regardless of whether they lived in a city or the bush. They are 1.2 times more likely to be overweight or obese compared with their nonindigenous counterparts.

Studies show that Aboriginal Australian babies are fully nourished by their mother's milk, but with so much processed food in their environment, they inevitably gain excess weight and become unhealthy when they move on to solid foods. Exercise is another large factor in why so many Aboriginals are overweight, as more than 70 percent of remote and nonremote Aboriginal Australians do little to no exercise. Diet and exercise are also contributors to the large number of Aboriginals suffering from cardiovascular disease and high blood pressure.

One group trying to make a difference in Aboriginal Australian health is the Fred Hollows Foundation, which has been collaborating with indigenous women in the Northern Territory to create a cookbook for indigenous Australians that can be used in remote communities and can help alleviate poor health due to diet. Aboriginal Australians' increased rate of obesity has led to an excessive occurrence of type 2 diabetes in the Aboriginal Australian community, making them four times more likely to develop diabetes than the nonindigenous Australian community. The first Aboriginal Australian case of diabetes occurred in 1923, but before that, there was no history of metabolic conditions among this community, as most hunter-gatherer Aboriginals were in good physical condition and their diet was healthy. After a group of diabetic Aboriginal Australians returned to a traditional lifestyle and cuisine, studies found that their health improved and their diabetes symptoms either lessened or disappeared. Alcohol is another factor in poor Aboriginal health, specifically in diabetes and cardiovascular disease. Studies have shown that although Aboriginals are less apt to drink alcohol than nonindigenous Australians, they are more prone to drink dangerous amounts of alcohol when they do imbibe. Between 2000 and 2004, injuries or diseases related to alcohol use led to the deaths of 1,145 Aboriginal Australians, with the median age of death around 35 years of age.

Leena Trivedi-Grenier

Further Reading

"Australian Indigenous Cookbook Promotes Healthy Tucker." Radio Australia Web Site. 2009. http://www.radioaustralia.net.au/pacbeat/stories/200910/s2708132.htm.

Australian Native Foods Research. Australia's Commonwealth Scientific and Industrial Research Organization's Web Site. http://www.cse.csiro.au/research/nativefoods/.

"Australia's Disturbing Health Disparities Set Aboriginals Apart." *Bulletin of the World Health Organization* 86, No. 4 (2008): 241–320.

"The Context of Indigenous Health." Australia Aboriginal Health Info Net's Web Site. January 2009. http://www.healthinfonet.ecu.edu.au/health-facts/overviews/the-context-of-indigenous-health.

D'Alusio, Faith. *Hungry Planet: What the World Eats.* Berkeley, CA: Ten Speed Press, 2005.

Dyson, Laurel Evelyn. "Indigenous Australian Cookery, Past and Present." *Journal of Australian Studies* 87 (2006): 5–18.

Haden, Roger. *Food Culture in the Pacific Islands.* Westport, CT: Greenwood Press, 2009.

Harney, Bill. *Yarns from an Aussie Bushcook.* Farmington, MI: Martensen, 1979.

Isaacs, Jennifer. *Bush Foods: Aboriginal Food and Herbal Medicine.* Sydney, Australia: Weldons, 1987.

Ramsden, Jessica. "Australia's Native Cuisine: A Study of Food in Contemporary Australian Society." Master's thesis, University of Adelaide, 2008.

Smith, Pamela A., and Richard M. Smith. "Diets in Transition: Hunter-Gatherer to Station Diet and Station Diet to the Self-Select Store Diet." *Human Ecology* 27 (1999): 115–33.

Afghanistan

Overview

Afghanistan is a landlocked, mountainous country situated at the crossroads of four major cultural areas: the Middle East, Central Asia, the Indian Subcontinent, and the Far East. It is bordered by Iran in the west, Pakistan in the south and east, Turkmenistan, Uzbekistan, and Tajikistan in the north, and China in the far northeast. Afghanistan was also a major crossroad on the ancient Silk Road that linked East and West and played a vital role in the exchange of ideas, religions, foods, and plants.

Afghanistan has had a turbulent history, which continues to the present day. Because of its geographic position Afghanistan has been invaded many times by armies from different places, each bringing its own influences on the culture. After a brief period of relative stability under King Zahir Shah (r. 1933–1973), since the late 1970s Afghanistan has suffered continuous conflict and war. The Russians invaded in 1980. After they left, the 1990s saw a brutal civil war and the rise of the Taliban. In 2001 the U.S.-led invasion toppled the Taliban, but the war against them continues.

Afghanistan, which became an Islamic Republic in 2001, has an estimated population of between 28 and 33 million. The population is made up of a number of ethnic groups, the main ones being Pashtun, Tajik, Hazara, Uzbek, Aimak, Turkmen, and Baloch. While the majority (99%) of Afghans are Muslims, there are also small pockets of Hindus and Sikhs, and there used to be a small community of Jews. Afghanistan has been a melting pot for a large number of cultures and traditions over the centuries, and the cuisine reflects its internal diversity and the tastes and flavors of its neighbors.

Food Culture Snapshot

Homayoun and Shakila live in a two-bedroom apartment in southwestern Kabul. Shakila works as a housekeeper for an Afghan engineer, and their apartment is attached to his house in the same compound. Her husband, Homayoun, is a chauffeur for the Ministry of Foreign Affairs in Kabul. They have five children, two boys and three girls, ranging from 7 to 16 years of age.

Their lifestyle is typical of an upper-working-class family in Afghanistan. Their day begins early in the morning. Shakila sends one of her children to the local bakery to buy bread (nan) for the family. With the bread they drink tea sweetened with sugar and perhaps some milk added. On special occasions they might have butter, yogurt, honey, or jam to go with the bread.

In the morning Shakila goes to the local bazaar to buy the ingredients for the main midday meal and the evening meal. The menu will be decided by what seasonal vegetables and fruits are available. She may buy meat (usually lamb) for the main dish. In winter and early spring vegetables and fruits are very limited, but onions, carrots, potatoes, cucumbers, oranges (including sour oranges), lemons, and bananas are usually available. In summer and autumn there is much more variety as eggplant, tomatoes, beans, okra, grapes, melons, watermelons, peaches, pears, apples, quinces, pomegranates, and plums come into season. In the bazaar Shakila may also buy dairy products and eggs if needed and also stock up on basic ingredients such as rice, flour, pulses, cooking oil, sugar, and tea.

Shakila tries to vary the main midday meal. Sometimes she makes a meat and vegetable soup to be eaten with nan or a rice dish, either plain white rice served with a meat or vegetable *qorma* (braised dish with yogurt and ground nuts), or a pilau (rice dish) cooked with meat or perhaps a sticky rice dish with lentils or beans called *shola*. For a change she may make *aush,* a noodle soup–like dish with beans and yogurt and flavored with mint.

Aush

Afghans often prepare this dish to help cure colds. They add plenty of garlic and lots of red pepper as they say it helps clear the head and chest. Afghans usually make their own noodles. The noodle dough is rolled out very thin, then rolled up tight and cut into fine strips with a sharp knife. The noodles are then tossed in a little flour and allowed to dry on a board. Dried noodles or ready-made fresh spaghetti, as in this recipe, can be substituted although the cooking time may vary. Canned chickpeas and kidney beans may also be substituted.

2 oz dry chickpeas

2 oz dry red kidney beans

8 oz fresh spaghetti or tagliatelle

2 c strained yogurt

Salt

Red pepper, according to taste

1 tbsp dried mint

For the Minced Meat

6 tbsp vegetable oil

2 medium onions, finely chopped

1 lb minced beef or lamb

½ c tomato juice (or water)

1 tsp ground coriander

Salt and pepper

Soak the chickpeas and beans in 4 cups water overnight.

Put the chickpeas and beans into a large pan with the water in which they were soaked and add ½ cup water. Bring to a boil, then reduce the heat and boil gently until cooked, adding extra water if necessary. Cooking time will vary according to the freshness of the pulses.

While the pulses are cooking, prepare the meat. Heat the oil in a pan over medium to high heat. Add the chopped onions, and fry over medium heat, stirring continuously until they are reddish-brown. Turn up the heat, add the meat, and stir well. Fry until brown. Add the tomato juice (or water), and bring to a boil. Add the coriander and salt and pepper to taste. Stir again, then turn down the heat and simmer for about half an hour or until the meat is cooked and the sauce is thick. Add extra water if the sauce becomes too dry.

When the meat and pulses are cooked, bring to a boil 3½ cups water in a large pan. Add salt and the noodles, and boil gently for about 10 minutes. Add the chickpeas, beans, strained yogurt, and some or all of the liquid from the chickpeas and beans, depending on how thick you want the soup. Add the dried mint, salt, and red pepper, and mix well. More water can be added if required. Leave on low heat for about 10 minutes or so to let the flavors blend. Serve the soup and top with a little of the meat. The remaining meat is served separately to be added to the top of each individual portion of aush.

The evening meal, usually eaten at around 6 or 7 P.M., generally consists of leftovers from lunch with the addition of a snack such as fried potatoes or *boulanee* (fried leek- or potato-filled pastries). Nan is served with every meal, and tea is drunk throughout the day and after every meal. When Shakila has unexpected guests, which happens quite frequently, she sends the children out to buy biscuits from the local bakery and perhaps some sweets, such as *noql* (sugared almonds). These are served with tea. For special occasions Shakila will make more elaborate food such as a pilau or the meat-filled dumpling-like steamed dish called *mantu* or the leek-filled boiled pasta *ashak*. She also likes to make a crisp sweet fried pastry called *goash-e-feel,* which means "elephant's ears." Fresh fruit is served after the meal.

Major Foodstuffs

Afghanistan is one of the poorest countries in the world, and many years of war and political instability have taken their toll, leaving the country in ruins and dependent on foreign aid. It is a land of contrasts, with vast areas of scorching, parched deserts; high, cold, inaccessible mountain regions; and extensive green valleys and plains. Generally the summers are hot and dry, and the winters are cold with heavy snowfalls, especially in the mountains. It is from the snow-capped mountains that water is available for irrigation. The plains and valleys are very fertile as long as there is water. With the diversity of its terrain and climate Afghanistan can produce a wide variety of foodstuffs.

Agriculture is the main source of income. Cereals such as wheat, corn, and barley are the chief staple crops. They are ground into flour and made into different kinds of breads and noodle-type dishes. A small amount of rice, another staple, is grown on the terraces of the Hindu Kush in the north and in the Jalalabad area in the southeast, although much has to be imported.

Vegetables, fruits, and nuts are cultivated extensively, and many are exported. Afghanistan is famous for its numerous varieties of grapes, from which green and red raisins are produced, and for its melons and watermelons. Other fruits include pomegranates, plums, mulberries, quinces, cherries, apricots, nectarines, apples, and pears. Bananas, lemons, and oranges grow in the subtropical region of Jalalabad. Vegetables include onions, potatoes, tomatoes, eggplant, *gandana* (a kind of allium similar to Chinese chives), spring onions (scallions), green beans, okra, cabbage, cauliflower, radishes, and numerous kinds of pumpkins, squashes, gourds, and zucchini. Nuts also play an important role in the Afghan diet. Walnuts, pistachios, pine nuts, and almonds are all used in cooking—in pastries, pilaus, and desserts—but they are also eaten on their own as snacks, often salted and mixed with dried fruits such as raisins and served with tea.

Afghans add spices and herbs to their food for flavor and fragrance; the results are neither too spicy nor too bland. Some spices are imported, but many herbs are grown locally. Saffron, although expensive, is the preferred spice for flavoring and coloring rice dishes and desserts. It is grown in Afghanistan, and its cultivation is being encouraged to try to persuade farmers to switch from growing poppies, which are processed into opium and are thus an enormous cash crop. Similarly, farmers are being encouraged to cultivate more quinces and pomegranates for export. Other popular spices include aniseed, cardamom, cassia and cinnamon, chilies, cloves, coriander, cumin, dill, fenugreek, ginger, nigella, black and red pepper, poppy seeds, sesame seeds, and turmeric. Asafetida, which grows profusely in the north of Afghanistan, is not used much in Afghan cooking but is an important crop, as much of it is exported to India. Herbs such as cilantro, dill, and mint are used extensively in cooking, especially in soups and stews. Garlic is also widely used. Other flavorings include rose water, especially for desserts. Roses grow abundantly in Afghanistan, and distilling rose water is a cottage industry.

Industry in Afghanistan is based on agriculture and pastoral raw materials. The major industrial crops are cotton, tobacco, madder, castor beans, and sugar. Sugar beets are grown in the north, and sugarcane is grown near Jalalabad in the southeast. *Nabot* (crystallized sugar) is a popular energy-boosting snack, especially with children. *Gur* (unrefined sugar) is used as a sweetener.

Lamb, which comes from the fat-tailed sheep, is the preferred meat, but beef, veal, goat, water buffalo, horse, and camel are also eaten. Chicken, which used to be a luxury and not always available, is liked, and today many chickens are imported (often frozen) from Iran, Pakistan, and India and are plentiful in the cities. Since Afghanistan is a Muslim country, pork is not eaten. Game meats such as quail, pigeon, duck, and partridge are eaten when available. All parts of animals are eaten including the heads, feet, and testicles. A sausage made from boiled horse meat using the innards as a casing is made and eaten by Uzbeks and Kirghiz in northern Afghanistan.

Fish is not a regular part of the Afghan diet even though many of the rivers and lakes teem with fish: brown trout, rainbow trout, *sheer mahi* (milkfish), catfish called *mahi laqa,* and carp (which were introduced to the Darunta Dam near Jalalabad with Chinese assistance in 1967). In winter some sea fish is imported from Pakistan.

Traditionally Afghans cooked with what is called *roghan-e-dumbah,* a fat rendered from the tail of the fat-tailed sheep, and *roghan-e-zard,* a clarified butter. Cottonseed oil is produced in Kunduz in the north and is used for cooking. Nowadays, much of the cooking medium is in the form of ghee (clarified butter) and vegetable oils, which are imported.

Dairy products play an important role in the Afghan diet, especially in the high mountainous areas where fresh vegetables and fruits are not readily available. Milk comes from cows, water buffalo, sheep, and goats. Most of the milk is made into butter (*maska*), cheese (*panir*), or yogurt (*mast*), which can be kept for longer periods. When the yogurt is strained, the remaining curds are called *chaka.* Chaka is often salted, dried, and formed into round balls that harden and resemble gray pebbles; these are called *quroot.* For use in cooking the quroot is reconstituted in water in a special bowl with a rough bottom surface, called a *taghora qurooti. Qymaq* is another milk product; it is a close relation to the *kaymak* of the Middle East and is similar to clotted cream. Milk is rarely drunk, but a refreshing drink called *dogh* (yogurt mixed with water and mint) is sometimes made.

Tea, green or black, is drunk copiously throughout the day and is always served after a meal. It is not usually drunk with milk except sometimes for breakfast, but it is often sweetened with sugar and flavored with cardamom. An Afghan custom is to have a first cup of tea with sugar followed by one without. Many people soak sugar cubes called *qand* in their tea and hold them in their mouths as they sip the tea. Affluent Afghans will serve fruit juices, sherbets, or bottled soft drinks, such as Coca-Cola and Fanta, with meals for guests. Bottled water (locally produced or imported) has recently become readily available in the bazaars.

Cooking

Many Afghans live in extended families, and this means that a large amount of food must be prepared each day. The shopping used to be the responsibility of the men, but recently women and children have taken on this role. The preparation and cooking of the food, which are very labor-intensive, are normally done by the female members of the household, the most senior woman usually being in charge with her female relatives helping. Affluent families have cooks, usually male, and for big parties and special occasions professional male cooks are hired.

The traditional Afghan kitchen is very basic. Few people have electric ovens, even in the cities. Cooking is done over wood or charcoal fires or in more recent times on burners fueled by bottled gas. Some large families may have a clay oven (tandoor) for baking bread. Refrigerators are also rare. Food is kept cool and fresh during the hot summer months in a range of clay pots and containers. In many households, especially in rural areas, there is no running water. All washing up is done outside, using water from a well. Sophisticated kitchen equipment such as electric mixers or grinders is practically nonexistent. Most Afghans do, however, have a range of pans (*dayg*) in different sizes, some quite large for cooking pilaus. The *awang* (mortar and pestle) is an essential piece of equipment for crushing garlic, onions, herbs, and spices, and all Afghan homes own one. Many Afghan families grind their own spice mixture called *char masala,* which is used mainly to flavor pilaus. The choice of spices varies, but the four most common ones are cassia (or cinnamon), cloves, cumin, and black cardamom seeds. Most families have a rolling pin for rolling out the dough for their pasta and noodle dishes. Affluent Afghans may have a pasta-making machine.

Afghans rarely measure out their ingredients. Recipes and techniques tend to be passed down from mother to daughter and are learned through practice and experience. Most kitchens do, however, have a range of pots with handles, called *malaqa,* which are used as measuring aids, and ordinary cups, glasses, and spoons are also used for measuring.

Food tends to be cooked slowly and for a longer time, especially meat dishes, as meat can be quite tough and this method of cooking helps brings out all the flavors of the ingredients. Some Afghans own a pressure cooker, which shortens the cooking time considerably.

Nan forms the basis of the diet of all Afghans, and it usually accompanies every meal to scoop up food or soak up juices. The word *nan* actually means "food" in Afghanistan. First thing in the morning the dough for the bread will be made. It is leavened with a fermented starter prepared from a small lump of dough from the previous day. Bread is left to rise before being baked in the tandoor or taken to the local bakery to be baked. A tandoor is a clay oven built into the ground that is capable of reaching temperatures far higher than an ordinary domestic oven does. The bread is cooked by slapping the dough onto the hot sides of the tandoor. When ready it is deftly removed using a hook or a stick. Breads are also cooked on a *tawah,* a curved, circular cast iron plate that is heated over a fire before the bread is slapped onto it and cooked on both sides. The plate is portable, and this method is especially used by the nomads. Bread cooked on a tawah is unleavened and known as chapati or *nan-e-tawagi.*

Noodle dishes are popular and resemble many of the noodle dishes found along the Silk Road. They are all made in the home, with some of the more complicated versions made only for special occasions, including mantu, which is closely related to the *man t'ou* of China and the *manti* of Turkey. Ashak, a leek-filled pasta, resembles Italian ravioli. Aush is the basic noodle dish, served much like a soup. *Lakhchak* is similar to lasagna.

Two types of rice are used in cooking: long grain and short grain. The long-grain variety is used for pilaus and *chalau.* Chalau is plain white rice that is served with a vegetable or meat dish. Pilaus are more elaborate and are cooked with meat and meat juices. They are colored by using browned onions, spinach, caramelized sugar, saffron, or turmeric. Very often vegetables, such as carrots, or fruits and nuts, such as orange peel, apricots, raisins, almonds, and pistachios, are used as a garnish.

Ashak, a leek-filled boiled pasta often served at special occasions. (Shutterstock)

Two methods are used for cooking long-grain rice. In the *dampokht* method the rice is boiled in just enough liquid for the cooking. With the *sof* method the rice is first parboiled in a large amount of salted water and then drained. Oil, spices, and a little more liquid (water or stock) are added, and the rice is finished off in an oven or on top of the stove or fire.

The basic short-grain rice dish is called *bata,* where the rice is cooked with plenty of water and a little oil until soft and sticky. It is served with a vegetable or meat qorma. Shola, another sticky white rice dish, is cooked in a similar way but can be savory or sweet. The savory version is cooked with meat and pulses. Sweet versions are often flavored with cardamom and rose water and studded with flaked almonds and pistachios. *Ketcheree quroot* (similar to the *kitchri* of India) is another version that is made with the addition of mung beans and served with a meat qorma and quroot.

Onions play an important role in Afghan cookery. Both white and red onions are used, but red ones are preferred as they give a thicker sauce and richer flavor. Onions are sometimes fried until very brown and soft, almost caramelized, before being ground for adding to soups, qormas, and pilaus to give flavor and color.

The Afghan housewife makes full use of fruits and vegetables in season and dries them or makes preserves, chutneys, and pickles. Pickles (*turshi*) are made from lemons, carrots, eggplants, and mixed vegetables. Apricots, peaches, cherries, bell peppers, cilantro, and mint are made into chutneys (*chutni*). Meat is also dried, especially in mountainous or remote regions where fresh meat is not always available in the winter months. *Landi* is a special type of dried meat. A fat sheep is slaughtered at the end of autumn and the wool is sheared off, leaving the skin with a thick layer of fat underneath. The whole carcass is then hung to dry. To make *gosht-e-qagh* (dried meat) the meat is cut into large chunks that are scored and rubbed with salt. The meat is then hung up in a warm, shady place to dry and let the juices drip out. After the process is repeated, the meat is hung in a cool place until needed.

Mantu, a traditional noodle dumpling often served as a part of *iftar*. (Imagevillage | Dreamstime.com)

Typical Meals

Although many people in Afghanistan are desperately poor and their diet and meals are generally very basic, most eat three meals a day: breakfast, a midday meal, and an evening meal. Breakfast is bread, sometimes in the form of *nan-e-roghani*, which is nan with oil added to the dough before baking. This is served with sweet tea, sometimes with milk added; for those who can afford it, the bread may be accompanied by cheese, qymaq (cream), honey, or jam. The midday meal usually consists of a main dish such as soup, noodles, or a rice dish, all accompanied by bread. Bread soaked in soup is the most common staple food of poor people. Bread is also eaten with grapes when in season. Another simple and traditional dish is *qurooti*. Quroot (dried yogurt) is reconstituted in water, and garlic, salt, and pepper are added. The mixture is boiled and eaten with bread with dried mint sprinkled on top. The evening meal is similar and often includes leftovers. Snacks such as *khagina* (a kind of omelet similar to frittatas and Spanish tortillas) are sometimes made for a quick lunch. Other popular snacks include fried savory pastries called boulanee stuffed with gandana or mashed potato. Desserts are a luxury and usually made only for special occasions.

The traditional mode of eating in Afghanistan is on the floor. Everyone sits on cushions around a large cloth or thin mat called a *disterkhan*. It is often the custom to share food communally. Three or four people share one large platter of rice with smaller side dishes of a meat qorma, kebabs, and a vegetable dish, perhaps spinach or okra, or a *burani* (see the following) made with eggplant or potatoes. A salad might be an accompaniment, as well as chutneys and pickles, to add piquancy to the meal. Nan is passed around for diners to tear off a piece.

Burani Bonjon

2–3 large eggplants

Vegetable oil for frying

1 medium onion, finely chopped

2 medium tomatoes, thinly sliced

1 green bell pepper, finely sliced in rings (optional)

Salt

¼–½ tsp red pepper

1–2 c strained yogurt

2 cloves garlic, peeled and crushed

2 tsp dried mint

Peel the eggplants, and slice them into rounds about ¼–½ inch thick.

Heat plenty of vegetable oil in a frying pan (eggplant soaks up a lot of oil), and fry as many slices of the eggplant as possible in one layer. Fry on both sides until brown. Remove from the pan, and drain on absorbent kitchen paper. Repeat with the remaining eggplant, adding more oil as necessary.

Fry the chopped onions in a little oil until reddish-brown. Arrange the eggplant, sliced tomatoes, and sliced pepper in layers in the frying pan, sprinkling each layer with some fried onion and a little salt and a little red pepper. Spoon over 2–3 tablespoons of water, cover the pan with a lid, and simmer over low heat for about 20 to 30 minutes.

Meanwhile, combine the strained yogurt, the crushed garlic, a little salt, and the dried mint. Put half of the strained yogurt onto a warm serving dish. Carefully remove the eggplant from the pan with a spatula, and arrange it on the yogurt. Dot the rest of the yogurt over the eggplant, and sprinkle over any remaining sauce (but not the oil) from the eggplant on top. Serve immediately with freshly baked nan or with chalau.

The traditional way of eating for most Afghans is with the right hand. Rice is formed, using the fingers, into small balls, which are popped into the mouth. Nan or chapati is also used to scoop up small portions of food. Even soup is eaten with the hands. Bread is broken into pieces and added to the soup to soak up the juices. Spoons may be used for eating desserts and yogurt. More affluent Afghans do use Western-style plates and cutlery.

All the dishes are served at the same time. Although there is no formal sequence of courses, generally all the savory dishes are eaten first. If there is a dessert such as *firni* (a rice or corn-flour milk pudding), it will be eaten as a final course. Fresh fruit is usually served after the meal. The meal ends with tea (green or black), usually without milk or sugar and often flavored with cardamom to aid digestion.

Eating Out

Afghans rarely eat in restaurants, although there are some that serve traditional Afghan food to locals. Most restaurants in major cities cater to foreigners or well-to-do Afghans. With the arrival of many foreign troops and aid workers since 2001, a great variety of restaurants opened in Kabul, including Chinese, Mexican, Thai, and French. Many have closed recently due to the deterioration of security. Street foods, *chaikhana* (teahouses, sometimes called *samovar*), and kebab stalls are, however, very popular with Afghans.

Street vendors, called *tabang wala,* sell a variety of tasty foods for people wanting a quick snack. A *tabang* is a large, flat, round wooden tray on which the vendor carries his wares and then stakes his claim to a particular street corner or patch. He may roast corn over charcoal or fry leek-filled pastries called boulanee. Passersby stop to taste his *shour nakhod* (salty chickpeas), red kidney beans, and boiled, sliced potatoes, all doused with a mint and vinegar dressing and served with brightly colored chutneys such as hot red pepper or tangy green cilantro. Other favorite street snacks are samosas and *pakaura* (vegetable or potato fritters). The passersby can quench their thirst with *kishmish ab* (red or green raisins soaked in water). In recent years the old-style tabang wala has been disappearing, and most of the street vendors today have a kind of mobile kiosk on wheels.

More permanent stalls in the bazaar sell *faluda* (a kind of vermicelli dessert), into which are added crushed ice and a custard made with milk and sugar thickened with salep (orchid bulb) and flavored with rose water and chopped pistachios; or *sheer yakh* (ice cream) can be added to the faluda instead. In winter fried fish is served with *jelabi* (a fried funnel cake–like sweet soaked in syrup) or a thick and hearty porridge of whole wheat and ground meat served with oil and sugar called *haleem. Kishmish panir* (cheese with red raisins), displayed on a colorful bed of vine leaves, is a popular street food in springtime.

The samovar, or chaikhana, are places where men can meet and chat over endless cups of tea served from a constantly boiling samovar in which the tea is made. Some are very basic and serve only tea. Others provide customers with a variety of refreshments and food, including the traditional but simple soup called *sherwa-e-chainaki* (teapot soup). Lamb, onions, split peas, fresh cilantro, salt, and pepper are put into a teapot, covered with water,

Military bases in Afghanistan are becoming more and more comfortable as is evidenced by this restaurant in Kabul. (Pavel Burian | Dreamstime.com)

and then left to simmer slowly among burning embers raked from either the charcoal brazier used for grilling kebabs or the fire of the boiling samovar.

Many chaikhana have kebab stalls attached. Kebabs are one of the main street foods all over Afghanistan. The kebabs are usually made from small cubes of lamb interspersed on the skewers with fat called *dumba* from the fat-tailed sheep and grilled over charcoal. The kebabs are placed on nan, *lawausha* (a larger but thinner type of nan), or chapati and often served with a salad of sliced onions and tomatoes with cilantro. For added flavor the kebabs are sprinkled with crushed dried sour grapes called *ghora,* salt, red pepper, and lemon if available. Other kebabs include *kofta* (minced meat), *shinwari* (lamb chops), and the specialty of lamb's testicles, considered by many to be an aphrodisiac. A specialty of Jalalabad is the fried *chappli* kebab, which is fiery hot and consists of minced meat, lots of gandana (Chinese chives), *noash piaz* (scallions), cilantro, and green chilies. *Chappli* means "sandal,"

and this kebab is named thus because of its resemblance to the sole of a sandal.

Special Occasions

Afghanistan is a Muslim country, and religion plays a very important part in the way of life. Afghans observe all religious days and festivals, which are based on the lunar calendar. Fasting is one of the five pillars of Islam, and during the holy month of Ramadan (Ramazan), Muslims refrain from taking any food or water between dawn and dusk. The fast is broken every day at sunset. This is called *iftar.* Afghans at first take a sip of water, and some will take a pinch of salt, but others eat a date. After this a large meal is served. It is ironic that during this month of fasting special and elaborate meals are prepared: soup; pasta or noodle dishes such as ashak or mantu; rice dishes in the form of chalau (plain white rice) and pilau; meat qormas; vegetable dishes; and pickles and chutneys. All this is followed by lots of fresh fruit and the inevitable tea. Before sunrise and after morning prayers, another much lighter meal will be eaten, usually consisting of bread and tea with perhaps some eggs, cheese, qymaq, or preserves.

The two most important religious festivals are Eid al-Fitr (also called Eid-e-Ramazan) which marks the end of Ramadan (Ramazan) and Eid al-Adha (known in Afghanistan as Eid-e-Qorban), which marks the end of the hajj, the pilgrimage to Mecca. At each Eid people visit their relatives to drink tea and eat nuts and sweets. Often special sweets and pastries are prepared: *halwa-e-swanak* (a kind of nut brittle), *sheer payra* (a rich milky sweet with nuts), goash-e-feel (literally, "elephant's ear"; sweet fried pastries, so called because of their shape and size). At Eid al-Adha many families sacrifice a lamb or calf. The meat is distributed among the poor, relatives, and neighbors.

Afghans celebrate their New Year (called Nauroz) on March 21, which is the first day of spring. Nauroz has its origins long before Islam, in the time of Zoroaster (founder of the Zoroastrian faith in Persia, ca. 18th–10th century B.C.). Special foods are prepared. *Samanak* is an ancient and traditional dish for the New Year. About 15 to 20 days before the New Year, wheat is planted in flowerpots, and the green shoots of the wheat are made into a sweet pudding. Other traditional dishes include *haft miwa,* a compote that traditionally contains seven different kinds of fruit and nuts (*haft* means "seven," *miwa,* "fruit"), and *kulcha Naurozee,* a biscuit made with rice flour. It is also the custom to prepare white and green foods at Nauroz such as *sabzi chalau* (white rice with spinach) and chicken.

New Year is also the time when Afghans like to go on picnics, which can be quite elaborate affairs. While the women prepare a feast of rice dishes, qormas, and salads and the men are in charge of making kebabs, children play and fly their kites. Bread and fruit are often purchased on the way.

The custom of *Nazr,* a kind of thanksgiving, is also observed at New Year. Sweet rice dishes called *shola-e-shireen* or *shola-e-zard* are prepared and distributed among the poor. Another dish often prepared for Nazr is *halwa,* made with either wheat flour, semolina, or rice flour, flavored with rose water and studded with pistachios and almonds.

Shola-e-Zard

This dish is particularly associated with the 10th day of Muharram (the lunar month of mourning, the 10th day being the anniversary of the massacre of Hazrat-e-Hussein, grandson of Muhammad, and 72 members of his family), when it is traditionally served with *sharbat-e-rayhan* (a sweet drink flavored with basil seed).

1 c short-grain rice

1–1½ c sugar, according to taste

¼ tsp saffron

1 tbsp chopped or flaked pistachios

1 tbsp chopped or flaked almonds

1 tbsp rose water

½ tsp ground cardamom

Soak the rice in water, well covered, for a couple of hours or longer.

Boil approximately 7 cups of water, and add the rice. The water should come up to about 4 inches above the rice. Simmer the rice in the water slowly, stirring occasionally, until the rice dissolves and becomes like jelly. This can take 1 to 2 hours, or perhaps even longer. Add the sugar, saffron, chopped pistachios and almonds, rose water, and ground cardamom. Turn down the heat to very low, and cook for another half an hour.

Pour the warm shola onto a large serving dish, and leave to set in a cool place for a couple of hours.

Afghans will find any excuse to have a party. Births, circumcisions, engagements, and weddings are celebrated in style, and many special foods are prepared. The birth of a child, especially the first male child, is a big occasion, and many guests come to congratulate the family. Lots of food is prepared. Special "hot" and nourishing foods are prepared for the mother to give her strength: *humach* (a flour-based soup), *leetee* (a flour-based dessert), *kachee* (a kind of halwa), aush (a noodle soup with plenty of garlic), and *shola-e-holba* (a sweet sticky rice dish flavored with fenugreek). On the 40th day after the birth a rich, sweet bread called *roht* is baked.

Engagements and weddings are festive occasions. Engagements are called *shirnee khoree,* which literally means "sweet eating." Traditionally the family of the groom brings sweets, goash-e-feel, and other gifts such as clothes and jewelry to the bride's family. The bride's family in return prepares and organizes the food for the party. Often special kitchens are set up in order to cope with the vast amounts of food to be prepared: pilaus, qormas, kebabs such as *shami* kebab or *do piaza* (usually shrimp or chicken stewed with lots of onions), ashak, mantu, boulanee, and lots of sweet dishes such as firni, *maughoot* (cornstarch pudding), shola-e-shireen,

sheer payra, and sweet pastries such as *baqlava* and the elaborate fried pastry called *qatlama.* A special tea called *qymaq chai* is often served. It is made with green tea, but by a process of aeration and the addition of bicarbonate of soda the tea turns dark red. Milk is added (and sugar too), and it becomes a purply pink color. It has a strong, rich taste. Qymaq (a kind of clotted cream) is floated on the top. Sugared almonds called noql are served with the tea.

Qabili Pilau

This pilau is probably the best known of all the rice dishes of Afghanistan and could almost be described as the national dish. It is a popular main dish and

Jamila Sharifi, the groom-to-be's mother, throws candy over the heads of bride-to-be Najilla Ahmadi and groom-to-be Dawood Sharifi to wish them all the best during their engagement party in Kabul, Afghanistan, 2002. (Getty Images)

is nearly always served as one of the rice dishes prepared for guests. There are, of course, many variations, as families have their own special way of making it. But common to all versions is the use of carrots and raisins. It can be made with lamb or chicken, the spices may vary, and other garnishes may be added such as lightly fried almonds and pistachios. This recipe is an Uzbek version.

1 lb (2½ c) long-grain rice, preferably basmati

6 tbsp vegetable oil

2 medium onions, finely chopped

2 lb lamb on the bone or 1 chicken, cut up

2 large carrots

4 oz raisins

2 tsp ground cumin

1 tsp black pepper

Salt

Rinse the rice several times until the water remains clear, then leave it to soak in fresh water for at least half an hour.

Heat the oil in a heatproof casserole over medium to high heat, and add the chopped onions. Fry until golden brown and soft. Add the meat (if lamb, trimmed of excess fat), and fry until well browned. Then add enough water to cover the meat, and salt, bring to a boil, turn down the heat, and cook gently until the meat is tender.

While the meat is cooking, wash, peel, and cut up the carrots into julienne strips. When the meat is done and you are ready to cook the rice, place the carrots and the raisins on top of the meat, and sprinkle with 1 teaspoon each of cumin and black pepper and some salt.

Drain the rice, place it on top of the carrots and raisins, and add enough water to cover it by about ½ inch. Add the second teaspoon of cumin and a little salt, bring to a boil, turn down the heat, cover, and boil gently for about 10 to 12 minutes until the rice is tender and the water has been absorbed.

Place the casserole, which should have a tight-fitting lid, in a preheated oven at 300°F for about 45 minutes. Or you can finish the cooking by leaving it over on very low heat on top of the stove for the same length of time.

To serve, mound the rice, meat, carrots, and raisins in a large dish.

Similar dishes are prepared for weddings except they are even more elaborate and more food is prepared as there will be a larger number of guests. *Abrayshum kebab* (*abrayshum* meaning "silk") is an unusual sweet often made for festive occasions such as weddings. It is made with egg in such a way that the egg forms "silken" threads, which are then rolled up like a kebab and sprinkled with syrup and ground pistachios. But perhaps the most traditional food served at weddings is *molida,* sometimes called *changali.* This special powdery sweetmeat made from flour, oil, sugar, and butter and flavored with cardamom and rose water is tasted by the bride and groom as they sit on their wedding throne during the ceremony. The groom first feeds his bride a teaspoon, then she in turn feeds him. Then the molida is served to the wedding guests. Sugared almonds (noql), symbolizing fruitfulness and prosperity, and other sweets, symbolizing happiness, are then showered over the newlyweds. For funerals it is tradition to serve halwa to the mourners.

Rice pilau being cooked over an open fire. (Maxim Tupikov | Dreamstime.com)

Diet and Health

Although much liked by Afghans, meat is expensive and sometimes eaten only once or twice a week. However, the bread is very nutritious, and when supplemented with soups, pulses. and vegetables it provides enough protein, carbohydrates, vitamins, and minerals for a fairly healthy diet. Desserts and sweets are a luxury, but fruits abound in summer and autumn. Afghan tastes favor a large amount of fat or oil in their cooking. Indeed, this is a sort of status symbol. Many Afghans, especially those now living in the West, have reduced their use of oil or fat and are much more conscious about a healthy diet.

Many people in Afghanistan still adhere in everyday life to the ancient Persian concept of *sardi/garmi,* literally "cold/hot." Like yin-yang in China, it is a system for classifying foods for the purpose of dietary health. In general people believe that eating "hot" foods can alleviate "cold" illnesses such as the common cold. "Cold" foods are prescribed to reduce fevers or hot tempers. "Hot" and "cold" here refer to the properties of the food, not the temperature. While there are some differences of opinion as to just what foods can be classified as hot or cold, there is a definite pattern. Hot foods are rich, warm in aroma, sweet, and high in calories and carbohydrates, whereas cold foods are generally characterized by acidity or blandness, have a high water content, and are low in calories. In Afghanistan hot foods include sugar and honey, fats and oils, wheat flour and chickpea flour, dried fruits, nuts, garlic and onions, fish, meat, eggs, and most spices such as chilies, fenugreek, ginger, turmeric, and saffron. Cold foods include rose water, milk and yogurt, chicken, rice, some pulses (such as lentils and kidney beans), fresh fruits (such as melons, grapes, pears, apples, and lemons) and vegetables (especially spinach, cucumbers, and lettuce), and most herbs (such as cilantro and dill). Both spices and herbs are valued by Afghans for their medicinal properties, and many are used to aid digestion or help cure and alleviate other illnesses.

Helen Saberi

Further Reading

Saberi, Helen. "Fish in Afghanistan." In *Fish: Food from the Waters, Proceedings of the Oxford Symposium on Food and Cookery, 1997,* edited by Harlan Walker, 259–63. Devon, UK: Prospect Books, 1998.

Saberi, Helen. *Noshe Djan: Afghan Food and Cookery.* Devon, UK: Prospect Books, 2000.

Saberi, Helen. "Public Eating in Afghanistan." In *Public Eating, Proceedings of the Oxford Symposium on Food and Cookery, 1991,* edited by Harlan Walker. London: Prospect Books, 1992.

Saberi, Helen. "Rosewater, the Flavouring of Venus, Goddess of Love, and Asafoetida, Devil's Dung." In *Spicing up the Palate, Proceedings of the Oxford Symposium on Food and Cookery, 1992,* edited by Harlan Walker. Devon, UK: Prospect Books, 1993.

Saberi, Helen. "Silk Kebab and Pink Tea." In *Look and Feel, Proceedings of the Oxford Symposium on Food and Cookery, 1993,* edited by Harlan Walker. Devon, UK: Prospect Books, 1994.

Saberi, Helen. "Travel and Food in Afghanistan." In *Food on the Move, Proceedings of the Oxford Symposium on Food and Cookery, 1996,* edited by Harlan Walker. Devon, UK: Prospect Books, 1997.

Australia

Overview

The only country in the world to encompass an entire continent, Australia is about the size of the continental United States and is home to primarily Mediterranean and tropical climates. With some of the oldest and most stable geology in the world, Australia's environment is characterized by enormous deserts with a few uplifted but eroded mountain ranges and a wetter tropical north. Australia was settled over 40,000 years ago by people presumed to have arrived over land bridges and through short sea voyages from Asia. They likely brought with them some foods and food-preparation techniques, but the first Australian cuisine was forged largely from native animals and vegetation. In more recent times the British claimed and colonized the continent starting in the late 18th century. The new settlers brought with them many nonindigenous crops and animals that would require transportation, transplantation, and adaptation to local conditions. They also opened the continent to settlement by migrants from throughout the world, all bringing their own ideas about food preparation and in many cases stock they intended to cultivate in their new home.

The current population is around 22 million people, of whom more than 6 million are migrants, who come from over 200 countries.[1] With such a diverse and multicultural background, Australian cuisine is elusive to define. Australians themselves take great pleasure in arguing about whether or not it exists, where it comes from, and who gets to decide its parameters. Food is more than a dinner conversation in Australia. Australians idealize their farming heritage, have a long history of cooking shows on television and cooking books on their shelves, and are in the midst of a boom in foodie culture, making heroes and rock stars out of local chefs and farmers. But still no one can definitively say what Australian cuisine actually is. The slippery nature of food and eating in Australia, and the debate itself, probably is the essence of Australian food culture.

🍽 Food Culture Snapshot

Ingrid and Christian are a typical middle-class couple in their mid-thirties. He is a software engineer and she is a psychologist, and they both hold full-time jobs. His father migrated from Holland, and three of her grandparents came to Australia from Great Britain. They just bought a house in the hills overlooking the city of Adelaide where they have lived all their lives, minus a few years here and there working or traveling overseas.

Typically, breakfast consists of a bowl of *muesli* (granola) with yogurt or toast spread with butter and Vegemite. Christian drinks espresso coffee (never instant or percolated), and Ingrid drinks tea with milk and sugar before they go to work. Australians are equally in love with tea and coffee, though the older generations and Asian Australians tend toward tea. For lunch they either bring sandwiches from home or buy a sandwich from the take-out shops in the food courts near their respective workplaces. Ingrid eats at her desk while continuing to work on most days. In the evenings they usually eat together, as Australians tend to eat in nuclear families.

On Saturdays, they shop for food. Ingrid prefers to do this together so that Christian can buy what he needs for the one night a week he is responsible for cooking. They put their stylish shopping trolley in the car and go to the Adelaide Central Markets in the middle of the city: a large warehouse of small food stalls filled with fresh fruit and vegetables, meats, and grocery items. On the fringes of the markets are breakfast places where they meet with friends for a bite to eat before shopping. Just outside the markets are the "eat streets" of Adelaide, giving the accurate impression that this quarter of the city is all about food.

Ingrid and Christian get their fresh fruit and vegetables as well as bread, cheese, olives, prepared dips, muslie, pasta, and rice from bulk bins. Christian goes to a seafood shop next to the stalls to talk to the staff about the freshest fish to buy for the curry he is making this week. He got the recipe online and thinks it approximates the one he ate on their last visit to Thailand. He also picks up some sausages for the barbecue they are attending that afternoon. Ingrid goes to the Asian grocery stall to get lemongrass and galangal for a *laksa* (noodle soup) she is making and on the way picks up a frozen lasagna at a little Italian-themed stall and pre-prepared roast at the German butcher's stall, both of which she can just throw in the oven on a weeknight. On the way home they stop at the supermarket to get their canned goods, jars of everyday items like vegemite, black tea, milk, and anything frozen.

While Ingrid does most of the cooking, Christian would never say it was her role, and he is the assistant cook on most nights. Preparing a meal is time for couples, the core of the household, to catch up on the events of the day and is usually timed for a 7 P.M. meal. The meal could be a stir-fry, a pasta casserole, or a recipe from any ethnic cuisine they have come across in their travels, seen on television, or heard about from friends. It usually contains meat, although Australia is home to an increasing number of vegetarians and a meat-free meal in a week is not unusual. Dinner is the biggest meal of the day unless there is a barbecue on the weekend, where a late lunch bleeds into the dinner hour.

Ingrid and Christian also aim to make healthy meals, which they define as low fat and low salt with a good balance of the major food groups in accordance with the dietary advice advertisements on television or discussed in the local media's food and lifestyle section. They gave up on meat pies and fish and chips down at the local take-out place years ago when the extra pounds started to show. Still, when they get take-out food (about once a week) or go out to eat (also about once a week), health is sacrificed for good taste and interesting cuisine at any number of Indian, Thai, Italian, Vietnamese, Chinese, Japanese, Greek, Argentinean, or modern Australian restaurants in their multicultural city. While Christian's and Ingrid's parents cooked more traditional fare while they were growing up, Ingrid now swaps recipes with her mother-in-law as changing cuisine is a stable feature of Australian foodways.

Major Foodstuffs

From a British colonial perspective, in the late 18th and 19th centuries, Australia was vast, water poor in the habitable south, and very far away from home. Indigenous food and cuisines developed by Aboriginal inhabitants were barely acceptable to colonists and thought a poor cousin to British fare. Some native meats such as kangaroo, wallaby, and possum could be cut and cooked into recognizable dishes, but more exotic fare such as banyan nuts, mountain pepper, and macadamia nuts was relegated to curiosities or used in recipes as substitutes for better-known ingredients. Even today the legacy of substitution exists. For example, the *quandong* (*Santalum acuminatum*), a member of the sandalwood family, is commonly referred to as the desert peach. Quandongs are not related to and do not look like nor taste overwhelmingly similar to the stone fruit in the genus *Prunus*. While migrants investigated the suitability of native plants and animals as food, they did not consider native plants and animals as an existing and functional system of food, nor did they consider Aboriginal cuisine fit for consumption. Even today "bush food" is viewed primarily as a provider of exotic ingredients to be incorporated into European or Asian dishes, rather than as a complete cuisine in and of itself. Instead, early colonists and migrants continued to bring British ideas about food and quickly rooted both plant and animal stock based on those ideas into Australian soils and culture. One of the first developments in Australian cuisine centered on how to transplant a British diet into what was viewed as a Mediterranean climate, both for the uses of the colonists and for export back to Britain.

With an abundance of land (much of it poor quality), a shortage of labor, and the need to aggregate production to make international exporting a viable business, Australians encouraged the development of large-scale commodity-production facilities for European food and agricultural goods. While this did not change what Australians ate, it did impact how much they ate. For example, one of the more successful industries in colonial Australia was grazing. As Michael Symons has detailed in *One Continuous Picnic,* the lack of a peasantry coupled with the high status afforded meat consumption in European dietary thinking encouraged the development of a prestigious and lucrative cattle and sheep industry. The success of the rangelands and the ensuing availability of inexpensive meat allowed even laborers to eat more meat than the typical British diet.[2] In the mid-19th century, the available meat supply allowed for 9.5 pounds (4.3 kilograms) of meat per person per week in New South Wales, slightly less than the government-set standard rations of 9.9–12.1 pounds (4.5–5.5 kilograms) per person. Records indicate that the working-class diet in Britain in the same period contained only 0.5–2 pounds (0.23–0.90 kilograms) of meat per person per week.[3] The transplantation of ideas about the importance and prestige of meat coupled with its abundance translated into changes in diet, and Australians typically ate meat with every meal.

Early Australians also planted familiar grains, fruits, and vegetables from their predominantly British diet. The wheat farms established throughout New South Wales, Victoria, South Australia, and eventually Western Australia entrenched a culture of dryland farming and ensured bread became the staple carbohydrate. The late 19th-century development of irrigation infrastructure throughout the Murray-Darling Basin allowed Australians to reliably establish water-dependent crops and pasturelands for dairying. This irrigation infrastructure largely exists today though it is overtaxed and is the cause of many of the environmental and freshwater-access problems Australians face. Dairying, for example, used about 1.5 billion gallons (5.4 gigaliters) of irrigation water per 1,000 hectares (2,471 acres) of land in the 2000–2001 agricultural year, which is a relatively high amount of water, given that vegetables used over 1 billion gallons (4.37 gigaliters) and wheat is farmed without irrigation. Furthermore, almost 480,000 hectares (1,186,000 acres), or 18 percent, of all irrigated land is dedicated to dairy farming.[4] All this is produced for essentially a luxury European suite of products: milk and various cheeses. The persistence of "thirsty" luxury foods such as dairy, stone fruits, and wine grapes in a water-poor country demonstrates the cultural persistence of maintaining a largely European foodscape in Australia.

While in southern Australia farmers were able to find or create suitable climates for European-style agriculture, the subtropical weather is more suited to traditional Southeast Asian fare and farming techniques. Early farmers persisted with largely European crops, limiting their initial range north and their success. However, two crops in the subtropics stood out as appropriate for the Australian domestic and export markets: sugarcane and bananas. Their consumption as part of a European food pattern was either well established or, in the case of bananas, rapidly becoming so. Even with these notable exceptions there is no doubt that the short heritage of Australian settlement shaped the Australian landscape into a European-styled foodscape. This development in the face of a very non-European environment and climatic conditions is a testament to the strength and creative adaptation of the tastemakers of colonial Australia. The notion of an Australian-shaped landscape, as opposed to one of wild native food, is central to Australian notions about eating "Australian," and therefore the maintenance of the existing local foodscape is central to notions of Australian cuisine.

Cooking

Many Australian critics have called what Australians did with this largely industrial and commodity-based foodscape "uninspiring." In her study of colonial Australian cookbooks, Barbara Santich noted that while Australian cookbooks adapted recipes to Australian conditions and native foodstuffs, they were still based on techniques from the home country, so much so that even the few bush foods used were incorporated into English recipes and not constructed as native cuisine.[5] According to Symons, this British cuisine translated into roughly a meal starting with soup, followed by a centerpiece of meat and two vegetables, and ending with a pudding, pie, or cake dessert until well into the 1950s.[6] Further research by Deborah Lupton suggests that this meal pattern persists in rural Australia even today.[7] Pork pies, lamb roasts, puddings, and sponge cakes are all familiar hallmarks shared with British cuisine. In addition, a few distinctly Australian dishes from the period are still widely enjoyed today, such as damper, a yeastless bread made over a campfire; pavlova, a meringue-based dessert; Lamingtons, small sponge cakes coated with chocolate and coconut; and ANZAC biscuits, hard sweet oatmeal biscuits (i.e., cookies) designed to store and ship well in packages.[8] There are also some Australian dishes such as the carpetbag steak (steak stuffed with oysters) and the kangaroo steamer (steamed kangaroo meat) that have fallen out of fashion.[9] Overall, the food industry and the cuisines promoted in cookbooks and periodicals during the first half of the 20th century emphasized adaptation to British fare with necessary concessions to the hotter climate of the continent. By the 1950s there was not yet a great divergence from British cuisine just as there was no great divergence from British culture.

Carpetbag Steak

Carpetbag steaks were last popular in Australia in the 1950s, but they are making a comeback as an authentic Australian creation and a dish that takes advantage of Australia's high-quality beef and seafood. The following recipe is per person.

1 thick scotch fillet (rib eye) steak

3–4 fresh shucked oysters

1 tsp Worcestershire sauce

Salt and pepper to taste

Butter to taste

Cut a pocket along the side of the steak about ¾ of the way into the steak. Season the fresh oysters with the Worcestershire sauce, salt, and pepper. Stuff the seasoned oysters into the steak, and secure with skewers or toothpicks that have been soaked in water. Grill the steak on a barbecue, basting with the butter, to each individual's preferences and serve.

In the mid-20th century, Australia began to contend with its geographic position as part of Asia but also as a continent with unique weather patterns and soil. This was coupled with the dismantling of policies designed to keep Australia "British" in a backhanded recognition that it was in fact not British. With the ending of World War II, Australia began once again to take in large numbers of migrants. While most of them were European, a significant number of them were not British but rather from Italian, Greek, and other southern European communities with their own entrenched ideas about what constituted a good meal. In his oral history *Wogfood,* John Newton details the challenges Mediterranean migrants faced in a new Mediterranean climate with a British food heritage.[10] He details the initial resistance and even racism associated with introducing elements of a new (and climatically appropriate) cuisine to predominantly British Australia. Thankfully, the new migrants persisted and contributed to the agricultural landscape and skills as well as the cuisine. Italian, Greek, and other Mediterranean produce and cuisines are ubiquitous in modern Australia. In fact, a perusal of current menus suggests that the prestige of Italian food, dish names, and techniques largely surpasses that of the traditional French high-brow influence in Australian restaurants inherited from the English.[11]

In the 1970s the Whitlam government began to officially dismantle the White Australia policy of immigration and assimilation in favor of an official policy of multiculturalism, which included a large intake of Southeast Asian migrants.[12] This had a tremendous impact on Australian cuisine and supplied Australia with new opportunities to adapt, adopt, and mould Australian cuisine from the enduring British food legacy. According to Cherry Ripe in *Goodbye Culinary Cringe,* these changes were coupled with an increase in acceptance and exploration of international cuisine as Australians started to travel and embrace their geographic location.[13] Furthermore, improved supply chains resulting from increased traffic with Asia and technological improvements in storage and transport have consistently brought more of the world's food products to Australia, allowing Australians to take culinary advantage of changes in political attitudes.

Since the 1970s Australians have done nothing but add to the variety in their shopping baskets. The post–World War II European migrants moved out of their home kitchens and into restaurants and cookbook production. With the opening of Australia's doors to Asian migration and travel, an influx of migrants enhanced the small but firmly entrenched Chinese community established during the 19th-century gold rush. Chinese Australian fusion cuisine, found even in small country towns, has been augmented by more ethnically accurate Chinese food. Indian cuisine can be increasingly found outside metropolitan areas, and the sophistication of urban Indian restaurants is rising as customers want to know "What *kind* of Indian food, from *where*?" As Australians have made Bali and Thailand tropical holiday destinations, a plethora of Indonesian, Malaysian, and Thai restaurants, cooking classes, and cookbooks have found success with Australian palates. *Nasi goreng* (Indonesian fried rice), laksa soups, and the jungle curries of northern Thailand are all at home on Australian urban eat streets and increasingly in the kitchens of middle-class Anglo-Australians, where you will also find a full set of family chopsticks in the cutlery drawer. Some of this variety has been driven by the natural impulses that drive all urban centers. These globalizing trends influence Australia more than other countries as over three-quarters of the

population lives in urban areas.[14] Urbanity may set the pace of innovation and acceptance of culinary multiculturalism in all countries, but it also largely defines the Australian population.

The cuisines of new Asian migrants still face some challenges. Not only is the foodscape still firmly established as European, but the geography, climate, and sparse population often hinder the availability of the required primary produce. While Australians might crave jungle curries, Vietnamese cold rolls, and other delicacies and they might be able to find newly migrated Australians to teach them how to construct these dishes, they cannot always find the *pac chi farang* and mint varieties needed to recreate them. Australian farmers have at long last started to grow subtropical Asian fruits and vegetables in the environmentally appropriate north and to expand the production of an Asian food base throughout Australia.[15] While many of these enterprises have Asian export markets in their sights, they also increasingly supply the domestic markets in specialty shops and sections alongside heritage tomatoes and specialty cheeses.

Though the variety of foods grown in the countryside is increasing, the food still has to get into the city. In many places the near duopoly of the two major grocery chains, Coles and Woolworths, hampers access to new and local foodstuffs due to their national supply-chain policies. However, most Australian cities have retained a market somewhere in the city limits. These markets, such as the Queen Victoria Markets in Melbourne, Paddy's Haymarket in Sydney, and the Central Markets in Adelaide, still cater to small stallholders and maintain a mix of primary produce, butcher, and *provedore* stalls (grocery purveyors). Though far from genuine farmers' markets, they provide an outlet for niche ingredients and imported specialties and a rallying point for food exploration. In addition, since the 1990s many outlying periurban areas have developed genuine farmers' markets aimed at increasing the variety of foodstuffs available to the public. For the most part these markets cater to urban or periurban customers who value the surrounding countryside and ideas about fresh, local, and pampered healthy food that they associate with it.

Typical Meals

Today, Australian kitchens are constructed along the same general lines as most modern European-influenced kitchens found all over the world. The kitchen will typically also contain cookbooks and magazines reflecting both Australian and ethnic foods. While many Australian cooks learned how to cook from their mothers, they are also aware of the explosion of culinary possibilities that were not contemplated a generation ago. The Australian media promote the contemplation of Australian cuisine. Cooking shows have been avidly watched for at least 40 years; a variety of Australian food magazines such as *Delicious, Epicure, Food and Wine, Gourmet Traveller,* and *Sumptuous* enjoy a wide readership; and there has been an explosion in Australian cooking books over the past 20 years. Alongside the expected set of pots and pans, Australian cooks are also familiar with woks, *tagines,* bamboo steamers, and a multitude of other cooking implements gathered from cuisines around the world. The refrigerator tends to privilege fresh over frozen foods, and most Australians shop weekly for their produce. The pantry will have a wide variety of spices and spice mixes gathered in attempts to master various dishes, but it will also inevitably contain some Australian staple favorites: vegemite, a yeast-based salty spread for toast; Milo, a chocolate powder for milk; and some variety of Arnott's biscuits (cookies) to serve with tea or coffee when guests arrive. If guests are very lucky, they might even be treated to a Tim Tam, an iconic chocolate-covered layered biscuit (again, a kind of cookie).

With both parents working in many families, the idealized Australian family meal is less of a common reality than in times past. While breakfast and lunch can be eaten on the run, out with friends, or as the increasingly popular "deskfast" (the meal you eat at your desk while working), dinner is at least discussed as something nuclear families should strive to have together. The patterns for such a meal are rooted in the old British ideal of a first course of soup, a second course of a meat centerpiece with two cooked vegetables, and a third course of pudding (the Australian sticky date pudding if you are lucky) or cake for dessert. While most Anglo-Australians would agree that this is a "proper" meal achievable only on occasional Saturday or Sunday nights, actual main meals are much more varied. To save time, most are served as single plates and take advantage of the faster preparation and cooking times of pasta dishes, stir-fries, and curries. Anything that fits within a family's time constraints can be found on the dining room table without a set pattern of consciously borrowed cuisines.

Even with the variety in Australian cooking, there are elements of rigid structure. For example, nearly every household in Australia has, effectively, a second kitchen. At a minimum it consists of an old brick incinerator retrofitted with a grill, a rickety table next to it, and an *esky* (a cooler) to keep the beer and sausages cold. At best, a quick perusal of backyard-renovation shows reveals that the ideal "other kitchen" is just off the back porch, complete with the latest gas barbecue, a spit for a leg of lamb, and a wok burner installed next to an outdoor sink and an electric bar fridge. This is an Australian man's kitchen, and while the women of the household can contribute salads and the occasional marinade, any woman found outdoors publicly cooking with fire leaves herself open to criticism and often replacement at the grill. Australian cookbooks, magazines, and advertising consistently discuss how men can improve their barbecuing techniques, such as selecting cuts of meat, better-quality sausages, and better cooking techniques as well as beer matching. These discussions are often mirrored around the grill as men, beer in hand, cook meat with fire.

The Australian barbecue is perhaps the most common and formally constituted meal. At its heart, it must contain sausages, bread on which to put the sausages, fried onions and tomato sauce as accompaniments, and beer. The sausages by no means have to be of good quality or "fancy," and the bread is expected to be sliced white bread. The meat is simply grilled and the onion fried on the hotplate of the barbecue. The beer only has to be cold. This simple and consistent barbecue formula can be found at any school fete, most voting booths, and many hardware stores on any given weekend. In backyards across Australia, the "sausage sizzle" forms the background of more elaborate barbecues to which the attending guests might add lamb or pork chops, cuts of beef and kangaroo, and chicken for the ladies. In general, salads are communal, but guests are expected to bring their own meat and drinks and to share any surplus with the host and others. Meat is put on the barbecue in shifts, usually organized by the host or a recognized master of the grill, and people are responsible for cooking the meat they brought and distributing it if necessary. A barbecue is more a type of party with its own rules of etiquette than it is a method of cooking.

Eating Out

At the turn of the 20th century Australia had about 20,000 restaurants and 20,000 take-out and fast-food outlets.[16] Australians eat one in every five meals outside their homes. This is split fairly evenly between takeout or fast food and restaurant dining.[17] Eating out is ubiquitous but not yet a national pastime nor the main source of food for most Australians. When they do eat out, Australians tend to eat ethnic, as in non–British-Australian, cuisine. In a 2009 survey of 1,500 consumers, most respondents nominated their preferred restaurants as Chinese, Italian, and Thai, whereas only 13 percent of respondents named Australian or British restaurants as favorite choices.[18] While much of this ethnic food has been altered to fit Western expectations for portion size, proportions of meat to starch, cuts of meats, and vegetables and variety of ingredients, the stated preference itself demonstrates not just an acceptance but a seeking of international cuisines.

Despite stated preferences, there are still places Australians nostalgically reflect on a distinctively Australian meal. Regardless of the level of highbrow sophistication in tastes, any Australian will be able to identify the best pub counter meal in their neighborhood. Australian pubs usually have restaurants, but they also serve a fairly standard menu of easy-to-prepare fast meals in the bar, commonly referred to as counter meals. Traditionally these are eaten while standing up or sitting on a stool propped against the main bar. A typical counter-meal menu includes chicken or veal schnitzels, meat

An Australian meat pie topped with a special sauce. (Shutterstock)

pies, burgers, and battered and fried fish, all served with thick fried chips and a suggestion of a green salad. Today, particularly in the cities, many pubs have become gentrified, and their menus have had a yuppie overhaul. If you scratch the surface, you can still see the great Aussie counter meal peeking through, even if you are eating Coopers ale-battered barramundi fillets with thickly sliced Tasmanian potato chips (fries) with a rocket (arugula) and pear side salad in the new beer garden of the local microbrewery.

Special Occasions

With regard to traditional British holidays, Australians have had to make many concessions to their hemisphere. Christmas is in the middle of summer in Australia. Increasingly, Santa wears board shorts, gives the reindeer a break, and is transported around by a koala and a kangaroo driving a red *ute* (truck). This makes sense to Australian children. Likewise, Australians are letting go of British traditions involving hot stoves and large baked birds in favor of an outdoor setting involving seafood and barbecues, as this makes sense to Australian cooks. The main meal of the Christmas holiday is typically a late lunch on December 25, served outside to take advantage of good weather. Cold hams; barbecued meat; crustaceans such as native lobsters, freshwater yabbies, or Moreton bay bugs; and a ring of giant prawns (never called shrimp) are hallmarks of Christmas lunch. Several British traditions that do not involve hot stoves have also survived, such as Christmas toffee date puddings and a plethora of traditional English boiled sweets. Across Australia, the idealized Christmas meal is an extended family summer picnic.

Meals at Easter generally follow a less elaborate version of the Christmas model. However, the treatment of Easter gifts has an increasingly Australian ring to it. One challenge facing Australian parents is reconciling the Easter bunny with the status of feral rabbits as a plague on the Australian landscape, decimating populations of native animals as well as crops. An increasingly popular solution to this problem has been to substitute the chocolate Easter bunnies available throughout the Western world with a chocolate bilby, a small, rabbit-like, endangered Australian animal. Easter also entails the exchange of large chocolate eggs, where the size of the chocolate egg is what really matters. Odd for a country so in love with British boiled lollies, Easter is almost exclusively about the chocolate. Even the traditional hot cross buns are now available in chocolate chip varieties.

Australia also has its own secular holidays, and while both Australia Day and the Queen's Birthday holiday are more associated with fireworks than meals, ANZAC Day, a memorial day for war veterans on April 25, does have a meal associated with the celebrations. After gathering around flagpoles throughout the country, Australians participate in a dawn service and then retire to a local park for an outdoor community breakfast, which is usually cooked and organized as a fund-raiser for local community groups and veterans organizations. The meal is striking in that it is the only time Australians tend to break the pattern of celebrating occasions with an outdoor leisurely midafternoon lunch.

Diet and Health

At the turn of the century, 60 percent of Australians age 25 and over were overweight, and 21 percent were obese.[19] Both adult and childhood obesity continue to be a growing concern in Australia. As in most Western countries, Australians seem to be suffering from what Australian thinker and author Clive Hamilton has diagnosed as "affluenza" and the overindulgences associated with an office-bound, consumption-based lifestyle.[20] Whether Australians blame the influx of American fast-food chains over the last 30 years, the long heritage of a starchy, meat-filled British diet, or the abundance of homegrown meat pies and take-out fish and chip shops more suited to an earlier, more active era, they are looking for solutions among the varied cuisines around them. Almost since settlement, Australians have discussed the merits of following a Mediterranean diet in their largely Mediterranean climate, as a matter of health. These discussions continue today. Added to them are recognitions of the health benefits Asian and other cuisines have to offer. Australians are doing what they have always done to answer the perceived health crisis: They are looking across the world for solutions they can cook at home, casting off what does not fit and wrangling what does into patterns of cooking that work in a "she'll be right" functional, fast-moving, and avidly discussed Australian cuisine.

Andrea MacRae

Notes

1. "Australia Facts," About Australia, http://www.about-australia.com/facts/.

2. Michael Symons, *One Continuous Picnic* (Carlton, Australia: Melbourne University Press, 1982 [2007]).

3. Barbara Santich, "Paradigm Shifts in the History of Dietary Advice in Australia," *Nutrition and Dietetics* 62, No. 4 (2005): 153.

4. Australian Government National Water Commission, "Australian Water Resources 2005," http://www.water.gov.au/WaterUse/Agricultural wateruse/index.aspx?Menu=Level1_4_4.

5. Barbara Santich, "The High and the Low: Australian Cuisine in the Late Nineteenth and Early Twentieth Centuries," *Journal of Australian Studies* 30, No. 87 (2006): 43.

6. Symons, *One Continuous Picnic.*

7. Deborah Lupton, "The Heart of the Meal: Food Preferences and Habits among Rural Australian Couples," *Sociology of Health and Illness* 22, No. 1 (2000): 98.

8. Barbara Santich, *Looking for Flavour* (Kent Town, Australia: Wakefield Press, 1996).

9. Santich, *Looking for Flavour,* 24–26, 115–24.

10. John Newton, *Wogfood: An Oral History with Recipes* (Milsons Point, Australia: Random House Australia, 1996).

11. Santich, "The High and the Low," 45.

12. Leslie F. Claydon, "Australia's Settlers: The Galbally Report," *International Migration Review* 15, No. 1–2 (1981): 109–12. See also Joanne Finkelstein, "The Taste of Boredom—McDonaldization and Australian Food Culture," *American Behavioral Scientist* 47, No. 2 (2003): 194.

13. Cherry Ripe, *Goodbye Culinary Cringe* (St. Leonards, Australia: Allen & Unwin, 1993).

14. Australian Bureau of Statistics, *Year Book Australia, 2006* (www.abs.gov.au), http://www.abs.gov.au/ausstats/abs@.nsf/Previousproducts/1301.0Feature%20Article72006?opendocument&tabname=Summary&prodno=1301.0&issue=2006&num=&view=.

15. For examples see the industry reports on Asian foods on the Rural Industries Research and Development Corporation site (www.rirdc.infoservices.com.au).

16. Finkelstein, "Taste of Boredom," 194.

17. Sensis, *Sensis Consumer Report—March 2009,* http://about.sensis.com.au/small-business/archived-reports/sensis-consumer-reports/, p. 14.

18. Sensis, *Sensis Consumer Report—March 2009*, p. 15.

19. Adrian J. Cameron, Timothy A. Welborn, Paul Z. Zimmet, David W. Dunstan, Neville Owen, Jo Salmon, Marita Dalton, Damien Jolley, and Jonathan E. Shaw, "Overweight and Obesity in Australia: The 1999–2000 Australian Diabetes, Obesity and Lifestyle Study (AusDiab)," *Medical Journal of Australia* 178 (2003): 427–32.

20. Clive Hamilton and Richard Denniss, *Affluenza: When Too Much Is Never Enough* (Crows Nest, Australia: Allen & Unwin, 2005).

Further Reading

Finkelstein, Joanne. "The Taste of Boredom—McDonaldization and Australian Food Culture." *American Behavioral Scientist* 47, No. 2 (2003): 187–200.

Lupton, Deborah. "The Heart of the Meal: Food Preferences and Habits among Rural Australian Couples." *Sociology of Health and Illness* 22, No. 1 (2000): 94–109.

Newton, John. *Wogfood: An Oral History with Recipes.* Milsons Point, Australia: Random House Australia, 1996.

Ripe, Cherry. *Goodbye Culinary Cringe.* St. Leonards, Australia: Allen & Unwin, 1993.

Santich, Barbara. "The High and the Low: Australian Cuisine in the Late Nineteenth and Early Twentieth Centuries." *Journal of Australian Studies* 30, No. 87 (2006): 43.

Santich, Barbara. *Looking for Flavour.* Kent Town, Australia: Wakefield Press, 1996.

Santich, Barbara. "Paradigm Shifts in the History of Dietary Advice in Australia." *Nutrition and Dietetics* 62, No. 4 (2005): 152–57.

Symons, Michael. *One Continuous Picnic.* 1982. Carlton, Australia: Melbourne University Press, 2007.

Bangladesh

Overview

The People's Republic of Bangladesh, located between Burma and India on the Bay of Bengal, has an area of 55,599 square miles (144,000 square kilometers) and a population of 142 million, making it the world's eighth-largest country in terms of population. The climate is tropical. Around 80 percent of the landmass is on the fertile alluvial lowland called the Bangladesh Plain, which receives heavy rainfalls during the monsoon season.

The territory that now constitutes Bangladesh was under the rule of various Islamic rulers, including the Moguls, from 1201 until 1757, when it passed into British rule. From then until 1947, the year in which India gained its independence from Britain, the territory was part of the Indian province of Bengal. In 1947, the region became East Pakistan, a part of the Islamic Republic of Pakistan. East Pakistan gained its independence from Pakistan in 1971 and became an independent country. The capital of Bangladesh, Dhaka, has a population of over 12 million people and is by far the largest city. The language is called Bengali.

Culturally and gastronomically, Bangladesh has much in common with the Indian state of West Bengal. The main difference is religion; whereas West Bengal is predominantly Hindu, around 85 percent of the inhabitants of Bangladesh are Muslim, 15 percent are Hindu, and 1 percent practice Buddhism or a tribal religion. Thus, most Bangladeshis follow Islamic food practices, which forbid the consumption of pork and alcohol. Only a small proportion of Bengali Hindus are vegetarian.

The country is extremely poor, with a per-capita gross domestic product of around US$600, and is predominantly agricultural. However, the cuisine of the affluent is one of most delicious on the subcontinent. For centuries, Bengal was a province the Mogul Empire, and the emperor's representatives, called nawabs, sought to emulate the rulers' lavish lifestyles and their sumptuous cuisine, which featured meat, cream, and aromatic spices and flavorings such as cardamom, cloves, and cinnamon. They found it unpalatable to eat rice without first frying it and perfected rich pilaus and *biryanis* (rice baked with meat and aromatic spices) laden with ghee (clarified butter) and decorated with nuts and dried fruits.

A uniquely Bangladeshi dish is *rezala,* made by slowly cooking pieces of goat or lamb with yogurt, milk, spices, and green chilies. It is often eaten with *Dhaka parota,* a large, round bread with 50 or 60 flaky layers and a crisp golden outside. Today, these dishes are mainly served at weddings and other feasts.

Rezala (White Lamb Curry)

2 lb goat or lamb meat, cut into 1-in. cubes

1 finely chopped onion

2 tbsp finely chopped ginger

1 tsp finely chopped garlic

3 whole green cardamom pods

2 2-in. pieces of cinnamon

2 cloves

½ c yogurt

1 tsp sugar

1½ tsp salt

½ c ghee (clarified butter)

Pinch of saffron, dissolved in ½ c warm milk

5–10 green chilies (to taste), split lengthwise with the seeds removed

Combine all the ingredients in a large pot, mix well, cover, and cook on low heat for half an hour. Stir the meat well, cover again, and continue to simmer until the moisture has evaporated and the ghee has separated from the meat. Add the milk with the saffron, and pour over the meat. Add the chilies, and cook over low heat for another half hour or until the meat is tender. Serve with rice pilau.

Food Culture Snapshot

Fazrul and Aysha Chaudhry are a middle-class couple living in Dhaka. Fazrul is a civil servant, and Aysha is a housewife. They have two children, Rashid (age 12) and Amina (age 14). The family starts its day with a bowl of *cheera,* flattened rice, served with sugar, fruits, yogurt, or milk, or sometimes a bowl of Western cereal and toast. Fazrul has lunch at his office canteen, while the children have lunch at school. Around 5 P.M. the family has an afternoon cup of tea with snacks and sweets. Sometimes friends and relatives drop in to visit. Dinner is typically eaten at 9 P.M. and includes rice, dal (stewed lentils), two vegetable dishes, and a meat or fish curry.

Major Foodstuffs

The main crop of Bangladesh is rice, and it is the staple of the diet. Instead of asking "Have you had lunch (or dinner)?" a Bengali speaker asks, "Bhat kheiicho?" (Have you eaten rice?). The development of new hybrids under the green revolution greatly increased rice production in Bangladesh. Average annual consumption is around 350 pounds (175 kilograms) per person. Most rice is parboiled before use. The most common way of preparing rice at home is by boiling it in water with no added flavoring, a preparation called *bhat*. On more important

occasions, rice is fried in ghee and cooked with spices, nuts, meat, and vegetables. The second dietary staple is wheat, which is grown in the western parts of the country. Consumption averages about 46 pounds (21 kilograms) per person. Wheat is ground into flour and made into breads.

The rich soil of Bangladesh produces a multitude of edible plants. Vegetables include eggplant, cabbage, cauliflower, beans, many kinds of gourds and squash, chilies, okra, amaranth, sweet potatoes, spinach, carrots, plantains, onions, radishes, and water lilies. All parts of the plant are eaten, including the leaves, roots, stems, flowers, and stalks. Potatoes, grown in the winter, account for more than 55 percent of all vegetable production and are widely eaten as a vegetable rather than a staple. Bangladeshis are said to be the world's second-largest potato eaters after the Irish. Sugarcane is widely cultivated and consumed.

Unlike in India, where lentils are a dietary staple, Bangladeshis eat relatively small amounts of lentils, about 9 pounds (4 kilograms) per person per year, compared with about 25 pounds (11 kilograms) in India. One reason may be the lower incidence of vegetarianism and the availability of protein in fish. The most commonly eaten lentils are *masur dal,* or red lentils.

Bangladesh abounds with a large variety of tropical and subtropical fruits. The most widely cultivated are mangoes, jackfruit, pineapple, bananas, lychee, citrus fruits, guavas, papayas, custard apples, sapodillas, coconuts, tamarinds, melons, watermelons, pomegranates, palmyras (a relative of the coconut whose small fruits are gelatinous when immature), plums, rose apples, and Indian jujubes (something like a date). Many fruits with no equivalents in the West grow wild in the jungle, among them the *latkan,* monkey jack, durian, rattan, river ebony, *garcinia,* water coconut, and wild date palm.

An important source of protein is fish, which is abundant in rivers, canals, floodplains, ponds, and lakes and in the Bay of Bengal. Both West Bengalis and Bangladeshis are famous for their love of fish: According to a proverb, *maacher bhate bangali,* which means "Bengali = fish + rice." Bangladeshis consume an average of about 25 pounds

Exotic fruits and vegetables on display at a market in Bangladesh. (iStockPhoto)

(11 kilograms) a year of seafood and 20 pounds (9 kilograms) of freshwater fish. Sea fish are generally considered less desirable than freshwater fish, especially those caught in rivers. Exceptions are pomfret and *bekti* (a delicate codlike fish), shrimp, and prawns. The most highly prized fish is *hilsa,* the national fish of Bangladesh. Related to the shad, it is a sea fish that swims upriver to spawn. It is very oily and bony and must be eaten with great care, using one's fingers. Other popular fish are *rui* (buffalo) and *magur* (catfish), which are pond dwellers; koi; "the climbing perch"; *chital* (featherback fish); groupers; croakers; and grey mullet. Dried fish is eaten mainly in coastal regions.

Because meat is expensive, consumption is very low (about 8 pounds, or 3.5 kilograms per year); meat is eaten by most Bangladeshis only on special occasions. The most common meats are beef, water buffalo, goat, and chicken. The establishment of large poultry farms has increased the availability of chickens and eggs.

Dairy products are an important source of protein. Around two-thirds of all the milk consumed in Bangladesh comes from goats, which are raised by the rural poor, especially women. Yogurt (*dahi*) is widely used as a marinade for meat, served as a side dish, or churned to produce butter. Cow milk and sugar are the main ingredients in Bangladeshi sweets.

Bangladesh is a major producer and exporter of chilies. Other spices grown in the country are ginger, garlic, turmeric, red pepper, and coriander.

Cooking

Kitchens in Bangladesh are simple by Western standards. Most cooking is done on top of a simple burner. The traditional stove is a small clay oven with a hole for inserting fuel and knobs on the top to hold the pot. Traditional fuels are charcoal, twigs, and dried cow patties. Today, middle-class households use a small cooktop with two burners fueled by bottled gas (propane). Sautéing and deep-frying are done in a wok-shaped pot made of stainless steel or cast iron, called a *karai.* A heavy, flat iron griddle with a wooden handle, called a *tawa,* is used for roasting spices and sautéing breads.

Spices can be dry-roasted and ground into a powder. Powdered or whole spices may be sautéed and added to a dish at the end of the cooking process to add flavor. For vegetables and dals, Bangladeshis use a spice mixture called *panch phoron* (five spices), a mixture of equal parts of fennel seed, *radhuni* (also known as celery seeds), nigella (*N. sativa,* sometimes called black cumin or onion seed), fenugreek, and cumin seeds. Panch phoron is typically added at the end of the cooking by frying it in oil or ghee and adding it to the dish. Spices can also be ground into a wet paste with onions, garlic, ginger, yogurt, coconut milk, or some other liquid that serves as the basis of a gravy, especially for meat dishes.

Pickling, an ancient technique, is essential in a country with a hot climate. It is a way of preserving fruits, vegetables, meat, or fish by impregnating them with acid, which discourages the growth of most microbes. In the coastal regions of Bangladesh, drying fish or salting them and sealing them in earthenware pots is a common practice.

Typical Meals

People in rural areas often start the day with *panta bhat,* boiled rice that is soaked overnight in water so that it becomes slightly fermented and is then mixed with salt and chilies. Other breakfast staples are *moori* (puffed rice), cheera (flattened rice), and *khoi* (popped rice), eaten with milk or yogurt and seasonal fruits. Middle-class city dwellers may have a breakfast of Western-style cereal or toast and eggs.

Traditionally, lunch was the main meal of the day, taken between 1 and 2 P.M. Before the days of outside employment, the entire family ate together, but today the breadwinner eats outside the home. A typical lunch centers around rice, supplemented by dal, vegetables, and, for those who can afford it, fish. Vegetable preparations include *bhorta* (boiled vegetables mashed and flavored with mustard oil and spices) and *bhati* (sautéed or fried vegetables). Fish can be fried; simmered in a thin, watery gravy (*jhol*); cooked with large amounts of onions (*dopijaji*); fried crisp; or made into a spicy chili-flavored dish called a *jhal.* Sweet chutneys, made from mango or tomatoes, and hot and sour pickles are standard accompaniments.

Because it is expensive, meat is not a common everyday dish even among the affluent. Meat is often eaten with a bread called *lucchhis,* made with a dough of white flour, oil, and water that is rolled into disks that are then deep-fried until they puff into spheres. A meal ends with yogurt, either plain or sweetened with sugar.

Throughout the Indian Subcontinent people take an afternoon meal called tea, and the Bangladeshis are no exception. Taken around 5 P.M., this consists of cups of black tea served with salty snacks and sweets. Sweets are one of the glories of Bengali/Bangladeshi cuisine and are distributed to friends and families on the occasion of births, engagements, weddings, success in examinations, and religious festivals. A traditional homemade sweet is *pantua,* deep-fried sausage-shaped rolls made of semolina, milk, ghee, and sugar syrup. Today, most people purchase sweets from sweet shops, some of them dating back to the 19th century. Bengali sweets are typically made from *chhanna*—the curd produced by separating milk with a sour substance (a technique that may have been introduced by the Portuguese in the 16th century). It is heated with sugar and ghee and flavored with cardamom powder, rose water, nuts, or orange rind. The apogee of the Bengali sweetmaker's art is *sandesh,* small fudgelike

A selection of traditional Bengali sweets, including jamun and mawa. (iStockPhoto)

delicacies made by pressing the dough into pretty molds shaped like flowers, fruits, or shells. There are more than 100 varieties of sandesh, with poetic names such as *pranahara* (losing one's heart), which is a specialty of Dhaka. Dinner is typically eaten very late, around 9 P.M. or even later, and is a smaller version of lunch. The standard drink taken with meals is water.

The meals of Hindu Bangladeshis are similar. One difference is that a meal typically begins with a bitter dish, such as *shukto,* made with diced bitter gourd, white radish, potatoes, beans, and other vegetables.

Eating Out

The subcontinent did not have a restaurant culture in the past; eating meals outside the house was a necessity rather than a luxury or source of pleasure.

However, from ancient times people bought savory items from stalls and street vendors, including *shingara* (deep-fried pastry shells filled with vegetables or meat), kebabs, curries, and salty snacks. Today, in Dhaka and other large towns, restaurants serve Thai, Italian, and Chinese food as well as American-style burgers and sandwiches. Sweet shops are ubiquitous in Bangladeshi towns, many serving local specialties.

Special Occasions

Meat is central to the feasts and festivals of Muslim Bangladeshis. The most important holiday is Eid al-Fitr, which ends the fasting month of Ramadan. Goats or cows are sacrificed, and elaborate dishes are prepared and served to friends and family and to the poor.

Hindu Bangladeshis celebrate Durga Puja in the autumn by building statues of the goddess. On the final day, Bijoya Dashami, people visit each other and bring sweets, including sandesh, *rosgollas* (cheese dumplings in syrup), pantua, *patishapta* (sweet stuffed crepes), and *malpoas* (fritters in syrup).

Malpoa

3 c sugar, divided

2 c water

1 c flour

¾ c milk

1 tsp fennel or anise seeds

1 c clarified butter or vegetable oil

Make a thin syrup with 2 cups sugar and the water. Set aside.

Mix the flour and remaining sugar, and then add the milk to make a smooth, thick batter. Add the fennel.

Heat the ghee or oil in a shallow pan, and pour 1 tablespoon of batter into the fat. Fry on both sides until brown. Remove with a slotted spoon, and dip into the syrup.

Chill and serve cold.

All communities celebrate the harvesting of new rice at community festivals. Typical dishes include *payesh,* a rice pudding made with *gur* (a gritty brown sugar made by boiling down sugarcane juice); a potato dish called *alur dam* with lucchhis; a dal made with yellow split peas and coconut; and sweets.

Bangladeshi weddings are lavish affairs to which hundreds or even thousands of guests are invited. The wedding banquet features as many meat dishes as the bride's family can afford. Traditionally it includes at least one biryani, *korma/qorma* (meat cooked in a fragrant yogurt gravy), rezala (meat slow-cooked in a piquant white gravy), Dhaka parota, *navrattan* (mixed vegetables), *shami* kebab (patties made of ground meat and chickpeas), fish curry or fried fish, yogurt and cucumber salad, bread, and many desserts, including rice pudding (*kheer*) in clay pots, *gulab jaman* (chhanna balls in a sugar syrup), *ras malai* (chhanna balls in a cream sauce), wedding cake, and tea.

Diet and Health

In addition to Western medicine, the traditional Ayurvedic and Unani systems are widely practiced in Bangladesh, especially at the primary health care level. An estimated 70 to 75 percent of people in the country still use traditional medicine to manage their health problems.

Ayurveda, the ancient Indian school of medicine, had its roots in the region. Ayurveda is holistic: It treats the entire individual, including one's mental, emotional, and physical makeup, not just the symptoms. Ayurveda also strongly emphasizes the link between health and diet. The goal of eating is to increase desirable qualities, reduce negative qualities, and introduce previously absent qualities.

Unani, the Muslim system of medicine, is offered by 4,000 qualified and professionally trained physicians, called *hakims*. Unani medicine is based on the humoral theory of Greek medicine, which assumes the presence of four humors in the body: blood, phlegm, yellow bile, and black bile. Every person is born with a unique humoral constitution, which represents his healthy state and determines his personality. When the amounts of the humors are changed and thrown out of balance with each other, it leads to disease. Restoring the quality and balance of humors is the goal of treatment, and diet plays a role in this. Certain foods are prescribed for certain ailments.

Colleen Taylor Sen

Further Reading

Banerji, Chitrita. *Life and Food in Bengal.* Delhi: Penguin Books India, 1991.

The National Encyclopedia of Bangladesh. http://www.banglapedia.org/.

Sen, Colleen Taylor, with Joe Roberts. "A Carp Wearing Lipstick: The Role of Fish in Bengali Cuisine and Culture." In *Fish: Food from the Waters, Proceedings of the Oxford Symposium on Food and Cookery,* edited by Harlan Walker. Totnes, Devon, UK: Prospect Books, 1997.

Brunei

Overview

A tiny jewel perched on the tip of Sarawak, Brunei became a force to contend with when oil was discovered around 1929. From ancient times it has always been regarded as one of the more progressive countries in the area, much spoken about by seafarers and sought after by colonials including Spain and Portugal, especially during the golden age of Sultan Bolkiah, head of the longest-running hereditary monarchy in the world, when Brunei ruled all of Sumatra, Borneo, and the southern islands of the Philippines. Brunei then stood alone as a proud monarchy. Only through James Brooke's subtle approach as Raja Brooke of Sarawak were the British colonials able to force a series of treaties on the royal house that, in typical colonial maneuvers, left Brunei as it stands today: two elongated slivers of land separated by a tract of Sarawak.

The present Sultan Haji Hassanal Bolkiah, a graduate of the Sandhurst military academy with close ties to British royalty, rules the country with absolute power and has kept the peace as his father did, while laying the foundations for independent rule from the British. The sultan is simultaneously ruler, prime minister, and minister for defense in a country that stresses the importance of Malay culture, Islam, and the monarchy in Darussalam, which means "Abode of Peace."

Of the population of 389,000, 68 percent are Brunei-Muslim, practicing a brand of Islamic fundamentalism. There is no income tax for anyone, including the 29 percent Chinese and 3 percent expatriates working in government and in the private sector, who enjoy generous pensions with many handouts from the government such as free overseas education, lifetime guaranteed jobs, and occasional cash bonuses when oil prices soar. Islam plays an overall decisive role in the country, today more than ever before.

Food Culture Snapshot

Mohamed Shafar and Noor Azna are a middle-class couple living in a government-subsidized townhouse in a suburb close to Bandar Sari Begawan, or BSB. Shafar, a teacher of information technology, and Azna, a dental nurse, both work in the city. They are saving for a deposit for a house of their own. As government employees they have the added advantage of interest-free loans.

After the 5 A.M. call to prayer, breakfast is a meal of toast and fried eggs splashed with some soy sauce, washed down with black coffee. Shafar and Azna travel together to work and on the way pick up a light lunch of rice or noodles from hawker stalls close to Shafar's office. Today it is a banana leaf–wrapped packet of *nasi lemak,* coconut rice with spiced whitebait *ikan bilis* sambal (a sauce made of the tiny fish) and slices of fresh cucumber. Azna prefers a simple *gado-gado,* a fresh vegetable salad with crisp pineapple, cucumber, and tofu cubes drizzled with a light peanut sauce.

Dinner is curried fish, tofu served with a spicy shrimp paste (*belacan*) sauce, and a stir-fry of mixed vegetables, served after evening prayers at about 7:30 P.M. Dinner plates are set on batik placemats with glasses of water on the side. There is no cutlery except for the serving spoons at each dish. While dining privately at home, people eat with their fingers or with chopsticks.

Major Foodstuffs

Although Brunei is self-sufficient in poultry and egg production, Chinese greens, and some seafood, almost 80 percent of Brunei's food is imported from Malaysia and Indonesia. Australia and the United States supply frozen and fresh halal beef and lamb, as well as most other goods including fresh ultrapasteurized milk in cartons and canned evaporated milk.

Pork, deemed *haram* (forbidden) for the Muslim market, is imported for the non-Muslims as pig rearing is banned here. Pork is clearly labeled and separated from halal meats in local markets and supermarkets with cold-storage facilities. The sale of alcohol is banned, although expatriates and non-Muslim residents are allowed restricted amounts when entering Brunei. Duty-free liquor is available on Labuan Island, Malaysia, a short boat ride from the capital, BSB.

A broad variety of foods is available to cater for the varied peoples living here. Food is available from the less expensive wet markets, where water is sprayed regularly to keep greens fresh for daily shoppers. Malay vegetable stalls specialize in fern shoots, small-leaved greens, lotus stems, spinach, varieties of sweet potatoes, and local herbs, especially the Vietnamese mint, galangal (*lengkuas*), lemongrass (*serai*), pink torch ginger (*bunga kantan*), kaffir lime leaves called *daun limau perut,* sweet potato leaves, various types of basil, banana flowers, the aromatic *pandan* (pandanus) leaf, and stacks of banana leaves, the aluminum foil of the East, used for wrapping and cooking. Shrimp paste is sold in cakes and packed in banana leaves to keep it fresh.

Asian greens are plentiful: Chinese bok choy, *kai lan* (Chinese broccoli) and *kang kong* (water convolvulus), long beans, green golf ball–sized eggplants, and green bitter melons are popular, as are garlic chives, onions, garlic, and spring onions. Here tofu products are also found, close to salted radishes,

Nasi lemak, the most popular food in Brunei that can be served during breakfast, lunch, dinner, and as a snack. (Hooelse | Dreamstime.com)

fresh bean sprouts, and noodles, including broad flat rice noodles and yellow wheat noodles. Coconut halves are freshly grated and pressed into coconut milk that is sold in plastic bags, where in a few minutes the heavier cream separates from the milky fluid.

During the April fruit season, a mad profusion of exotic fruits are available: The strong smelling durians, mangosteens, green and yellow mangoes, pomelo and other citrus, watermelons, longans, and rambutans will satisfy every palate. On the main roads, seasonal stalls are piled high with rambutans, durians, and mangosteens to attract the shoppers in passing traffic. These fruits have short shelf lives and have to be disposed of quickly.

Seafood is the preferred protein, eaten at least three times a week. At the fishmongers, customers find snapper, mackerel, small red-spotted whiting, black and white pomfret, *kembong,* anchovies dried into ikan bilis, and shoals of prawns sitting amid shaved ice next to crates of blue swimmers and live mud crabs.

A halal section with meat on hooks and fresh poultry is slightly less expensive than the chilled meats at the cold-storage supermarkets. Spice stores specialize in curry powders and pastes, tamarinds, and dried prawns as well as flours—local sago flour from the sago-palm core and glutinous rice, wheat, and tapioca flours—and wines, cooking oils, and Chinese vinegars.

Cooking

The food eaten in Brunei is similar to the food of Malaysia as the inhabitants of these places are basically the same people eating a blend of food influenced by Indian and Chinese traders who traveled through from the 11th century on and who married their styles with local herbs and Malay cooking using woks brought with them. Although the food is intricate to prepare, the kitchens are basic, with cupboards for storage and counters. A gas burner with two or three rings, a coconut scraper stool with a protruding goose-necked scraper with prongs for scraping coconut halves, and a granite mortar and pestle for grinding herbs seem sufficient. A sharp Chinese cleaver tackles the slicing and chopping, done on a large chopping board from a tree trunk. Garlic, onions, and chilies are dry-roasted and then pounded before being added to meat and fish. Vegetables are stir-fried, sautéed, or stewed in soups or sometimes mashed into pureed sambals with chili, ginger, and garlic. Tamarind sours a curry without any tartness, and tofu is used by Chinese and Malays especially as its health-promoting properties are known and respected.

Malay cooking is spicy, reflecting Indian and Arab styles with tasty sambals, curries, and elaborate rice, meat, and vegetable dishes with a Mogul bent, while Chinese meals are sauce based. Various methods of cooking are used: stir-frying, stewing, steaming, and boiling. There are few salad dishes. Rice or noodles forms the main meal, and these are eaten twice, even three times a day, with a small quantity of meat or fish, which is sliced thinly and tossed with vegetables or served on its own.

Typical Meals

Meals are eaten with the fingers of the right hand, managed by pinching off pieces of fish or meat and mixing them with some curry sauce, some vegetables, and a small amount of rice. The thumb acts as a shovel. The palm of the hand should remain clean. Everything is sliced into small pieces for holding small portions for eating.

Bruneians are used to eating smaller portions of meat or fish cooked with vegetables. In most of Asia, the main carbohydrate (in this case, rice) is served on a dining table along with three or more vegetable dishes. Etiquette decrees that one never takes a second helping unless invited by the hostess.

Typical meals may be fried rice cooked with fresh prawns and Chinese vegetables with a chili stir-fry base or rice noodles called *mee-hoon,* chock-full of dried prawns, mushrooms, and leafy greens. Tofu or tempeh (fermented soybeans) is often added for texture. Chicken rice steamed in chicken stock is served with a sweet chili sauce. Indian roti with a soupy lentil and vegetable curry is commonly served at lunchtime. Malay dishes are stronger flavored with lemongrass, galangal, and chili. A good example is the *laksa,* a soupy curried coconut soup flavored with lemongrass, galangal, and chili. In contrast, Chinese meals are less spicy. Steamed prawns and fish with slivers of ginger are popular, as well as chicken wings steeped in wine, beef slivers cooked in a black bean sauce, and *yong tofu* (tofu puffs stuffed with fish paste served in a rich brothy soup).

Malay festive dishes include slow-cooked beef *rendang* cooked in 12 spices. Fried fish and prawn sambals are served in spicy sauces. Chicken *satay* (strips of meat on a skewer) is typical of the region. When entertaining guests, noodle dishes are served in Chinese bowls with chopsticks, but when a rice meal is served, forks and spoons are laid with paper napkins. Knives, traditionally considered a sign of aggression, are never placed on the table.

Prawn Sambal

2 lemongrass bulbs, finely chopped

4 cloves garlic, finely chopped

2 red onions (to yield 1 c chopped)

1 tbsp dried prawns, soaked in hot water

1 tbsp chili paste or Indonesian *sambal oelek*

¼ c vegetable oil

1½ c coconut milk

1 lb peeled green shrimp

Salt, sugar, and fresh lime juice to taste

Garnish of cilantro leaves

Collect all the chopped ingredients, and pound roughly in a mortar and pestle with the dried prawns and the chili paste.

Heat the oil in a wok, and add the blended mixture. Stir until the aromas are fragrant and to prevent sticking at the bottom of wok. Add the coconut milk, mix, and simmer to reduce mixture to a thick pouring consistency, then add the shrimp and allow to cook for 3 to 4 minutes until shrimp turn pink. Season with salt, sugar, and fresh lime juice, and garnish with cilantro leaves.

Eating Out

Restaurants attached to the hotel chains serve high-quality halal meals and a tantalizing mix of local and foreign steaks and pasta dishes everywhere. Malay and Chinese restaurants and coffeehouses are available for those who want to enjoy a meal cooked outside the home. Asians prefer to eat at small stalls and take-out cafés that serve a variety of cuisines. They are normally found in the busy parts of the city. Often a family with pajama-clad children in tow can be seen at a late-night market, enjoying a "past-bedtime" bowl of piping hot fish congee (rice porridge). It is also possible to sample Brunei's official dish, the *ambuyat,* a starchy sago flour boiled into a thick pasty mush, eaten with a

two-pronged bamboo sticks called *chanda* and accompanied with many spicy sambal dips to flavor the pottage.

People snack at any time of day, buying from many portable stalls that move to serve commuting office workers throughout the day. Here, cakes and noodles are available 24/7, and even a unique version of cappuccino: coffee *kopi tarik,* sweetened with condensed milk, then frothed by pouring from a distance. This is served in a plastic bag threaded through with the ubiquitous pink raffia as a handle.

Special Occasions

Ramadan is the most important Muslim festival. It is a month of fasting, the end of which (Eid al-Fitr) is celebrated with a general open-house invitation to friends and colleagues, who come to pay their respects to the family. Clothed in their best, Muslim families in silken *kain songket* cloth sarongs and batik shirts invite their guests to a heavily laden buffet table laden with celebratory food including rendang, saffron or biryani rice, and glutinous rice coconut cakes. No alcohol is served, but fresh lime barley or commercial fizzy drinks like Coke or orange crush are an acceptable alternative to tea.

Children greet their elders by bowing low, hands held to their hearts, addressing them as aunt or uncle, a custom that defers to elders in the community. To call an adult by his common name would be an unpardonable offence. Shoes are left on the doorstep Brunei-style, where one can be fully dressed without shoes.

Chinese New Year, celebrated similarly by Chinese the world over, begins with a New Year's Eve dinner where ancestors are remembered and "lucky" dishes—including prawns for happiness and fish with black moss fungus—portend good luck for the New Year. Firecrackers are lit to dispel bad luck, and children receive lucky red packets of money.

Diet and Health

The spices and herbs used in Brunei, Malaysia, and Indonesia have been used for centuries for their health-giving properties, long before people started using them in cooking. Spices like turmeric, cinnamon, ginger juice, the Asian pennywort or *gotu kola,* and asafetida are now being seriously researched to determine their healing properties as the locals have used them for centuries with positive results. Brunei is also a well-informed country, where health authorities remind the people of health issues, such as the dangers of the cholesterol in coconut milk, and encourage active exercise classes. In BSB, the capital city, many gymnasiums offer affordable exercise classes to encourage the younger office workers to keep trim. Brunei has its fair share of joggers and Hash House Harriers, as in any part of the world, but unless the sedentary lifestyle gets to them, balanced meals with large helpings of vegetables will continue to be advantageous to health.

Carol Selva Rajah

Further Reading

Selva Rajah, Carol. *The Essential Guide to Buying and Using Essential Asian Ingredients.* Chatswood, Australia: New Holland Press, 2002.

Selva Rajah, Carol. *Heavenly Fragrance: Mastering the Art of Aromatic Asian Cooking.* Singapore: Periplus, 2008.

Selva Rajah, Carol. *Makan, lah.* Sydney, Australia: Harper Collins, 1997.

Selva Rajah, Carol. *Malaysian Cooking.* Singapore: Periplus, 2010.

Solomon, Charmaine. *The Asian Cookbook.* Sydney, Australia: Weldon Hardie, 1997.

Cambodia

Overview

Cambodia shares many culinary traditions with the neighboring countries of Thailand, Laos, Vietnam, and Indonesia. This reflects the power of the Khmer Empire in the 9th to 15th centuries, spreading the influence of this Indianized kingdom beyond the borders of present-day Cambodia. The royal tradition of palace food centered in the temple complex of Angkor Wat had a profound influence on Thai palace food. Thai and Khmer palace cooking share the elaborate flavoring pastes based on herbs and spices that enrich their curries, soups, and stews. Cambodian dishes are likely to contain more aromatic spices such as cardamom, star anise, cloves, and nutmeg, common in the islands, along with lemongrass, ginger, galangal, coriander, and wild lime leaves. Most dishes make less use of the fiery hot chilies that dominate Thai cooking.

The Khmer in Cambodia make up about 90 percent of the population. Theravada Buddhism is the dominant religion in Cambodia, although in the war years under the Khmer Rouge, religious practice was forbidden and culinary skills all but disappeared, as the country faced a constant state of near starvation.

The Mekong River and its delta in southern Vietnam is the longest river in Southeast Asia, forming boundaries and bounty for communities living in southern China, Thailand, the Lao People's Democratic Republic, Cambodia, and Vietnam. The Mekong and its tributaries create rich alluvial soils ideally suited for wet-rice agriculture. The Khmer built their earliest civilizations around the Mekong River and the freshwater lake, Tonle Sap. The great

Tonle Sap represents the largest reserve of freshwater fish in the world in the rainy season. This is reflected in the fish dishes that accompany most Cambodian meals today.

Food Culture Snapshot

Nary and Chayim owned a rice mill in the town of Siem Riep, near the famous site of Angkor Wat. As successful entrepreneurs of Chinese and Cambodian ancestry, they had made a comfortable life for themselves and their four grown children. Their rice for daily meals came from their own land, worked by their children's families. The daughters knew how to make the side dishes of grilled fish, soups, and stir-fried vegetables they consumed from ingredients grown on their own land. In the 1960s and early 1970s, they would drive into Phnom Penh several times a year to visit the family of Nary's brother, who worked for the government in the diplomatic corps. When he was not overseas, he set a European table and had his wife and servant prepare French dishes for his dinner every night, including French bread and French wine with his meals. Nary enjoyed these occasional meals, but Chayim missed the richly flavored fish curries his family prepared at home.

After 1975, when the Khmer Rouge took over the country, Nary's brother and his family were executed, and Chayim disappeared. Nary and her children were separated and sent to work camps, where they barely survived; somehow, they survived the starvation rations and heavy workload. Eating only a few grains of rice and insects, Nary made it through the war years and now lives in a more modest style in her daughter's home in a village near Siem Riep. Here, she teaches her grandchildren how to make the dishes she remembers from her childhood—grilled fish, soups delicately flavored with lemongrass, and steamed cakes.

Major Foodstuffs

Cambodians prefer long-grain nonglutinous rice as their main staple. Rituals accompany the skilled technical practices of rice production, ritual work that must be accomplished for a good harvest. These important rice rituals were probably established to support the complex irrigation systems that flourished during the powerful Khmer Empire. Irrigated wet rice varieties are the most productive but rely on canals, irrigation systems, terracing, and other labor-intensive techniques to produce large yields. These were not maintained under the Khmer Rouge leadership, who knew little about the day-to-day work of rice farming.

Fish and fermented fish products are also critically important to Cambodian diets. Freshwater fish, sea fish, and shellfish are the major sources of protein for most meals. The Mekong River has supplied people from Cambodia with a steady supply of river fish for centuries. Snakehead, snapper, catfish, and mackerel are popular fish in the country. In Cambodia, the Tonle Sap (Great Lake) supplies a large variety of freshwater fish for much of the population especially during the rainy season. In November, when the waters of the Tonle Sap crest and begin to run backward, freshwater fish are scooped up in quantity. Cambodians process this fish in a variety of ways, including making a preserved fermented fish product, *prahok,* in order to make full use of the seasonal surplus all year long. The fish and shellfish are also sun-dried and salted.

Vegetables such as green beans, bamboo shoots, squash, eggplant, and wild and cultivated greens are served in soups; stir-fried with onions, garlic, meat, or fish; or served raw or lightly steamed with fermented fish products as dipping sauces. They are key ingredients in dry and wet curries. Eggplants come in a wide variety of forms, from long green or purple plants used for grilling or stir-fries to tiny bitter pealike plants flavoring curries. Other popular

vegetables include banana blossoms, bitter melons, lotus, bok choy, rapini, napa cabbage, sweet potatoes, and green onions or scallions. Chinese chives and bean sprouts (from soy and mung beans) garnish a wide variety of side dishes. Cambodians enjoy a wide range of tropical fruits and include preserved lemons in many savory dishes. They honor the durian as the king of fruit and the mangosteen as the queen, and they enjoy fruit as a snack or with salted fish and rice as part of a simple meal.

Cooking

In the decades after World War II, it was common for urban middle-class and elite households in Cambodia to have servants, including cooks who were trained to prepare French dishes; children from these households may never have learned to cook and would have to learn Cambodian recipes from cookbooks as adults. The disruption of war and famine in the 1970s and 1980s further eroded the transmission of traditional knowledge of Cambodian cooking. Cambodians who fled the country as refugees may have carried with them treasured family recipes and cooking techniques.

Cambodian meals include steamed rice with a number of accompanying side dishes. Many side dishes are grilled or stir-fried, but some specialties such as chicken or fish *amok* (with a thick coconut sauce) are steamed. Curries and wet or dry stews are cooked with aromatic flavoring pastes. Many ingredients such as chilies, garlic, and shallots are dry-roasted before cooking to intensify their flavors. Sesame seeds mixed with salt and black pepper can be dry-roasted and ground, with or without dried chilies, to enhance dishes served with rice. Lemongrass and galangal can be added to the mixture. In Cambodia, stir-frying is usually the last step in preparing a dish to go with rice. Vegetables are washed and dried, cut evenly, and cooked quickly over high heat in small amounts of oil with meat, fish, and seasonings, as in this simple but tasty dish:

Cambodian Pork and Eggplant Stir-Fry

This simple eggplant stir-fry could be made with other vegetables as well.

3 eggplants

2 tbsp oil

5 cloves garlic, coarsely chopped

½ lb ground pork

2 tbsp fish sauce

1 tbsp sugar

Ground black pepper

Small bunch of garlic chive blossoms, cut in 2-in. lengths

Prick eggplant and grill or roast for 40 minutes until soft. When cool, peel and mash the flesh. Stir-fry garlic in oil until golden, and add pork. Add fish sauce, sugar, and pepper. Add eggplant and chives, stir-frying until well mixed, and serve with rice.

Typical Meals

In the capital city and major towns, a wider range of meal options including baguettes and noodles are available from food vendors for breakfast and snacks. Most rural Cambodians eat rice with side dishes for all meals. A special stew or thick soup made for an evening meal might be heated up and eaten for breakfast with rice the next morning.

Cambodian meals are served all at once, rather than in courses, unless the meal contains French-style dishes, in which case the European pattern of courses is followed. Cambodian meals do not usually begin with appetizers. The Western category of appetizer might better be understood as the food to go with drinks, often snack foods purchased from street vendors—or side dishes without rice. When there are several side dishes, it is appropriate

A typical meal found in Cambodia from a popular restaurant. (Anyee | Dreamstime.com)

to take a small amount from one side dish at a time rather than pile a selection of all side dishes on a plate of rice at once. The latter is considered both rude and foolish, as mixing the side dishes makes it difficult to appreciate the taste contrasts and to personalize mouthfuls. Dry and wet condiments are placed directly on rice or on the side of the plate.

Accompanying most Cambodian meals is a sauce or paste made from fermented fish or shellfish. Fish sauce is also a crucial ingredient in most Khmer dishes. A thicker form of fermented fish, called pra-hok in Khmer, is served as a dish with rice, often accompanied by raw or lightly steamed vegetables. Fermented catfish or snakehead fish provides the distinctive salty taste in Khmer dishes. Fermented fish products can be served alone as a condiment or made into more complex sauces by adding a number of herbs and spices.

Caramelized Fish

This technique of caramelizing fish is also popular in Vietnamese cooking; the caramelizing process probably has its origin in French techniques.

1 trout, cleaned and filleted

3 tbsp sugar

1 tbsp water plus 1 c water

2 cloves garlic, chopped

1 tbsp fish sauce

Black pepper

3 green onions, chopped

Cut fish into strips and set aside. Make a caramel sauce by browning 1 tablespoon sugar in 1 tablespoon water in a skillet. When it is brown, slowly add 1 cup water and stir until it is an even brown color. Add chopped garlic, the remaining sugar, and fish sauce, along with the fish steaks. Simmer, and turn the fish when it is cooked on one side and the sauce thickens. Remove from heat, and garnish with black pepper and green onions. Serve with rice.

Eating Out

While French restaurants once flourished in the towns and cities of Cambodia, the years of war reduced their numbers, and they do a good business only in the capital of Phnom Penh, where visitors have the cash to eat out on a regular basis. However, street foods have returned to the towns and cities in the form of vendors close to central markets and small noodle shops. Night markets in the capital sell foods like chicken, beef, or pork *satay* (thin strips of meat on a skewer), sausages, fried bananas, glutinous rice cakes, grilled squid, baguette sandwiches, fried or fresh spring rolls, salty or sweet fried doughnuts, and rice porridge.

Fried or grilled meats, sausages, and deep-fried snacks including insects such as crickets and grasshoppers may be offered at small drinking shops frequented mostly by men. As the economy recovers, more lakeside, riverside, and seaside restaurants feature regional specialties of fried, smoked, grilled, or salted fish.

Special Occasions

Cambodians celebrate life-cycle events such as births, weddings, and funerals as well as the round of Buddhist holidays that fit with the agricultural cycle. New Year's celebrations in April are always occasions for festive meals. Grilled fish with special relishes is popular on such occasions, as well as grilled packets of glutinous rice with coconut milk and bananas wrapped in banana leaves.

The Khmer Rouge disrupted the cycle of Buddhist rituals that used to be integrated into the rural agricultural cycle. Where temples are flourishing, rural and urban households cook rice at dawn for distribution to monks on their early-morning alms rounds. This means that boiled rice is available for family breakfasts. The best dishes the family can afford are prepared for the monks early in the morning; later, the family and neighbors can enjoy the rest of the dishes for their breakfast meal. Some families prepare special food for the monks only on the days when religious services are held in the community temples of Cambodia.

Diet and Health

There are few food cultures more ideally suited to human health than the Cambodian diet based on rice, fish, fresh vegetables, and fruit. However, the war years disrupted the development of the once-famous Cambodian cuisine associated with the ancient Khmer Empire.

Cambodia faces severe problems with malnutrition, with many communities and households eating less than the minimal calories recommended. Most of the available calories come from rice. The World Food Program estimates that a third of the population is undernourished. The infant mortality rate of 98 deaths per 1,000 live births is dropping, as is the under-five mortality rate (143 per 1,000). But malnutrition remains a significant problem in the country. International assistance has focused on immunizations, food supplements in schools, and vitamin A supplementation. Few households use iodized salt, which means that iodine deficiency and goiter are still common.

When Cambodians fled their country as refugees, escaping war and the repressive regime of the Khmer Rouge, healers known as Khru Khmer offered a variety of traditional medical services in the refugee camps, including massage and herbal therapies.

Penny Van Esterik

Further Reading

Alford, Jeffrey, and Naomi Duguid. *Hot Sour Salty Sweet.* Toronto, Canada: Random House Canada, 2000.

Brissenden, Rosemary. *Southeast Asian Food.* Singapore: Periplus, 2007.

"Cambodia." Asian Recipe. http://Asiarecipe.com/Cambodia.html.

De Monteiro, Longteine, and Katherine Neustadt. *The Elephant Walk Cookbook.* Boston: Houghton Mifflin, 1998.

Van Esterik, Penny. "Food and the Refugee Experience: Gender and Food in Exile, Asylum, and Repatriation." In *Development and Diaspora,* edited by P. Van Esterik, W. Giles, and H. Moussa, 61–74. Dundas, Canada: Artemis Press, 1996.

Van Esterik, Penny. *Food Culture in Southeast Asia.* Westport, CT: Greenwood Press, 2008.

Central Asia

Overview

Central Asia, including the province of Xinjiang in China, is a massive territory, more than half the size of the United States. The newly independent states of Uzbekistan, Turkmenistan, Tajikistan, and Kyrgyzstan are situated east of the Caspian Sea, west of China, south of Russia, and north of Afghanistan and Iran. (A fifth state, Kazakhstan, just to the north, is covered in a separate article.) Central Asia is generally regarded as a vast, imprecise zone, simultaneously connecting and dividing the continents of Europe and Asia. Turkic and Iranian peoples are the dominant cultural groups of the region.

Far from the moderating influence of oceans, the main geographic features of the region are steppe, desert, and mountains. Most of the land is desert in Uzbekistan (two-thirds), Xinjiang (two-thirds), and Turkmenistan (four-fifths), in addition to semiarid plains. Kyrgyzstan and Tajikistan are mountainous regions; towering ranges from 16,000 to 26,000 feet radiating out from the Pamirs form the border separating Central Asia from India and China.

For Central Asian non-nomadic (sedentary) society, the vibrant culture of Iran was the primary creative inspiration, with later Arabic and Chinese contributions. Most recently, 150 years of Russian control in the Soviet era have considerably altered the foodways. The varied Central Asian cuisine also forms the foundation of cookery in modern-day Turkey. The mountains, steppes, and deserts divided people into two lifestyles—scattered settlements in river valleys and along oases on the one hand, and nomadic pastoralists on the other. The swath of territory along the Silk Road—the network of exchange routes linking Asia and Europe—forms the heart of Central Asia, more specifically Uzbekistan, with its fabled cities of Samarqand and Bukhara.

Central Asian cuisine is as elusive as identifying the boundaries of the area itself. From Xian (the starting point for the Silk Road in China) to Istanbul on the threshold of Europe, the variety of dishes gradually diverges from one region to the next. Yet the similarities are more striking than the differences. Hospitality—symbolized in the *dastarkhan* (a Turkic word for "tablecloth," or "great spread")—is foremost among the common culinary cultural traits. More like a bountiful holiday table setting, dastarkhan refers to the prolific assortment of prepared dishes laid out for an honored guest.

The ancient Eastern hospitality, the ritual of the dastarkhan, flatbread, lamb, and cumin unite this area and its immense collection of traditions and produce, as well as setting Central Asian cuisine apart from Chinese, Indian, and European fare. Central Asia has been home to countless ethnic groups and kingdoms throughout the ages. While the new nations of Central Asia attempt to draw ethnic and cultural distinctions between themselves and their close neighbors, the region is a fascinating mix of Mongol, Turkic, and Iranian ancestry. Today, Central Asia is home to almost 80 million people. Turkic ethnic groups dominate post-Soviet Central Asian demographics, accounting for almost 65 percent of the population. Tajiks of Iranian extraction, Russians, and others make up the remaining ethnic groups.

Of all the Central Asian political units, Uzbekistan remains among the most distinctive in dress, language, culture, traditions, and customs. This contributes to a well-defined concept of identity in the post-Soviet world, due in part to the enormous Uzbek population and centuries of sedentary life. The Turkmen and Kyrgyz nomads were forcibly settled and collectivized by the Soviets—their culture, in essence, confined to unfamiliar apartment walls.

Central Asian nomadic groups keep sheep and goats as well. Cattle and camels are also herded, even though most cattle could barely survive the winters without fodder. The main source of protein in the nomadic diet is milk products, especially kumiss, yogurt, *ayran* (yogurt mixed with water), and *qurt* (or *qurut;* air-dried cheese).

In terms of culinary cultures, it is possible to divide the region into multiple categories: nomadic or urban, highland or lowland, and Mongol, Turkic, or Iranian. Kazakhstan, Kyrgyzstan, and Turkmenistan represent the subsistence nomadic diet based on meat and dairy products. The settled Turks—Uzbeks and Uighurs (from western China)—form another Central Asian tradition. Their core cuisine includes pilafs, kebabs, noodles, stews, tandoori breads (flatbreads cooked on the side wall of a cylindrical clay oven), and savory pastries. The Eastern philosophy of harmony and balance permeates the cuisine, underlying the preventative and medicinal qualities of food. The third culinary group is Iranian, encompassing Tajikistan and southern Uzbekistan, extending into parts of northern Pakistan and India. Rice dishes, stewed vegetables, extensive spices, and lavish sweets mark this cuisine. Despite attempts at classification and definition of all the varied features or regional variations, the uniformity of lifestyle, customs, and history produces a singular identifiable culinary culture.

🍽 Food Culture Snapshot

The Abdurakhmanov family lives in a downtown two-bedroom apartment in Tashkent, the capital of Uzbekistan. Gulmira is an accountant, and Ramiz is a dentist. Aziza is their nine-year-old daughter, and Surat is their five-year-old son. The family gathers on the weekends for meals at the grandmother's house, which contains a traditional gardened courtyard and detached kitchen. On Fridays, they prepare Central Asian pilaf with rice, mutton or beef, chickpeas, onions, and carrots. The other favorite outdoor meal is shish kebabs (*shashlyk*) of lamb, beef, or chicken.

Central Asian cuisine is extremely labor-intensive, requiring long preparation and cooking times. Therefore, it is quite common for the Abdurakhmanova to eat modestly throughout the week and make a special effort when guests come over or for the Friday meal. Ramiz, like most Muslim men, visits the mosque to participate in community worship on Fridays, and that evening is considered their family time at home or with the extended family at grandmother's house. She is fortunate enough to have a modest three-bedroom home with a courtyard. They take their weekend morning and evening meals outside in the shade. A raised square platform or dais with a low table in the center is the main place for enjoying family meals. In the heat of summer, it is fairly common to eat bread, fruit, and tea all day to stave off hunger and have only one large meal a day.

Their essential staples in the household are rice, flour, mutton, beef, onions, carrots, potatoes, tomatoes, and cucumbers. For a one-week period, the Abdurakhmanovs buy roughly 8 pounds of potatoes, 4 pounds of tomatoes, 4 pounds of cucumbers, 3 pounds of rice, 2 pounds of pasta, 2 pounds of flour, 2 pounds of carrots, 2 pounds of meat, 1.5 pounds of sugar, 1 pound of onions, 1 pound of bell peppers, 1.5 quarts of oil, and a dozen eggs. In autumn they add pumpkin and fruits.

For breakfast, the family eats buckwheat kasha (from the Russian influence) or rice porridge with milk and sugar. The weekly repertoire of dishes made by Gulmira includes pilaf and the pasta dishes of *manti, chuchvara,* and *khanum.* Manti are large steamed dumplings with a mutton and onion filling. Chuchvara are smaller boiled dumplings with a similar filling to that of manti. Khanum is also a steamed noodle roll with a mutton or pumpkin filling. Gulmira also regularly makes *samsa* (savory pastries) and soup. Other starch staples include store-bought flatbread, fried homemade flatbread (*gilmindi*), and spaghetti noodles. Green tea is consumed all day long, usually with bread or sweet biscuits.

Major Foodstuffs

The rich, mildly seasoned, and celebratory qualities of Central Asian cookery reflect the nomadic, Eastern, and Islamic customs of the region. The high courtly style of Persian cuisine, famous for its perfumed rice dishes and fat-tailed sheep, heavily influenced the regal cities of Samarqand, Bukhara, and Merv. Central Asian cuisine also incorporates the distinguished cooking methods of China with its reliance on woks and steaming. Grilled meats, yogurt, and stuffed vegetables are similar to those found in the Middle East. Rice pilaf, shashlyk, noodle dishes, flatbreads, and *halva* are among the most recognizable dishes. Dishes that may seem unusual to the Westerner include green turnip salads, pumpkin or mung bean stews, horse sausage, and hearty kebabs of liver and sheep fat. The Russians introduced beets, potatoes, and vodka, and the modern era brought pizza, beer, and ice cream sandwiches.

Grains form the dietary basis for most Central Asians; those that are grown in significant quantities are wheat, rice, millet, and barley. Millet is brewed into a beerlike drink called *boza* in Kyrgyzstan. Alfalfa, oats, barley, and sorghum are grown mainly for fodder. Chickpeas (*nokhat*) and mung beans (*mosh*) are the standard legumes found in soups and rice dishes. The most common use of grain is in the form of wheat flour for breads. Rice and noodles are the other starchy mainstays. Flatbread (*non*) is present at every meal. Non was traditionally made at home, although now it is increasingly sold at markets or communal bakeries. The standard non is simply a mixture of wheat flour, water, yeast, and salt. The dough ferments and proofs overnight, then is baked in a tandoor before dawn. European-style dark and white wheat-bread loaves have become common in urban areas through Russian influence.

Rice pilaf (*palov*) is the flagship of Central Asian cookery. In its most basic form, it is a dish with rice, meat, onions, and carrots. However, it has a much greater cultural significance. Pilaf is intimately bound to hospitality, community, and identity. Pilaf provides nourishment as well as a glimpse into the Central Asian psyche. For Central Asians, pilaf signifies hospitality, celebration, and solemnity, and it is a weekly ritual.

From the earliest times, a paste of flour and water has formed the basis for many meals. Turkic nomads have added dough to their dishes for centuries. *Sutli atala* is an Uzbek milk soup thickened with flour, while a similar dish in Tajikistan is called *atolai kochi. Manpar* are small bits of pinched dough, or sometimes small, square noodles, in a meat soup. The varieties of noodles and filled dumplings make Central Asian cuisine especially diverse. *Laghman* is a thick noodle dish served with a soup or dry with meat, peppers, tomatoes, and onions.

Chuchvara in Uzbek, or *tushbera* in Tajik, are the Central Asian version of Russian *pelmeni* (ravioli-like dumplings), filled with meat and onions. A special spring treat is *koq chuchvara,* a filling made with any mixture of greens available—sorrel, spinach, mint, cilantro, dill, basil, thyme, parsley, celeriac, garlic, green onion, arugula, or shepherd's purse—and topped with yogurt.

The savory meat pastries in Central Asia are similar to those found in Russia, which is not surprising since many have the same source and the same name. A Kazan Tatar dish, *belishi* (Russian *belyashi*), is a fried dough with a mincemeat and onion filling similar to *chebureki,* a dish eaten throughout the former Soviet Union. Central Asians also use the tandoor to make triangular or round samsa

Samsa is being baked in a tandoor, the traditional Central Asian oven. (Monsteranimal | Dreamstime.com)

(Uzbek) or *sambusa* (Tajik) with the standard mutton and onion filling.

The Central Asians remain true to their pastoral heritage as manifested in their sizable livestock herds. The principal products from cattle, sheep, and goats are dairy products, leather, meat, and wool. Central Asia is renowned for the vibrancy of its fermented dairy products. The region can claim kumiss, fermented mare's milk, among its best-known contributions to world cuisine.

Some yogurt is made with naturally occurring bacteria, while other yogurts are made by adding a bacterial culture to fresh cow, ewe, goat, or even camel milk. *Katyk* is made by heating milk and then allowing it to sour naturally. Both yogurt and katyk are served as an appetizer and used frequently as a garnish in soups and stews. Ayran is a salty mix of yogurt and water, especially refreshing in the summer.

The primary sources of protein in Central Asia are mutton, beef, poultry, and eggs. Goat and camel meat are less common. Pork is usually raised and eaten by Slavs, Koreans, and Germans who live in the area. Mutton is the most important meat, and unless otherwise specified, almost all recipes and menus that list meat denote mutton. Throughout Central Asia fat-tailed sheep are esteemed for their meat, fat, milk, and wool.

Meat is most commonly served as kebabs made from beef, mutton, liver, mincemeat, and chicken. It is also found in pilaf, soups (*shorpo, shurva, sorpa*), stews (*kovorma*), and salads. Horse meat and horse sausage are consumed mainly in Kyrgyzstan. *Chuchuk* or *kazy,* sausage made from horse meat, is considered a delicacy.

In regard to state vegetable production, all four Central Asian countries grow huge quantities of tomatoes and potatoes. Almost all produce is locally grown, and the bazaars have a tremendous selection of fruits, vegetables, and nuts. The chief vegetables are tomatoes, peppers, onions, cucumbers, and eggplant. Some kinds of vegetables that are virtually unknown outside Central Asia include green radishes (*turp*), yellow carrots (actually a type of turnip), and dozens of pumpkin and squash varieties. Pumpkin is found in stews, samsa, and manti. Vegetables most often are grilled or stewed. A salad

made from fresh tomato, onion, and hot pepper (*achik-chichuk*) is enjoyed throughout the warm months, and turp salad accompanies the main dish in the winter. Among the legumes, chickpeas and mung beans are the most prevalent.

Hundreds of varieties make melons the principal fruit export, famous throughout the region for their unique flavor. Fruit, fresh or dried, is eaten throughout the day for between-meal snacks. Grapes, too, are generally eaten fresh since Islam discourages the production of wine. The superiority of Central Asian fruit has been hailed over the ages. Early travelers to Central Asia, western China, and Iran never failed to mention the selection of luscious melons. Grapes, apples, quinces, and melons compose the largest fruit crops of the region. The spring is eagerly awaited for all the new plants, herbs, vegetables, and fruits that begin to appear. The fresh, young grape leaves are stuffed with a rice and meat mixture in a fashion almost identical to that found in Middle Eastern cuisine.

Apricots, strawberries, cherries, figs, and peaches are other fruits that appear in the early warm months. Toward the end of the summer, the fruit

Dressed in traditional Central Asian attire, a vendor of locally grown melons poses at his stand in the marketplace of Samarkand in present-day Uzbekistan, 1911. (Sergei Mikhailovich Prokudin-Gorskii Collection | Library of Congress)

orchards bloom with apples, quinces, persimmons, and pears. The final growing season produces the legendary melons, as well as pomegranates, lemons, and mandarins. Pomegranate seeds are mixed into salads, and one effortless dish combines only onions and pomegranate seeds. Citrons, similar to lemons, are native to Central Asia and have a thick, aromatic rind.

Central Asian cuisine is characteristically mild, but piquant sauces, garlicky relishes, and even whole peppers are added for punch in some regions, especially in the Fergana Valley. Rendered sheep fat is the general cooking oil, often mixed with cottonseed oil. Cottonseed oil has a strong and distinctive taste, and Central Asians bring it to the smoking point before adding the food, in the belief that the heat purifies the oil and seasons the wok. Vegetable oils are becoming more popular, but olive oil and butter are not traditional cooking fats. The main seasoning comes from black cumin, red and black pepper, barberries, coriander, and sesame seeds. The Uzbek cumin (*zera*) is smaller, darker, and more pungent than the seeds found in the West. Barberries are an acidic fruit, gathered in the autumn from an ornamental shrub. They contain vitamin C and, used in moderation, impart a tartness to any pilaf or stew. Cilantro (*kinza*) and parsley are the primary herbs, although dill, celeriac, and a pungent basil are broadly available.

Green tea (*koq chai*) reigns as the main beverage in Central Asia. It is the drink of hospitality, of leisure, and of health. Countless cups are consumed throughout the day. Green tea is served at every meal, and it is always the right time for a cup of tea. Central Asians prefer to drink it straight, but sugar is customarily offered to guests.

Dessert in general is another European borrowing. Sweet dishes are, however, part of teatime. An addictive mixture of walnuts and raisins is a frequent offering with tea. Endless varieties of halva, fruits, and confections—including sugar-coated almonds and crystallized sugar (*novvot*)—also make an appearance at teatime. Dried fruit is combined with honey, walnuts, pistachios, or almonds into many dessert recipes. In Uzbekistan, *chakchak* is fried dough fingers coated with honey, and *urama* is fried spiraled strips of dough dusted with powdered sugar. *Boorsok* are unsweetened triangular pieces of leavened, deep-fried dough that are served with tea in Kyrgyzstan.

Cooking

Today's food-production and cooking techniques differ little from those employed by the ancients. Wives, mothers, grandmothers, and other women of the household spend a considerable portion of their day shopping for and preparing meals at home. There are few women in the workforce, and those who work are also expected to prepare the family meals. Women are responsible for all of the cooking except on those occasions when the men want to demonstrate their proficiency with the flame. Nomadic women make most of the dairy products, although the men sometimes help milk the horses. Central Asians cook over open flames in *qazans* (wok-shaped cauldrons) for deep-fat frying, frying, stewing, and simmering. Street vendors and home cooks still grill kebabs in braziers over glowing coals, make bread and samsa in tandoor ovens, and make dumplings (manti) in a bamboo or aluminum steamer (*qasqan*). The brazier, or grill, for cooking shashlyk is called a *mangal*. The preparation of Central Asian dishes resembles in many respects Chinese methods of cutting, cooking, and seasoning foods. All vegetables are cut according to strict traditional guidelines—shredded, diced, sliced, and so forth—depending on the dish. For the main courses, meat and vegetables are also fried before stewing (for pilaf or *shavlya*—a meat and rice porridge) or boiling (for stock for *laghman*—noodles). Among widely used dishware are *kasa* (a deep plate) and *piala* (a handleless teacup), round and oval serving platters, china teapots, and trays, as well as ceramic and wooden dishes.

In nomad cookery, the amount of equipment is minimal because it must be transported from location to location to follow the grazing herds. Furthermore, there is no luxury of electricity or running water. The iron qazan is the most indispensable cookware, used for cooking pilaf, soups, and even bread. If the qazan is shallow, it may be turned over a flame to create a convex cooking surface to produce flatbreads among other things. Many parts of the sheep and goat—especially the cleaned, emptied stomach—are used for holding milk products or producing cheese. The main dairy products are milk, yogurt, ayran, kumiss, butter, and qurt made from the milk of sheep, goats, yaks, and even camels. Large (up to 10 gallons), sealable aluminum storage cans are one modern convenience the nomads have adopted for storing liquids or oil.

Considering the region's history of borrowing, adopting, and contributing elements of culture, the foodways and culinary arts of Central Asia are bound to flourish if their esteemed traditions of hospitality keep pace with the introduction of new foodstuffs. In the short time since independence, Central Asians have fostered a new national consciousness, developed a distinct identity, and cooked up increasingly distinct culinary boundaries through the savvy use of national cuisine.

Typical Meals

The four countries of Central Asia have populations that exhibit a mix of urbanized, Sovietized, nomadic, Russian, Turkic, and Iranian cultures and influences. While the apartment kitchen epitomizes Russian daily meals, the open flame sets Central Asian food apart. Fire is the preferred method of cooking for the region's staples of pilaf, kebabs, samsa, and flatbreads. Increased contact with the outside world pushes some Central Asians to adapt their eating habits and mealtimes to conform to world patterns. Restaurant culture, European convenience foods, imported Turkish and Iranian dishes, and inexpensive Chinese cookware and equipment have all contributed to the changing foodways.

For the sake of simplicity, meals in Central Asia may be crudely divided into two groups—urban and rural. The meals of the city or apartment dweller have taken on many Russified elements, such as the number and timing of meals. The rural group, including the remaining nomads of Kyrgyzstan, has experienced a tremendous change of lifestyle but generally maintains much of the basic foodways of its forefathers. Three meals a day are standard for both nomads and city dwellers, with every meal including tea and flatbread (non). For breakfast, fresh cheese or honey may be added, but the meal is normally light. Lunch, usually a soup, may be taken at home, or a quick snack can be bought from street vendors.

The largest meal is usually eaten in the evening. The meal customarily starts with a prayer. After the prayer, diners make a passing gesture across their eyes with two hands as if they are washing their face. The men are expected to break and distribute the flatbread. Tea is first offered to everyone who passes a threshold in Central Asia, and a whole subset of customs exists surrounding the preparation, presentation, and consumption of tea. Green tea is predominant and the drink of hospitality. Black tea is preferred in Russian regions. Green tea is generally served straight, but sugar, milk, salt, or even butter may be added depending on individual preference. An entire portion of the cuisine—samsas, bread, halva, and various fried foods—is dedicated solely to teatime.

The nomads of Central Asia live in portable felt dwellings called yurts. The nomadic evening meal, as in antiquity, is the most substantial and often consists of mutton or beef. The traditional Kyrgyz dinner table is low and round and covered with a cloth. It is usually positioned near the center of the yurt. Diners sit around the table on decorative felts topped with long, narrow mattresses or pillows for comfort. The place of honor is reserved for the elderly, guests, or the head of the family. The daughter-in-law sits near the tea urn and serves the guests. These customs are still preserved, especially in rural areas. The visitor is first served kumiss (mare's milk) or ayran (yogurt and water). Kyrgyz prefer green tea (koq chai) during the summer. It is served in the morning, before and after lunch, and in the evening with fresh milk. *Aktagan* is one type of Kyrgyz tea drink, made with milk, butter, sour cream, and salt. Turkmen consume large quantities of meat, cereals, grains, dairy products, legumes, and fruit. Bread makes up a significant portion of the diet, especially in the rural areas. Their traditional bread is *chorek*, a tandoori flatbread.

Uzbeks normally have three or four meals a day— breakfast, lunch, afternoon snack, and dinner.

Selling bread at the Russian bazaar in Turkmenistan. (Travel-images.com)

Traditionally, freshly made green tea is served at the beginning and end of every breakfast, lunch, and dinner. Baked goods, sweets, and tea (sometimes with milk or cream) are served for breakfast. It is fairly common for the Tajiks, Turkmen, and Uzbeks to have a dining room that is devoid of furniture, with only a brightly colored wool carpet hanging on the wall. The tablecloth, or dastarkhan, is laid out on the floor or on low tables, and everyone eats on pillows surrounding the tablecloth. For both lunch and dinner, flatbreads, sweets, and fruits are served first, with tea. Then a hot dish is served, and fresh fruit follows as dessert. Desserts are generally the tea adjuncts—raisins and nuts, lightly sweetened cookies, multiple variations of halva, fruits, and confections. Pastries and layer cakes are a European addition. The Uzbek winter diet traditionally consists of vegetables, dried fruits, and preserves to provide the necessary vitamins throughout the season. Hearty noodle or pasta-type dishes are common chilly-weather fare. Nuts (walnuts, peanuts, pistachios, and almonds) and honey are eaten separately or used in sweets and desserts. Even in the middle of winter, melons, apples, pomegranates, pumpkins, and other products of the fall harvest are available in the market, almost up until the spring harvest.

Bairam Palovi (Uzbek Wedding Pilaf)

3 lb mutton or beef

4½ c vegetable oil

5 onions, sliced

2 lb carrots, cut in matchstick strips

2½ qt water

1 c chickpeas, canned

¾ c raisins

Salt, black pepper, cumin, coriander, turmeric, and barberries to taste

5 c rice

Cut meat in pieces, and sear in hot oil. Add sliced onions. After a few minutes put in carrot strips and mix. Add water, chickpeas, raisins, salt, and spices; simmer for 25–30 minutes. Add rice and additional water as needed to rise to ½ inch above the rice. Cook, uncovered, until water evaporates. Cover and cook on low heat 30–40 minutes or until meat is tender and rice is fully steamed. Stir mixture, remove the meat, and cut into small uniform-sized pieces. Serve rice in a mound on a large platter topped with the meat pieces.

Eating Out

Central Asian cuisine, if it has a reputation at all beyond the borders of the former Soviet Union, is considered a poor cousin to Turkish food. Anyone who has traveled to the area has undoubtedly experienced Soviet-era service and low-quality dishes in the few restaurants operating before the five Central Asian states became independent. The restaurants presented a very meager imitation of the diverse local cuisine. Scratching only the surface may give the impression that the region offers little more than pilaf, shashlyk, and a few miscellaneous noodle dishes. Nothing could be further from the truth, reinforcing the argument that restaurants are a poor source for judging a nation's culinary culture.

Central Asia has a rich tradition of hospitality, expressed through food in its teahouses and caravansaries along the Silk Road for over a millennium. A caravansary is a way station that provided shelter for trade caravans, a hostel and a place for nourishment for road-weary travelers and their camels. The Silk Road attracted merchants moving east and west laden with goods for exchange and sale from the 2nd century A.D. until the

15th century A.D. In Central Asia, all the roads converged, bringing the area into contact with Chinese, Indian, Persian, Slavic, and Middle Eastern traders and cultural influences. The teahouse (*chaikhana*), based on similar establishments in China, remains to this day a social institution where a community or neighborhood gathers over green tea and traditional Central Asian dishes of pilaf, shashlyk, and noodle soup (laghman). The chaikhana is the foundation of Central Asian culinary culture, especially in Uzbekistan. Always shaded, preferably situated near a cool stream, the chaikhana is a gathering place for social interaction and fraternity. Robed men congregate around low tables, centered on bedlike platforms adorned with local carpets, to enjoy a meal and endless cups of green tea. In addition to providing nourishment, shade, fellowship, and relaxation during the sweltering summer months, the chaikhana helped preserve many aspects of Central

Asian heritage and cultural identity, which were obscured by 150 years of Russification. Almost every neighborhood has a mosque and a community teahouse, both influential social institutions. The chaikhana functions as a quiet retreat, a social center, a sacred place, a restaurant, and a men's club. The village or community elders gather here to share news, discuss business, make decisions, and comment on family and cultural matters.

The restaurant culture in a Western sense has still not firmly taken hold in the region, mainly due to a strong and preferred tradition of domestic cookery. Because Central Asian cuisine is so labor-intensive and the distribution system is heavily regulated by the state, it has yet to become profitable to open a great number of new restaurants featuring local cuisine. Furthermore, for Western tastes, Central Asian cuisine tends to be too heavy in the use of oil and animal fat. More important, foods prepared

Men sitting at a dais, a low table (*Khiva*), in Uzbekistan. (Travel-images.com)

in commercial kitchens for sizable groups can in no way compare to the outdoor cookery of pilaf made in large woks over open flames, shashlyk smoked over coals, and samsas (savory pastries) baked in tandoor ovens.

In general, restaurant dishes have been artificially assigned to courses of the Russian model: hot and cold appetizers (*zakuski*), a first course (*pervoe*) or soup (*sup*), a main course (*vtoroe*), and dessert. Sometimes the diner is simply told the final amount of the bill; other times a sum total is scribbled on a notepad. Only recently have restaurants begun to present an itemized check. Appetizers generally consist of caviar, samsa, horse meat, tongue, assorted fish, spicy Korean vegetable salads, and seasonal fruit. The primary soups are laghman (mutton, vegetables, and thick noodles), *shurpa* (with potatoes instead of noodles), manpar (pasta bits like thick noodles), and borscht. Pilaf, shashlyk, cutlets, and manti (mutton- or pumpkin-filled dumplings) are the usual main course. Tea and coffee are served at the end. Pilaf, manti, and kebabs are available on almost every other street corner throughout Central Asia.

Special Occasions

Ramadan (Ramazan) is the most renowned Muslim holiday, a monthlong ceremony of prayer, fasting, and charity occurring in the ninth month of the year. No food or drink is allowed during daylight hours. All foods, however, are permitted from sunset to sunrise. The Quran dictates to "eat and drink until the black and white thread can be discerned at dawn." Ramadan (Uraza in Uzbek) is a working holiday, but work schedules may be seriously disrupted or altered.

In Uzbekistan, the largest festival and holiday is Eid al-Adha (also called Qurban-Hait or Qurban Bayram), eagerly awaited all year. Eid al-Adha occurs 70 days after Ramadan, to celebrate God's mercy in providing the sacrificial lamb. The holiday has special importance for the pilgrims performing the hajj, or journey to Mecca.

Nauruz Bayram is the ancient, pre-Islamic holiday celebrating the coming of spring on March 21, the vernal equinox. Although sometimes called the Muslim New Year, it has no basis in Islam. Nauruz has its origins in an Iranian folk holiday with roots in Zoroastrianism. Traditional dishes in Uzbekistan include *koq samsa*, koq chuchvara, *halim, nishalda,* and *sumalak. Koq* means "green" in Uzbek, and the savory pastries and small ravioli-like dumplings are made with all the spring greens that abound in the mountain valleys. Wheat porridge (halim) is made from boiled meat and wheat grains, seasoned with ground black pepper and cinnamon. Nishalda, a meringue flavored with licorice root, is also popular during Ramadan. Sumalak is a bread made of sprouted wheat.

Koq Chuchvara (Uzbek Green Dumplings)

Dough

4 c flour

1 egg, hard-boiled and chopped

1 c water

1 tsp salt

Filling

1½ lb mixed greens and herbs: sorrel, spinach, mint, cilantro, dill, basil, thyme, parsley, celeriac, garlic, green onion, arugula, shepherd's purse

12 oz onions, finely diced

1 egg, hard-boiled and chopped

4 oz butter or animal fat

Black pepper and salt to taste

Chop the herbs, and combine well with onions, boiled egg, butter, and seasonings. Make a stiff dough out of the flour, salt, egg, and water; let stand for 30–40 minutes. Roll out dough ¹/₁₂ inch thick and cut into 2-inch × 2-inch squares. Place a touch of filling in the center, fold dough corner to corner, and pinch edges—completely enclosing filling. Boil in salted water until they float, no more than 4 minutes.

Serve in broth or drained with yogurt or sour cream; sprinkle with black pepper.

The Central Asian republics continue to celebrate the Soviet holidays of New Year's Day, International Women's Day, May 1, and May 9. May 1 was known as the International Day of Workers' Solidarity, only recently officially renamed Spring and Labor Day. The Celebration of Victory Day in World War II is marked on May 9, the day of Soviet triumph over Nazi Germany in 1945. They have also added Nauruz, Islamic holidays, independence days, constitution days, and a handful of nation-building holidays. Some of the older seasonal celebrations in Uzbekistan and Central Asia, directly related to food and survival, are experiencing a cultural revival: Erga urug kadash (planting festival), Khosil bairami (harvest holiday), Mekhrjon (bounty of nature celebration), Uzum saili (grape day), and Kovun saili (melon day). These days are marked with feasts, folk songs, and prayers.

Weddings in Central Asia may follow some Russian/Soviet traditions, but every cultural group has its own unique way of celebrating this special day. Families with nomadic roots, living in Western-style dwellings, may erect yurts to celebrate weddings and funerals. In Uzbekistan, prior to the wedding, representatives from the groom's family visit the bride's house to formally ask for her hand. The event is culminated in a ritual called *non sindirish* (breaking of bread). The date of the wedding is agreed upon. At the end of the evening, the bride's family presents each representative with a dastarkhan, two flatbreads, and sweets, as well as gifts for the groom's family. The party continues at the groom's house, where the presents are examined and the treats enjoyed. The couple is now considered to be engaged. On the day of the wedding two pilafs are cooked: one at the groom's house and one at the bride's house. The typical Uzbek wedding pilaf contains rice, mutton, chickpeas, raisins, onions, carrots, barberries, cumin, and turmeric for a golden color. Tajik wedding pilaf is very sweet—with sugar, dried fruit, and orange peel—to ensure a sweet life for the couple. The bride ceremoniously leaves her house for the groom's house, and the main party continues there.

In Central Asia, a pilaf ritual takes place on three main occasions: the wedding day, the 20th day after a death, and the one-year anniversary of a death. It involves not only relatives and friends but the entire neighborhood (*mahalla*). On the eve of the event, a carrot-cutting (*sabzi tugrar*) party takes place, usually with a concert (for weddings only) and a feast, during which the roles for the next day are assigned by the elders. The pilaf is cooked just before dawn so it is ready by the time the morning prayer is over. Wedding and funeral feasts are prepared and served by men only. Folk music calls the neighborhood to the table. The ritual begins with bread and tea, and then pilaf is served. Each platter is to be shared by two guests. Once guests are finished with the food, they leave and their places are taken by new arrivals.

Diet and Health

In Central Asia, food is not only treated as a source of nourishment and fuel but also valued for its preventative and curative role. Specific nutritional problems include the lack of affordability of certain healthful and essential food items, the suspect quality of some foodstuffs, and the absence of public awareness of what constitutes a healthful and balanced diet.

Vitamin A and C deficiencies are common in Kyrgyzstan because the people eat fewer fruits and vegetables than do Uzbeks, Tajiks, and Turkmen. One concern in Tajikistan is the prevalence of thyroid deficiencies due to a lack of iron in the diet. Turkmen depend heavily on bread for calories, with only seasonal consumption of vegetables and fruit, resulting in a deficiency of protein and fat. Overall per-capita food consumption in Uzbekistan actually increased between 1992 and 1996, except for milk products. Uzbek consumption of meat increased, while bread intake has remained relatively stable since 1992.

Central Asians loosely maintained a diet based on the ancient Greek humoral practices as propagated by the Muslim philosopher ibn Sina (born near Bukhara in Uzbekistan) in the 11th century. This theory holds that the body has four humors (blood, yellow bile, black bile, and phlegm) that determine health and disease. The humors were, in turn, associated with the four elements: air, fire, earth, and water, which were neatly paired with the qualities hot, cold, dry, and moist. According to that theory, a proper and evenly balanced combination of humors characterized the health of the body and mind; an imbalance resulted in disease. Combining local wisdom with traditional Chinese thought, Central Asians consider foods to have either "hot" or "cold" as well as "dry" or "moist" qualities in regard to both medicinal and nutritive functions. The inextricable relationship between diet and health forms the basis for the humoral theory of medicine, which still holds considerable sway in individual food choices in the region. The layperson in Central Asia can still classify most foodstuffs as having hot or cold properties.

The major health-related problems in Central Asia are low life expectancy, cardiovascular disease, high rates of tobacco and alcohol use, and general nutritional deficiencies. These, combined with diets high in fat and low in antioxidants, mean that the conditions for cardiovascular disease are ripe. Central Asians consume well below the recommended average daily calories for the European region. Acute malnutrition among children remains high, resulting in disorders caused by lack of micronutrients such as iron and iodine. Carbohydrates in the form of bread and potatoes make up a larger part of the diet than in the past as the consumption of fats, milk products, fish, and eggs has declined. Still, the saturated fatty acids of animal fat make up a large portion of total calorie intake. According to recent reports by the World Health Organization, the Central Asian republics, while still in need of improvement, experienced some positive health results since the early 1990s. The Kyrgyz appear to have the best relative health in the region. In general, they eat a more healthful diet, smoke less, and are less frequent drinkers. Muslims in Central Asia, according to recent research, were significantly less likely to drink frequently or smoke.

Glenn R. Mack

Further Reading

Allworth, Edward, ed. *Central Asia, 130 Years of Russian Dominance, A Historical Overview.* Durham, NC: Duke University Press, 1998.

Allworth, Edward. *The Modern Uzbeks: From the Fourteenth Century to the Present; A Cultural History*. Stanford, CA: Hoover Institution Press, Stanford University, 1990.

Bacon, Elizabeth E. *Central Asians under Russian Rule: A Study in Cultural Change*. Ithaca, NY: Cornell University Press, 1980.

"Central Asian Food: The Good , Bad and the Inedible." Uncornered Market. http://www.uncorneredmarket.com/2008/02/central-asian-food-good-bad-inedible/.

Hopkirk, Kathleen. *A Traveller's Companion to Central Asia*. London: John Murray, 1993.

Mack, Glenn R., and Asele Surina. *Food Culture of Russia and Central Asia*. Westport, CT: Greenwood Press, 2005.

Paksoy, Hasan Bülent, ed. *Central Asia Reader: The Rediscovery of History*. Armonk, NY: M. E. Sharpe, 1994.

"Silk Road Seattle—Traditional Culture: Food." http://depts.washington.edu/silkroad/culture/food/food.html.

Soucek, Svatopluk. *A History of Inner Asia*. Cambridge: Cambridge University Press, 2000.

Zubaida, Sami, and Richard Trapper, eds. *A Taste of Thyme: Culinary Cultures of the Middle East*. London: I. B. Taurus, 2000.

China

Overview

The People's Republic of China is the largest country in the world in terms of population, with 1,320 million people; it is the second largest in area, at 3,696,100 square miles. Taiwan, an island (and some neighboring small islands) that is generally considered to be legally a part of China, is a de facto independent country with 23 million people on 14,000 square miles. In addition, Chinese food and culture have followed Chinese emigrants all over the world, especially to Southeast Asia, where Chinese food has profoundly affected local foodways.

China stretches from the Pacific Ocean to the vast deserts of Central Asia, and from the tropics to the latitude of southern Canada. It is the most geographically varied country in the world, with tropical rain forests, high mountain tundras, waterless deserts, dry dusty plains, and vast riverine landscapes now dominated by rice. Critically important is the monsoon climate, which brings summer rain and winter drought. Rain is very heavy in the far south and southeast, diminishing steadily toward the northwest and far west. China is a major biodiversity center; western China has the most diverse fauna and flora of any temperate region in the world. China is still an agricultural country first and foremost, with extremely varied farming and livestock herding. All this means that Chinese agriculture and foodways can be extremely diverse.

The historic core area of China, the "18 provinces," extends from the southern border to just north of Beijing, the capital. This core can be ecologically divided into north, east, south, and west. Over recent centuries China has added the northeast

(Manchuria), Inner Mongolia, Xinjiang (Chinese Central Asia), and the vast mountain area of Tibet.

China's population is largely Han, a group that has at least eight major languages and thousands of local dialects. The national language, Putonghua, is called Mandarin in most Western literature; closely related are Cantonese, Shanghainese, and other local languages. China has 56 recognized minority groups, each with its own language (or group of related languages) that may be distantly related or quite unrelated to the Chinese language family. The largest minority is the Zhuang, speaking a language very close to Thai. Other minorities include Tibetans, Mongols, Tungus, Koreans, and Turkic speakers including the Uighurs. Each minority has its own food culture.

🍽 Food Culture Snapshot

Wu Zilian and his wife, Ni Guifei, are farmers in southern China. (Surnames come first, and women traditionally do not change their names at marriage.) They consider themselves traditional in foodways but have adapted somewhat to changing times.

They need to get to the fields by 7 A.M. and get their son off to school, so breakfast is early; they eat *ju* (congee), which is rice boiled down to thin porridge, with some peanuts, pickled vegetables, and small dried fish and soy sauce mixed in. From the shop next door they buy *yutiao*, strips of dough fried like doughnuts or churros but usually unsweetened. Sometimes they dunk these in the congee or in warm soy milk. With all this they have hot tea; they are still glad to be able to buy decent-quality tea. They recall the old days where there was only hot water or, somewhat more recently, a dark brew made from old leaves and twigs.

They work hard in the fields till noon, then stop for a fairly substantial lunch of soup noodles and stir-fried greens. After taking it easy during the heat of the day, they finish up several projects and head home by 5 P.M. Ni Guifei goes to her small refrigerator, a prized possession, and gets out a piece of fish and a small bit of pork. She then turns on the small gas stove—another prized possession; she was raised breaking up firewood to burn in a clay bucket. She puts on a large pot of rice. On top of it goes the fish, in a small metal bowl, with ginger, slivered green onions, and a bit of oil over it; the fish will steam in the vapor coming up from the boiling rice. She slices the pork fine and stir-fries it with garlic, pickled soybeans, and assorted vegetables picked from the garden. There is still plenty of tea in the pot. Dessert is fruit from a neighbor family's orchard; they grow oranges, tangerines, and peaches.

This is the daily round, but over the last 15 years they have gradually added cookies, crackers, cheap candy, and store-bought white bread, first as rare luxuries, then as increasingly common snacks. Now, some mornings they eat bread and store-bought spread of some sort for breakfast. They drink sodas regularly, and Wu has a beer or two whenever there is a special occasion.

Such occasions are more common than they used to be, and they involve the whole family—and, usually, some friends and neighbors—eating stewed chicken and duck, roast pork, highly spiced vegetable dishes, and a number of sweets. Bean curd (tofu), once inevitable at such events, is getting rare; people say it is too low class for modern times. The couple says that people aren't as healthy as they used to be, but their son is old enough to have his own opinions and prefers the new ways.

Their neighbor's son, Wang Xifeng, lives a very different life indeed. He went to the city many years ago and prospered in manufacturing. He lives in a large house near Shanghai, with all the modern Euro-American conveniences, from a full kitchen to a flat-screen television. He still eats rice, but many of his calories now come from oil, meat, sugar, and wine, frequently con-sumed during the course of splendid business lunches and dinners. If he eats vegetables, they are the finest tender young sprouts. He is fully familiar with foreign foods, from McDonald's hamburgers to French wine and Indian curry. Lately, he has taken to eating white bread and jam for breakfast, instead of congee.

Major Foodstuffs

China is famous for rice, which indeed is by far the most common food, but the north and west of the country are not good rice land. They therefore depended until recently on wheat, maize, and several species of millet. Today, rice is grown much farther north than of old, and it is sold everywhere, making it much more important in these other regions. Conversely, wheat is also more common and available, and it has increasingly gained ground against rice in the south and east. Western foods like crackers and white bread have made wheat much more visible in the food system. Maize, disliked because of its perceived low nutritional value and poor fit with Chinese cooking methods, has become an animal food. Other grains, being less productive, have almost disappeared.

The classic divide between wheat and rice split China in half at the Yangtze River (or a bit north of it). South of the Yangtze Valley, rice dominated; north of it, wheat ruled; in the valley itself, people grew rice in summer and wheat in winter and had plenty of both. Rice now grows as far north as southern Manchuria, thanks to development of ever more quick-growing varieties.

China's major protein source until recently was the soybean, a native of northern China. Soybeans require processing to be nutritionally very valuable, and traditionally they were turned into soy sauce, fermented pastes, pickled beans, and bean curd. Bean curd is made by grinding the beans, boiling the resulting meal, and precipitating the protein, letting the oil and starch go off with the water. The bean curd is thus a highly concentrated protein food. However, in recent decades, China has self-consciously tried to raise consumption of meat, and this has come at the expense of lower-status bean curd. Today, not only is the soybean largely an animal food, but China's production of soybeans is dropping, as urbanization wipes out farmland and more productive grain and vegetables take over what is left. China now imports soybeans from Brazil and elsewhere.

Today, the main protein source is pork; China has two-thirds of the world's pigs. Fish are important and are largely produced by aquaculture (fish farming); China invented aquaculture about 2,500 years ago. China's marine and river fisheries have been decimated by pollution and overfishing, and they no longer supply what they once did. As elsewhere in the world, chicken production has rapidly increased through battery production in huge industrial farms. Ducks are locally common. Beef is not a traditional food but is available. Sheep are common and often dominant in the north and west, especially Xinjiang and Tibet. Camels, donkeys, yaks, horses, goats, and all sorts of game animals and wildlife have been pressed into service for meat.

With the exception of nomadic herders in Inner Mongolia, Tibet, and remote parts of Xinjiang, Chinese peoples very rarely ate dairy products until recently. Today, yogurt, milk, and cheese are available, primarily in cities, but are still somewhat unusual as foods. Virtually no one in China, not even the nomadic herders, can digest lactose (milk sugar) except in early childhood, but using fermented milk products like yogurt overcomes this problem; the real reasons for lack of dairying were lack of pastureland and the settled people's traditional rivalries with the herders.

The universal, dominant, and culturally very important vegetables are Chinese cabbage greens, which come in countless forms, from Beijing celery cabbage to the tender mustard greens of the south. Some are coarse and cheap, and some are exceedingly delicate and expensive. Improvements in farming and in available varieties have led to rapid expansion of the other popular vegetables, including many kinds of beans, peas, squash, onions, garlic, chives, carrots, huge Chinese radishes, cucumbers, and many others. Beans and peas are often grown for the young sprouts, which are among the favorite foods. The Chinese love vegetables, often above

all other foods. After 1600, the Spanish, Portuguese, and later Dutch and English brought New World foods to East Asia, and thus the Chinese acquired and enthusiastically adopted maize, tomatoes, white and sweet potatoes, peanuts, chili peppers, and many other foods. More recently, they have borrowed still more, and few indeed are the foods that cannot be found in China today. One might even find *k'anistel* (*Pouteria campechiana Baehni*), a rare fruit domesticated and grown by the Maya of Mexico, in Taiwanese markets (under the name "heavenly peach").

More usual and traditional fruits include many native to China that are now known worldwide: oranges, tangerines, peaches (native all across Central Asia), plums, jujubes ("Chinese dates"), melons, and others. Apricots abound in the west. Closely related is the native Chinese flowering apricot or *mei* (*Prunus mume; mume* is the Japanese name), perversely miscalled "plum" in most translations. Its small, sour fruits are used in pickles, sauces, and salt preserves and as such have gone worldwide in recent decades. Among nonnative fruits, first and foremost is the watermelon, which came from Africa via Central Asia in the medieval period. It is another true favorite food, being not only sweet but also a source of delightfully cooling and refreshing liquid on a hot summer day (and Chinese summers are scorching).

Nuts are combined with fruit in the category *guo;* they include walnuts, pine nuts, almonds, and others. Some are largely medicinal. Pine nuts are recognized as healthful and are supposed to contribute to long life. Apricot kernels (ground up), *torreya* nuts, and acorns treat respiratory irritation. Foxnuts (the seeds of a water lily) are thought to cool and clean the body. Lotus seeds are both healthful and good fortune, since the lotus is sacred in Buddhism and the Chinese word for lotus, *lian,* sounds like a word for "abundance." The underwater stems of the lotus (sold as "lotus roots" in markets), when boiled, produce sticky threads, so that when a stem is broken and the pieces are pulled apart they remain connected by the sticky threads; at Chinese weddings, there is a tradition for someone to break a lotus stem and pull, saying something like "no matter how much this couple is apart, they will always stick together." This sort of use of foods as metaphors is universal in Chinese culture, and it is hard to imagine a Chinese wedding or Chinese New Year celebration without lotuses and many other foods that call forth wordplay.

Oil has been crushed from seeds for over 2,000 years. In early times the commonest was from Chinese cabbage seeds (very close to modern canola oil). More recently, soybeans, peanuts, maize, and other foods have come into service. Sesame oil is used for its fine flavor.

Spicing is light but pervasive. The characteristic flavor mix, the real "signature spice" of Chinese food, is soy sauce, ginger, garlic, Chinese "wine," white pepper (made from young black peppercorns by removing the skin), Sichuan pepper (a different species than black pepper), fermented soybeans or soybean paste, and chili peppers. Only the first three of these are really universal; the others are common and widespread. Chilies vary with the area; they are almost unknown in the north and far west but so heavily used in Hunan and Sichuan that dishes there are often unbearably hot to the uninitiated. (Sichuanese restaurants outside the homeland generally tone this down many notches.)

The famous Chinese drink is tea, but it came to China from the area of northern Burma and northeastern India in the early Middle Ages and spread slowly. Not until around 1100 was it listed as a necessity, and it was actually quite rare except among fairly affluent households until the 20th century. Ordinary people made do with hot water—everyone realized that unboiled water was unsafe—as well as fruit juices and soy milk. Commonest of all, however, was soup, which used to be found at almost every meal because it provided the necessary liquid. Banquets in hot, sweaty southeastern China often included three different soups.

Chinese "wine" made from rice is technically a beer or ale, but it is stronger than beer and not carbonated, so it seems more like a true wine. The Chinese have been distilling for over 1,000 years (possibly 2,000 years) and probably invented distillation, and they thus have a range of drinks similar to whiskey and vodka, with names like *maotai* (fermented from sorghum) and *sanshu* ("triple-distilled").

Finally, China was a great center of fermentation technology. Soy products were the most varied and important ferments, but alcoholic drinks, pickles, fermented teas, preserved grains, meats and sausages, yogurts, and countless other products made use of a vast variety of yeasts, beneficial bacteria, and similar microorganisms. These not only preserved the food but also made it more digestible and provided necessary nutrients, including vitamin B_{12}, often otherwise absent from Chinese diets.

Cooking

Chinese cooking is a cooking of scarcity. Until recent decades, not only food but also fuel, oil, water, and even time for cooking were all scarce and often expensive. Thus, techniques that use a great deal of fuel and take a long time, like baking, are relatively uncommon.

China's famous and distinctive cooking method is stir-frying (*chao*): cutting ingredients into small pieces and stirring them in extremely hot oil for a brief period. The oil is heated, sometimes until it catches fire, before the food is put in—the flavorings first, then the main items. This method saves both oil and fuel; the cooking is almost instantaneous. Experts will cut the ingredients in such a way that surface area is maximized, for example, by thin slicing. This speeds the cooking even more. Sparing of meat is often done by using a few small cubes of highly flavorful ham or cured pork in a large dish of vegetables.

However, by far the commonest cooking method is boiling. Rice has to be boiled, and so does millet (a former staple). Wheat is usually eaten in the form of boiled noodles; these and related soup-with-starch dishes like won ton (*huntun,* soup with dumplings) are almost a religion in much of eastern China. The Chinese have had noodles for thousands of years. Soups, stews, ordinary and medicinal teas, and whole boiled chickens and ducks join the list of boiled foods.

The third most common method of cooking is steaming. It is economical not only because little plates of food can be steamed on top of boiling rice but also because steamers full of little dishes can be stacked over pans of boiling water, so that large amounts of small food items can be steamed very quickly and simply. Almost unique to Chinese cooking are steamed buns: wheat bread buns, leavened with various kinds of baking powders and steamed rather than baked. These are staple foods in much of the north. They can be solid dough (*mantou*), or they can be stuffed with meat, sweet paste, or vegetables (*baozi*). If the filling is wrapped in thin dough instead of leavened bread, the result is *jiaozi* or something similar such as *xiaomi* (the *siu mai* of Cantonese restaurants). Fish is very often steamed, as are even small plates of meat. Deep-frying is rare but widespread, especially for dumplings of many sorts.

Typical Meals

Breakfast was traditionally congee or some other grain porridge, with savory additions. In the north it often involved steamed buns. A more substantial breakfast, often later in the day, consists of *dianxin*—the Cantonese pronunciation *tim sam* gives us the "dim sum" of Cantonese restaurants. *Dianxin* means "to dot the heart," equivalent to "to hit the spot" in English. These are rich snacks—typically steamed but very often baked or fried, so that they are more expensive and a great deal higher in calories than most Chinese food. They were traditionally the food of workers who needed a lot of calories quickly; they had no time to eat a whole big bowl of congee but had to eat enough to sustain backbreaking labor for a full day. Now, dim sum are the great moneymakers of many a Chinese restaurant, and their high levels of calories, fat, and carbohydrates contribute to the rise in problems with rich food.

Lunch on a nonworking day is often a main meal eaten around 1 P.M., but working all day away from home is no new thing in China, and thus the tendency has always been to have a bowl of soup noodles (*mian*), a plate of fried noodles (*chaomian*) with vegetables and a bit of meat, a plate of rice with a cheap topping, a large wrapped dumpling, or something else that is quick, easy, and cheap. The quick-noodle lunch has now gone worldwide, thanks not only to Chinese technology but also to elaborations such as Japanese ramen and Vietnamese *pho*.

Several bamboo steamers and plates of dim sum. (Shoutforhumanity | Dreamstime.com)

The main meal is eaten as soon as people finish work and return home in a very hungry condition. It almost invariably involves a major grain base (*fan*) with several side dishes (*cai;* literally, "vegetables") to use as toppings. Cantonese has a distinctive word, *sung,* for dishes used as toppings for rice. Fan is so essential that the usual way of saying "to eat" is *chi fan,* "to eat fan," and the standard greeting around mealtime is "Have you eaten fan yet?" Chinese people generally do not feel that they have eaten unless they have had a good solid bowl of this starch staple. After a banquet without rice they will often seek out a bowl of it, saying that they "haven't eaten yet."

In most of China, the grain is now rice, but remote parts of the north and west may still use wheat dumplings or other foods. Boiled millet, sorghum, sweet potatoes, and other lower-rated staples are now largely a memory. A typical family dinner involves enough rice to give everyone a couple of 12-ounce bowls or more, with a dish of fish or meat, a dish of greens, and a dish of some other vegetable or a vegetable with meat. Small nibbles may come before dinner and some fruit after, but appetizer courses and real desserts are strictly for banquet occasions.

Snacks, known as *xiaochi* ("small eats"), are extremely frequent. Children especially need them after school and at other critical moments. In addition to the more serious and expensive dianxin, small eats can be crackers, cookies, small baked tarts, nuts, seeds, fruit, sodas, and indeed almost anything small and easy to carry, up to and including yet another bowl of noodles.

Chinese cuisine is classically divided into five regional variations, following the classic division of the world into the four directions and the center. No one has ever defined the "central" cuisine very well, but the four directions certainly have their marked differences.

The north is the realm of wheat, sheep, Beijing or celery cabbage, and hearty meals where vinegar and other sour flavors are often pronounced. The range of vegetables was traditionally rather small, but diverse grains were available. Lately, rice has become common, replacing most of the minor grains.

The east centers on the Yangtze Delta and is characterized by complex dishes that are often oily or sweet. The river and sea afforded an enormous quantity and variety of seafood until recently; now, long-distance fisheries have to supply the demand. The hot climate makes stews and soups desirable, to replace liquid lost in perspiration. Tea was popular and the subject of connoisseurship.

The west is China's land of spices, with chili peppers and the Sichuan pepper dominant. Hunan and Sichuan in particular are the home of a fiery cuisine. River fish are common, but food tends to run to mountain specialties, including pork, bamboo shoots, mushrooms, and deciduous fruits and nuts.

Farmers tend to the rice harvest in southern China. (Corel)

The south is the most complex area, with many subtraditions. Classic gourmet cooking is centered on Guangzhou and more recently on nearby Hong Kong. This is the most rice-dependent region of China; rice yields three harvests a year and traditionally supplied fully 90 percent of calories. Otherwise, fish, pork, duck, chicken, and an enormous variety of vegetables dominate.

Within these regions, different provinces and even counties have their own foods. Yunnan in China's far southwest has its own dishes and produces the best hams in China if not in all Asia. The Chaozhou (Teochiu) region in Guangdong Province has a very distinctive cuisine that makes much use of goose, duck, crab, taro (a root crop), and sweet pastes and sauces. Chinese are highly aware of regional cuisines and specialties. For centuries or even millennia, travelers have brought back "local country products" from the regions they visited, as gifts to the home folk. (This custom has spread to Japan, where it has become a vital social function.)

China's minorities all have their own cuisines. The Mongols and their neighbors in the north and west depend heavily on sheep and consume yogurt and kumiss (fermented mare's milk). "Mongolian barbecue" is not really a Mongolian dish; it was created in Beijing in the early 20th century. The Turkic and other settled peoples of Xinjiang traditionally live on Persian-style bread, rice pilaf (with fruit, carrots, and lamb cooked with the rice), roast lamb, noodles with boiled lamb, and fruit, especially grapes and melons—they produce the best melons in China, if not in the world. Tibetan everyday food includes butter, tea, roasted barley meal, and dairy products such as yogurt; festive food involves dumplings (momo, similar to jiaozi), meat stews, and noodle dishes. The Yi of the Liang Mountains in Sichuan traditionally depended heavily on buckwheat pancakes but now are switching to rice. The southern border peoples such as the Thai-speaking groups depend on rice and vegetables, with the usual range of meats when affordable.

Stir-Fried Greens

1 tbsp oil

2 cloves garlic, minced

½ in. ginger, minced fine (optional)

2 lb greens, usually one of the following: bok choy, baby bok choy, *gailaan* ("Chinese broccoli"), mustard greens, spinach, or turnip greens (any greens will do)

Soy sauce to taste

Heat the oil over a very hot flame. Add the garlic and ginger. Fry till the garlic begins to brown. Meanwhile, coarsely chop the greens, if needed; small leaves like spinach do not need to be chopped. Add to hot oil, and stir rapidly till wilted. Add ¼ cup water, turn down to a very low flame, and leave to cook for about 15 minutes, stirring occasionally and checking to prevent sticking and burning. The cooking time depends on how tender the greens are, so check them often—when they are tender, add a dash of best-quality soy sauce, stir, and then serve immediately; overcooking ruins them.

Sweet and Sour Fish

Everyone knows sweet and sour pork, but the dish was originally made with fish and was more refined than the usual modern forms.

1 whole cleaned fish (1½ lb), with firm white flesh (rockfish, sea bass, or the like)

5 c cooking oil

1 tbsp garlic, chopped

Marinade

1 tbsp Chinese "wine"

2 green onions, chopped fine

½ in. fresh ginger, scraped, crushed, or chopped fine so as to present maximum surface area

Salt to taste

Sauce

1 package hawthorn-paste tablets (available at Chinese markets)

2 tbsp brown or white sugar

2–3 tbsp clear rice vinegar

2 tbsp soy sauce

¼ tsp sesame oil

Salt to taste

½ tsp cornstarch to thicken (lotus rhizome starch is more traditional, and better, but hard to find)

Optional

Chopped pickled Chinese leeks (*rakkyo;* available from Asian markets)

Pine nuts, roasted or fried

Green pepper, pineapple, and so forth (modern cooks add these, but they are not traditional)

Marinate the fish in the marinade for 20 minutes. Deep-fry in the oil for about 10 minutes. Take out and drain.

Stir-fry the garlic in just a little oil (1 tablespoon) and then add the sauce ingredients, including the Chinese leeks if you can find them. Cook till thick (ca. 5 minutes). Pour over the fish, and serve. Decorate with pine nuts, if desired.

The red color and unique sweet-sour flavor originally came from the hawthorn paste. Almost no one uses it now, but it is worth trying. Modern cooks use a bit of tomato sauce, or just food coloring, to get the red color of the hawthorn paste.

Red-Cooked Pork

Red-cooked pork is a favorite slow-cooked dish, best in winter when one needs the heat and calories.

2 tbsp cooking oil

3 cloves garlic, minced fine

3 lb pork in chunks about 1 to 2 in. square

6 c water

6 tbsp soy sauce

3 tbsp Chinese "wine"

1 tbsp sugar

1 star anise star

1 cinnamon stick (Chinese "cinnamon," actually cassia, if you can find it)

Dried tangerine peel (known as *gu pi,* "very old skin," in Chinese markets), about 2 square in., in pieces

3 green onions, slivered

About 1 in. ginger, crushed or minced fine

Heat the oil in a large stewpot (cast iron is good) till very hot. Stir-fry the garlic, then add the pork and brown quickly. Then add the rest of the ingredients, and simmer for 3 hours till the sauce cooks down and thickens somewhat.

Eating Out

For centuries, China has had an astonishing number and variety of eating-out options. Until recently, every busy street was lined with small stalls that provided quick snacks of dumplings, noodles, or fruit. Street-stall cooking could get quite elaborate, as in old Hong Kong or the Chinese neighborhoods of Singapore. Some street stalls became more famous than almost any restaurant. Contrary to travel-book myth, street-stall food was usually extremely good and thoroughly safe, being cooked fresh and on the spot.

Restaurants vary from tiny lunchrooms to the vast "wine palaces" and "wine towers" that have become familiar worldwide in recent years. Quality does not vary with price or size, and the best food is often found in a tiny one-room place or street stall

A food vendor at the night market in China.

that specializes in a single dish and has perfected it. Gourmets know that X has the best wonton, Y the best duck, and Z the best mustard greens. A significant amount of conversation concerns such matters, not only in China itself but as far away as Sydney's Chinatown and California's San Gabriel Valley. This lore is often written down, and books from the early medieval centuries on have preserved names and addresses.

Special Occasions

Any important event is celebrated with a banquet. This is literally a sacred tradition; it traces back to ancient times, when gods, spirits, and deceased ancestors had to be entertained with sacrifice rites. The divine beings usually ate only the spirit of the food; the living shared the feast by eating the material parts. China's great culinary tradition developed at least in part through the need to entertain the divinities with the finest that could possibly be provided. In ordinary life, business deals, family rites of passage, and any fortunate occasion must be celebrated with a good dinner. More spectacular are weddings, 60th birthdays (when a full cycle of the Chinese calendar has been completed), and major holidays.

For banquets, all economy is thrown to the winds. This is the time for whole roast pigs, whole boiled ducks and geese, baked buns, great quantities of fat meat, and the most expensive vegetables. Quantities of expensive spices, fine wine, sugar in various forms, and other choice flavorings bring out the best in these items. The goal is to lavish attention on the guests, to satisfy them and make them as comfortable as possible. This is investment, not loss; the guests will reciprocate, either with a return invitation or with help in business or other matters. With increasing affluence in the last few decades, banqueting has gotten somewhat out of hand. It is often seen as a drain on the economy. It invites corruption; favors asked in return for an invitation can be shady ones. Worst, it has doomed the reputation of Chinese cuisine as one of the world's healthiest. Following the rise of banquets has come a rise in heart disease, diabetes, and other conditions that can be brought on by chronic overindulgence in rich foods.

The Chinese New Year begins (theoretically, at least) on the second new moon after the winter solstice. Lunar months are counted from this date, 30 days to the month. New Year is the major festival of the year. Foods that bring luck (like the lotus seeds) are eaten, as well as roast pork and any other luxuries that a family can afford. After that, there was a traditional period of three days before a fire could be lit, and people had to live on leftovers from the New Year feast. This is no longer observed by most households.

Every month brings festivals of one sort or another, and many have traditional foods. The Dragon Boat Festival, the fifth day of the fifth lunar month, is celebrated with *zongzi,* dumplings of sticky rice, meat, and spices wrapped in leaves and steamed. The Midautumn Festival, celebrating the autumn new moon on the 15th day of the eighth month, requires moon cakes. These are round wheat cakes stuffed with sugar, seeds, and other ingredients. They became particularly popular after the future Ming Emperor Zhu Yuanzhang supposedly stuffed moon cakes with messages calling for revolution, in his successful rebellion against the Mongols in 1368. This legend assumes that the Mongols did not share the Chinese tradition and so did not buy the moon cakes. Today, more edible stuffings dominate. Most are fatty and cholesterol-laden, but a recent movement has promoted more healthful moon cakes.

Diet and Health

The traditional Chinese diet of roughly milled or whole grains, vegetables, and bean curd was extremely healthy. Diabetes, heart disease, and other conditions that can be caused or made worse by food were almost unknown. A major study found that traditional Chinese almost never had these conditions, or even high blood pressure or high blood cholesterol. The only problem with the diet was getting enough to eat, but that was a major one before modern agriculture, transportation, and storage. Probably most deaths in China before 1970 were due to malnutrition or starvation, or were caused by parasites and diseases carried by polluted water and sometimes by foods themselves. Locally, some cancers were caused or made worse by poorly preserved or poorly cooked foods, or by local minerals that got into food.

Chinese medicine has always focused on food, for the very good reason that malnutrition and starvation were the commonest killers throughout most of China's history. The first recourse in illness is eating the diet considered appropriate. Given this reality, it is not surprising that Chinese nutritional science reached a high level at quite early times. Medical texts more than 2,000 years old preserve nutritional lore, though of rather varying quality. Early medical books record successful nutritional therapies for beriberi (vitamin B_1 deficiency), acute diarrhea, and general debility, as well as pointing out that pine nuts are notably more conducive to long life than a primarily grain diet. (The pine nuts are high in protein and minerals lacking in grains.) The books advise a balance between yang (the hot, dry, sunny aspect of nature, dominant in males) and yin (the cool, moist, shady aspect, dominant in females). Flavors, staple grains, and other medical influences were classified in fives, the five flavors being sweet, sour, salt, bitter, and rank (possibly an early anticipation of the discovery of the umami flavor in modern times).

Basic to Chinese medicine is the concept of *qi* (pronounced "chee"), literally "air" or "breath" but expanded to include the vital spirits thought to animate and nourish the body. A good flow of qi is necessary to health. Deficiency or blockage causes disease or makes it worse. So does imbalance between yang and yin (types of qi) or between any other forms of qi. Much (perhaps, theoretically, all) Chinese medical treatment involves getting the qi back in order, as well as more direct symptomatic treatment.

The Greek school of medicine that traces back to Hippocrates (fifth century B.C.) and was perfected by Galen (ca. 129–210 A.D.) reached China fairly early from the Near East and fused with Chinese concepts; the fusion process appears in sixth- and seventh-century medical texts. Galen's concern with hot, cool, dry, and wet naturally fused with the yang/yin concept and complemented the fivefold classification system.

Herbs used in Chinese traditional medicine sit on a prescription. (Hyhoon1210 | Dreamstime.com)

Foods continued to be classified in all these ways, climaxing in the great herbal *Bencao Gangmu* by Li Shizhen (ca. 1593 A.D.). However, ordinary people found the heating/cooling, yang/yin dimension much more salient and useful than the others. Today, traditional Chinese still think in these terms. Heating foods are, most obviously, those that provide the most calories (literal heat energy for the body). These are fatty foods, very sweet foods, baked foods, strong alcohol, and the like. One can also understand why foods that cause burning sensations, like chili, black pepper, and ginger, are "heating." Also catalogued among the hot foods are those with "hot" colors: red beans or brown sugar. Cooling foods are those that are very low in calories (like most vegetables), those that feel "cooling" in the sense of being astringent and puckery, and those that are very watery—getting wet chills you, and drinking cold water cools you down, so watery foods are thought to be cooling. Also cooling are things that are cold colors (green or icy white, for example), especially if they look like ice (for example, rock sugar, white radishes). The perfect balance point is cooked rice, and anything similar to it—white potatoes, white-fleshed fish, soup noodles—is also considered to be at the balanced or temperate point.

The more heating foods tend to be served in winter, when people need the calories, and also at feasts, which are "hot" occasions (consider the English phrase "a hot time"). The more cooling foods go best in summer. This is especially true of foods like watermelon and cucumber that are genuinely cooling. They stay cool during the day and in prerefrigeration times were about the only things that did in China's blistering summers.

On the whole, this system kept people healthy. The classic "hot" condition was scurvy, which seems like burning. It involves redness, rash, sores, infections, constipation, and other things that seem like the result of too much heat. It was cured by eating cooling foods, notably vegetables. It is actually caused by a lack of vitamin C, which abounds in Chinese vegetables, so these foods really did cure it. Conversely, the commonest "cold" conditions were anemia (iron deficiency) and tuberculosis; they involve pallor, weakness, and often a low body temperature. Anemia is cured, and tuberculosis can be alleviated, by eating strengthening foods seen as "warming," notably red meat and organ meats. Empirically, the Chinese found that things like pig liver and wild duck meat—particularly rich sources of iron—were especially effective. Some attention was paid to drying and wetting foods, but they remained minor in the system.

Far more important was the purely Chinese concept, over 2,000 years old and probably much older, of *bupin,* "supplementing foods." These are foods that are high in protein and minerals but low in fats and carbohydrates, and thus easy to digest while extremely nourishing. They are particularly recommended for women who have just given birth, for anyone convalescing from major injury or sickness, and for elders who want to stay as hale as possible.

They were originally things like pork, pig liver, duck, and game meats generally. At some point Chinese doctors found that certain odd items like tendons, mushrooms, sea cucumbers, and similar sea life worked well, and they generalized to assume that anything similar to these was a bupin. Moreover, it was logical to suppose that the odder an item looked, the more it might help, because there was a belief that odd appearance showed an abundance of qi. Thus, odd-seeming items like edible bird's nests (the nests of a tropical swift that secretes a proteinaceous substance), ancient misshapen fungi, and weird-looking or rare animals (turtles, raccoons, or dogs, for example) are considered bupin. In recent years this has proved a disaster for the species in question. Traditional conservation and management measures, very effective in many cases, have been abandoned, and overhunting is wiping out everything even remotely bupin. Perhaps the biggest irony is that none of these oddities works any better than—or, indeed, as well as—the traditional red meat and pork liver. People rarely eat bupin unless they feel the need, and modern medicine is replacing the more exotic ones.

The bupin belief grades into a belief in the magical power of some powerful animals like tigers and stags. Air-breathing catfish, which can live out of water and are very difficult to kill, are cooked as a cancer remedy, in hopes that they will transfer their tenacity of life to the patient. Another important belief is the idea that some foods are cleansing (*jing*). These are largely herbal remedies that, when taken in medicinal tea, make the body feel refreshed, cooled, and harmonized. So far, very little research has investigated their actual effects on the system. They do not "clean one out" in the sense of purgatives and emetics—both well known to the Chinese and considered a wholly separate matter.

An example of successful nutritional therapy that is being discovered worldwide is the Chinese wolfthorn plant, *gouqi* in Chinese (*Lycium chinense*). This common shrub has edible but tasteless leaves and small berries that are similar to and closely related to small tomatoes. The leaves and berries have the distinction of being among the richest in vitamins and minerals of any common food. They are thus grown for tonic use, typically in stews of pork, pork liver, Chinese wine, ginger, black vinegar, and other nutritious and strengthening items. These stews are fed to women who have just given birth and to convalescents. A significant percentage of Chinese living today owe their lives to them. The berries, dried, were always a staple of Chinese medicine stores. Recently they have appeared in markets worldwide. From America to Australia, one can now buy a pound bag of goji berries at the corner store, at least if the corner store has much selection of dried fruit. Another nutraceutical that has gone worldwide is wormwood (*Artemisia* spp.). It is used in China to kill intestinal worms and other parasites, including the organisms that cause malaria. One active ingredient, artemisinin, is now the drug of choice for malaria in much of the world.

E. N. Anderson

Further Reading

Anderson, E. N. *The Food of China.* New Haven, CT: Yale University Press, 1988.

Buell, Paul D., E. N. Anderson, and Charles Perry. *A Soup for the Qan.* London: Kegan Paul International, 2000.

Campbell, T. Colin, with Thomas M. Campbell II. *The China Study.* Dallas, TX: Benbella Books, 2005.

Cheung, Sidney, and Tan Chee-Beng. *Food and Foodways in Asia: Resource, Tradition and Cooking.* London: Routledge, 2007.

Hu Shiu-ying. *Food Plants of China.* Hong Kong: Chinese University of Hong Kong, 2005.

Huang, H. T. *Science and Civilisation in China.* Vol. 6. Cambridge: Cambridge University Press, 2000.

Newman, Jacqueline. *Food Culture in China.* Westport, CT: Greenwood Press, 2004.

Newman, Jacqueline M., and Roberta Halporn, eds. *Chinese Cuisine, American Palate: An Anthology.* New York: Center for Thanatology Research and Education, 2004.

Roberts, J.A.G. *China to Chinatown: Chinese Food in the West.* London: Reaktion Books, 2002.

Simoons, Frederick J. *Food in China: A Cultural and Historical Inquiry.* Boca Raton, FL: CRC Press, 1991.

Hmong

Overview

The Hmong are members of an ancient tribe that existed in relative obscurity for thousands of years. There has never been a Hmong nation-state. According to Hmong oral tradition (there was no written language before the 20th century), the Hmong were originally Mongolians, great horsemen who were separated from the main Mongol population by years of skirmishes with the Chinese and the subsequent building of the Great Wall. Chinese manuscripts from as early as 2700 B.C. bear out the claim, specifically naming the Miao, as the group is known in China, as one of the tribes that were considered a threat to the dominant Han Chinese.

Contemporary Hmong are, indeed, excellent horsemen and blacksmiths and are known for their skill at animal husbandry. Although the legend of the Hmong having been separated from the Mongolians has traditionally been met with skepticism, mitochondrial DNA studies demonstrate that the Hmong are, genetically, more closely related to the Mongol populations north of China than to other peoples living closer to Hmong villages.

Over centuries, as the Han Chinese population grew both in size and power, the Hmong were forced south and east into ever more marginal territories. They eventually retreated to a mountainous area in the southern part of China, with significant spillover into the region that would eventually become North Vietnam, Laos, and Burma. In the aftermath of the Vietnam War, the Hmong of Laos fled to the United States, Canada, France, and Australia, continuing a nearly 3,000-year diaspora.

Although they are separated in time and space, Hmong people in all these different places maintain their identity as Hmong, as opposed to the nationality of the country in which they happen to reside. Hmong culture and identity transcend everything else, which is why the Hmong people have resisted assimilation for thousands of years. Hmong culture is complicated. It requires commitment and energy to keep speaking an outnumbered language, to maintain a belief system that is out of the mainstream, and to stay true to clan rules even when they are in conflict with the dominant society. Only a truly remarkable culture could sustain the hardship and pressures that the Hmong have endured and yet remain intact.

There are an estimated nine million Hmong in China, the homeland. Although this may seem like a large population, it is a drop in the bucket. The overall population of China is 1.29 billion. The Hmong population is spread out among eight provinces in southern China, but about four million live in the Guizhou Province.

In Laos, there are only about 400,000 Hmong left, compared to more than one million prior to the Vietnam War. They are stubborn survivors of war and genocide, still clinging to a hardscrabble life as subsistence farmers who hardly grow enough food to keep themselves alive. Their only cash crop is opium, which is legal under a special agreement with the Laotian government.

In the United States, there are about 200,000 Hmong, all refugees from Laos and their descendants. The largest population center is in California, with Fresno as the main metropolitan area in

Va Vang (left) walks with the shopping cart as her sister Bao Lee (right) leads the way while they buy groceries at Costco in Fresno, California. The Vangs are among thousands of Hmong refugees who fled Laos for Thailand 30 years ago and now reside in the United States. (Getty Images)

the state. This article concentrates on the Hmong refugees now living in the United States.

🍽 Food Culture Snapshot

The Xiong family lives in a house in a working-class neighborhood in Fresno, California. The household is composed of a husband and wife, the husband's mother, and five of their six children, ranging in age from 26 to 10 years old. The 26-year-old son is married, and his wife and baby also live in the home, where they have converted the garage into their private space. A 20-year-old married daughter lives with her husband's family under similar conditions, only a few blocks away. The husband, wife, and mother-in-law came to California in the late 1970s as refugees from Laos. The children were all born in America. Everyone

in the family who is old enough to hold a job does so. Because of their lack of education and poor English skills, both husband and wife hold low-paying, blue-collar jobs. Their working-age children make as much money as their parents and add their earnings to the household budget. There is a high value placed on education, and the dining room has been converted into a study hall, with a computer and study desks. The family eats in the living room, with some members sitting at the table and others on the couch. In the modest kitchen, there is a dinette set to seat another three to four diners.

On Saturday morning, everyone in the house piles into the minivan for the weekly outing to the farmers' market. There, they can buy fresh vegetables from Hmong farmers who live in the vicinity, such as Chinese long beans, oriental eggplant, bok choy, bitter melon, daikon, lemongrass, black nightshade, Hmong cucumbers, and *opo* (a type of bottle gourd). They also pick up some glutinous rice, a few live chickens, and freshly caught fish. One of the benefits of living in an ethnic enclave the size of Fresno, especially in Fresno County, where there are approximately 2,000 Hmong/Lao family farms, is that fresh vegetables are available in season. There is even a Hmong American extension agent stationed in the county, who helps farmers adjust crops that originated in the tropical rain forest to the arid conditions of central California. The family is able to purchase most of the foods it prefers at the farmers' market during most of the year. There is also a network of small Hmong-owned markets and convenience stores in the area, as well as a few large Asian supermarkets.

While at the farmers' market, individuals in the family purchase ready-made food. Some choose breakfast burritos, while others get hot dogs. One of the interesting things about Hmong culture is that the adherence to "being Hmong" does not extend to food. These are people who have learned over the past 3,000 years to accept whatever food is available, sort of a "when in Rome, do as the Romans do" attitude about food.

Once home, the girls and women go to the kitchen to start cooking dinner while the boys and men work on projects around the house. Most cooking chores are traditionally the work of women, although men do much of the heavy work, such as hunting, fishing, slaughtering large domestic animals (such as pigs), pressing the juice out of sugarcane, and making rice beer.

Major Foodstuffs

The Hmong have never developed a sophisticated cuisine. Food is a simple thing in this complex culture, and the Hmong have always been quite willing to adopt the foods of the dominant culture. There are a few constants, however. The staple food, and the basis for all meals, is rice. In fact, the Hmong phrase for "Let's eat" is *peb noj mov*—literally, "Let us eat rice." There are many types of rice, chosen for special occasions, based on budget, or by personal preference. Families consume so much rice that they purchase three to four 25-pound sacks of rice at a time. One favored variety is jasmine rice, which has a nutty flavor. The favorite rice for desserts and special occasions is glutinous rice, which is usually referred to as sticky rice, because it is sticky enough to roll into small balls.

The best food is, simply, whatever is freshest. When Hmong refugees first came to the United States, they were unfamiliar with the concept of refrigeration. They were used to harvesting fresh food every day for immediate use, with the exception of rice. The refugees found the very idea of shopping only once a week or so and keeping the food in the refrigerator to be disgusting. The idea of buying meat and then freezing it to be thawed and cooked later was unacceptable to them.

Hmong refugees will eat many sources of protein: fish, pork, beef, chicken, venison, and other wild game. Hunting and fishing are favored activities for both men and women. Pork is the highest-status meat. In Laos, it was reserved for special occasions, but the convenience of purchasing smaller amounts at the supermarket has resulted in pork being eaten for everyday meals. Chicken and fish are probably the most commonly eaten protein sources, partly because chickens are also used ceremonially, for healing and other shamanic rituals. Fish is free and can be caught for same-day consumption, which is highly valued. It can also be bought fresh at the Asian supermarkets and farmers' markets.

Fruits and vegetables are important foods but not as important as meat. The Hmong eat a wide variety of vegetables, many of which have already been listed. They don't limit themselves strictly to vegetables from Southeast Asia and are willing to try any new fruit or vegetable. Favorite fruits include mangoes, peaches, pineapple, bananas, and papaya. The primary carbohydrate is rice. Sweets are not part of the traditional diet, except for the occasional sticky rice cakes sweetened with sugarcane juice. This has changed since moving to the United States, and both children and adults consume sweets and soft drinks.

Cooking

The traditional way to cook rice is to first soak it, then rinse it, then steam it, then rinse it again, and then steam it again. It is a long process but results in very fluffy grains of rice that do not stick together. More westernized Hmong women, who hold jobs outside the home, use a rice cooker for convenience, although they admit the rice is not as fluffy.

There are two main cooking methods: boiling and stir-frying. In Laos, most families cooked all their meals in one cooking pot, or crucible, hung over a fire. Since moving to the United States, cooks have become comfortable with American cooking methods, and many cooks find the process of stir-frying several dishes for each meal to be efficient and satisfying for serving their typically large families.

Typical Meals

The basic meal consists of rice in a large bowl in the center of the table, surrounded by smaller side dishes. Most of the side dishes are vegetable dishes. One or two dishes contain meat, when available. The preferred meat for most meals is pork, with chicken a close second. Chicken is also important for healing rituals. Families in Asia eat from the same dishes, dipping in with chopsticks, forks, spoons, or fingers. Families that have moved to the Western world are more apt to have adopted the concept of separate dishes for each family member and guest, with serving utensils for reaching into the communal pot. The dishes may be boiled or stir-fried.

A good meal begins with soup. It may be as simple as "rice soup," which is simply the leftover water from the second steaming of rice. Rice soup is commonly eaten when food is in short supply or as a medicine for sick individuals. It is considered plain but nutritious. Another type of soup is "sour soup," which can be eaten as is or form the basis for other recipes. Sour soup is a fermented dish that is unique to the Hmong and gives the food a distinctive flavor. Every family has a crock or jar that is used exclusively for sour soup. It should be kept on hand as a pantry staple.

Sour Soup

Mince a collection of vegetables, such as cabbage, carrots, leeks, and radishes together, and place them in a large crock or jar. Mix in glutinous rice flour, pepper, and salty water. Cover the jar, and set aside for several days.

Here is a recipe for a popular main course:

Zeub Nfsuab (Boiled Pork and Mustard Greens)

8 c water

2 lb pork shoulder

1¾ lb mustard greens

Bring water to a boil in a large saucepan. Add pork, and reduce heat to low. Cover and simmer gently until meat is fork-tender, about 1½ hours. Remove meat, trim fat carefully, and cut meat into bite-size pieces. Let the broth cool, then skim fat, reserving ¾ cup for use in other recipes.

Wash greens and cut into 2-inch pieces, removing coarse stems. (Stems may be saved for pickling, if desired.)

Put ¾ cup of defatted meat broth in a pan. Add greens and pork, and simmer until greens are wilted, 5 to 10 minutes.

Hmong foods tend to be heavily spiced with Thai peppers, lemongrass, garlic, green onions, ginger, mint, fish sauce, pickled vegetables, and a variety of other herbs and spices. There is a preference for sour flavors, as evidenced by sour soup, but sourness is not the only flavor. Foods can also be spicy, sweet, pungent, and/or salty. Pickled vegetables are another notable item, because it is another possible link to Mongolia. Although cucumbers and pickling date back about 4,000 years, to ancient India, they were quickly adopted by the Tatars of Mongolia.

Alcoholic beverages are popular with men, but women usually limit their drinking to special occasions—when they sometimes drink heavily. One popular drink is made, not surprisingly, with fermented rice. It has a flavor similar to beer. This drink is called sweet rice—usually said with a knowing grin.

Eating Out

There is a running joke in the Hmong refugee community that there are no Hmong restaurants, a reference to the spartan quality of the cuisine. It's almost true. There is a significant number of Hmong-owned restaurants, but they are usually presented as Chinese restaurants, with classic "Chinese" dishes, such as chop suey. Some Hmong dishes are usually on the menu as well, but they are hidden among the Chinese dishes. There are also about three openly Hmong restaurants in the United States. One is in Fresno.

When Hmong refugees go out to eat, they are usually not interested in eating Hmong food. In fact, there is no distinctive preference, although Vietnamese restaurants are favorites. Otherwise, the typical "when in Rome" attitude prevails, and restaurants are chosen based on convenience, price, and other factors, such as the chance to see and be seen by other people in the community. Hmong refugees enjoy trying the foods of other cultures and, besides Vietnamese restaurants, will happily frequent Mexican restaurants, mainstream American family restaurants, Chinese restaurants, and the ethnic restaurants that have been opened by the chefs of other ethnic groups. Hmong refugees and Latinos live in the same neighborhoods and get along quite well. The Hmong have adopted many Latino foods, such as tortillas, churros, and jicama. Hmong foods are beginning to enter the mainstream, with the opening of a small number of restaurants in Minneapolis, the Central Valley in California, and Chicago. These restaurants offer some Hmong dishes along with Vietnamese, Thai, or even Philippine cuisines.

Special Occasions

The most important celebration of the year is the Hmong New Year, which takes place after the harvest in the autumn. Traditionally, it lasts 10 days. In the United States, it has been changed from a 10-day event to a full season, lasting approximately from Halloween to New Year's Day. For example, the Fresno Hmong New Year is generally held between December 26 and January 1. The Atlanta Hmong New Year is held on Thanksgiving weekend. The Seattle Hmong New Year is typically held the first weekend of November. This allows people an opportunity to visit New Year celebrations in several cities over the course of a season.

Hmong New Year is a joyous occasion. In the traditional religion, which is a combination of animism and ancestor worship, it is also a time for important rituals. The rituals that are done to appease the ancestors and release the souls of the dead are done in the home. There are also thousands of Hmong who have converted to Christianity. They also hold smaller family get-togethers in the New Year tradition but are more apt to sing gospel music than to sacrifice a chicken to the ancestors. Nonetheless, most of the celebration of the New Year is done in huge parties where literally everyone in the community comes together for singing, dancing, eating, and mixing.

The food of the Hmong New Year season is best described as "abundant" and is served from buffet tables that are crowded with all kinds of foods, either brought potluck-style or purchased from a caterer. One traditional treat is the sticky rice cake, which is made by sweetening glutinous, or sticky, rice with sugarcane syrup and forming it into a bite-size patty. The patty is wrapped in a banana leaf and roasted, making a pleasantly browned confection. Another popular treat is rice beer, which the adults in the crowd enjoy thoroughly.

The Hmong New Year has changed, however, and in the United States it reflects the American lifestyle. It celebrates ancient traditions, but it is also influenced by the American and Western concepts. Feasting is one of the traditional aspects of the Hmong New Year that continues to this day, except that some of the food and other customs are different from in Laos. For example, there are both private and public aspects to the celebration. Families entertain out-of-town guests and invite friends over for dinner in the private celebrations. This is the time to slaughter the New Year's pig, or *npua tsiab,* which has been raised for this specific purpose. In urban areas, it is difficult to raise and slaughter the npua tsiab, which is one of the reasons that so many Hmong families have moved to rural areas.

Bao Lee (left) helps her sister Va Vang kill chickens for a special Hmong New Year feast on December 12, 2004, in Fresno, California. (Paula Bronstein | Getty Images)

Both Christians and followers of the old religion mix freely in the public celebration. At the public celebration, there is, increasingly, paid entertainment instead of long-winded renditions of folktales and recitations of traditional poetry. While many of the women still wear traditional clothing, the men are more likely to wear Western-style business suits. Business is conducted at the party, politicians shake hands and kiss babies, and community groups set up booths and pass out flyers.

The food at the Hmong American New Year represents adaptation to life in multicultural America. There might be a range of food, from fried chicken and noodle soup to ice cream and donuts. There might also be tacos, churros, Thai and Chinese foods, green papaya salad, and Lao *khao poun* mixed in with the Hmong smoked pork and sticky rice cakes.

The Hmong in China hold two special, food-related holidays. The first is Chixin Jie, the New Rice Tasting Festival, in July. This festival celebrates the rice harvest. To express gratitude to the spirits, the newly harvested rice is steamed and eaten with newly harvested vegetables and freshly caught fish. Some of the rice is also made into wine for the festival. The theme is freshness, which relates directly to the high value placed on fresh foods.

The other festival is called the Sister Rice Festival, sometimes referred to as the "First Valentine's Day." This festival, a celebration of spring and an annual mating ritual, is based on the folktale of the seven sisters. The sisters in the story were lonely, because there were no marriageable men on their mountain. On a neighboring mountain, separated by a river, there were seven lonely brothers. The bearded god, Zhang Guolao, who carried a tubular bamboo drum, took pity on them. He instructed the girls to dye glutinous rice into colors, using flowers and leaves of mountain plants. The dyed rice was then rolled into balls containing meat or fish. The god then brought the brothers across the river, where the sisters presented them with small bamboo baskets filled with the colored rice balls. And they lived happily ever after.

In modern-day China, the Sister Rice Festival is a colorful reenactment of the folktale. Single women still go into the hills to collect flowers and leaves to dye small balls of sticky rice. They sometimes insert highly symbolic gifts into the colored rice balls, which are arranged in small bamboo baskets. When suitors come to call, they take these love tokens as messages from their intended mate. For example, a small bamboo fishhook means, quite literally, "Let's hook up and get married quickly."

Diet and Health

Food and diet, health and disease, are controversial topics within the Hmong refugee community. Some of the older people try to maintain a traditional diet, but so much has changed that it seems impossible. For example, pork, once reserved for special occasions, is abundant, but it does not taste the same. Refrigeration, so much a part of American life, changes the flavors of food. The need to go out and work for wages results in very different time issues than when living in a village and supporting oneself by raising one's own food.

In some ways, traditional Hmong food customs, such as the emphasis on freshness and plenty of vegetables, help keep the group healthy. But others, such as a perceived value in being fat (a sign of plenty) and the uncritical acceptance of other foods, have the opposite effect. The Hmong in America are suffering from diseases that they did not know existed 30 years ago, and not everyone agrees on the reasons.

One of the more positive traditional practices is the tender custom of caring for a woman during the first month after the delivery of a baby. During this time, the mother is considered vulnerable and must eat a special diet for protection and to regain her strength. The diet is made up of boiled chicken with special, healing herbs. She is not allowed to work during that month, and rest is required. It is best for the husband's mother to cook and care for her daughter-in-law for the first month after delivery, which is a nice benefit for young women who, otherwise, must serve their mothers-in-law. The women say that the diet is monotonous but important. A public health study conducted by the National Institutes of Health (NIH) showed that maternal and child deaths among Hmong refugees were surprisingly low.

One negative result of the access to an abundance of food in the United States is a high rate of obesity and diabetes. In Laos, food was sometimes in short supply. There was never a surplus of food, and people adjusted to living on a low-calorie, low-fat, plant-based diet. In that environment, a fat baby was a healthy baby. When the Hmong moved to the United States, they delighted in how easy it was to have fat babies and fat children. Some of the adults also became overweight, and a high rate of diabetes, previously unknown, is the outcome. Diabetes educators find that it is difficult to work with Hmong patients, because their cultural beliefs are in conflict with Western medicine. A study in Minnesota found that Hmong refugees with diabetes do not accept that it is caused by food. Rather, they see it as a result of their refugee experience, of the loss that they have suffered. In their belief system, they are "out of balance here."

Hmong American children have learned about hot dogs, hamburgers, tacos, pizza, and other Western-style foods through their school lunch programs, and they often demand those foods at home, resulting in an especially high intake of foods that are high in calories and low in nutrients. The best efforts of nutrition educators sometimes are stymied by cultural differences. For example, one public health office took care to hire a registered dietitian with a master's degree, who was Hmong and from the local community, in an earnest effort to improve the diet and health status in the area. It looked like a win-win situation, with a culturally appropriate yet scientifically trained care provider. The dietitian did her best, concentrating on prenatal health, diabetes, weight control, and heart disease, but her advice fell on deaf ears among her clientele. The reason: She came from a low-ranking clan.

There is a high level of mistrust toward American doctors. Western medicine is cold and intrusive in comparison with the more familiar shaman. Even individuals who have converted to Christianity tend to fear and avoid American doctors. To make things more difficult, there are only 13 last names, one for each clan. There is a limited number of first names as well, resulting in many people having the same name. This causes confusion at pharmacies and health clinics, resulting in treatments and prescriptions being confused on a semiregular basis. In one example, a man with kidney problems went to see his doctor. The doctor gave him an appropriate prescription, but the pharmacist got his prescription switched with that of another man with the same name. As a result, the man suffered kidney failure. His doctor suggested dialysis, but there was a rumor circulating among the Hmong that dialysis was just a way for the doctors to collect blood that they wanted to drink. The myth of the vampire doctor started during the Vietnam War and has never really gone away. The man refused treatment until he was so weak that his American friends just picked him up and carried him to the emergency room. When his wife was notified, she came to the hospital and screamed at their American friends that the doctors just wanted to kill her husband, until a nurse, who also happened to be Hmong, managed to calm her down. In this case, the man recovered, but every time a Hmong person dies in the hospital it helps perpetuate the myth of the vampire doctor.

A group of local Hmong farmers proudly display their crop of dikons near Fresno, California. (Andy Sacks | Getty Images)

There is a higher rate of kidney stones and kidney failure in the Hmong population than in the general population. The reasons are unclear, but one possible cause is high protein intake combined with low water intake. It is also possible that there is a genetic enzymatic imbalance that is widespread in this small population, similar to the tendency, in some families, to develop gout due to a genetic tendency to build up uric acid in the system. Even so, the problem might be alleviated by eating less protein and drinking more water.

Most Hmong people who now live in the United States have adjusted the traditional diet to Western standards. For example, they will keep frozen meat in the home freezer, although they still prefer meats and fish that are as fresh as possible. The preference for fresh fruits and vegetables remains, however, and those foods are to be found at Hmong-owned booths at local farmers' markets, as well as from Hmong people who have moved to rural areas where they can farm. However, most Hmong homemakers still cook rice with every meal and prefer the flavor of pork to beef, flavored with traditional spices such as coriander, lemongrass, and monosodium glutamate.

Deborah Duchon

Further Reading

Culhane-Pera, Kathleen A., Cheng Her, and Bee Her. "'We Are Out of Balance Here': A Hmong Cultural Model of Diabetes." *Journal of Immigrant and Minority Health* 9, No. 3 (2007): 179–90.

Culhane-Pera, Kathleen A., and Mayseng Lee. "'Die Another Day': A Qualitative Analysis of Hmong Experiences with Kidney Stones." *Hmong Studies Journal* 7 (2006): 1–34.

Duchon, D. A. "'Home Is Where You Make It': Hmong Refugees in Georgia." *Urban Anthropology and Studies of Cultural Systems and World Economic Development* 26, No. 1 (1997): 71–92.

Faller, H. S. "Perinatal Needs of Immigrant Hmong Women: Surveys of Women and Health Care Providers." *Public Health Reports* 100, No. 3 (1985): 340–43. http://www.ncbi.nlm.nih.gov/pmc/articles/PMC1424761/.

Ikeda, Joanne P. *Hmong American Food Practices, Customs, and Holidays.* Chicago, IL: American Dietetic Association; Alexandria, VA: American Diabetic Association, 1992.

Molinar, Richard, and Michael Yang. *Guide to Asian Specialty Vegetables in the Central Valley, CA.* University of California Cooperative Extension in Fresno County. http://cefresno.ucdavis.edu/files/4902.pdf.

Scripter, Sami, and Sheng Yang. *Cooking from the Heart: The Hmong Kitchen in America.* Minneapolis: University of Minnesota Press, 2009.

Yang, Kou. "An Assessment of the Hmong American New Year and Its Implications for Hmong-American Culture." *Hmong Studies Journal* 8 (2007): 1–32.

Hong Kong

Overview

Food is so intimately woven into the fabric of Hong Kong's society that it is part of the standard greeting when one encounters family, friends, and acquaintances. Hong Kong is a gourmet's paradise where one can eat, and eat well, 24 hours a day, seven days a week. The choices range from some of the best street food in Asia to haute fusion cuisine at the restaurants of world-famous chefs.

Hong Kong, which means "fragrant harbor" in Cantonese, after the incense that used to perfume the island, was once just a small fishing village. The deep natural harbor and its location as the gateway to southern China ensured its destiny as a busy entrepôt, but it has suffered a tumultuous history in the last two centuries. After the Chinese lost the Opium War, Hong Kong was ceded to the British and in 1842 became a Crown Colony. After the Chinese lost the Second Opium War, the Kowloon Peninsula south of Boundary Street was also ceded to Britain. In 1898, faced with an increasing French influence in southern China and worried about the colony's security, Britain obtained a 99-year lease of Lantau Island and the adjacent northern lands, which became known as the New Territories. These three agreements formed the territory that is collectively known today as Hong Kong. The territory was briefly occupied by the Japanese during World War II and in the last century has experienced waves of immigration, first from mainland Chinese fleeing the newly established Communist government, and then a steady flow of Indian and Pakistani entrepreneurs, Vietnamese refugees in the 1980s and 1990s and, since its return to Chinese sovereignty in 1997,

internal migration from the mainland. Under its period of British rule, Hong Kong became a thriving port that attracted tradespeople, immigrants, refugees, Commonwealth expatriates, and others from all over the world. Throughout the territory's transformation, the dominant culture (and population, which is 95% Han Chinese) has remained unmistakably rooted in Chinese practices, traditions, and preferences, but its complicated history can be clearly observed in Hong Kong's rich and eclectic food culture.

🍽 Food Culture Snapshot

Wendy and David Chan live in a modest but high-rise apartment close to the bustling shops, restaurants, and businesses of Mong Kok. Wendy and David were born and raised in Hong Kong, although David was educated abroad. David works in the family's import-export business. Wendy also works there part-time while raising their two boys. The Chans employ a maid to help with household chores and cooking but also eat out frequently. Their lifestyle and foodways are typical of well-educated, bilingual, and well-traveled middle-class Hong Kongers. Their background has influenced their diet, which embraces foodstuffs from both East and West.

David usually gets up at 7 A.M. and goes straight to work. He picks up a hot breakfast along the way, which usually consists of a bowl of rice porridge (congee) with scallions, preserved duck eggs called *pei dan*, and lean pork. Sometimes he stops by a storefront and buys a small package of *ju cheong fun*—rolled rice crepes that are doused in soy or hoisin sauce, sprinkled with sesame and scallions, and dressed with peanut sauce. This he takes back to work and eats at his desk. An occasional coffee drinker, David might also purchase a small eight-ounce cup of coffee with sugar to perk him up. Meanwhile, Wendy prepares breakfast at home for herself and the boys. The boys favor cold cereal with milk and buttered toast. Other times Wendy will ask their Filipina domestic helper, Josephine, to pick up something from the bakery the night before. This is usually an assortment that includes sweet and savory options: soft glazed rolls with ham and egg sandwiched in between; glazed buns stuffed with roast pork (*cha siu bao*); sweet buns with a cookie-like crumble top and custard filling, known as pineapple buns for how the crumble resembles a pineapple; light, sweet rolls split in half, filled with sweetened whipped cream, and sprinkled with toasted coconut (*lai yeo bao*); or plain semihard rolls known as *ju tsai bao,* or "piggie rolls," which are eaten with butter and jam.

The boys buy what they wish for lunch at the school cafeteria. The cafeteria offers ham and cheese sandwiches, curried soup noodles, or stir-fried rice or noodles. If they are really hungry, they might buy a *fan hup,* or "rice box," which contains a meat of choice, a vegetable, and a sauce, all over a large helping of rice. Wendy and David also eat out for lunch and usually choose to go to the large food court in the basement of their office building to get a quick "set meal" of a soup, a rice, a vegetable, and a meat for a modest price.

At around 4 P.M. someone in David and Wendy's office is sent downstairs for an afternoon tea break. The designated courier takes orders from everyone and returns shortly with an assortment of *lai cha* (strong hot tea usually sweetened with condensed milk), coffee, and a few colorful bubble tea drinks (tea, coffee, or juice-based beverages with large brown tapioca pearls mixed in). The boys, meanwhile, have been let out of school and head to the nearby 7-Eleven with their friends to buy drinks and processed snack foods such as BBQ potato chips, shrimp crackers, Japanese candies, or ice creams. They might also stop at one of the hawker stalls (street vendors) near their school. Some favorites include curried fish balls (fish paste formed into Ping-Pong ball–sized balls) on skewers, waffles slathered with peanut butter and margarine

folded inside paper bags, and fried stinky (fermented) tofu served with sweet hoisin sauce.

Dinner is the most important meal of the day for a busy family like the Chans because it is when everyone sits together to share a meal and their day. As Wendy is at work in the afternoon, it is Josephine's job to visit the local market when it opens at 10 A.M. That way, the family ensures they have the best selection of meat, fish, and produce.

Major Foodstuffs

Hong Kong is often described as a crossroads of East and West, which translates into the foods available for purchase as well. The region's proximity to other Southeast Asian neighbors, long history of attracting visitors, and continued role as a major trading port have meant that Hong Kongers today have developed a wide-ranging palate that demands foodstuffs from all over the world. Land is at a premium, the cost of living is high, and labor is expensive, so the territory must import most of its food in any case. Chinese cuisine, and especially the regional preferences of neighboring Canton, is the one that maintains the strongest influence, however, and this is reflected in the major foods that are consumed in Hong Kong.

Located just north of the Tropic of Cancer, Hong Kong is subject to the annual monsoons that irrigate the rice paddies of Southeast Asia. Rice is thus the preferred staple in Hong Kong, with noodles of all types also consumed regularly. Rice paddies used to be a common sight in Hong Kong, but rapid urbanization and an exploding population have changed this. Rice must now be imported, with fragrant jasmine rice from Thailand preferred above other types.

Like other cuisines at cultural crossroads, the geography of Hong Kong has played an important part in its food culture. Seafood, whether captured from the South China Sea at its doorstep or imported from far away, is beloved by all Hong Kongers. Hong Kong seafood markets are exhilarating sights to behold, with what seems to be every edible creature piled, dumped, stacked, and laid out to satisfy every possible craving. Aside from a huge variety of fish—frozen, swimming in tanks, or simply gasping for air on wet tarps laid out on the pavement—there is every size and shape of clams, mussels, oysters, crabs, lobster, shrimp, crayfish, sea urchins, sea eels, and more. Some of the more spectacular specimens in markets are huge, almost lobster-like mantis shrimp, long-bladed razor clams, prehistoric-looking rockfish, pricey abalone, and the unmistakably phallic-looking geoduck clam. The Cantonese also love frogs, which can be found in the "wet" seafood section of markets. These are piled into small wire cages, from which they are removed and skinned and gutted upon request.

Walk through any of Hong Kong's markets, and the variety of fruits for sale year-round is equally stunning. Fruit is flown in daily from the rest of Southeast Asia, China, Australia, New Zealand, North and South America, and beyond. Hong Kongers adore fruit and usually end their meals with it. Apples, oranges, and grapes are popular, as are tropical fruits such as the impressive jackfruit, with its long (some up to four feet!), hard, spiky body; the gorgeous pink and green dragon fruit with its white flesh and black, kiwilike seeds; the succulent Cantonese lychee and longans that have inspired classic poems; the neat purple billiard ball–like mangosteens; crisp-juicy Asian pears; fragrant papayas; honeyed Thai mangoes; and more.

Hong Kongers, like their mainland cousins, are enthusiastic vegetable eaters. No meal is considered complete without a vegetable dish. Chinese broccoli (*gai lan*), mustard greens, napa cabbage, and bok choy and its more svelte relative *choy sum* are some of the most popular leafy greens. Chinese eggplant,

A large variety of fish and seafood on display at a vendor's shop at the popular Nelson Road outdoor market in Hong Kong's Kowloon district. (Lee Snider | Dreamstime.com)

white Chinese turnips, starchy taro root, and lotus root are commonly seen on Hong Kong menus and may be fried, boiled, steamed, sautéed, braised, and so on. Additionally, while technically not a vegetable, mushrooms of all kinds are embraced, with the meaty oyster mushroom fetching premium prices whether dried or fresh.

Soybean products are omnipresent in Hong Kong markets and menus. Soy milk, known as *dou tseung,* is popular beverage that is consumed either hot or cold and can be purchased from small cafés or in bottles from stores. Tofu in its many forms is used in soups, stews, braises, stir-fries, and desserts. Fresh and dried tofu "skin," which forms on the surface of soy milk as it is boiled, is used to add textural interest to vegetarian dishes and soups. Perhaps its most interesting use is in Buddhist vegetarian cuisine, where the skins can be used to imitate duck or chicken, both texturally and visually. Soybeans themselves are not commonly eaten whole, except perhaps as a bar snack or at Japanese restaurants.

Cooking

Preparation of meals in Hong Kong relies on the same set of equipment and techniques as on the Chinese mainland. Chinese cooking does not involve a lot of specialized equipment, but the most basic kitchen will have three items: a wok, a meat cleaver, and a heavy cutting board. The wok is the workhorse of the Hong Kong kitchen and is used for everything from steaming to braising, stir-frying to deep-frying. The best woks are made of cast iron, and the 14-inch diameter size is sufficient for the average household. A large meat cleaver, usually made of carbon or stainless steel and with a wooden handle, is also standard in every Chinese kitchen. While it may appear unwieldy, the Chinese cleaver is extremely versatile and can accomplish cutting tasks that range from a fine mince to chopping bones. As the cleaver is a weighty knife, it is necessary to have a heavy and stable cutting board. Traditional boards were made from round wood taken from a slice of a single tree trunk and were so large that they should be more accurately described as blocks. Modern boards are made of a dense, heavy-duty rubber or plastic material that is not as thick but can still meet the downward chop of a cleaver into bone without bouncing off the counter.

Hong Kong kitchens tend to be tiny, which limits the number of appliances that can be crammed into them. Refrigerators are diminutive and simple compared to the high-tech behemoths found in North American kitchens, which means that daily grocery shopping is a must for anyone who eats at home regularly. Since open markets are available in every neighborhood, though, shopping is not the same kind of chore in Hong Kong as it would be in North America's car-centric society. Fresh food items tend to be purchased in open markets, while dry goods, processed or frozen foods, and household goods are purchased in supermarkets. Most shopping is done on the way home from work, or if the household employs a maid, she (maids are almost always female) will do the shopping during the workday. Microwaves are not ubiquitous as they tend to take up a lot of room, and those who have them tend to limit their use to reheating, rather than cooking, food. Households without microwaves reheat food the old-fashioned way by steaming it in a wok or giving it a quick stir in a pot. Actual stoves are not available in every household; many contain cooktops with single or double burners that stand on top of the counter and may be hooked up to a gas tank that must be exchanged regularly. Set-in cooktops will be attached to a gas supply line. Chinese home cooking does not feature many roasted or baked dishes; that, combined with the lack of space, means that ovens are not common either. Even households that do have kitchens large enough for a proper stove and oven rarely use them unless there is an interest in preparing Western dishes or in baking.

One appliance that is universal, however, is the rice cooker. Rice being an important staple, having the rice cooker can help free up a burner, which is especially important if there is only one burner. The rice cooker can cook large amounts of rice at once without requiring any attention. As a bonus, small dishes of food can be steam-cooked by placing them directly on top of the rice while it is cooking, saving space and energy. The food also flavors or perfumes the rice in the process.

In terms of technique, stir-frying is perhaps the best-known Chinese cooking method. To stir-fry, a small amount of oil is placed in a wok over high heat. Evenly cut pieces of meat and/or vegetables are then placed in the wok and quickly tossed together. The high heat and the round-bottomed shape of the wok allow heat to conduct quickly and evenly over a large surface area, resulting in a very quick method of cooking that seals in flavors and nutrients. This was particularly desirable in the days when firewood still had to be collected as it was an energy-efficient way of preparing food.

Steaming is popular and is a simple, healthy method of preparation that brings out the true flavors of the food. The setup for steaming usually involves placing a small stainless steel wire rack at the bottom of a wok and filling the wok with boiling water up to the height of the rack. A plate of the food to be steamed is then lowered gently onto the rack and a cover placed over the wok until the dish is done.

Other important techniques include clay pot cooking, braising, double steaming, and slow-simmered soups. All of these techniques belong to the larger body of Chinese cooking methods as well but are an integral part of how Hong Kongers cook. Clay pot cooking is exactly that—food is cooked in earthen pots whose interiors are typically glazed black, with a small sturdy handle to one side and a matching lid. These are especially suitable for long braises because of the material's ability to conduct and retain heat evenly, minimizing burning. One popular use for clay pots is in preparing *bo tsai fan,* or clay pot rice. Rice and water are measured into the pot, with seasoned meat and vegetables settled on top to cook with the rice. It is a literal one-pot meal, with the pot acting as an attractive serving bowl as well. Braising differs from Western braising only in the choice of ingredients for the liquid, with soy sauce being a common base flavoring. Double steaming is a method usually reserved for preparing expensive delicacies such as shark's-fin or bird's nest soups. Ingredients are placed inside a ceramic jar with water, this is in turn placed inside another container, and the whole contraption is gently steamed for several hours. This technique minimizes the loss

Traditional soup found in Hong Kong made with meat, vegetables, and noodles. (Shutterstock)

of moisture while cooking and so is considered ideal when there is a need to preserve the nutritional and medicinal benefits of expensive ingredients. Double steaming is often used when making *tong sui,* Cantonese dessert soups that incorporate herbal medicines and are consumed for their nourishing and beautifying benefits.

Soups, both savory and sweet, hold a special place in Hong Kong food culture. Similarities can be drawn between the healthful, comfort-food qualities of chicken noodle soup and the body of Cantonese-style slow-simmered soup recipes (*lo foh tong*) that Hong Kongers draw on. The Chinese herbs that are present in almost every recipe create soups that are believed to counteract everything from overwork and poor diet to post-pregnancy health problems and asthma and are the ultimate expression of caring when prepared for family and friends.

Typical Meals

Most meals consumed at home are primarily Cantonese influenced, reflecting Hong Kong's geography and the majority Cantonese population. Chinese home meals are eaten communally, with all the dishes placed at the center of the table and everyone taking small portions to go with their individual portions of rice throughout the meal. Thus, when eating at home, there are no courses because everything is placed on the table at once. At formal banquets there will be courses, but they, too, are placed in the center of a large table, albeit at intervals. The dishes remain on the table until they are empty, so by the end of a banquet all 9, 12, or 13 courses may be present in the middle of the table.

The basic structure of a meal is predicated on the belief that a healthy, balanced meal consists, at a bare minimum, of a meat dish, a vegetable dish, and a soup, or *leung sung yat tong,* meaning "two side dishes and one soup." This is, of course, in addition to jasmine rice. If guests are expected, dinner will be much more elaborate, with at least one seafood dish, usually steamed fish, and some roasted meats such as barbecued pork (*cha siu*), crispy-skinned roasted suckling pig, honey-lacquered roast duck, roast pigeon, or soy-braised chicken, purchased from special roasted-meat vendors.

The vegetable is usually the simplest dish, with a dark leafy green such as bok choy or choy sum quickly boiled and served with a dressing of oyster sauce or stir-fried with garlic. The meat dish might feature modest home-style dishes such as sliced beef stir-fried with onion, sweet and sour pork with bell peppers and pineapple, or steamed chicken with mushrooms and ginger.

Seafood is a little more expensive, so a family may have fresh fish less often. Salted fish and shrimp are usually used as condiments as part of a larger dish, although sometimes salted or dried fish and cuttlefish will be steamed and eaten plain. Hong Kongers prefer to purchase fish as fresh as possible. Still swimming is best, and a fresh fish is a must if guests will be present. The fish, gutted and descaled but with head and tail still intact, is typically steamed in the wok with ginger, scallions, and soy sauce and doused with hot oil to bring out the flavors.

Depending on what kind of soup is being prepared, ingredients such as dried nuts, seeds, or roots; fresh or dried fish; fresh or preserved vegetables; and/or meat may be included. Fresh fruit is usually eaten for dessert, and as noted earlier, the average Hong Kong fruit bowl may contain anything from apples and oranges to lychees, durians, and mangosteens.

Eating Out

Eating out is also a very important part of the local food culture. Tiny apartments and long workdays (most people work a half day on Saturday and even schools require morning attendance) mean that Hong Kongers have little space or time to socialize. Restaurants provide much-needed social spaces in this inescapably cramped city.

Hong Kong's food culture, like that in other Southeast Asian cities, begins on its streets. Street-food vendors, known as hawkers, can be found on the streets and in the markets throughout the territory. Most require some sort of vending license, although some operate illegally and take their chances with the authorities, leading to desperate scrambles whenever a uniform happens along. Common foods sold are chestnuts roasted in giant woks of hot coals; stinky tofu (which can be smelled a block away); *boot tsai go*, which are small, sweet steamed puddings studded with mung beans or adzuki red beans; and mock shark's-fin soup, made of similar flavoring ingredients but with vermicelli replacing the strands of cooked shark's fin. Waffles—both the familiar square-holed variety and the "little chicken egg" type known as *gai dan tsai*—are very popular with children. Both are made from waffle batter. Gai dan tsai is cooked in an iron with little half-moon indentations that result in the "egg" look and is eaten plain, pulled apart piece by piece. Regular waffles are smeared with peanut butter and/or butter. Dragon beard candy—finely pulled sugar rolled around bits of crushed peanut, toasted sesame, white sugar, and coconut that resembles silk cocoons—was a typical hawker treat but is now a rare sight. Pulling sugar into gossamer strands takes practice and skill, but this dying art can no longer command a living wage.

Dai pai dong are beloved institutions and an important part of the local food culture. These informal, affordable outdoor eateries usually consist of rickety plastic or cheap metal tables and chairs set on the pavement. The kitchen doles out simple Cantonese favorites such as congee, soups, noodles, and stir-fries, as well as small snacks such as *jung,* the Chinese tamale-like dumpling. The menu is usually in Chinese. Open early in the morning through the wee hours, dai pai dong are frequented for every meal of the day.

As Hong Kong is a city that never sleeps, it seems inevitable that there is a proper mealtime—the fourth in a standard day—to sustain those who keep going long after the sun sets. *Siu yeh* (both characters mean "night") is the term used for a small meal taken late at night, after dinner has already been eaten. It is usually eaten with friends after an evening out or a long night at work. Larger and more formal restaurants tend to close after 10 or 11 P.M., so more casual Hong Kong–style cafés, hawker stands, or dai pai dong are the usual venues for siu yeh.

There are several categories of cafés in Hong Kong. The Hong Kong–style ones, known as *cha chaan teng* (literally, "tea diner"), serve casual Cantonese dishes similar to what is available at dai pai dong, with the addition of "Western" items such as steak, pork cutlets, ramen noodles or macaroni with Spam and a fried egg, plain buttered toast, or French toast. In Hong Kong French toast is two slices of deep-fried bread with peanut butter in between, served with English golden syrup and margarine. These cafés also serve a variety of classic Hong Kong beverages such as iced lemon water with simple syrup, hot or cold malted drinks sweetened with condensed milk, and "fleecies"—red bean ices made of sweetened red beans with condensed milk and ice

A typical dai pai dong, or street restaurant, in Hong Kong. (Shutterstock)

or topped with ice cream. Casual, cheap, and ubiquitous, cafés are popular for a quick, casual meal or snack.

More upscale Western-style cafés in Hong Kong serve only *sai chan,* or Western cuisine. Dishes on the menu here are derived from no specific Western country but are adjusted for local tastes, earning this style of cooking the nickname "soy sauce cuisine." Most will offer a three-course set meal consisting of a soup, a main course, and a dessert. Clam chowder, cream of asparagus, borscht, and minestrone are popular options for the soup course, while wok-fried spaghetti with meat sauce or sizzling iron plates of steak are the usual main-course options. Dessert usually consists of a scoop of ice cream, mango pudding, or Jell-O.

Although there are international fast-food chains, Hong Kong also has its indigenous category of fast-food establishments. The two largest chains are Café de Coral and Fairwood. Diners order and pay up front at the cashier and then take their receipt and a tray to a cafeteria-style line to claim their meals. Well-lit, consistent, and inexpensive, these places also offer items similar to those at cha chaan teng and set-meal deals that can include home-style slow-simmered soups.

Large banquet/seafood restaurants sit at the top of the pecking order in local cuisine. *Yum cha,* meaning literally to "drink tea," is served in the mornings. It is a beloved activity on weekends, when entire extended families get together around a table to enjoy dish after dish of small bites known as dim sum. Classic dim sum include *ha gao,* steamed shrimp dumplings; *siu mai,* steamed pork dumplings; cha siu bao, barbecue roast pork buns; and *daan tat,* custard egg tarts. Weekday mornings in these large restaurants belong to Hong Kong's senior citizens, who start their days lingering over a bamboo steamer or three of dim sum, a pot of black tea, and a newspaper. Most choose a favorite restaurant and become familiar with the servers and fellow patrons, and it becomes an important part of their daily social routine. In the evenings, the restaurants' kitchens cater to wedding banquets and dinner parties, serving more elaborate items not usually made at home such as abalone with mushroom, winter melon soup with the hollowed-out melon serving as the tureen, lobster, shark's-fin soup, and roasted meats.

Mock Shark's-Fin Soup

This popular street snack is also easy and inexpensive to make at home. All ingredients can be found in well-stocked Asian groceries. Be careful not to overcook the vermicelli or overthicken the soup; it will become gummy.

Serves 4

6 oz lean pork butt, trimmed

8 c chicken stock

2 tbsp ginger, julienned

½ oz dried snow ear fungus, rehydrated and shredded

6–8 shiitake mushrooms, fresh or dried and rehydrated, julienned

7 tbsp water chestnut starch

8 tbsp cold water

2 tbsp oyster sauce

2 tbsp dark soy sauce

Sesame oil and white pepper, to taste

2 packages dried vermicelli, rehydrated in cold water and cut into about 2-in. sections

2 eggs, beaten

Red rice vinegar and extra julienned ginger, to serve

1. Rinse and dry the pork. Blanch pork in boiling water for 5 minutes. Rinse, drain, and place in pot with chicken stock and simmer for half an hour, skimming off any foam that rises to the surface.

2. Remove pork from stock. Reserve stock, and set pork aside to cool, and then pull the meat apart with a fork.

3. Heat a little oil in a wok, and sauté ginger, snow ear fungus, and mushrooms until soft and fragrant. Add reserved stock, and bring to a boil.

4. Meanwhile, dissolve water chestnut starch in the water and set aside.

5. To the wok, add oyster sauce, soy sauce, sesame oil, and white pepper, to taste. Thicken the soup with water chestnut solution to desired consistency. Stir in vermicelli. Bring to a boil, and pour in beaten eggs, stirring quickly to create thin strands of cooked egg.

6. Serve hot with red rice vinegar, ginger, salt, and white pepper on the side.

Japanese sushi and noodles, Thai cuisine, Vietnamese soups, Korean barbecue, and French haute cuisine are the top cuisines favored by Hong Kongers, although chances are good that one can find at least one option for even the most esoteric cuisine. Fusion cuisine is very trendy and one of the more expensive dining options in Hong Kong, with the restaurants themselves often located within luxury hotels.

Hong Kong is a city prone to trends of all kinds. Food trends are no exception. Sometimes these trends may begin in other Asian cities, as was the case with Portuguese egg tarts, little puff pastry shells filled with egg custard. Originally from neighboring Macau, they first became a huge sensation in Taiwan and Singapore in the 1990s. The craze soon caught on in Hong Kong as well, where people lined up for hours in front of bakeries that couldn't turn them out fast enough. Other crazes have followed since with foods such as Japanese-style cheesecake (so light and moist as to be compared to the lightest pound cakes), Taiwanese bubble tea, and "crunch" cake (an angel food cake–like base with a light layer of frosting, topped with crunchy meringues).

Special Occasions

Banquet halls are where Hong Kongers celebrate their life events. In a society where face and status are important, the bigger the event is, the better one looks. In a city where people don't like to host dinner parties because of lack of space, the expansive banquet halls are a necessity.

Births are celebrated by hosting a *mun yuet jau,* or "full-month banquet," so named because it is held when the child reaches one month of age. This custom arose because communities were used to experiencing high infant mortality rates. Babies would not be named or formally welcomed into the family until this time, when they had survived the most dangerous period of their lives. Close friends and family are invited to the typically nine-course banquet, which ends with a noodle dish (the length symbolizes longevity), red-dyed hard-boiled eggs, and slices of red-dyed ginger. Nutritious eggs and the warming properties of ginger are both believed to help women recover from childbirth, while red is the color of happiness, luck, and prosperity. In the old days, red eggs were sent to friends and family to announce the birth. Birthday banquets are usually reserved for those aged 60 and older, when people get together to celebrate the person's health and longevity and to pay their respects to an elder. Long egg noodles are served at the end of these banquets, too, along with *sau bao* (long-life buns), steamed little white buns stuffed with sweet lotus seed paste and painted with a rosy flush to resemble peaches, another symbol of longevity. Children's birthdays are marked with cakes from one of the Western-style bakeries; the cakes are filled with fresh fruit and iced with whipped cream.

There are no particular foods associated with funerals; however, it is customary for the bereaved family to host a *gai wai jau,* or a "stomach-easing banquet," for those who attended the funeral. This meal, held to celebrate the deceased's journey to heaven, is vegetarian and traditionally consists of only five courses—much shorter than the minimum nine of happier occasions.

Weddings are the most elaborate celebrations of all. Prior to the event, the bride's family is expected to distribute *loh poh beng,* "wife cakes," to those invited. These heavy little cakes are filled with winter melon or almond paste and are encased in pastry made flaky with pork lard. They used to serve as the wedding announcements and invitations, but in hectic Hong Kong, the preferred method is to enclose "cake cards" with the red-and-gold wedding invitations. These cards are later redeemed at the bakery that issued them for whatever the recipient desires. The wedding banquet itself is an opportunity for the family to put on a show of prosperity and wealth, so the larger the event, and the longer and more expensive the menu, the better. During the meal, the wedding party goes from table to table to personally toast all their guests and thank them for coming. Bottles of champagne, scotch, and cognac are placed at each table for this express purpose.

Diet and Health

To Hong Kongers, food is never eaten just for the sake of filling the belly. Every food is believed to possess innate qualities that can ultimately affect the natural balance of a body's system. When poor diet, stress, and other hazards of 21st-century life throw the body out of balance, Hong Kongers rely on food as medicine to put them back on track. This understanding is grounded in the Taoist principle of yin-yang. There is no positive without a negative, no light without dark, no male without female. This is true of everything in nature, including food, and only when all elements are present in equal amounts can balance and harmony be achieved. Thus, every food is ascribed a property—hot or cold, damp or dry, nourishing or neutral—and when eaten will have a corresponding effect on the body.

The structure of the basic Chinese meal is based on this idea, and ingredients are combined in recipes according to their properties. For example, bok choy on its own is very cooling and not suitable for someone with a cold or weak constitution. Cooking bok choy with ginger, which is a warming food, counterbalances this property. This is most evident is in Cantonese soup recipes where complex combinations of ingredients are simmered slowly together to create tonics that are curative or prophylactic, as the case may be. Ingredients may be purchased in markets and at special herbalist shops where Chinese doctors are available to listen to patients' pulses and prescribe brews tailored to individual needs. The shops are distinguishable by the cases of dried food items that line the walls and entrances, as well as by their unique smell—briny and musty, with an undertone of bitter medicine.

Hong Kong being a busy town, there is a fast-food option for those too busy to eat right and make their own soups—herbal tea shops. They are recognizable by large copper-colored urns with taps dispensing a variety of brews. The urns are usually placed near the front of the shop, with bowls of tea already poured and available to passersby for a quick fix. If one chooses to enter and sit, a larger menu of soups and teas is available to treat everything from fatigue to poor digestion, and others claim beauty benefits. A subtype of these shops sells the popular—and expensive—turtle pudding. Made from turtle shell and a mixture of Chinese herbs, this black, mild-tasting pudding is believed to flush toxins from the body.

Karen Lau Taylor

Further Reading

Cheung, Sidney C. H., and Chee Beng Tan. *Food and Foodways in Asia: Resource, Tradition and Cooking.* London: Routledge, 2007.

Halvorsen, Francine. *The Food and Cooking of China: An Exploration of Chinese Cuisine in the Provinces and Cities of China, Hong Kong, and Taiwan.* New York: Wiley, 1996.

Hom, Ken. *Fragrant Harbor Taste: The New Chinese Cooking of Hong Kong.* New York: Simon & Schuster, 1989.

India

Overview

The Republic of India occupies most of the landmass called the Indian Subcontinent or South Asia, which also includes the republics of Pakistan, Bangladesh, and Sri Lanka and the independent kingdoms of Nepal and Bhutan. India is a federal republic consisting of 29 states and six union territories. India is the world's seventh-largest country in area and, with more than a billion people, is second only to China in population. Some Indian states are larger than most countries and have distinctive languages, ethnicities, cultures, and cuisines.

Religion and geography play a key role in determining what Indians eat. More than 80 percent of the population is Hindu, but 13.5 percent—138 million— are Muslims, making India the world's second-largest Muslim country after Indonesia. The population also includes 24 million Christians, 19 million Sikhs, 8 million Buddhists, 4 million Jains, and small communities of Parsis (Zoroastrians), animists, and other religious groups. While it is a common belief that Indians are overwhelmingly vegetarian, in reality only 30 percent of the population has never eaten meat. However, because meat is expensive, most people are de facto vegetarians who eat meat and fish rarely. On average, Indians get 92 percent of their calories from vegetable products, including 70 percent from cereals, and just 8 percent from animal products (meat, dairy products, and eggs). Very few Indians are vegans.

🍽 Food Culture Snapshot

Robin and Anu Das live in an affluent neighborhood of South Delhi. Robin, a Bengali originally from Calcutta, is a freelance documentary film director; his wife, Anu, a Punjabi from Amritsar, is a freelance writer who helps Robin with his work. Their lifestyle and foodways are typical of middle-class cosmopolitan urbanites whose diet includes dishes from different parts of India as well as the West.

Robin and Anu start their day at 9 A.M. with *dalia,* a porridge made from cracked wheat, or perhaps a bowl of oatmeal or cold cereal, together with toast, a piece of fruit, and a cup of tea. For the Dases, as for many Indians, lunch is the largest meal of the day. It generally includes fried or stewed fish (reflecting Robin's Bengali origins), dal (boiled spiced lentils), one or two fried or boiled vegetable dishes, and rice. Around 5 P.M. the Dases have an afternoon snack of tea and biscuits (cookies). If guests drop by, they will purchase Indian sweets, European pastries, and fried snacks from a bakery. Dinner is around 9 P.M. Roast chicken, cooked Western style without any spices, or a roast of mutton, is served instead of fish, together with Indian or Western-style breads, boiled vegetables, dal, and fruit for dessert.

With globalization, things are changing rapidly in India. According to Anu, people are much more health conscious than in the past, so that meals are much smaller than the multicourse meals their parents enjoyed and butter and oil consumption is reduced. Even a decade ago, shopping would take several hours since it meant visiting a number of outdoor markets and small shops—one for fish, another for meat, a third for vegetables, and a fourth for dry goods like rice and flour. Today, people do one-stop shopping at supermarkets that carry not only all these items but also once-exotic "foreign" vegetables (such as broccoli, bell peppers, and asparagus), frozen foods, cold meats, other prepared foods, and even imported goods such as olive oil and Italian pasta. Robin and Anu also eat out much more than their parents did, both in restaurants serving Thai, Italian, and Indian regional cuisines and in fast-food outlets.

Major Foodstuffs

India is a predominantly rural country, and most Indian food is still produced regionally or locally. Only 2 percent of India's agricultural output is processed, so most meals are made from scratch. India has an enormous diversity of climates, soils, and weather systems. The states of Punjab and Haryana, called the breadbasket of India, are wheat producers. The northeastern states of Bengal and Assam to the east produce two, and sometimes three, crops of rice each year. Much of western India (Rajasthan, part of Gujarat) consists of barren deserts where only millets, sorghum, and other "coarse grains" grow. Consequently, in northern India, the dietary staple is wheat, ground into flour and made into bread, whereas in the east and south, the staple is rice. Indians prefer rice varieties with long, slender grains that retain their shape when cooked. The best known is basmati.

Another dietary staple are legumes—lentils (there are more than 50 commercial varieties), peas, chickpeas, and beans. In Hindi, both the raw ingredients and the boiled dish made from them are called dal. Almost all Indians eat dal every day. The combination of grains and lentils provides most of the amino acids our bodies need to stay healthy.

Minerals and trace elements are provided by vegetables. Potatoes, tomatoes, green peppers, winter squash, corn, okra, and other popular vegetables were brought by the Portuguese from the Western Hemisphere and Africa beginning in the late 15th century in the so-called Columbian Exchange. During their 300-year rule, the British introduced cabbages, cauliflower, lettuce, carrots, green beans, and navy beans.

Indigenous vegetables include bitter melons (*karela*); many varieties of squash and gourds, including the bottle gourd (*lauki* or *lau*), ash gourd, (*petha kaddu*), a small green gourd (*parwal*), and snake gourd (*chichinda*); eggplant (*brinjal* or *baingun*); long green beans (*seema*); white radishes (*mooli*); and various kinds of leafy greens, collectively called *saag*.

Milk and its products are an important source of protein. In North India milk is drunk by itself or boiled with tea and spices to make *chai*. Milk solids are pressed and cut into cubes to make *paneer*, a mild cheese that is a meat substitute in vegetarian dishes. Yogurt (*dahi*) is widely used as a marinade for meat, served as a side dish, or churned to produce butter. Because butter is perishable, it is made into clarified butter, called ghee, by cooking it over low heat until all the water has evaporated. Ghee is the preferred cooking medium in India, but oils made from mustard seeds, sesame seeds, peanuts, coconut, corn, and sunflower seeds are also used in different parts of the country.

The most distinctive feature of Indian cuisine is the addition of spices and seasonings to most dishes. The most widely used are turmeric, cloves, coriander, cumin, black pepper, cardamom, cinnamon, ginger, fenugreek, nutmeg, poppy seeds, saffron, mustard seeds, and, of course, chilies. Although Indian food has the reputation of being hot, in reality both the degree of hotness, which comes from chilies and pepper, and the spices that are used depend on the dish and regional and individual preferences. For example, mustard seeds and fenugreek are standard in South Indian vegetarian dishes, while highly aromatic spices such as cloves, cardamom, nutmeg, and cinnamon are essential ingredients in North Indian meat and rice dishes. Onions and garlic, sautéed in oil, are the starting point for many dishes but are avoided by some Hindus.

India is a fruit lover's paradise. Virtually all the fruits and berries cultivated in temperate climates grow in the cooler parts of the country, including peaches, plums, apricots, mulberries, strawberries, and apples. Most tropical and semitropical fruits flourish there, including bananas, mangoes, citrus fruits, jackfruit, papayas, guavas, sapodillas, custard apples, and pineapples.

Sugarcane cultivation and sugar refining are native to India. The stems are crushed to extract the juice, which is boiled down to make solid brown

Vendor of dried fruit in New Delhi, India. (Shutterstock)

sugar, called *gur* or jaggery. It is combined with milk products to make many Indian sweets.

Hindus and Sikhs avoid eating beef, since the cow is highly valued for its many contributions, and cow slaughter is banned in most parts of the country. The most popular meats are mutton, a word used for the flesh of both goats and sheep, and chicken. The meat of pigs is forbidden to Muslims and is generally avoided by non-Muslims as well.

Fish is a dietary staple in certain regions. Bengalis prefer freshwater fish from rivers and ponds. Popular varieties include *hilsa* (which is a kind of shad), carp, catfish, the perchlike *bekti,* pomfret, and kingfish. In Kerala, sea fish are widely eaten, including varieties of sardines, mackerel, pomfret, seer, squid, and prawns. Shrimp (called prawns in Indian English) are considered a delicacy, and several varieties are caught in Indian waters.

Water is served with meals. Milk and buttermilk are popular drinks in northern and western India, including *lassi,* yogurt mixed with water and spices. Bottled soft drinks are popular among the young. Tea boiled with milk and spices is popular in North India, while coffee is mainly grown and consumed in the south.

Cooking

Preparing Indian food is very labor-intensive. In an Indian joint family, where several generations live in one household, the senior woman supervises the food preparation, aided by her daughters and daughters-in-law. Affluent families have cooks.

Indian kitchens are simple by Western standards. Most cooking is done on top of a simple burner. The traditional stove, a *chula,* is a small U-shaped clay oven with a hole for inserting fuel and knobs on the top to hold the pot. Traditional fuels are charcoal, twigs, and dried cow patties. Today, middle-class households use a small cooktop with two burners fueled by bottled gas (propane).

Sautéing and deep-frying are done in a wok-shaped pot made of stainless steel or cast iron, called a *kadhai.* Many households own a pressure cooker, which considerably shortens the time needed to cook curries. A heavy, flat iron griddle with a wooden handle, called a *tawa,* is used for roasting spices and grilling and sautéing breads.

In North India, spices, onions, garlic, and herbs are crushed using a small rolling pin on a stone slab. In South India, a mortar and pestle are more commonly used. Modern cooks use electric grinders and blenders. Spices and flavorings are often ground early in the morning for the day's meals. Whole spices are kept in a spice box next to the stove.

Spices can be dry-roasted and ground into a powder, called *garam masala,* or "warm seasonings." This is stored in airtight bottles. A few pinches are added to a dish just before serving. Ready-made garam masalas are sold commercially and are sometimes called curry powder. Powdered or whole spices may be sautéed and added to a dish at the end of the cooking process to add flavor. Spices can also be ground into a wet paste with onions, garlic, ginger, yogurt, coconut milk, or some other liquid and used to make a gravy.

A uniquely Indian technique is called *bhuna.* After frying spices, garlic, onions, ginger, and perhaps tomatoes in a little oil, the cook sautés pieces of meat, fish, or vegetables in the mixture and then adds small amounts of water, yogurt, or other liquid a little at a time, stirring constantly. Other common techniques are sautéing and deep-frying. Since most households do not have ovens, roasted and grilled foods, such as kebabs (pieces of meat impaled on a stick and grilled over hot coals or in a tandoor, a large clay oven), are purchased outside.

Pickling, an ancient Indian technique, is essential in a country with a hot climate. It is a way of preserving fruits, vegetables, meat, or fish by impregnating them with acid, which discourages the growth of most microbes.

Typical Meals

Describing a typical Indian meal is difficult in view of the region's great regional, religious, and social diversity. However, there are certain commonalities. Most Indians who can afford it eat four meals a day: two main meals—lunch and dinner—and two supplementary meals—breakfast and a light snack in the late afternoon, sometimes called tea or *tiffin.*

Rural people start the day with a hearty breakfast or early lunch to prepare for the day's labor. In cities, most people enjoy a light breakfast, followed by a large lunch either at home or at the office or school, a light afternoon tea when family members return home from work or school, and a dinner eaten at 8:30, 9:00, or even later. In southern India, breakfast is the main meal of the day.

Traditionally, Indians sat on the floor for meals, sometimes on a carpet or raised stool. The food is prepared for each meal and served hot. Breads are always cooked on the spot and slid onto each diner's plate. The traditional plate is a *thali,* a circular metal tray with raised edges. Liquid dishes and yogurt are served in little metal bowls, called *kathoris.* In South India, banana leaves are used. Today, many families use Western-style plates and utensils, especially in cities.

The time-honored way of eating is with the fingers of the right hand. If bread is part of the meal, the diner breaks off a piece, uses it to scoop up a small portion of the food, and pops it into his mouth. For rice or vegetables, the tips of the fingers are used to form a little ball of food. A diner never touches the food or plate of another person.

Indian meals do not normally have a sequence of courses. Everything arrives more or less at once, although certain dishes may be served together. An Indian meal is centered around a cereal—wheat, rice, or some other grain. The second main component is lentils, generally served as a spiced souplike dish called dal. Generally, thick dals are eaten with bread, and thinner, more watery dals with rice. Relatively small amounts of meat, fish, and vegetables are added to enhance the taste and qualities of the main grain. Additional flavors come from yogurt; sweet and sour fruit and vegetable chutneys; sweet, sour, or pungent pickles; and salads. Sometimes seasonal fruit is served at the end of a meal. In many parts of India a meal ends with buttermilk or yogurt as an aid to digestion.

Dal Makhani

The thick, rich dals of the northern states of Punjab and Haryana are famous all over the subcontinent. They are made from black gram beans (often called black lentils though botanically unrelated to the true lentil), chickpeas, black-eyed peas, or kidney beans simmered for a long time over a slow fire until they become thick and then flavored with spices and cream. *Dal makhani* has been called India's favorite lentil dish.

$^2/_3$ c *urad* dal (whole black gram beans)

3 tbsp red kidney beans

1-in. piece of ginger or 3 tsp ready-made ginger paste

4 cloves garlic or 3 tsp garlic paste

4 tomatoes, pureed in a food processor or blender

1 tsp chili powder

4 tbsp ghee (clarified butter) or oil

½ c cream

Wash the beans and soak overnight. If ready-made ginger and garlic paste are not available, grind the ginger and garlic together with a little water to make a paste. Drain the water from the beans, and place in a large pot with 6 cups fresh water. Add salt, half the garlic and ginger paste, and 1 tablespoon ghee, and simmer until the beans are cooked. Mash lightly. Remove from the fire. Heat the remaining ghee and cook the tomatoes, chili powder, and the rest of the ginger and garlic paste until the ghee separates from the mixture. Add the mixture to the cooked beans, and cook over low heat for 20–25 minutes, mashing occasionally with a spoon against the side of the pot. Add the cream, and cook for 15–20 minutes more.

Within this basic framework there are wide variations depending on religion, region, social class, and affluence. For the very poor, a meal means a handful of boiled rice with chilies or vegetable peels, or roasted chickpea flour mixed with salt and green chilies. According to a recent survey, 35 percent of respondents said that at least once in the past year they or someone in their family did not have two square meals a day.

Less than a third of Indians are vegetarians, although the regional proportion varies from 2–3 percent in the states of Kerala and West Bengal to 45 percent in Gujarat and 62 percent in Haryana and Rajasthan. Because a vegetarian diet is associated with spiritual serenity, meat is avoided by swamis, yogis, and their followers. Some people also avoid garlic and onions for the same reason. Almost all Hindus and Sikhs avoid beef. Pork and alcohol are forbidden to Muslims, and although pigs are not explicitly proscribed for Hindus, many avoid pork as well. However, even people who are not vegetarians eat very little meat by Western standards; meat is a condiment, a flavoring of the starch, rather than the focal point of a meal.

The following are examples of typical meals in middle-class families in three regions of India. The food of Punjab and Haryana, rich agricultural states in northern India, is simple, robust, and closely linked to the land. In rural areas, the day may start with a hearty breakfast of sautéed bread called *parathas,* sometimes stuffed with potatoes, cauliflower, or grated radish. Sometimes breakfast is supplemented with *halwa,* a dish of grated vegetables cooked in butter and sugar syrup.

Lunch and dinner consist of bread and butter, dal, yogurt, a vegetable dish, and, for nonvegetarians, a chicken or mutton currylike dish. Paneer is combined with peas and other vegetables in curries or grilled on sticks. Spicing is straightforward, featuring coriander, cumin seeds, and red chilies. Rice is served mainly on special occasions. The region is renowned for its thick, rich dals flavored with spices and cream.

In Gujarat in western India, breakfast is served around 7 A.M. and includes tea with wheat or millet bread; *papri* (crisp little squares made from chickpea flour); or puffed rice. For lunch, Gujaratis eat flatbreads called *rotla* and *rotli* lightly sautéed on a griddle and traditionally made from millet or sorghum flour. Other dishes are a sautéed vegetable or vegetable stew, followed by plain boiled rice and dal or *kadhi,* a spicy yogurt curry thickened with chickpea flour. Gujaratis always add a pinch of sugar to dishes and may serve milk- or lentil-based sweets as part of the meal itself. Dinner, typically served at 8:00–8:30 P.M., is smaller than lunch. Sometimes it features a thick bread called *bakri* and a vegetable or a one-dish meal, such as *khichri,* a dish of boiled rice, lentils, and vegetables and nuts.

In southern India, the core cereal is rice. Breakfast is an important meal for Hindus and typically features *idlis* (soft, steamed, disk-shaped cakes) or *dosas* (flat, round, crispy crepes lightly sautéed in oil). The doughs are made by grinding rice, black lentils, and water into a paste. The standard accompaniments are *sambar*—a spicy lentil soup that sometimes includes vegetables—and coconut chutney. The standard breakfast drink is strong filtered coffee mixed with milk. Another popular breakfast dish is *uppuma,* a semolina porridge with tomatoes and onions.

Lunch features boiled white rice, accompanied by two or three seasonal vegetables (potatoes, plantains, eggplants, cabbage) sautéed with mustard seeds, fenugreek, and red chilies in a little oil or cooked in a gravy; a thin, very hot lentil soup called *rasam;* pickles; perhaps a salad of cucumber or bean sprouts; and mango or other fruit in season. A meal always ends with yogurt mixed with rice. Dinner is similar to lunch but generally simpler, and the dishes do not repeat those served at lunch. Often dinner includes *pappadums,* crispy lentil wafers.

Hyderabad, the capital of Andhra Pradesh, has a large Muslim population. A breakfast in a middle-class Muslim household might include parathas served with fried eggs, an omelet, or minced meat and/or sautéed potatoes. Lunch could feature bread or rice, a meat dish (beef or mutton) made with a gravy, dal, and yogurt. Dinner would be similar to lunch with the inclusion of a vegetable. On special occasions, *pulao* or *biryani* (richly spiced rice dishes with vegetables or meat) might be served.

Eating Out

Until the middle of the 20th century, India did not have a restaurant culture. Eating out was tolerated as a necessity rather than valued as a luxury or a new experience. Concerns about pollution prevented many Indians from eating in public places. Cooking and entertaining at home were facilitated by the presence of many women in a joint family and, for the wealthy, abundant servants.

There were exceptions. Large temples have always had kitchens that prepared vegetarian meals for pilgrims, and some became famous for their food, especially the temples at Udupi in Karnataka. In the 19th century, the temples' cooks started migrating to other parts of India where they opened small vegetarian restaurants; today, some South Indian restaurants have the word *Udupi* (sometimes spelled Udipi) in their names. In the mid-1930s K. K. Rao opened Woodlands Restaurant in Madras to serve this food in a more elegant setting. One of its specialties was an enormous yard-wide, paper-thin dosa, today a popular restaurant dish.

The first Indian restaurant in the modern sense was Delhi's Moti Mahal, opened in 1947 by Kundan Lal Gujral, a Hindu refugee from Pakistan. He invented tandoori chicken—chicken marinated in spiced yogurt and roasted in a tandoor, a large clay oven. Moti Mahal also served kebabs (meat on skewers that is grilled in the tandoor), butter chicken (tandoori chicken in a tomato sauce), and tandoor-roasted breads, called nan. Moti Mahal spawned many imitators, including the Kwality and Gaylord chains, whose menu expanded to include so-called Moghlai dishes—rich meat-based dishes—and Punjabi dishes.

Chinese restaurants are very popular in India and have their roots in Calcutta's Chinatown. Standard dishes include chicken corn soup, chili chicken, sweet and sour pork or lamb served in a dark red, very spicy sauce, and noodles.

Indians love to snack, and every town and village has many roadside vendors and shops selling samosas (small pastries filled with vegetables or meat), meat and vegetable patties, kebabs (meat grilled on skewers), and other savory items. Mumbai is famous for its crunchy spicy snacks, such as *bhelpuri,* a mix of crispy noodles, puffed rice, tomato, onion, boiled potatoes, coriander, and tamarind chutney. Kolkata is known for its sweet shops.

Today, people are discarding their old taboos, and India's rapidly growing middle class has the money, time, and desire to eat out at trendy restaurants that serve Thai, Italian, and Indian regional cuisines as well as at fast-food chains. McDonald's, Pizza Hut, Dominos, Kentucky Fried Chicken, and other Western fast-food chains have outlets throughout the subcontinent and have adapted their dishes to local

Snack vendor at the Amber Palace Courtyard, Jaipur, India. (Corel)

tastes and customs, with such dishes as McAloo Tikka, a vegetarian fried potato patty, and chicken curry–topped pizza. Spending on restaurant meals doubled in the past decade to five billion dollars a year and is expected to double again in five years.

Special Occasions

India has been called the land of feasts, fasts, and festivals. All groups celebrate seasonal and harvest festivals, religious holidays, and life transitions, such as weddings, births, and deaths, by eating certain foods, avoiding them (fasting), or sometimes both.

On festival days, large Hindu temples prepare elaborate vegetarian feasts featuring hundreds of dishes. Hindu deities have favorite foods, usually sweets, which are offered to them during ceremonies in the temple and are afterward distributed to worshippers. For example, the festival Janmashtami, observed in the early autumn, commemorates the birth of Lord Krishna, who as a child loved milk, ghee, and yogurt. Thus, devotees celebrate this day by eating *bhog kheer,* a rich rice pudding, or *shrikand,* a thickish pudding made from strained yogurt, sugar, and cardamom. Ganesh Chaturthi celebrates the birthday of the elephant-headed god Ganesh, who is always depicted holding a *modaka*—a steamed rice dumpling filled with coconut, sugar, milk solids, and dried nuts. On this day, devotees eat and serve modakas along with another of Ganesh's favorite foods—*laddoos,* fried balls made from flour, ghee, sugar, and nuts, raisins, or sesame seeds.

The most colorful Hindu festival, Holi, is celebrated on the day of the full moon in March. Special foods include sweets, snacks, and a mildly intoxicating milk drink called *thandai.* The Indian equivalent of Christmas is Diwali, the Festival of Lights, which celebrates Lord Rama's return to his kingdom after 14 years in exile. Because this symbolizes the victory of good over evil and light over darkness, little lamps are lit everywhere and people exchange lantern-shaped sweets.

In Punjab, the harvest festival Lohri is marked by eating sheaves of roasted corn from the new harvest as well as laddoos and other sweets. South Indians observe the harvest festival Pongal by eating a dish of that name made by boiling rice in milk with jaggery, cashew nuts, ghee, and coconut.

Laddoos

One of the most popular Indian sweets often associated with Hindu festivals, laddoos are balls made of chickpea, rice, or wheat flour; ghee; sugar or jaggery; and other ingredients, such as nuts, raisins, and sesame seeds. Often they are made from little drops of fried chickpea-flour batter that are soaked in sugar syrup and shaped into balls. The following recipe is easy to make.

1 c chickpea flour

1/3 c ghee or melted butter

1 c ground jaggery or powdered sugar

1/2 tsp ground cardamom (purchased as powder or made by grinding a few green cardamom pods, shells and all)

2 tbsp chopped almonds, cashew nuts, and/or raisins

Sift the chickpea flour. Heat the ghee over high heat until it starts to smoke, then lower the heat to medium and add the flour. Stir it well until the flour starts to turn brown and releases a fragrant aroma. Remove from the heat, add the sugar, and mix well. When it cools down slightly, add the cardamom powder and nuts, mix well, and form into small balls around 1½ inches in diameter using your greased palms. Set aside to harden.

Many Hindus fast, either individually or communally, as a form of worship, a petition to a god for a favor, an instrument of self-discipline, a means of attaining spiritual merit, or a form of physical cleansing. Some people always fast on certain days of the month. Fasting can mean total abstention from food and water or a restricted vegetarian diet.

Fasting is one of the five pillars of Islam. During the month of Ramadan, Muslims avoid taking any food or water between dawn and dusk. The fast is broken every day at sunset with a sip of water, dates, and perhaps a little fruit, a custom called *iftar.* This is followed by a large meal featuring meat dishes such as biryanis, a richly spiced meat and rice dish, and *haleem,* a sticky stew of pounded meat and grains. The end of Ramadan, called Eid al-Fitr, is celebrated with great fanfare. People visit the mosque, give food and alms to the poor, and prepare special sweet dishes, such as *sewian,* a vermicelli pudding, and *sheer korma,* a sweet pudding made from vermicelli, milk, saffron, sugar, spices, and ghee.

Indians of all communities devote much energy and wealth to arranging and celebrating their children's marriages. Many prewedding rituals involve offering food to prospective in-laws. The amount and quality of the food served at wedding meals are symbolic of a family's prestige. The traditional wedding banquet was prepared by caterers and held in a large tent. Guests sat in long rows with banana leaves in front of them, while teams of servers ladled food onto the leaves. Today, however, wealthy and even middle-class people hold wedding receptions in large hotels, where the food is served buffet style and people sit on chairs and at tables.

When there is a death in a Hindu family, all eating and cooking activities stop until the body is cremated. A household's normal food patterns are suspended for 10 to 13 days, depending on the community, and many restrictions are observed, such as taking only one meal a day, eating only vegetarian food, and eliminating spices. When the mourning period ends, a lavish feast is held for family and friends. Hindu widows traditionally become vegetarian and in the old days were expected to lead very austere lives.

Diet and Health

"You are what you eat" is a central tenet of Indian medical and philosophical systems. The best known of these is Ayurveda (which means "science of life" in Sanskrit), the ancient indigenous Indian system of medicine that is enjoying a vogue in the West. In Ayurvedic theory, all existence is made up of five elements: earth, water, fire, air, and ether (or space). They in turn manifest themselves in three *doshas* that govern all human biological, psychological, and physiological functions. The doshas determine

personality and disposition as well as basic constitutions. But they keep the body and mind healthy only as long as they can maintain their flow and balance. When the doshas are underproduced or overproduced, disease can result.

An important method of controlling doshas is proper eating. According to the legendary physician Charaka (b. 300 B.C.), "Without proper diet, medicines are of no use; with a proper diet, medicines are unnecessary." After evaluating their patients' conditions, Ayurvedic physicians prescribe certain foods to restore the flow and balance.

Moreover, food should be "alive" in order to give life to the eater. Raw food is more alive than cooked food. Leftovers should be heated up as soon as possible or, ideally, avoided altogether. Spices should be ground freshly for each use. Ayurveda is not vegetarian; in fact, meat, especially venison, is even recommended for certain ailments, as is wine.

Once a disease has developed, it is treated by an appropriate diet recommended by the physician. This regimen always begins with fasting, "the first and most important of all medicines." Once the acute stage of the disease has passed, the patient is given appropriate medicines derived from plants and herbs. Some of these ancient remedies were later adapted by Greek and Western medicine, such as reserpine, extracted from *Wauwolfia serpentina,* which is still prescribed for reducing blood pressure.

A parallel, although distinct, attitude to food is found in yoga, which is not just a series of physical

Herbs commonly used in the practice of Ayurveda. (Shutterstock)

postures but a profound philosophy of life aimed at the development of a balance between body and mind in order to reunite the individual self with the Absolute. People who aspire to spiritual advancement are supposed to eat vegetarian *sattvic* foods that render the mind pure and calm—fresh fruits and vegetables, wheat, rice, cow milk, cucumber, green vegetables, nuts, and clarified butter—and avoid onion and garlic as well as meat. *Rajasic* foods, recommended for warriors, stimulate energy and creativity but also passion and aggressiveness. They include fish, chilies, wild game, goat, eggs, coffee and tea, white sugar, and spices. *Tamasic* foods fill the mind with anger, darkness, confusion, and inertia and are to be avoided. They include meat, leftovers, fast foods, fried foods and processed foods, tobacco, alcohol, and drugs.

In yet another classification that is more a part of folk medicine, all foods are classified as either "hot" or "cold" and are to be eaten or avoided depending on the time of year, an individual's constitution and state of health, and other factors. However, there is no consistency or logic in the way foods are classified as hot or cold, and there are wide regional variations. For example, most lentils are considered cold foods in western India but hot foods in the north.

Muslims practice their own system of medicine, called Unani, which is based on the humoral theory of Greek medicine that assumes the presence of four humors in the body that determine physical health and temperament. Digestion plays a central role, and minor and even some major ailments can be prevented by eating certain foods and eating in a proper manner. People are also advised to eat foods that have the opposite quality to their temperament.

Colleen Taylor Sen

Further Reading

Achaya, K. T. *Historical Dictionary of Indian Food.* New Delhi, India: Oxford University Press, 1998.

Achaya, K. T. *Indian Food: A Historical Companion.* New Delhi, India: Oxford University Press, 1994.

Bharadwaj, Monisha. *The Indian Pantry.* London: Kyle Cathie, 1995.

Burnett, David, and Helen Saberi. *The Road to Vindaloo: Curry Books and Curry Cooks.* Totnes, UK: Prospect Books, 2008.

Collingham, Lizzie. *Curry: A Tale of Cooks and Conquerors.* New York: Oxford University Press, 2006.

Indian Foods Co. http://www.indianfoodsco.com.

India Tastes. http://www.indiatastes.com.

Jaffrey, Madhur. *A Taste of India.* New York: Atheneum, 1988.

Sen, Colleen Taylor. *Food Culture in India.* Westport, CT: Greenwood Press, 2004.

Indonesia

Overview

Indonesia is located in Southeast Asia and shares land borders with Malaysia, Papua New Guinea, and East Timor. Indonesia is the world's fourth most populous nation, consisting of 240.3 million people with more than 250 ethnic groups. There are more than 17,500 islands, 6,000 of which are inhabited. Main islands include Java, Sumatra, Kalimantan (shared with Malaysia and Brunei), New Guinea (shared with Papua New Guinea), and Sulawesi. Other, smaller islands include Bali, Lombok, Sumbawa, and the Maluku Islands (the Moluccas).

Indonesia's religions include Islam (86.1%), Protestantism (5.7%), Catholicism (3%), and Hinduism (1.8%). Islam, Catholicism, Protestantism, Buddhism, and Hinduism are the five religions officially recognized by the Indonesian government. Indonesia has the largest Muslim population in the world. The spread of Islam was influenced by increased trade links between Southeast Asia and the Muslim world. This increase was further generated by emerging demand for spices in late-medieval Europe. Java and Sumatra became regions where Islam was dominant by the end of the 16th century.

Many ethnic groups largely influenced the creation of unique regional food cultures in the country. Since the Srivijaya kingdom, an ancient Malay kingdom on the island of Sumatra, started trading with China in the seventh century, Indonesia has been an important trade region for its abundant natural resources. The Indian merchants brought with them the Hindu and Buddhist religions as well as dried spices such as cardamom, cumin, and caraway. Chinese traders and immigrants contributed soybeans, noodles, and the technique of stir-frying, while Arab traders introduced kebabs and Arabian spices such as dill and fennel. Meanwhile, Europeans, including the Dutch, Portuguese, and Spanish, fought each other for control of the Spice Islands of Maluku. Spanish and Portuguese traders brought produce from the New World before the Dutch finally colonized Indonesia for three and a half centuries. During that time, the colonists imported potatoes, cabbage, cauliflower, carrots, string beans, and corn in order to have food habits relatively similar to those in their home countries. The Japanese invasion during World War II ended Dutch rule of Indonesia, and two days after the surrender of Japan in August 1945, the Indonesian declaration of independence was proclaimed by Sukarno and Hatta, who were appointed president and vice president.

Indonesia has an incredible diversity of ethnicities, religions, and natural resources in its over 782,000 square miles (about 2 million square kilometers). *Bhinneka Tunggal Ika* (Unity in Diversity), the official national motto, can be applied to the description of the modern Indonesian food culture. Even within a single province, many distinctive food cultures exist. Today, Indonesian food culture continues to influence the cuisine of its neighboring countries such as Malaysia and Singapore.

Food Culture Snapshot

Muhammad and Ani, a young Minangkabau couple, live in Jakarta Selatan (South Jakarta). They are originally from Sumatera Barat (West Sumatra) and are devout

Muslims. Muhammad owns a small business, and Ani helps in his business. Muhammad and Ani attempt to preserve their traditional Minangkabau food culture while living in Jakarta. In the Minangkabau culture, people have three meals a day, and food is normally prepared in midday to be consumed as lunch, dinner on that day, and breakfast the following morning. Ingredients are purchased in a local market near their house. The main ingredients of Minangkabau food include rice, fish, coconut, and chili peppers. With Muhammad's middle-class income, they can also afford to purchase beef and chicken for their meat dishes. They never eat pork, which is a *haram* (unlawful) food for Muslims.

Around 7:30 A.M., they have breakfast, which consists of fried banana with boiled glutinous rice and grated coconut. Muhammad loves to sip *teh-telur*, a mixture of raw egg and Sumatran tea they brought from their hometown. Lunch is the most important meal in the day for Muhammad and Ani. The core component of their lunch is rice. Ani spends a couple of hours to make hot and delicious *rendang*, a traditional Minangkabau meat dish made of beef cooked in a generous amount of coconut milk and spices such as ginger, galangal, turmeric leaf, lemongrass, and red chilies. *Kangkung* (water spinach) boiled with coconut milk is also served as a side dish.

The durian season has started, and Muhammad and Ani enjoy durian as a midafternoon snack and feel slightly nostalgic. Durian trees were right next to their house when they grew up in West Sumatra. Now Ani goes to a local market to get fresh durians. The durian is a huge fruit with a fearsome spiked shell. Inside it is yellowish and creamy with an aroma that is reminiscent of stinky cheese or feces, but it is nonetheless delicious.

Around 6:30 P.M. guests, originally from East Java, arrive in their house and enjoy rendang, tempeh (fermented soybeans), and kangkung. When Ani was in West Sumatra, she never cooked tempeh, which is originally from Java. Now, in Jakarta, Ani frequently enjoys tempeh as a relatively inexpensive and nutritious protein source. Papaya and rambutan (a spiked fruit similar to the lychee), another favorite fruit of Indonesians, are purchased in a local market and served at the dinner table. Muhammad, Ani, and their guests talk about a new Chinese restaurant located inside a shopping mall

in Kuningan, a fast-growing district in Jakarta's Golden Triangle. Because of globalization, Chinese foods have become very popular in Jakarta. Historically, Chinese brought soy sauce, soybean cake, Chinese vegetables, and stir-frying ingredients and techniques, contributing to the present Indonesian cuisine. Today, middle-class Indonesians in urban areas, such as Muhammad and Ani, experience both authentic Chinese foods at fancy restaurants and delicious street foods of Chinese origin at *warung* (food-hawker stalls).

Major Foodstuffs

Indonesia has a huge diversity of ethnicities, religions, and natural resources. About 6,000 species of plants are used in local traditional foods.

Rice

Indonesia is one of the world's leading rice producers. Just as in other Asian countries, rice is also a main staple food throughout the country, with more than 440 pounds (200 kilograms) per person consumed each year. Rice is perceived to be essential for survival, to be easy to store and cook, and to give strength during pregnancy and delivery. In Bahasa Indonesia, the official national language of Indonesia, there are four different words for rice: *Padi* is rice on the stalks, while *gabah* is unhulled rice that is separated from the stalks. When it is hulled, it is then called *beras*. Finally, *nasi* is the cooked end product. Also, the word for cooked rice (*nasi*) is synonymous with the word for a meal. There are two common types of rice consumed in Indonesia: *nasi putih* (long-grain white rice), which is served as a plain cooked rice, and *nasi ketan* (glutinous rice), which is used for making cakes and snacks. During harsh times, cassava, which is perceived to be of lower quality than rice in some parts of the country, is substituted for rice. Interestingly, when the price of rice increased during the economic crisis of 1997, rice consumption increased.

Other Starches

Sago (a starch that accumulates in the pith of the sago palm stem), corn, and cassava are also con-

Boy working at a rice paddy, Bali, Indonesia. (Corel)

sumed as carbohydrate-rich foods in some parts of the country. Sago and corn are commonly consumed in the eastern part of the country, such as in Papua, Maluku, and Sulawesi. Cassava and sweet potatoes became important staple foods in Maluku and Papua. *Kerupuk,* cassava chips, are popular and consumed as a side dish or snack in Indonesia.

Animal Proteins

Islam precludes the use of pork in many parts of the country. The main animal meats consumed by Muslims include beef, chicken, and goat. The Hindu Balinese consume pork, including *babi guling* (roasted suckling pig), and avoid beef. *Sate* (kebabs) is a common meat dish, including Indonesian sweet and sour beef sate with peanut sauce (*sate daging sapi manis pedas sambal kacang*). *Sate kambing* (goat sate) and *sate ayam* (chicken sate) are also popular. A chicken soup with noodles, called *soto ayam,* is a popular soup in the country. Each household has its own recipe that has been passed down from generation to generation.

Indonesia is also known as a maritime country. Its national fish consumption was 57 pounds (26 kilograms) per capita in 2008 according to the *Jakarta Post.* Fish and shellfish, including shrimp, mussels, crab, and squid, are often prepared with abundant seasonings such as coconut, tamarind, chili peppers, and herbs.

Plant Sources

Nuts and pulses, especially soybeans, are important protein sources for many Indonesians. In addition to *tafu* (tofu), which is originally from other Asian countries, tempeh, a fermented soybean cake using *Rhizopus* molds as a starter, is uniquely Indonesian. The use of a fermentation processing technique may be attributed to the adaptation of tofu to the tropical climate of the country. Originally from Java, tempeh became popular throughout the nation in the 20th century. Peanuts, originally from South America, have become an important part of the Indonesian cuisine. Peanuts are used for sauces for sate, *gado-gado* (a vegetable salad with peanut sauce), and other traditional Indonesian dishes.

Gado-Gado

Sambal Kacang (Peanut Sauce)

1 c roasted peanuts

3 large cloves garlic, chopped

4 shallots, chopped

1 tsp shrimp paste

Salt to taste

2 tbsp peanut or vegetable oil

1 tsp red chili powder

1 tsp brown sugar

1 tbsp soy sauce

2 c water

1 tbsp lemon juice

1. Grind the roasted peanuts into a fine powder using a coffee grinder.

2. Blend the garlic, shallots, shrimp paste, and salt in a food processor to make a paste. Heat the oil in a medium-sized nonstick frying pan. Fry the blended paste in the oil for 3 minutes on medium heat. Be careful not to burn the paste.

3. Add the chili powder, brown sugar, soy sauce, and water to the paste. Bring the mix to a boil, then add the ground peanuts. Simmer about 20 minutes or until the sauce becomes thick. Stir occasionally.

4. Add lemon juice just before use.

Vegetables

1 c cauliflower florets

1 medium carrot, peeled and thinly sliced

1 c cabbage, shredded

1 c snow peas

1 c bean sprouts

Garnish

4 lettuce leaves

A few sprigs of watercress

2 medium potatoes, boiled in their skins, then peeled and sliced

½ cucumber, thinly sliced

4 eggs, hard-boiled

4 green onions, sliced diagonally

Bring about 2½ quarts of water to a boil. Place the cauliflower and carrots in the boiling water, and boil about 2 minutes. Using a slotted spoon, remove them and place in a colander. Rinse under cold water until cool.

Repeat the procedure with the cabbage, snow peas, and bean sprouts, but let them stay in the boiling water for just 30 seconds. Drain well.

To serve, arrange the lettuce and watercress around the edge of a serving dish. Then place the vegetables in the middle of the dish. Arrange the boiled eggs, sliced potatoes, and sliced cucumber on top.

Drizzle the warm sambal kacang over the top, and sprinkle with the green onion.

Indonesians enjoy a variety of unique tropical fruits such as durians, mangosteens, rambutans, passion fruit, jackfruit (often eaten young), and tamarinds. Other tropical fruits consumed in many parts of the world, such as mangoes, papayas, and bananas, are also popular in Indonesia. The durian, native to Indonesia, is called the "king of fruits." Locals enjoy eating fresh durians that have been ripened on the tree. The flavor of durian may be unfamiliar to most people who are not from Southeast Asia, but locals enjoy the flavor of the durian very much, and even some tourists fall in love with it. The exotic and complex odor of the durian comes from different sulfur and ester compounds.

Many fruits are cooked or used for juice in Indonesia. *Pisang goreng,* Indonesian banana fritters, is a popular snack across the nation. Soursop, called *sirsak,* is used to make fresh juice. Avocado "juice" with chocolate syrup (*jus apulkat*) is another popular drink unique to Indonesia, more like a smoothie since an avocado cannot be juiced. Passion fruit syrup, called *sirup markisa,* is a specialty in Medan, North Sumatra.

Many types of vegetables are also consumed in Indonesia. Vegetables and spices in Indonesia are closely associated with the country's immigrant history. The Dutch introduced cabbage, cauliflower, carrots, string beans, and potatoes to Indonesia. Chinese traders brought mustard greens, mung beans, and Chinese cabbage. Kangkung (water spinach) is a popular aquatic green and has a pleasant flavor and texture.

Many spices and herbs are also used throughout the country. The Indonesian islands of Maluku, also called the Spice Islands, contributed to the introduction of native spices to Indonesian cuisine—of the greatest culinary world importance are cloves from Ternate and Tidore and nutmeg from Ambon (Amboyna). India also brought cumin, coriander, ginger, and caraway to the country. Dill and fennel came with Arab traders. Today, common spices and herbs include turmeric, cloves, nutmeg, cinnamon, ginger, galangal, lemongrass, *salam* leaves (also called Indonesian bay leaf), and lemon leaves.

Finally, coconut is an important staple food in many parts of Indonesia and is extensively used for meat and vegetable dishes, desserts, and street foods. The extensive use of coconut milk is especially found in Minangkabau cuisine (in West Sumatra), as well as in Minahasan (in North Sulawesi)

Traditional Indonesian soup made with rice and coconut milk, *lontong opor.* (Willy Setiadi | Dreamstime.com)

cuisine. It is a great lubricator and provides oil, flavor, and texture when it is thickened.

Beverages

Indonesia is famous for its high-quality coffee. It is currently the fourth-largest coffee producer, following Brazil, Vietnam, and Colombia. Coffee beans have mainly been grown on the islands of Java, Sumatra, and Sulawesi since the 17th century when the first coffee plantations of arabica were established under Dutch rule. Today, Indonesia produces mainly robusta coffee, around 80 percent of its total output. At the same time, the international market is dominated by arabica coffee, accounting for 70 percent of global demand.

Kopi luwak is a coffee product unique to Indonesia. Kopi luwak is made from coffee berries that are eaten by, and pass through, the digestive tract of the Asian civet cat and are then extracted from its excrement. Recent research has demonstrated that the animal's digestion process makes the coffee beans harder, more brittle, and darker in color than the same type of bean that hasn't been eaten. Because producing kopi luwak is a very labor-intensive process, kopi luwak is very expensive, ranging from $100 to $600 per pound, and is exported to the United States, Japan, and Europe.

Cooking

Each island and region has its own culinary characteristics. The people of Java, on the one hand, are known for their generous use of sugar in their cooking. On the other hand, the Sumatrans usually enjoy extremely hot foods. In general, common methods for preparing food across the islands include frying, grilling, simmering, steaming, and stewing, often with coconut milk. *Oseng-oseng* and *tumis* (cooking in small amounts of cooking oil and water) and *sayur bening* (cooking in water with added refined sugar) are also common cooking methods used in Indonesia.

While many Indonesians living in Jakarta may have access to ready-made processed foods, many who live in rural areas still cook everyday meals in a traditional way. Many Indonesians use firewood for cooking, and few own a refrigerator. A gender difference in food preparation exists in Indonesia. Women in general cook everyday meals. In Minangkabau, men prepare beef dishes for special occasions. At the same time, the head chefs in all Minang restaurants are men.

Rice is an important part of the Indonesian meal. Rice is steamed and commonly served with other side dishes. Besides plain rice, nasi goreng is a popular fried rice in Indonesia. Rice, especially glutinous rice, is also used to make traditional cakes and snacks.

Vegetables are often steamed, fried, or boiled. They are also eaten raw. Gado-gado is a popular Javanese vegetable salad with peanut sauce. Herbs and spices are cooked to make *sambal,* a condiment popular in Indonesia and other Asian countries. *Sambal ulak* (spiced chili paste) is made of red chilies, onions, garlic, sugar, lime peel, oil, and salt. *Sambal rerasi* is a popular shrimp paste used for many Indonesian dishes. Sambal is used for meat, fish, and vegetable dishes. It is also added to fruits to make a spicy fruit salad called *rujak.*

Coconut provides oil, flavor, and texture when it is thickened. It is extensively used in some parts of the country, such as Minangkabau. Fish and meat are cooked with coconut milk and spices. Rendang is a great example of a meat dish cooked with a generous amount of coconut, herbs, and spices. Minced meat is cooked with herbs and spices and is simmered gradually on low heat until the coconut milk is reduced. In Java, people enjoy cooking meat and vegetables in a *wajan* (wok) with a generous amount of coconut milk and spices.

Typical Meals

It is difficult to describe a typical meal in Indonesia, which has such great diversity of regional cuisines. The meal patterns also vary across the country. For example, while patterns of three mealtimes a day are common among the Minangkabau people, two main meals are found in rural West Java. Breakfast is an important meal for most Indonesians. Rice is

a major food item for breakfast in most parts of the country and is served in different forms. One of the popular dishes served for breakfast is *lontong sayur,* which consists of cooked vegetables in coconut milk with rice cake. *Lontong* is an Indonesian rice cake. The vegetables and fruits used for lontong sayur include chayote (*labu siam*), long beans, young jackfruit, green papaya, and carrots. *Bubur* (porridge), especially *bubur ayam* (chicken porridge), is another popular breakfast item. Indonesians also enjoy nasi goreng, an Indonesian fried rice, and *nasi pecel,* a Javanese rice dish served with cooked vegetables and peanut sauce, for breakfast.

Lunch is the most important meal of the day for many Indonesians. The core component of their lunch is steamed rice. Indonesians eat steamed rice with a meat, chicken, fish, egg, goat, or soybean dish, as well as with vegetables, soup, and sambal. These main dishes vary across the nation. Pork dishes, such as babi guling (roast suckling pig), are consumed in Bali. In Maluku and Papua, where sago palm, cassava, and sweet potatoes are the staple foods, *papeda* (thick sago porridge) is a popular dish consumed with fish. An Indonesian supper is lighter than lunch, and something leftover from lunch is often consumed for supper.

Snacks are consumed between the two large meals in the morning or afternoon. Or the same foods eaten as snacks can also be served after a meal as dessert. In urban areas, snacks are more varied and consumed more often than in rural villages. *Pisang goreng* (banana fritters), *tape ketan* (fermented sticky rice), *tape telor* (fermented cassava), and *klepon* (rice cake with grated coconut) are some popular snacks.

Eating Out

Eating out at a restaurant is still not very common among Indonesians. However, just like other Asian countries, Indonesia is proud of its variety of street foods for breakfast, lunch, dinner, and light snacks, which are sold by street vendors or at a warung (a local food stall), the social center of villages and towns in Indonesia. In big cities, in addition to local foods, many traditional dishes from various regions across the nation are served at warung. The types of street or warung food offered vary across the islands, but there are some universal street foods found throughout the country. *Bakso,* or meatballs, one of the most popular street foods in Indonesia, are usually served in a soup bowl with noodles, fried *wan ton,* vegetables, and condiments. *Soto* (soup) and sate (kebabs) are other popular street foods that demonstrate a regional variation. For example, *banjar soto,* from South Kalimantan, is spiced with lemongrass and sour, hot sambal, accompanied with potato cakes, whereas *Bandung soto* is a clear beef soup with daikon pieces.

It has been argued that the Javanese cuisine has dominated because thousands of Javanese migrate to other regions every year and often make a living by selling foods. Hence, soto ayam, *sate madura* (chicken on skewers), and *mie bakso* (meatball soup) are found at warung outside the island of Java.

When it comes to more formal restaurants, both locals and tourists enjoy *nasi Padang* restaurants, which serve a Minang cuisine that originates from West Sumatra. They are famous for their spicy food and their unique way of serving and "recycling" the food. Padang restaurants can be found throughout the country. In a nasi Padang restaurant, dozens of small dishes filled with spicy and flavorful foods are displayed on the table. These foods include dishes such as *gulai ikan* (fish curry), *sambal cumi* (squid in spicy sauce), fried tempeh, soto Padang (crispy beef in spicy soup), and sate Padang (a Padang-style *satay* with a yellow sauce). The best-known Padang dish is *rendang sapi,* a spicy beef stew with coconut milk. Customers have many dishes to choose from and pay only for the dishes that they have eaten.

Due to globalization, locals in urban areas have started to enjoy eating out at a restaurant much more often than before. Numerous American fast-food chains and expensive Japanese restaurants are now found in big cities such as Jakarta. Chinese restaurants, whether sophisticated ones at five-star hotels and at huge multistory office buildings or modest noodle parlors, are perhaps one of the most popular non-Indonesian restaurants in Indonesia. Food hawkers also serve Chinese foods at a modest price. Chop suey, fried noodles, noodle soup, and rice porridge are just a few examples of delicious Chinese foods sold by hawkers.

Special Occasions

There are plenty of holidays related to religion in Indonesia. Ramadan (Puasa) is the most important time of the year for Muslims in Indonesia. After fasting from dawn to dusk, people get together with their families and friends and enjoy delicacies for breaking the fast, or *buka puasa,* at the Ramadan bazaar or at home. After a monthlong observance of fasting, Muslims in Indonesia celebrate Eid al-Fitr (called *Lebaran* or *Hari Raya Puasa*) with special dishes such as *ketupat* (blocks of rice cooked in coconut leaves), rendang, and *dodol* (a sweet toffee made of glutinous rice, coconut milk, and sugar).

Bali, the most popular island for tourists in Indonesia, is home to the largest Indonesian Hindu population. Because of that, the Balinese Hindu elaborately celebrate Hari Raya Nyepi, the Hindu New Year. It is a day of silence, fasting, and meditation for many people in Bali, and tourists are not allowed to leave their hotel on that day. On New Year's Eve, food is prepared for the following day (particularly homemade pastries and sweetmeats), when Hindus refrain from all activities, including food preparation. Streets are deserted.

Selamatan is a special occasion unique to Indonesia. It is not a religious feast. Rather, it is a way of expressing family and neighborhood solidarity before a significant event. *Selamatan* means thanksgiving, blessing, and grace. Following the prayer, *nasi tumpeng,* a cone-shaped mountain of steamed yellow or white rice, is sliced at the top and served. White rice is cooked in coconut, and the yellow rice is colored with turmeric, a popular spice in Indonesia.

Every year, Indonesians celebrate Hari Proklamasi Kemerdekaan (Independence Day) on August 17. It is a fun event for children. *Krupuk* (shrimp chips)-eating contests and other events for children take place. Women make nasi tumpeng surrounded by various foods such as *sayur urap* (spicy vegetable salads), roasted chicken, coconut beef, *bergedel*

Traditional Indonesian rice dish called *nasi tumpeng*. (Deepta Sateesh | Dreamstime)

(potato patties), salt fish, and dried tempeh to celebrate this important day for every Indonesian.

Diet and Health

While there are approximately 2.56 physicians per 1,000 people in the United States, the physician/patient ratio is much lower in Indonesia, only 0.13 physicians per 1,000 people, according to 2006 statistics. People, especially rural women in Indonesia, primarily rely on home remedies to prevent and treat illness within the family. *Dukun* (traditional healers) also play an important role in the traditional medicine system.

Jamu is a traditional herbal medicine commonly consumed by Indonesians. Different types of jamu

are used to maintain physical fitness, as well as to cure certain kinds of illness. Jamu has been sold in the form of powders, creams, pills, and capsules, and its market has expanded to outside of the country. The ingredients include ginger, cinnamon, turmeric, galangal, papaya leaf, and guava leaves and flowers.

Research has shown that some pregnant women consume *jamu cabe puyang,* which reduces tiredness; bitter jamu (*jamu pahitan*), which increases appetite; and *jamu sawanan,* which prevents disease. However, some women avoid the use of jamu during pregnancy to avoid possible side effects, including the contamination of the amniotic fluid.

Similar to other developing countries, Indonesia is experiencing a nutrition transition, which is characterized by rapid changes in dietary habits, as well as a double burden of disease, in which noncommunicable diseases are becoming more prevalent while infectious diseases remain undefeated. Indonesia's leading causes of death have shifted from infectious diseases to more chronic diseases, especially cardiovascular disease. In 2002, cardiovascular disease was the leading cause of death, accounting for 22 percent of all mortality. Infectious diseases such as tuberculosis and lower respiratory infections remain major causes of death in Indonesia. Diarrheal diseases and pneumonia are still leading causes of death among children under five. In general, there has been a rapid increase in consumption of meat, eggs, milk, and processed foods, while the consumption of cereal products has decreased.

There has also been a nutrition transition for indigenous people, who used to be foragers. For example, the Punan people who reside in Kalimantan have drastically changed their dietary habits through globalization and urbanization. They used to consume sago palm, their staple food, along with berries, wild boars, and other wild animals. Nowadays, the consumption of fat and processed foods has increased, and overweight has become an issue among periurban Punan women.

Micronutrient deficiencies, called "hidden hunger," remain a public health issue among certain populations. A recent study suggests that nonpregnant women are at greater risk of clinical vitamin

A deficiency, such as night blindness, in families that spend more on rice and less on animal and plant-based foods. Prevention of iodine deficiency continues to be a challenge in the country, where fortification of salt with iodine has not always been successful in some areas of the country. Moreover, the recent food price increase has affected the nutritional status of people in Indonesia. The cost of staple soybean-based products such as tofu and tempeh rose by about 50 percent in 2008. Child malnutrition, including hidden hunger, is on the rise.

Although fat consumption has increased slightly, there is a movement to maintain the traditional diet in Indonesia rather than adopting highly processed global or fast foods. A recent study of contemporary Minangkabau food culture in West Sumatra suggests that their traditional use of coconut may encourage the consumption of fish and vegetables, and, therefore, a well-balanced diet.

Keiko Goto

Further Reading

Afdhal, A. F., and R. L. Welsch. "The Rise of the Modern Jamu Industry in Indonesia: A Preliminary Overview." In *The Context of Medicines in Developing Countries: Studies in Pharmaceutical Anthropology,* edited by S. van der Geest and S. R. Whyte, 149–72. Dordrecht, the Netherlands: Kluwer, 1988.

Campbell, A. A., A. Thorne-Lyman, K. Sun, S. de Pee, K. Kraemer, R. Moench-Pfanner, M. Sari, N. Akhter, M. W. Bloem, and R. D. Semba. "Indonesian Women of Childbearing Age Are at Greater Risk of Clinical Vitamin A Deficiency in Families That Spend More on Rice and Less on Fruits/Vegetables and Animal-Based Foods." *Nutrition Research* 29, No. 2 (2009): 75–81.

Dounias, E., A. Selzner, M. Koizumi, and P. Levang. "From Sago to Rice, from Forest to Town: The Consequences of Sedentarization for the Nutritional Ecology of Punan Former Hunter-Gatherers of Borneo." *Food and Nutrition Bulletin* 28, No. 2 (2007): S294–S302.

"Food in Indonesia—Indonesian Food, Indonesian Cuisine." Food in Every Country. http://www.foodbycountry.com/Germany-to-Japan/Indonesia.html.

Hartini, T. N., R. S. Padmawati, L. Lindholm, A. Surjono, and A. Winkvist. "The Importance of Eating Rice: Changing Food Habits among Pregnant Indonesian Women during the Economic Crisis." *Social Science Medicine* 61, No. 1 (2005): 199–210.

Kuliner Indonesia. http://kulinerkita.multiply.com/reviews/item/42.

Lipoeto, N. I., Z. Agus, F. Oenzil, M. Masrul, and N. Wattanapenpaiboon. "Contemporary Minangkabau Food Culture in West Sumatra, Indonesia." *Asia Pacific Journal of Clinical Nutrition* 10, No. 1 (2001): 10–16.

Marks, C. *The Exotic Kitchens of Indonesia: Recipes from the Outer Islands.* New York: M. Evans, 1993.

Owen, S. *Indonesian Regional Food and Cookery.* New York: St. Martin's Press, 1995.

Technical Information Services (TIS)/King Mongkut's University of Technology, Thonburi (KMUTT). "Cassava Starch and Derived Products in Indonesia." http://www.aseanbiotechnology.info/Abstract/23004315.pdf.

"Vegetables of Indonesia." http://www.seasite.niu.edu/indonesian/Themes/Vegetables/Main/Default.htm.

Von Holzen, H., and L. Arsana. *Food of Indonesia: Authentic Recipes from the Spice Islands (Food of the World Cookbooks).* Hong Kong: Periplus, 1999.

World Health Organization. "Mortality Country Fact Sheet 2006." http://www.who.int/whosis/mort/profiles/mort_searo_idn_indonesia.pdf.

Japan

Overview

Japan is a group of over 3,600 islands that is 2,174 miles (3,500 kilometers) long, roughly the area of California but without its expanse of habitable terrain. Steep mountains cover over 80 percent of the four main islands of (from north to south) Hokkaido, Honshu, Shikoku, and Kyushu. Surrounded on all sides by the sea or the mountains, the Japanese naturally look to these sources for their food and lyrically refer to food as the delights of the seas and the mountains (*umi no sachi, yama no sachi*). Hokkaido as well as northern and western Honshu have a cold temperate climate with heavy snowfall for over half of the year, beginning as early as October and melting only in April. The rest of Honshu and Shikoku have a cool temperate climate, while southern Kyushu and the Okinawan islands have subtropical to tropical climates. The four seasons are regular and clearly defined. Monsoon rains occur between May and July. There is also a clear set of seasons in the seas around Japan: Certain species of fish appear at regular intervals and are best eaten at particular times.

Close to 100 percent of the population is ethnically Japanese. There are well-established historical minorities: Ainu, Koreans, Chinese, and Ryukyuans. Recent immigrants—from Brazil, Southeast Asia, and Europe and North America—have also added to the mix. Japanese religion is a blend of Buddhism and a native polytheistic religion called Shinto. Both emphasize purity, naturalness, and simplicity in daily life, and this philosophy has had a major effect on food-preparation practices and preferences, including, notably, less consumption of meat and milk products. Over 90 percent of the population is urban (until the start of the 20th century, some 80 percent were rural), and only about 5 percent of the population engages in full-time farming.

The modern Japanese family is small: usually one or two children. Most families live in what, by American standards, are very cramped quarters: three rooms, one or two serving for living, studying, and sleeping and one combination dining-kitchen area. The living zone is usually floored in fine woven straw mats (*tatami*) and is converted to a sleeping zone at night by folding any furniture away and bringing out sleeping quilts (*futon*) from built-in storage closets. The dining-kitchen area and one room often have Western-style furniture: a dining table, chairs, and armchairs. The traditional style of living "on the floor" is being superseded by more Western-type (though still Japanese-sized) accommodations and furnishings.

🍽 Food Culture Snapshot

Ken and Chie Tanaka live in a middle-class neighborhood of Tokyo. Their apartment is in a 10-story building that is part of a huge apartment complex near the terminal of a city feeder line of the railway. The complex includes a large shopping precinct (*shôten-gai*) with a large department store and several supermarkets, along with a covered market selling everything from food to electronics. Ken works in an office in downtown Tokyo and commutes for an hour daily. Chie works part-time in a nearby small business. Their only child, Matsu, is seven years old and attends primary school. Their lifestyle is typical of most blue- and white-collar salaried workers.

They start their weekdays around 7 A.M., with breakfast consisting of bread or toast, jams, a fried egg, and a small sausage, along with coffee for the adults. Matsu gets orange juice and cold cereal. On Sundays Chie sometimes cooks a Japanese-style breakfast of grilled salted salmon slices, crisp nori seaweed, fresh rice, miso soup, and fermented beans (natto), the last of which Chie, who is from western Japan, does not partake of.

They each eat lunch at work or school. Matsu has a lunch that Chie prepared according to school guidelines: a small fried cutlet, a seaweed roll, a small mound of pickles, a piece of fruit, and a candy bar. Most of these she buys ready-made from the supermarket, which offers a wide range of these side dishes for children and adults. The food is placed in half of a small lunch box, and she fills the compartment in the other half with cooked rice. Chie prepares a similar though larger lunch box for herself on some days. On others she and her coworkers order bowls of noodles from a neighborhood shop. Ken usually leaves work for about half an hour at lunchtime. He goes to one of the eateries around the office. He pays for a set meal of grilled fish or meat, rice, pickles, and soup and receives a token in exchange. The waiter accepts the token and brings the meal, and after a quick meal, Ken heads back to the office.

Chie shops on the way home from work, splitting purchases between the neighborhood supermarket and the small shops and stalls in the market. For exotics and special occasions she may shop in the basement supermarket of the large department store, where prices are higher but there is a large range of luxury foods, including tropical fruits and specialties from Japan's provinces.

The family tries to eat dinner together, but Ken often works late. Dinner may be cooked rice, grilled or cooked fish or meat, soup, cooked vegetables and pickles, and a sweet for dessert, sometimes from a ready-made pack. It may also be Western foods such as spaghetti or pizza, or a Japanese variation of curry called kareraisu, which Matsu adores.

On weekends the family tries to eat together and often goes out to one of the specialty restaurants in the shopping precinct. Sometimes they simply order out at one or another of their favorite neighborhood restaurants: noodles in soup or sushi. They also do more serious shopping for food on the weekend: Like many families they have a large freezer compartment designed to accept the standardized ready-made meals they buy from the supermarket once a month. Heavy items such as 22-pound (10-kilogram) bags of rice and plastic barrels of miso and pickles will be delivered by neighborhood shops. Chie had signed up for a fresh produce delivery service, which provided vegetables and mushrooms from named farmers, but rising costs have forced her to terminate this.

Major Foodstuffs

Traditionally, the three major sources of calories in Japan were rice (the most highly prized food), vegetables (either cooked or pickled), and fish (either fresh, pickled, dried, or made into fish sauce). The staple is still rice cooked without any flavoring. Rice is sometimes prepared as fried rice (that is, after cooking, small pieces of vegetables, fish, or meat are added) or as sushi rice (slightly vinegared and either formed into a ball with a topping or tossed with bits of fish and vegetables into a sort of salad), or it is cooked with beans, taro, or some other vegetable. Special varieties of rice with a very high starch content are steamed and pounded into a gluey, doughy consistency called mochi, which is a requirement for many kinds of rituals. The proportion of rice in the modern meal has declined throughout Japan as foreign foods have proliferated. Households with older people probably still eat rice three times a day. Younger people tend to have rice once, perhaps twice a day.

Japanese eat a large number and variety of noodles. Japanese-style noodles, made of wheat or buckwheat, are eaten in soup or with dipping sauces, hot or cold. The choice of meat, seafood, or vegetable toppings is vast. Italian-style pasta is widely eaten. Wheat-based Chinese-style noodles (râmen) are highly popular in soup or stir-fried. Popular garnishes include slices of flavored bamboo shoots, fresh bean sprouts, and thin slices of roast pork.

Ameyoko market in Ueno District in Tokyo, Japan. Ameyoko, once an entertainment district for U.S. Marines, now an exotic, classic Asian market. (Shutterstock)

Variations include fermented soybean paste (miso) flavoring and a seafood garnish. Bread is commonly eaten for breakfast instead of rice, and as a snack. Bakeries make a variety of rolls and buns, both plain and with fancy fillings ranging from cheese and curry to melon and green-tea flavors.

Soybeans were an important source of protein in premodern periods and are still an important food component. Green soybean pods (edamame) are cooked and eaten as a snack, but most of the crop goes to produce three important ingredients: soy sauce (shoyu), tofu, and miso. Soy sauce is used to flavor food during cooking and as a table condiment. Plain tofu is an element in a variety of dishes. Small cubes garnish *misoshiru* soup and many other dishes as well. Tofu is so plastic that a great many dishes incorporate some form of tofu, which can fool the eye, and even the tongue, into

believing it is meat or some kind of vegetable. Tofu also comes in the form of deep-fried cakes called *abura age,* which may be filled with meat or vegetables. Soybean milk can be gently simmered to form a film on its surface called *yuba,* used to wrap various fillings; the resulting roll is simmered in flavored broth or added to stews. Eastern Japan also favors a fermented-soybean dish called natto (beans suspended in a sticky paste), which is mixed with freshly beaten raw egg and soy sauce and poured over steaming hot rice.

Partly as a result of the adoption of Buddhism by the Japanese people in the seventh century A.D. and partly as a result of ecological considerations, the Japanese have evolved a complex and rich repertoire of purely vegetarian dishes in which a wide array of roots, fruits, seeds, leaves, bulbs, and other parts of plants are used in imaginative ways. There are many methods to prepare, cook, pickle, and serve vegetables: Various forms of pickling, light simmering in broth, and quick poaching are the most common.

The brassicas—cabbages, radishes, and turnips—are probably the most commonly used. Other familiar vegetables are bean sprouts, carrots, onions, squashes, and Japanese leeks. More exotic and relatively less well known are chrysanthemum flowers and leaves, *konnyaku* (devil's-tongue root), taro, burdock root, yams, and Japanese angelica. Over the centuries, native vegetables have been augmented by imports that have become naturalized to become intrinsic parts of Japanese cuisine: Small purple eggplants, tomatoes, sweet potatoes, and sweet and chili peppers have been adopted, as well as young flax plants, potatoes, and European cabbage. Japanese farmers have domesticated many varieties of mushrooms, and fungi constitute a major agricultural crop. Ten varieties are widely cultivated commercially, and some are known outside Japan. Perhaps the most well known is the brown, thick-fleshed shiitake, widely available all year round, fresh or dried. It is a component of soups and stews, is grilled and eaten on its own, and serves as a garnish for other foods. *Shimeji, enokitake* (enoki), *hiratake,* tree ears, *nameko, maitake,* and button mushrooms are also common. Supplementing the cultivated fungi are those collected from the wild. The most notable of all Japanese fungi is the pine mushroom (matsutake; *Armillaria edodes*), avowedly the most delicious and aromatic of all. This fungus has only recently been successfully raised commercially. Choice matsutake are the Japanese counterpart of the European truffle.

The Japanese love fruit, and, in fact, the word used today for cakes and candy was, early in history, used for fruit. Perhaps the most beloved fruit is the mandarin orange (*mikan*), and large orchards cover many of the temperate areas in Japan. There are also several unique varieties of grapes, from the tiny-berried, intensely sweet Delaware to choice plum-sized seedless varieties. Apples, persimmons, Asian pears (*nashi*), watermelons, melons, strawberries, and exotic fruits, such as loquats, are common

and have been eaten by the Japanese for centuries. Continuous agricultural improvement has resulted in new varieties such as Mutsu and Fuji apples, crisp 20th-century Asian pears, the supersized seedless Pione grape, and, a gift-giving novelty, conveniently cubic watermelons.

Fruits are sold in small mounds or baskets by greengrocers, and it is as small mounds of four or more fruit that they are offered to the deities at temples and shrines. Imported fruits are highly prized, ranging from bananas, mangoes, and pineapples from Central America and Southeast Asia to exotic fruits such as mangosteens and lychees.

Cooking

Day-to-day cooking is usually done by housewives. Magazines, cooking clubs, and many television shows offer clues for variety and nutrition, which is very important since multigenerational households are rare. Japanese eat out a great deal, so the other major figure in food is the professional chef. Professional chefs come in many types, specializations, and even grades (like many Japanese arts, chef schools award graded ranks to their trainees). There are schools of traditional cooking, and a high-quality chef is usually able to trace his lineage from pupil to student for many generations.

Most kitchens have relatively modest cooking arrangements. Refrigerators are generally small by U.S. standards, and working surfaces are very limited. Cooking is done on a countertop gas range. Built-in ovens are rare, though houses and apartments built in the past 30 years often have built-in ranges and ovens, and larger refrigerators are becoming more common. Countertop labor-saving devices, including ovens, mochi makers, bread machines, and yogurt makers, have proliferated. Japanese kitchens include a large variety of knives. Rectangular knives with very thin blades are used for slicing and peeling vegetables. Thicker triangular blades are used for meat and fish. The edges of these tend to be beveled on one side only, which allows a better control of the cut. Most kitchens will have at least one vegetable knife and two of the triangular blades: a short one for smaller fish and cuts, a long one for long, smooth slicing of items such as sashimi. Long chopsticks for cooking—stirring, whipping eggs, frying—and shorter ones for eating at the table are the most common implements.

To preserve the natural flavors of foods and their colors, and to present them visually in the best possible way, Japanese food often requires extensive preprocessing before cooking actually starts. Cuts have been developed to suit the characteristics of each type of vegetable and the cooking requirements for each dish. Many dishes require that a vegetable or fish be cut in a specific way to encourage even transmission of heat, ensure uniform distribution of flavor, and showcase natural textures. For example, an asymmetric and diagonal cut (*rangiri*) made by rolling a vegetable during cutting will create more facets than achieved by static square cutting, thereby exposing more of the vegetable to the hot cooking liquid. Each type of fish has its own special needs, and the good cook will be equipped with a series of very sharp knives and will need a great deal of practice to get the cut perfect: Cutting fish for sushi is quite different from cutting fish for grilling, for instance. Because of the importance of cutting, a chef is usually titled *itamae* (behind the counter), meaning the one responsible for the actual slicing of fish into its components. Since the eighth century, imperial chefs, and specialist chefs at some Shinto shrines in Kyoto, still carry out an annual ritual of slicing fish, using nothing but a pair of large chopsticks and a sharp knife.

Simmering and quick poaching are used, notably for vegetables. Fish can be served raw as sashimi or sushi. Smaller whole fish may be grilled, poached, or stewed. Meat is stir-fried, deep-fried in batter, or grilled. Chicken is often cut into small pieces and grilled on small skewers (yakitori). Long oven baking is rare.

Japanese cooks use relatively few spices. Mountain-ash berry, dried Japanese lime zest, sweet liquor (mirin), and soy sauce are often used for Japanese-style food. Western food is flavored with the full range of imported spices, though Japanese tend to prefer foods that are less aggressively seasoned.

Stews are well represented. Many are flavored with miso. They may contain meat, vegetables, fish, and mushrooms, in many combinations. Sumo wrestlers live on a diet of *chanko-nabe* stew, which includes all of the above plus mochi and liberal splashings of sake, to put on bulk.

Typical Meals

Typical meals in Japan can be categorized as rice-centered meals (most household meals), no-rice meals (which equate often to snacks), and rice-peripheral meals (which equate to feasts). Daily home meals often (almost always in the recent past) consisted of plain cooked rice, soup, and side dishes including fish, pickles, vegetables, and sometimes meat. Nowadays, fewer Japanese eat rice at every meal. Eating out includes snacks such as noodles or confectionary. Festive meals, often eaten at special restaurants, include many side dishes but almost always end with a bowl of rice and a bowl of soup.

Breakfast in Japanese households may be Western or Japanese style. Japanese-style breakfasts are more time-consuming and are more and more confined to weekends and nonworking days. Most households, particularly those with younger couples and couples with children, eat a Western-style breakfast. Children have corn flakes or some other cereal, milk, fruit, and yogurt. Adults tend to have toast and butter, eggs (fried, scrambled, or in an omelet), and slices of vegetables such as tomato or cucumber. There is also usually a slice or two of ham or a few small sausages. Adults drink coffee and store-bought orange juice, and the children have milk.

Japanese-style breakfasts are more complex: Steamed white rice, a bowl of misoshiru soup, and pickles, usually either giant radish (*takuan*), pickled plum (*umeboshi*), or short-pickled cabbage, form the centerpieces of the meal. Sheets of dried laver (nori) cut into standard one-inch by three-inch strips are used to wrap rice and awaken the taste buds. Commonly, a Japanese-style breakfast will also include a slice of salted grilled salmon (or some other fish) and a raw egg, which is beaten in a small bowl and poured on the hot rice. In eastern but not western Japan, a popular breakfast dish is fermented beans (natto), which are mixed with either the soup or the rice. Preparing all the little side dishes is time-consuming, and, unsurprisingly, most busy housewives, who might have to go to work themselves, prefer preparing quicker Western-style breakfasts.

The midday meal in most Japanese households is lighter than the evening meal, and more diffuse, since most household members are at work or at school. For the stay-at-homes it might mean little more than a bowl of noodles or some other light meal. Midday meals thus fall into three different types. People at home will usually eat a light meal of some sort. People at work will either bring a boxed lunch or eat at the company canteen, if there is one, or at a nearby restaurant, usually one that caters to working people and sells set lunches: salt-grilled fish, fried fish or meat, and stir-fried vegetables with rice and soup.

The main meal for most Japanese is the evening meal. The composition of such a meal varies of course according to taste, but it will almost always contain, or conclude with, plain rice. This is also likely to be an event where etiquette is preserved and where the entire family eats together, although many commuters arrive home too late to join their family at meals on weeknights.

A huge variety of box lunches (obentô) are available in Japanese cuisine, and they are popular for people working away from home, whether at work or traveling for leisure, as well as for special occasions. They consist of a plastic box divided into many irregular compartments, each with a few morsels of one food type. One compartment almost always contains rice, often with a pickled plum inserted to preserve freshness. Many box-lunch ingredients can be bought ready-made from department stores and supermarkets. The simplest of box lunches—oigiri—is little more than a ball of vinegared rice surrounding a piece of pickle or dried bonito shavings, sold in plastic containers at all supermarkets and convenience stores. More complex ones served at homes or restaurants can have many compartments, and even several stacked boxes. They are

nominally intended for people who are in a hurry or are traveling. The stations of interurban trains usually have station boxed meals (ekiben) for sale, which are hugely popular.

Kamo/Niku Namban Soba (Duck or Beef and Noodle Soup)

4 servings of soba (buckwheat noodles) or udon (thick wheat noodles)

2 breasts of duck or ¼ lb beef per person, cut into 1-in. x 2-in. fillets and then very thinly sliced

1 leek, sliced into ¼-in. rounds

4 c dashi stock

1 tsp grated ginger

6 c water for the noodles, plus 1 c water

4 large Asian soup bowls

Grill the duck (if using) skin side up until the skin is golden brown. The meat of the duck will be uncooked.

Remove from the grill, and slice across the duck breast into slices about ¼ inch thick.

Warm the dashi to a mild simmer. Slide in the duck or beef, the leek, and the ginger. Keep on a very slow simmer, but do not allow it to boil.

While the duck is grilling, boil 6 cups of water in a pot. When boiling, put in the noodles. Allow water to return to a boil. Pour in an additional cup of water (and a bit more if necessary) so that the boiling subsides. As soon as the water starts boiling again, remove from the heat, drain the noodles, and divide them among the four bowls. Ladle in a measure of stock, the leeks, and finally the meat on top of the noodles. Serve immediately.

Eating Out

Japanese sociologists argue that the Japanese eat out a great deal because Japanese houses are small and not suited for entertaining. Whatever the cause, Japanese do like to eat out a lot and there is a bewildering array of choices. Eating-out establishments range from carts and traditional Japanese-style restaurants (with or without geisha entertainment provided by women in formal traditional dress), through snack bars of various descriptions, to restaurants that combine foreign ideas with Japanese tastes.

Carts selling street foods are particularly common around train stations, where there are many potential customers. Street foods include *takoyaki* (chopped octopus puff-balls), *taiyaki* (waffles in the shape of a *tai* fish filled with sweet bean jam), and *manju* (Chinese steamed buns stuffed with a mixture of meat, bamboo shoots, and leeks or with sweet beans). A typical after-hours pick-me-up for tired roisterers is *oden,* a stew of brown tubes of fish paste (*chikuwa*), sweet potato and white potato slices, bundles of tied kelp (*kombu*), peeled boiled eggs, white and pink half-moon slices of fish paste (*kamaboko*), yuba (a skimmed soy-milk solid) tied with bow knots of dried gourd, small taro tubers (*satoimo*), and devil's foot root jelly (*konnyaku*). This is consumed with mustard and washed down with beer or sweet potato liquor (*sochu* or *shochu*—which can also be distilled from barley or rice).

There is a wide range of other foods that are more often eaten out than in. Many of these are best eaten at a counter, where the counterperson can serve morsels, sometimes one by one, and gauge the customer's satisfaction. Such foods include fresh or pickled fish on mouthfuls of vinegared rice (sushi), which comes in two varieties: Edo (Tokyo) style, made of fresh fish sliced to order and placed on rice balls, or in rolls or cones, and Osaka style, made of pickled fish and rice compressed in square molds. Sashimi are choice cuts of fresh fish. Tempura is another food best eaten at a counter, consisting of morsels of vegetables, fish, and seafood deep-fried in a light batter. This is served with a sauce of stock (dashi), grated radish, grated ginger, and light soy sauce.

Fish and other foods can be consumed in specialist *robatayaki-ya,* where diners sit around sand pits filled with glowing charcoal. Robatayaki-ya provide different grilled foods, as the taste and expertise of the cook and the demands of the customers dictate. *Yakitoriya* specialize in providing chicken bits on skewers, somewhat like the shish kebab of

A sushi chef making sushi at a restaurant in Japan. (Shutterstock)

the Middle East. Yakitoriya are common, perhaps because the investment is small: a narrow charcoal grill, just wide enough for standard bamboo skewers, some cuts of chicken, and a refrigerator full of chilled beer, and voila! yakitori. Grill bars come in a wide variety of styles to fit any purse. Smaller shops have a more limited choice of tidbits, but the small size offers an opportunity to talk with the owner as he grills the food. Larger places have much wider menus, and new types of grilled meats and other food are added all the time. For vegetarians there is a wide array of vegetables: shiitake mushrooms, asparagus, leeks, or cubes of tofu topped with a spread of thick tea- or miso-flavored paste and then grilled (*dengaku*).

Shared-pot restaurants serve one-pot dishes that are notable for their conviviality. Ceramic *donabe* and cast iron *tetsunabe* are deep-bellied, covered pots used for cooking soupy stews, of which the most common version is *shabu-shabu* (roughly "swirly" or "swish"). A quantity of stock is heated, then placed in the pot over a tabletop burner. When the liquid is roiling , fish and meat are added. Each diner takes out tidbits and dips them in a dipping sauce—Japanese lime and soy sauce is very common—before conveying them to the mouth. As the stock absorbs the meaty flavor, vegetables—Chinese cabbage, shiitake mushrooms, enokitake mushrooms, sliced leeks, carrots, chrysanthemum leaves, bean sprouts, or any vegetable that will cook quickly in liquid—are added and consumed. Finally, once the soup is fully flavored, thick udon noodles, which absorb flavor well, are added and consumed as well. Sukiyaki is supposed to have originated as a quick cooking method for farmers or soldiers out in the field, who used a hoe blade as a makeshift grill. Today, it is cooked using a special cast iron, flat-bottomed pot in which thin strips of beef are cooked in sweet rice liquor (mirin), lime juice, and soy liquid and eaten dipped in beaten raw egg. The sauce is thinned with sake, and then vegetables and bean gelatin noodles (*harusame*) are added.

Japanese enjoy both Japanese (*wagashi*) and Western (*yôgashi*) confections. Japanese confections are based largely on two major ingredients. Mochi is glutinous rice that is made by steaming and then pounding sticky rice into a thick paste somewhat like chewing gum. Very similar to marzipan in Europe, mochi is very plastic: It accepts and blends flavors and colors and can be shaped into anything from lifelike peaches to little statues of dogs. Cooked beans are sweetened and serve as a common filling, and sometimes coating, for mochi

Restaurant, Tokyo, Japan. (Corel)

confections. Other sweets are made of jellies from seaweed and translucent bean noodles. Wagashi are almost universally served with green tea, often in *kisaten* (tea shops) dedicated to the purpose.

Western confectionary covers the entire range of types and geographic locations, from delicate petit fours, through the entire range of Austrian, Italian, and German cream cakes and cheesecakes, to American fruit pies. These are either made at home or, more commonly, bought in one of the many Western-style bakeries and confectionaries found in every Japanese town.

Feasts, or banquets, punctuate and are part of most social life. The standard meal consisting of rice, soup, and side dishes can also be expanded into a full banquet or feast in which the entire corpus of cooking styles available to the Japanese cook can be brought into play. Obviously such banquets are indulged in only on special occasions, and they are very rarely undertaken at home. A banquet starts with an appetizer of small delicate tidbits (*zensai*) followed by a clear soup (*suimono*) intended to awaken the appetite, and possibly some sashimi: The delicate flavor of fresh raw fish is best appreciated when one is not completely hungry but before the taste of other foods dulls the palate.

The central dishes of a banquet come in a fixed order. A grilled dish (*yakimono*) starts the process. This is followed by a soft steamed dish (*mushimono*), which contrasts with the stronger flavors of the grilled food, and then a dish of vegetables or fish simmered in stock (*nimono*). Softer foods are followed with a crisp, fried item (*agemono*), and the oil is subsequently cut and the mouth freshened by vegetables or fish dressed in vinegar sauce (*sunomono*). The banquet then concludes with a rice dish, usually plain steamed white rice but sometimes rice with included materials: beans, chestnuts, or flavoring (*gohanmono*), which is accompanied by a heavier soup, usually misoshiru, and pickles (*tsukemono*). Finally, most modern banquets conclude with a sweet (*okashi*) and green tea.

The most refined form of dining—*kaiseki*—is that surrounding the tea ceremony. The practice of ritually drinking tea was originally imported from China, where it is still practiced today. But the Japanese, partly under the influence of Buddhism, made this ritual their own. Kaiseki cooking, strongly influenced by Buddhism, eschews meat to a large degree and encourages the use of delicate morsels of food that would complement the bitter-blandness of tea, as well as the refined atmosphere of the tea ritual itself. Nature enters into the kaiseki by minute attention to the types of plates used as well as the types of foods, which are to fit each season. Brightly colored plates and bowls are used in summer, and more somber colors in winter. In the fall, there are various evocations of the season such as decorations of red maple leaves, flying geese, or chrysanthemums, which flower in October. Spring utensils feature plum blossoms or some fresh greenery. There are even differences in the shape of utensils: Summer bowls and dishes tend to be airy, open mouthed, and often flat. Winter dishes tend to be solider, with thick vertical walls, and often lidded. A full kaiseki banquet is likely to have one or more dishes for each of the categories of Japanese cooking. Unsurprisingly, a full tea ceremony and banquet can take up an entire day.

Western-style fine-dining establishments have proliferated throughout Japan, which boasts numerous Michelin-starred restaurants as well.

Special Occasions

The Japanese enjoy and practice a variety of rituals, festivals, and holidays. In addition to traditional festivities that are related, at some level, to the divine, Japan as a nation also celebrates a number of purely civil holidays. At the core of every festive day in Japan is the concept of sharing food—often in the form of a full feast but, at a minimum, a sharing of rice or even a bite of seaweed, and wine, with the deities (*kami*) or ancestors (*hotoke*). As a consequence, few Japanese festivals do not include food, whether formally presented at a shrine or temple ritual, eaten at home with family or friends, and perhaps a visiting deity, or consumed from one or more of the street stalls that populate every festival.

New Year (*oshôgatsu;* December 31–January 3) is both a national and religious holiday, the most important of the year. Most businesses close for a few days. On the eve of the New Year (December 31), shrines and temples hold special services, and many people dressed in kimono visit a favorite shrine and temple, particularly at midnight, when the temple bells toll out the 108 Buddhist sins. This is the time to consume special New Year foods (*oseichi*), to decorate the entrances of homes with cut green bamboo poles wrapped in straw rope and decorated with pine branches and oranges (*kado matsu*), and to visit friends and family. New Year food is traditionally packed in special three-tiered square lacquered box trays (*jûbako*) decorated with an indication of the season: pine needles or branches, plum blossoms, and bamboo leaves, all indicating the approach of spring and the turn of the year. The foods themselves refer to the season as well, whether through a well-placed pun on the name (kombu [kelp] = *yorokobu* [felicitations]) or by their color or shape. Red, green, white, and gold colors predominate. For example, slices of red and white fish paste (kamaboko) might be alternated in a checkerboard pattern. Pink cooked whole prawns might be placed next to erect, hollowed-out spears of cucumber filled with brilliant reddish-orange fresh salmon roe. Mandarin oranges, whose plentiful seeds hint at fecundity, might be filled with brilliant gold-colored jelly. Lotus root, chicken breast fillets, and taro bulbs or burdock roots are fried a golden color or glazed with golden sauce and added to the trays. The arrangements of these boxes are so delicate and pleasing to the eye that many households keep the traditional three (sometimes four) box trays for display only, bringing in piled plates for actual consumption. Many of the individual foods are extremely time-consuming to make. Threading boiled golden gingko nuts individually on a pine needle, or cutting carrot slices into the shape of a plum blossom, requires a great deal of time and skill. So, in modern Japan, one can purchase either an entire tray or the more finicky preparations from the many supermarkets and particularly from the elite department stores.

Perhaps the single most important food of the New Year is *ozoñi*. This New Year's soup is based on the finest *ichibandashi* (stock made from shaved

Japanese ozoñi, a traditional soup served for New Year's celebrations. (Shutterstock)

bonito and kombu), often flavored with a strip of decoratively cut Japanese lime whose intense aroma fills the bowl. Besides the stock, the single most common ingredient in ozoñi is pounded and roasted rice cake.

Other national festival days include the Doll Festival (Hinamatsuri) during which parents of girls set out the *hina-ningyo* dolls, which portray an ancient imperial court, complete with emperor and empress, ladies-in-waiting, ministers, and musicians. Young girls entertain one another with drinks of *amazake* (a sweet, slightly fermented drink made of rice gruel), colored rice cakes, and red rice cooked with beans. One month after Hinamatsuri is the boys' turn. During the Boy's Festival (Tangonosekku) people eat rice dumplings (*chimaki dango*) of special rich rice wrapped in a bamboo leaf in the shape of a demon's horn, and also steamed and pounded-rice cakes wrapped in oak leaves called *kashiwa mochi.* During spring, office parties, families, and friends will have formal blossom-viewing picnics (*hanami*). Seasonal foods, including cakes in cherry-blossom shape, can be bought from many shops and are consumed under the blossoming trees. Many Japanese families celebrate Obon, the day of the dead, by a visit to the family graves, where the favorite foods of the recently departed are offered on the graves.

Life-cycle events—birth, adulthood, marriage, death, and a number of others—are celebrated in Japan and characterized by specific foods whose shape, coloration, or associations recalls the event. For example, families moving to a new neighborhood will often offer their neighbors—the three houses opposite and one on either side (*mukai sangen, ryodonari*), as the Japanese saying has it—packets of noodles (or tickets for a free meal at the neighboring noodle shop). *Soba* means both noodles and neighbors, and by offering the gift they are asking to become members of the local community. Special ritual foods may be offered to children on their third month, and to adults upon reaching their 60th birthday.

Red and White Salad

¼ c dashi stock

¼ c rice vinegar

1 tbsp sugar

½ daikon radish, peeled (use the upper half of the radish)

carrots, peeled, roughly the same quantity as the radish

2-in. piece of kombu (kelp), soaked in cool water for 15 minutes (the dry kombu will expand into a large leathery sheet)

Make the sweet vinegar the day before: Warm the dashi. Add the vinegar, then dissolve the sugar in the liquid. Allow to cool.

The next day, with a sharp, thin vegetable knife, cut the radish into a four-sided prism shape. Slice the prism into ¼-inch slices. Cut each slice into ¼-inch strips. Cut the carrots the same way.

Place the vegetables in a bowl, salt thoroughly, then knead with the hands for about 5 minutes. Allow to rest for a few minutes, then squeeze handfuls of the vegetables gently over a colander, and discard all liquid. Place the squeezed vegetables into a clean bowl.

While radish and carrots are resting, drain the kombu and slice it into thin strips. Combine all the vegetables.

Add one-third of the sweet vinegar. Mix by hand, then lightly squeeze handfuls of the vegetables over a colander once again. Discard the liquid. Return the vegetables to a clean bowl (glass is ideal).

Add the rest of the vinegar to the vegetables. Add the kombu. Mix all ingredients by hand, then allow to rest overnight before serving as side dish or salad.

Diet and Health

Most Japanese recognize that the key to healthy life can be found in two things: exercise and diet. The Japanese diet as a whole is apparently, with some reservations, extremely healthy. Scientific evidence is emerging that certain foods—kombu and nori, tea, shiitake mushrooms—have health benefits above and beyond their caloric value. The evidence is clear, if nothing else, in the actuarial tables. Notwithstanding the stresses of living in modern Japan, the Japanese consistently come at the head of the life-expectancy tables. Some of the features of Japanese cuisine that have a positive effect on health include the following:

A high proportion of vegetables in the diet: Traditional side dishes are largely based on lightly cooked vegetables: blanching, light steaming, and quick cooking in preference to heavy frying or long stewing. Thus, both caloric value and vitamins are maintained, and more roughage persists in the diet.

Low fat consumption: On the whole Japanese prefer to simmer or grill foods. Deep-frying, though available, is only one of a range of food-preparation methods.

High fish consumption: Japanese have traditionally consumed fatty fish, leading to an increase in high-density lipoprotein (HDL) cholesterol and a decrease in low-density lipoprotein (LDL) cholesterol. Seaweed—lavers, kelps, and true seaweed—which Japanese consume on a regular basis, has beneficial properties, apparently including anticarcinogenic abilities.

Freshness: The Japanese insistence, on the whole, on consuming fresh food, or at least food that has come as quickly as possible from the producer to the consumer (problems of hygiene and modern mass production aside), probably has beneficial aspects as well.

Small servings: Small portions, and lengthy service of desirable meals, have meant that the diner has the time, the emotional resources, and the leisure to savor each morsel and to digest food properly. Japanese meals, consisting of many small portions, ensure that the digestive process is not being put under stress.

Health-promoting foods: There seems to be substantial evidence of active health promotion by foods as diverse as tea, kelp (kombu), and shiitake mushrooms, among others. Tea—green (unfermented), oolong (semifermented and smoked), and black (fermented) types—is regularly consumed by most Japanese: Tea is available at work and school breaks, packed for travelers, and as a part of most meals. There are also strong claims by Japanese scientists that consumption of kelp, both cooked and fresh, may help in suppressing absorption of cancer-inducing chemicals. *Katsuobushi* (dried fermented skipjack tuna) flakes (from which dashi, the stock that is heavily used in Japanese cooking, is brewed) have the property of reducing blood pressure, and some studies have shown that the flakes themselves contain amino acids that act to suppress high blood pressure.

In contrast, there are some negative effects of the Japanese diet. These include the following:

High salt levels: Since salt pickles are a major component of the Japanese diet, along with miso, which is brewed with salt, high rates of stomach cancer and high blood pressure are recurring problems in Japan. The Japanese government has taken those findings seriously and has run several campaigns to reduce salt consumption.

Industrial food: Since the end of World War II, the Japanese populace has been affected by a series of problems such as outbreaks of *E. coli,* contaminated milk, and overconsumption of sugar, which have been traced to industrial processes in food manufacturing. Food manufacture is pervasive, and many Japanese households consume large proportions of ready-made meals and industrially produced food. An indication of the extent of factory-processed food is the Japanese government's authorization of the production of purely artificial food bars. Made by biochemists from chemicals and fermentation, they yield full nutritional value with very little taste.

Refined foodstuffs: Until well into the modern era, few Japanese families ate refined white rice as a staple. The process of polishing the rice removes the husk and the germ, which together provide vitamins and protein available only in brown rice. White rice was a desirable commodity, not necessarily an item of daily consumption. White rice is now commonly available, and refined foods such as fish paste (kamaboko), from which much of the vitamins have been removed, are eaten very frequently.

Sugar: The Japanese have become addicted to sugar, and the consumption of sweets in Japan, notably among children, has increased. High consumption of many sweet foods and candies available to Japanese children has contributed to poor dentition among Japanese as they become adults and has also encouraged obesity, which is currently becoming a problem among Japanese children.

Michael Ashkenazi

Further Reading

Ashkenazi, Michael, and Jeanne Jacob. *The Essence of Japanese Cuisine: An Essay on Food and*

Culture. Richmond, Surrey, UK: Curzon Press, 2000.

Ashkenazi, Michael, and Jeanne Jacob. *Food Culture in Japan.* Westport, CT: Greenwood Press, 2003.

Cwiertka, Katrzynka. *Modern Japanese Cuisine: Food Power and National Identity.* London: Reaktion Books, 2006.

Ishige, Naomichi. *The History and Culture of Japanese Food.* London: Kegan Paul, 2001.

Okakura, Kakuzo. *The Book of Tea.* Rutland, VT: Charles Tuttle, 1956.

Tsuchiya, Yoshio. *A Feast for the Eyes: The Japanese Art of Food Arrangement.* Tokyo: Kodansha International, 1985.

Kazakhstan

Overview

The Republic of Kazakhstan is the ninth-largest country in the world by landmass, about the same size as western Europe or Texas, but it is only the 62nd most populated, containing nearly 15.5 million people, about 60 percent of whom live in cities. North to south it stretches from the western Siberian plains to the Central Asian desert and the edge of the Silk Road; east to west it stretches from the Altai Mountains to the Volga. A landlocked country bordering two landlocked seas—the Caspian and the Aral—it neighbors China to its east, Kyrgyzstan, Turkmenistan, and Uzbekistan to the south, and Russia to the north and west.

Historically, the Kazakhs are a nomadic people, a mixture of Turkic and Mongol tribes who migrated to the area in the 13th century. Russia conquered part of Kazakhstan in the 18th century and the remainder in the 19th, and it became a Soviet republic in 1936. The Soviet Union's "virgin lands" project in the 1950s and 1960s had the twin effects of causing extensive immigration from Russia and other Soviet republics and of bringing to an end much of the traditional nomadic living and farming practices of the previous centuries. Among these Soviet immigrants were workers for the local industries and prisoners of the gulag, much of which was located in the steppes of Kazakhstan. Kazakhstan gained its independence in 1991, and many of the immigrant communities returned home. Today, although the country prides itself on accommodating 120 nationalities, the population is predominantly a mixture of native Kazakhs (approximately 55%) and Russians (approximately 30%), with Uzbeks, Tartars, and Ukrainians the next-largest groups. Russian and Kazakh are the official languages. About 44 percent practice the Russian Orthodox religion, and 47 percent of the population is Sunni Muslim. All of these populations have had their own influence on the food of the nation.

Kazakhstan's economy outstrips all of the other Central Asian states combined. Rich in natural minerals (it is said that almost every element in the periodic table can be found in Kazakhstan), it has a particular wealth of deposits of petroleum, natural gas, coal, copper, iron ore, lead, zinc, bauxite, gold, and uranium. It retains a strong relationship with Russia, and ever since independence has leased 2,316 square miles (6,000 square kilometers) of land around the Baikonur Cosmodrome to Russia for continued use in its space program. Its main agricultural products are grain—largely spring wheat—and livestock—sheep, horses, and cattle—although its continental climate means that it also has good conditions for growing a wide variety of fruits and vegetables in summer. Generally speaking, Kazakhstan is a nation of meat eaters, with between 30 and 50 percent of daily calories coming from meat and 50 percent from starches.

🍽 Food Culture Snapshot

Sholpan and Talgat live in an apartment in central Almaty, with their young daughter and baby son. A little over a year ago, when his mother died, Talgat's father came to live with the family. As the youngest son, Talgat is responsible for his parents and his sisters when the need arises. Both Sholpan and Talgat are middle-class urban professionals who work full-time, and they have regular help from an older woman, Gulfiya, who comes into their home to assist with cooking, cleaning, and child care.

Although both adults work, it is Sholpan's responsibility to take care of the family home and to shop for and prepare their meals. Home cooking is an essential component of their family life, extending even to the traditional fruit compotes or cordials that are always in a bottle in the fridge should anyone be thirsty. Talgat's favorite is made from dried apples and barberries simmered in water over a low flame, with the addition of raspberries in summer and dried apricots or raisins in winter.

Staple foods that are usually in the larder include fresh and preserved meats in the form of sausages and smoked meats, rice, eggs, wheat flour, ready-made breads and biscuits, and pickled fish, as well as a wide variety of fruits and vegetables in season. Nuts and dried fruits from the region are another important staple.

Sholpan and Talgat are typical of others in their social group in thinking that fruits and vegetables purchased from a supermarket are simply not fresh. The vast majority of fresh produce is still bought in outdoor or farmers' markets, which are centrally located, or from street vendors who bring their produce of the day into town to sell. Dried fruits and nuts are also best from the market. The impressive new supermarkets tend to be used for bulk purchases—or by the many foreigners working in the larger cities.

Major Foodstuffs

Traditionally, the most important foods for Kazakhs were meat and dairy, and these continue to play a prominent role on Kazakh tables. Sheep, horse, and camel are the traditional meats, and beef is popular. Wild goat is still relatively commonly consumed in rural areas, though the population of *saiga,* or long-nosed antelope, which used to be a staple, has dropped to the extent that it is now protected. Poultry is less frequently consumed than red meat but is becoming increasingly popular, especially chicken and duck. Meat is bled at slaughter, and the animal's head faces west in keeping with halal practice (Mecca is west of Kazakhstan). Camels are slaughtered on their knees, presumably since the animals are so tall. A carcass is usually divided into 12 pieces, each of which has a traditional owner when the meat is served: the head and pelvic bone for guests, kinsmen, and the elderly; the liver and tail fat to all of the in-laws; the breast/brisket for the son- or daughter-in-law; the anklebone for the son-in-law; the rump for a friend; the large intestine for the herdsman; the heart, fat, and cervical vertebrae for the girls; and the kidneys and neck vertebrae (and the ears from the head) for the children.

Horse is an especially important meat. In fact, everything about horses is redolent of Kazakhstan, and there are few more uplifting sights than a herd of horses galloping together across the steppe. Superb horsemen, Kazakhs breed different herds of horses to work, milk, and eat. Horseflesh is often the main meat in traditional Kazakh dishes, and it is also made into a wide array of sausages and preserved meats, each with a different flavor, texture, and balance. Horses raised for eating are encouraged to develop extensive deposits of fat, as this is particularly prized, especially the yellow fat from mountain-fed horses (lowland horses are leaner, and their fat is whiter). On the whole, the fattier the sausage the better. One sausage type, *kazy,* is made from the long strips of meat and fat from the ribs, seasoned with garlic, salt, and pepper and threaded in large, long, whole pieces into the guts. The meat and fat for *shuzhuk* is chopped before being seasoned with salt, pepper, and garlic and stuffed into guts. *Karta* is made from the thickest part of the rectum, which is washed carefully so as not to break up the fat that surrounds it and is then even more carefully turned inside out so that the fat is encased inside. Whole preserved meats include *zhal,* the oblong accumulation of fat from underneath the horse's mane, which is cut off with a thin piece of flesh and then salted, and *zhaya,* which is the salted upper muscular layer of the hip with up to 4 inches (10 centimeters) of fat. *Sur-yet* may be made of any part of the horse's flesh cut into in a piece of between 1 and 2 pounds (0.5 and 1 kilogram) and salted. All of these will be either dried or smoked, and all are boiled for up to two hours before use.

Sheep are an important meat source, and fattiness is also prized in this meat. The sheep are bred to have particularly fat rears, and this fat, as well as fat from the tail, is an important ingredient in many dishes as well as being eaten in its own right. The most expensive *shashlyk,* or kebabs, are those with the most fat included. Mutton is also preserved in sausages such as *kyimai,* a blood sausage, and *ulpershek,* made of the heart, aorta, and fat. No part of the animal is wasted. Children collect the knuckle and anklebones to play a throwing game called *asikya*—historically, this was also used to help them learn how to count. Men may be given one of these bones on their wedding day to symbolize hope for a son.

Although it borders two inland seas (the Caspian and Aral), Kazakhstan is landlocked, so as much freshwater as sea fish is consumed. Sturgeon, carp, and pike perch are particularly common, the former eaten for both its meat and its eggs—caviar. Sturgeon and carp are farmed, and in recent years programs have been put in place to try to repopulate the Aral Sea with Aral and Syr Darya sturgeon. As result of Russian and other northern European influence (especially German), salmon is eaten, and pickled fish in many forms is common, usually herring.

Milk from cows, mares, and camels is consumed in the form of milk, yogurt, cream, and cheeses, all of which may be fresh, soured, or fermented. In the countryside, beestings (the first milk after the birth of a calf), or *uyz,* are commonly consumed either boiled and drunk as a warm liquid or boiled, cooled, solidified, and eaten in slices. Fresh milk is usually drunk boiled and is sometimes added to black tea. Slightly fermented milk drinks are traditional, especially kumiss made from mare's milk, *shabat* from camel milk, and *airan* from cow milk. Slightly yogurty and sour, sometimes with a slight fizz, these drinks are refreshing and nourishing and a typical start to a meal or offering to a guest. Both kumiss and shabat are highly recommended for their health-giving properties, renowned for being good for the digestion and the liver, and even a cure for tuberculosis. Boiled soured milk from cows and mares is often strained and formed into small balls that are left to dry in the sun. The resulting *kurt*

is eaten as a snack alone or with tea, or diluted in broth or porridge.

Fresh fruit in season is plentiful and prized. In summer, there is a profusion of raspberries and currants of every color, peaches, apricots, melons, and watermelons. Many of these are dried for use in winter, too, the local dried fruits being supplemented by a vast array of imported dried fruits from southern neighbors, especially Uzbekistan, Kyrgyzstan, and Tajikistan. The sheer variety of differently prepared dried raisins, apricots, cherries, and plums from multiple fruit varieties make Kazakh markets a jeweler's shop of glowing color. Autumn is one of the more important fresh fruit seasons, for Kazakhstan is famous as the birthplace of the apple. Most apples eaten in the world today originate from its wild *Malus sieversii,* and the old capital, Almaty, is named for the apple—*Alma-ata* means "father of apples." Although many of the ancient orchards have been lost since independence, apples remain an important crop. Ranging from the highly scented and enormous Aport apple, which can be as large as a baby's head and will grow only on the land around Almaty, to the tiny wild crab apple, they are eaten fresh, dried, or made into brandy.

Alongside displays of dried fruits one finds an equally astonishing array of nuts, grown locally and imported. Almonds of every size, walnuts, cashews, pistachios, and even nutty little apricot kernels are sold in markets everywhere and served as snacks at home. A wide variety of honeys are also sold for consumption and for health. Unlike its Silk Road neighbors, however, Kazakhstan does not have a huge market in spices and herbs. In its markets, meat, dairy products, dried fruits and nuts, and fresh fruit and vegetables predominate. In summer, a profusion of the sweetest tomatoes are on sale; all year, onions, cabbage, seasonal greens, and fresh herbs, especially parsley and cilantro, are available. The influence of several immigrant communities can be found in the most commonly consumed salads: Russian beetroot salad and spicy Korean carrot salad.

With 70 percent of its agricultural land under cultivation, Kazakhstan is the sixth most important global wheat exporter, and wheat is grown in great quantities for the internal markets as well as for export. Wheat flour is consumed as bread, pasta, or noodles and is the key ingredient in the casing for different types of dumplings and pies. Bread is an important staple food, and there are numerous local breads, many of them the round, flattish, leavened loaves called *non* or *nan* with a distinct raised edge and attractive center decorated with a stamped pattern. Despite the name, these breads are not the same as the flat, unleavened Indian nan. Nan may be plain (*taba nan*), or it can include some fried onions rolled into the outer rim, or have sesame or nigella seeds strewn on the surface, or have a little tail fat added. Highly decorated smaller versions of this loaf, called *damdy nan,* are often served in restaurants. This type of loaf may also be enriched with egg to make *salma nan.* Egg-enriched puffy fried breads, or *baursak,* are very popular, and these, too, may be either simply savory or sweetened with sugar (*yespe baursak*) or, for a more complex preparation, have curds added and be boiled before frying (*domalak baursak*). Many of the dumplings that Kazakhs love to eat are made with leavened dough: *Samsa* are stuffed with meat, rice, and onion, shaped into half-moons, and baked; *belyashes* are shaped into small rolls, stuffed with meat or fish and onion, and fried; and *cheburek* are made in rounds, stuffed with meat and onions with the edges pinched together, and fried. Russian dumplings, *perogi* or *pelmeniy,* are also popular. *Manti* are more Chinese in style, made with a thinner, unleavened, wheat-based dough and steamed. *Gutap* dough is also unleavened but enriched with butter, the filling is rich in egg and herbs, and the square fritters are deep-fried. Many of these may be served with a sour cream sauce.

Rice is another important starch grown in the country and the basis for one of the national dishes, *plov.*

Bread sellers in Shymkent, Kazakhstan. (Travel-images.com)

Plov

This is a classic of Kazakh cuisine. Although it is clearly related to the typical rice dishes or pilafs common throughout Central Asia, plov has its own particular characteristics. Carrots are the main flavoring agent, and it rarely contains dried fruits (unheard of in most of its cousins). It is much less highly seasoned than other similar rice dishes from along the Silk Road. Typically, any meat can be used, though red meats are preferred. Lamb, including the fat from the tail, is the most common option, though some restaurants offer horse, and beef is popular with many families making it at home.

14 oz medium-grain white rice

2.2 lb lamb or beef, chopped into small cubes

3 tbsp sunflower or corn oil

2 pinches ground coriander

1 medium onion, peeled and sliced

2.2 lb carrots, cut into strips

2 tbsp ground mixed spices (cumin, coriander, cinnamon)

3½ c water

6 cloves garlic, peeled

Wash the rice until the water runs clear, and soak it in water. Heat the oil on high heat, and fry the lamb or beef until very well cooked, about 30 minutes, adding a couple pinches of ground coriander to reduce the smell of the meat. Add the onion, and fry for 2 minutes, then add the carrots and the spice mix. Fry for about 20 minutes until the carrots begin to caramelize. Turn down the heat to low, and add the water and a teaspoon of salt. Turn the heat to high, cover with a lid, and bring to a boil. Add the garlic and then the rice, which should be pushed gently under the surface of the liquid but not stirred. Replace the lid. Cook for 20 minutes, until the water is absorbed and the rice is cooked. Tip out onto a large dish, and serve with a tomato and onion salad.

Every meal ends with something sweet. Chocolate- or vanilla-flavored light sponge cakes, sandwiched together with jam, covered in sweetened cream, and brightly iced, are commonly bought at bakeries and served as desserts or with tea. Local factories produce a vast array of brightly wrapped boiled sweets in fruit, nut, and chocolate flavors. There is a thriving chocolate-making industry, and locals take rightful pride in the quality of the beautifully wrapped bars.

Cooking

Preparing Kazakh food is fairly labor-intensive. Although dishes tend to be composed of relatively few ingredients, meals are composed of multiple dishes, so a lot of chopping and mixing is required. In most households cooking is a female occupation, the responsibility of the senior woman in the house, aided by her daughters or daughters-in-law as required.

Middle-class Kazakh kitchens are somewhat simpler than Western kitchens. The room itself tends to be small, and the main piece of equipment is a domestic stove with an oven and surface burners (either electric or gas). The majority of cooking is done on the burners, and in many lower-middle-class households the oven is put to use as an additional storage area for pots and pans rather than as a means of cooking. Poorer households without these facilities continue to use the traditional dried-cow-dung fire. Some rural households have a clay oven in their backyard, used for baking bread and meats, but this type of oven is traditionally Uzbek, not Kazakh. The Kazakh "oven" is a more temporary affair made of two large, heavy metal pans of similar size, one used as a lid for the other, buried in the cow-dung fire. Grilling is done over charcoal outside.

Deep-frying and sautéing are done in large, deep frying pans; boiled dishes, especially meat-based stews, are made in large cast iron or steel saucepans, or *kazans*. Dumplings are steamed in large multi-layered pans called *kaskans*. Narrow rolling pins or a large broom handle are used to roll out bread or pasta dough. Handleless china cups or soup bowls, called *pialas,* are used for measuring volumes of about 1 cup (200 grams) dry and 8.5 fluid ounces (250 milliliters) of liquid ingredients. Spices are bought ready-ground, and often ready-mixed, from the market, so milling and crushing are not usually done at home.

Typical Meals

Most Kazakhs in urban and rural areas eat three meals a day, the largest of which is dinner. All meals are accompanied by tea, either black or green. Black tea may have milk added. Breakfast is usually eaten at home; it consists of tea and either bread with jam, honey, or cheese, plus hard-boiled or scrambled eggs, or a thin porridge with sweet toppings of jam or raisins. Some savory items are interchangeably consumed as either breakfast or lunch foods: breads stuffed with chopped eggs and greens or cabbage, or pancakes spread with a thin layer of minced lamb and rolled. Lunch is light and often eaten outside the home—perhaps manti or samsa, or soup (*sorpa*), or Korean-style salad bought from a street vendor or small restaurant. In many offices, people will bring in leftover food from home to eat at lunchtime.

Hospitality is a critical part of Kazakh life, and dinner tends to be an important time for this. The dining table in most homes is always set with two three-tiered plates of dried fruits, nuts, and sweets, ready for any guest who happens to visit. A typical meal for guests might start with savory baursak, little hollow doughnut-like fried puffed breads, and some salads—perhaps *sveyko nay*, made of grated beetroot and finely minced garlic; *mimosa*, or crab salad, made of chopped crab, hard-boiled eggs, rice, cucumbers, and sweet corn with a dill dressing; and a tomato and onion salad with garlic, this last one essential if plov, the Kazakh pilaf, is on the menu. Plov is traditionally made with horse or fat mutton, but many families prefer their plov made with beef. A soup of some kind, either fish or meat broth, will probably be served along with the meal. Every dish is placed on the table, and guests are exhorted to help themselves before the family begins eating. Mainly homemade up to this point, the meal may turn to purchased items for dessert. Along with tea with hot milk there will be a profusion of sweetmeats: dried fruits and nuts; fresh fruit (watermelon, raspberries, pomegranates, according to season); fruit jams, eaten by the teaspoonful; and cake, perhaps *midovi,* a honey cake with cream. Any cookies or chocolates brought by the guests will also be served.

Eating Out

Kazakh cities have numerous restaurants, and eating out is a popular pastime, with large groups meeting for business or social entertainment. In the summer, many restaurants have large open-air seating areas with live music to encourage parties to stay and enjoy the hospitality—and order more food. Many restaurants offer typical foods of the region, in particular Kazakh, Uzbek, or Georgian dishes. Although some of these restaurants specialize in a particular cuisine, many of them offer a broader range of dishes from the region.

Other Asian restaurants are also popular, especially Korean and Chinese, and there are a few Indian and Thai restaurants in the major cities. In many cases local ingredients are used to prepare classic dishes on these menus. The meat wrapped and steamed in a banana leaf in a Kazakh Thai restaurant is as likely to be horse meat as chicken.

Snacking is extremely popular, and many of the local foods lend themselves to the quick street-food treatment. Several of the favorite meat and vegetable dumplings, in particular manti and samsa, are readily available in markets, on the street, and in small, fast restaurants that let you drop in for a quick bite. One is also never too far from an open-air grill that has been wheeled into position in a park or on a street corner and is loaded with shashlyk, which are then served with bread, sliced onion and tomato, and a spicy sauce. Typical Western fast food is also available, and the local McBurger chain is a popular choice, but local foods seem to remain the preferred option for most snacking outside the home.

Special Occasions

The traditional Kazakh feast is known as the *dastarkhan,* which is literally the word for the tablecloth on which food would be laid out but is better translated here as a festive table. The dastarkhan is an expression of the importance of sharing generous hospitality with family, friends, and guests. Based on the nomadic tradition of the early Kazakh peoples, it has sheep as its centerpiece. Before the feast begins, the table is decorated with the snacks always laid out on a Kazakh table: dried fruits, nuts, and sweets. Guests are offered kumiss, fermented mare's milk; shabat, fermented camel milk; or airan, liquid yogurt, to drink. The small, puffy fried breads called baursak are served. The rest of the meal is focused on the meat, starting with the sheep's head. Traditionally this is presented to the most senior person at the table, who carves it and serves the other guests according to their status. Older people and children are taken particular care of—the children usually get the ears. *Beshbarmek* follows. This is a dish of boiled meat, in this case mutton or lamb, served in whole pieces on the bone on a dish of broad noodles and stewed onions. The meat is again served to the guests according to the most suitable part for them (pelvic bone or leg for elderly guests of honor, the cervical vertebrae to the girls), and each person has a soup bowl of the broth that the meat and pasta were cooked in, known as sorpa, which is served in small soup bowls called pialas. Black or green tea is served.

Beshbarmek

This dish is simple and filling. With the use of good ingredients and a healthy appetite, it is quite delicious. The same recipe can be used with any red meat: horse, beef, or mutton, depending on availability and preference. Horse will produce the leanest result, mutton the fattiest. Many families and restaurants prefer it made with mutton.

1 large, fat piece of mutton on the bone (approximately 4 lb)

4 onions

Salt

Pepper (optional)

1 egg

1 c water

4½ c white flour

Place the meat, a little salt, and one peeled whole onion in a large saucepan, cover with water, bring to a boil, and simmer until cooked—approximately 2 hours—frequently skimming off any scum that rises to the surface.

About an hour into the cooking of the meat, slice the remaining 3 onions thinly. Skim some fat and bouillon from the meat pan, and place into a smaller saucepan. Add the sliced onions, bring to a boil, and simmer gently until the onions are soft but not disintegrating. Season with salt and a little pepper if desired.

Now make the pasta. Beat together the egg and water with 1½ pinches salt in a large bowl. Gradually add the flour, and mix together with your hands, kneading firmly and scraping the dough from the sides of the bowl as you go. Keep adding flour and kneading until the mixture doesn't stick to the sides of the bowl any more—approximately 4–5 minutes. Tip out onto a large, clean work surface, and roll and knead it hard into a springy ball. Return to the bowl, cover, and let rest for 15 minutes. Flour the work surface. Cut the dough into 4 pieces, sprinkle each piece liberally with flour, and knead each for about a minute. Form 4 neat balls, pressing each one flat and allowing it to bounce up again. Then, take one ball at a time and press it flat with the knuckles, turning over and over in flour, and finally roll out through the lasagna setting of a pasta machine. Cut the pieces into long rectangles. Remove the cooked meat from the pan, and boil the pasta pieces in the broth until cooked, approximately 4 minutes.

To serve, place a generous layer of boiled sliced onions on a large dish. Cover with the pasta and then the rest of the onions. Place the meat on top, and take the dish to the table where the guests can help themselves. The broth should be served alongside in individual soup bowls, and the entire dish is eaten with a spoon.

Nauryz, the spring equinox at the end of March, is another important celebration, whether marked at home in the city or back in the family village. Of course, the sharing of food plays a crucial role.

Traditionally, every household makes its *nauryz koje,* a thin, savory porridge made with seven ingredients: ground wheat, water, tail fat and the pelvic bone from a sheep, pieces of kazy (horse-meat sausage), garlic, and salt. Neighbors invite one another to their houses to taste some. It's also a time for sweets: *tary/tara,* or dried wheat fried in tail fat with honey and served with hot milk, and *chak-chak,* a kind of extra-small baursak drenched in honey and sugar that has been boiled to the hard ball stage, perhaps decorated with walnuts or raisins.

Islam has influenced the traditional feasts of the Uighur and Dungan communities (groups of Turkic and Chinese origin). Shek Beru is held just before Ramadan; traditionally, a sheep is slaughtered and shared with neighbors, with a particular focus on sharing with the elderly and the poor. After the fast, Oraza Ait is a period of feasting and celebration in which traditionally one would visit 40 houses to taste food and share hospitality over a period of about three days. On the day of Oraza Ait itself, children visit the mosque to eat a special fat pancake called *kokidi* that is prepared for them.

To mark a year since a significant death, for example, that of a parent, many families will follow the old Kazakh tradition of *as beru,* a special meal to celebrate the person's life and the end of mourning. In many families the meal must include baursak, as the smell of the frying as the breads puff up in the hot oil is supposed to reach the spirit in heaven.

Diet and Health

As in other former Soviet states, life expectancy in Kazakhstan improved during President Gorbachev's anti-alcohol campaign of the mid-1980s; fell sharply beginning in 1992; and then began to improve again after 1997. Compared to other newly independent states, its infant and maternal mortality rates remain relatively high, as are its rates for cancer (especially lung cancer, in line with rising tobacco use) and infectious and parasitic diseases such as tuberculosis and hepatitis. The rate of cardiovascular disease in Kazakhstan is higher than in the rest of the region, due to the high rate of consumption of saturated fatty acids and salt. Male life expectancy, at 59 years, is 11 years lower than that for females.

In common with other Central Asian countries, the core thinking on diet and health is based on the Galenic humoral theories popularized in the region by ibn Sina's *Canon of Medicine* in the 11th century. Many Kazakh dietary beliefs continue to center on helping to digest the large amounts of saturated fat in the diet. Green tea, sweets, fresh herbs, and fruit all help with the digestion of protein. Green tea also provides valuable antioxidants and vitamins that are helpful in balancing the animal-product-heavy diet. Nonetheless, vitamins A and C are found to be lacking in many people's diets.

Jane Levi

Further Reading

Akshalova, Bakhytgul. *Kazakh Tradition and Ways.* Almaty, Kazakhstan: Dyke Press, 2002.

Chenciner, Robert. "Kazakhstan—Horsemeat and Two Veg." Polo's Bastards. 2005. http://polos bastards.com/pb/kazakhstan-horsemeat.

Fergus, Michael, with Janar Jandosova. *Kazakhstan Coming of Age.* London: Stacey International, 2003.

The National Cooking of Kazakhs. Almaty, Kazakhstan: Kaysar, 1990.

Ward, Susan. *Russian Regional Recipes: Classic Dishes from Moscow and St Petersburg; the Russian Federation and Moldova; the Baltic States; Georgia, Armenia and Azerbaijan; and Central Asia and Kazakhstan.* London: Apple Press, 1993.

Korea

Overview

The Korean War (1950–1953), which was both a civil war and a proxy war for China, Russia, the United States, and the United Nations, who were involved in a larger cold war, ceased in a stalemate. An armistice was signed, and two distinct political nations were formed on the tiny Korean Peninsula in northeastern Asia.

North Korea (the Democratic People's Republic of Korea) is a Socialist state with a single-party dictatorship. The country has been extremely isolated since the end of the war. South Korea (the Republic of Korea) is noted for its rapid transition from an agrarian society to an industrialized country with a large and stable middle class.

North and South Koreans are ethnically and linguistically homogeneous. Regional dialect variations are relatively minor, and all are mutually intelligible. On the surface, the peninsula appears to have enjoyed relative peace for thousands of years; dramatic foreign invasions, although significant, have not punctuated Korean history as frequently as in many other parts of the world. However, the peninsula is located at a crossroads for northeastern Asia, and much of Korean history is about the resistance to incursions by larger or more aggressive neighbors: Chinese, Japanese, Russians, Mongols, and Manchurians.

During Korea's Chosun dynasty (1392–1910), Toyotomi Hideyoshi, who had recently unified Japan, demanded Korean assistance to attack China. Korea refused. In 1592, an army of 150,000 Japanese troops invaded the peninsula. Internal resistance, with aid from Chinese troops, quickly ended the invasion in 1593. The Japanese returned in 1597 but were again expelled by the Koreans and Chinese in 1598.

The Ming dynasty of China, which had been able to send massive numbers of troops to Korea in the 1590s, declined rapidly from internal disorder. The Manchu, a non-Chinese people from just north of Korea, ruled China beginning in 1644. The Manchus invaded Korea in 1627, and Korea negotiated a tributary relationship with the Manchu (Qing) dynasty. Manchu people had a long history of territorial disputes with Koreans, as well as a shared dynasty, the Parhae Kingdom (719–926).

The Meiji government of Japan (1868–1912) adopted Western expansionist philosophies and once again attacked China and Korea. The First Sino-Japanese War (1894–1895) was fought over control of Korea; the Russo-Japanese War (1904–1905) was fought over control of Manchuria and Korea. Japan defeated both China and Russia, and Korea became a Japanese protectorate in 1905. In 1910, representatives of both governments signed the Japan-Korea Annexation Treaty, and the emperor of Korea ceded sovereignty to the emperor of Japan. In contemporary Korea, the treaty is referred to as a coerced—and hence null—treaty; the day it was signed is popularly referred to as the "national day of shame."

Although Japanese occupation ended in 1945, Korea continued to dispute the legality of the treaty. In 1965, representatives from both countries signed the Treaty of Basic Relations, which also included a clause nullifying the previous treaty. This may seem like splitting hairs, but Korean identity is rooted in the idea of having successfully maintained cultural autonomy throughout its history as a tiny country surrounded by cultures who all developed formidable military capacity at one time or another. This stubborn sense of uniqueness permeates the culture, including cultural identity related to food.

Late Chosun-era reformers began incorporating Western ideas of progressive histories and Social Darwinism. Between 1905 and 1910, Korean scholars raced with competing Japanese colonial historiographies and textbooks to create a national narrative, *minjok*. Minjok as "people-family" became minjok as "race-nation" to forge a collective history of Koreans bound to a nation-state. The first leaders of North and South Korea came of age within this zeitgeist. Minjok forked into two distinct paths: North Korea's *juche* (self-reliance) policies and South Korea's continued use of minjok to fuel the country's remarkably rapid transition to modernity.

In 1948, Syngman Rhee became the first president of the Republic of Korea with U.S. support. He was born into a *yangban* (landed gentry or aristocratic) family and received the requisite classical Korean neo-Confucian education of all socially elite men. He learned English at a Methodist school and earned degrees from Harvard and Princeton. Rhee was actively anti-Communist and perceived as invested in maintaining status-quo power structures.

Kim Il Sung led North Korea from its founding until his death in 1994. He was raised in a religious Protestant household of modest means. His family moved to Manchuria (present-day northern China) during the Japanese occupation. There, Kim joined various anti–Japanese occupation and Communist organizations. Apparently, he rejected the traditional Korean feudal system at an early age. He returned to Korea in 1945 with a Soviet-backed army, gained peasant support, and quickly organized a domestic army. In 1948 Kim Il Sung became the leader of the Democratic People's Republic of Korea with Russian support.

Both the Republic of Korea and the Democratic People's Republic of Korea claimed to be the only legitimate government for the entire peninsula. Larger cold war issues aside, the internal problems on the peninsula had to do with the extreme socioeconomic stratification under the traditional feudal system. Wealth, status, and power were in the hands of just a few, while the vast majority of the population were peasants or indentured servants. The lower classes had almost no opportunity for upward mobility based on a heredity system of wealth and title perpetuation.

The political upheavals and economic changes of the 20th century created a significant Korean diaspora. For the first time in history, a people that had coterminous ethnic and linguistic borders for thousands of years began scattering around the world. Currently there are about seven million Koreans living outside of the peninsula. The largest populations are in China, Japan, the United States, and the former Soviet-bloc countries, with smaller populations in the Middle East, Latin America, Australia, and Europe. Everywhere Koreans went they took kimchi, the culturally iconic food for all Koreans.

Korea has a subarctic climate with four distinct seasons: spring, summer, autumn, and winter. Autumn and spring are temperate. The contrast between summer and winter is the most striking. Summers are hot and humid from maritime winds. In the winter, cold, dry air from the Mongolian plains creates below-freezing temperatures. When Korea was a preindustrialized, agrarian country, kimchi was the primary way of preserving vegetables for consumption during the bitter cold winter months.

Korean cuisine is both a reaction to the tyranny of geography and climate and an ingenious use of the same factors. Long before refrigeration and industrial foods, Koreans had to figure out how to keep foods from spoiling rapidly during the summer and how to store foods for the barren winter months. Salt from the sea was plentiful, so pickling was the answer to both.

Commercial production of kimchi began in the 1960s. South Korea instigated an international trade dispute with Japan when *kimuchi* (the Japanese pronunciation of kimchi) was proposed as an official food of the Atlanta Olympic games. At the same time Japanese manufacturers of kimuchi were increasing their share of international markets for kimchi. Kimchi received official certification from the CODEX Alimentarius Commission in 2001, giving Korea control over international standards

A plate of pickled cabbage, or kimchi, beside a traditional pickling jar from Korea. (Shutterstock)

and guidelines, a moment that was hailed as a cultural victory.

The Kimchi Museum in Seoul lists about 200 historical and contemporary kimchi recipes, made from various vegetables and seasonings. However, the most ubiquitous type is made with salted napa cabbage seasoned with red pepper flakes, chives, garlic, and salted fish. It is basically a spicy and garlicky sauerkraut: salted cabbage transformed through a process of lactofermentation into a more nutritious and digestible food with an extended shelf life.

🍽 Food Culture Snapshot

Kyoung-Mi Choe and Jung-Ho Baek moved to a suburb of Seoul after they decided to raise a family. Seoul has a population of over 10 million residents; even the suburbs are densely populated. Real estate is very tightly utilized, and kitchens tend to be small. Kyoung-Mi and her husband, Jung-Ho, were born in Seoul, but their parents are from southern provinces. Kyoung-Mi works as a pharmacist and Jung-Ho as a software developer. Their lifestyle and diet are representative of educated urbanites living in Seoul and include dishes from different regions of Korea as well as Western foods.

They begin their day at 6:30 A.M. with a breakfast consisting of the three most basic components of a Korean meal: boiled short-grain rice, kimchi, and soup. They both eat lunch with coworkers at around noon. Kyoung-Mi's boss orders Chinese takeout for the entire staff. Jung-Ho eats fast food for lunch with his coworkers. He has a McDonald's *bulgogi* burger; the patty is seasoned with a Korean barbecue marinade. Dinner is the largest meal of the day. The main components are rice, napa cabbage kimchi, and a soup of *dwenjang* (a miso-type bean paste). The remainder of the *banchan* (side dishes) are purchased from various vendors or at the supermarket.

Kyoung-Mi and Jung-Ho purchase the bulk of their household staples at a megamarket such as Carrefour or Costco. The rest of their pantry items are purchased at *shijang* (open-air markets), minimarkets, and specialty stores. Most of Seoul is comprised of mixed-use commercial and residential neighborhoods; even in suburban areas, stores are densely packed within and around large apartment complexes. Side streets with single-family homes are dotted with minimarkets, small specialty stores, and mom-and-pop restaurants. Seoul's public transportation is extensive, fast, and consistent. Shopping and eating out are very convenient, and delivery services are extensive.

Major Foodstuffs

During the Chosun dynasty, Korea was divided into eight provinces. Natural borders of mountains and waterways separated the provinces. Before modern transportation, travel between provinces and throughout the peninsula was difficult. Provincial styles of cooking developed based on local climates and available resources. Each province became known for different styles of kimchi and specialty dishes.

Traditionally, the most important kimchi making was done in late autumn. *Kimjang* was a culinary event, a process that involved many family members over a two- to three-day period, when enough kimchi was made to last from late autumn until early spring. For three to five months of the year, kimchi was the primary source of vegetables for agrarians. As winter continued, food scarcity and rationing became predictably problematic. A portion of the kimchi was stored in outdoor freezers, essentially a hole in the ground, to extend its shelf life and ensure a steady supply of food in late winter.

In South Korea, Kimjang is no longer a necessity and has become more a symbolic preparation event. Industrialized agriculture, government policies, and trade agreements have obliterated food-security issues. The country enjoys a year-round supply of fresh vegetables and foods from imported sources and domestic farms that utilize greenhouse technology during winter. Small kimchi refrigerators with adjustable temperature settings are used to store kimchi throughout the year.

North Korea accomplished temporary food self-sufficiency by industrialization of its agricultural system and through price-controlled trade with the Soviet Union. However, there were always reports of food rationing, with Pyongyang, the capital, receiving preferential provisions. While other Communist countries adapted to reforms, Kim Il Sung stubbornly adhered to his self-reliance policies. The country has had widely reported food-security issues since the early 1990s. The famines of 1995 were initiated by natural disasters and then worsened with the collapse of the Soviet Union. During the remainder of the decade, the country was plagued with repeated famines. Food insecurity and famine conditions persist to this day.

The traditional Korean diet is based on cereals and vegetables, with the bulk of protein coming from soy products, seafood, and sea vegetables. Historically, cooking oil and animal fats were extremely scarce, so Korean cooking makes very little use of frying. In South Korea, consumption of animal proteins increased dramatically with economic growth. From 1980 to 2003, per-capita consumption of beef, pork, and chicken increased from 25 pounds to almost 70 pounds per year. Dairy consumption increased by 2,450 percent from 1969 to 1987.

Rice is the staff of life in Korea. The word *bap* (cooked rice) is synonymous with food. Boiled short-grain rice is eaten everyday, at almost every meal, unless noodles are served. Rice and kimchi are the two most basic components of a Korean meal. Sweet rice is used in a limited number of savory dishes. It is more commonly ground into flour and used for rice cakes.

Common vegetables include radishes, napa cabbage, peppers, carrots, onions, burdock, mushrooms, squash, gourds, potatoes, lotus root, bamboo shoots, bellflower roots, leeks, watercress, *rocambole* (a type of garlic), shepherd's purse (a green related to mustard), and chives. Common fruits are Asian pears, apples, tangerines, persimmons, *yuja* (Asian citrus), Concord grapes, and melons.

Soybeans are an important component of the diet. Fresh beans are eaten as a snack; soybean sprouts are eaten in saladlike preparations or in soups. *Dubu* (tofu or bean curd) is eaten cold or fried, used as filler for meat stuffing, and added to soups and stews. Toasted and ground soybean flour is sprinkled on rice cakes or mixed with water and drunk as a cold beverage.

Soybeans are also used to make the three essential sauces of Korean cooking: *kanjang, dwenjang,* and *kochujang* (*jang* means "sauce"). Traditionally the sauces were made once a year in a series of related processes. Dwenjang and kanjang are made first. Blocks of *meju* (fermented soybeans) are covered with water, salt, and malt syrup. A few jujubes (also known as red or Chinese dates) and whole red peppers are added for seasoning. Oak charcoal is added to the mixture for color. After two months of curing, the meju will have crumbled and softened to become dwenjang (fermented bean paste, similar to miso). The liquid that is strained off is kanjang, or soy sauce. Kochujang, a red pepper paste, is made last, since it contains soy sauce.

It is hard to imagine Korean cooking without red chili peppers. However, these are a relatively new introduction with two possible routes of entry:

Koreans who met Portuguese Jesuits in Beijing during the 16th century, or a Dutch shipwreck on the island of Cheju-do in the mid-17th century. During the Chosun dynasty, accounts documented new vegetables and fruits from foreign lands including pumpkins, sweet potatoes, white gourds, apples, watermelons, and the chili pepper. Before the introduction of red chili peppers, cockscomb flower (*Celosia cristata*), safflower, and violet mustard were used to tint foods red. The most common type of pepper in Korea is a long finger-type variety. It is used fresh or dried in powder, flakes, or shredded into fine threads.

Mung beans are another important legume. Mung bean sprouts are prepared the same way as soybean sprouts. Sweetened mung beans are used in rice cake preparations. Ground beans are used to make pancakes, and the starch is used to make cellophane noodles. Wheat flour is used for savory crepes, pancakes, noodles, dumplings, and batters.

Seafood is abundant in Korea. Preservation techniques include brining, salting, and drying. Tiny salted fish and tiny shrimp are used in kimchi sauces. Dried anchovies, kelp, and other seaweed are common home-cooking items. Roasted laver is ubiquitous. Fish is usually salted and fried or added to stews.

Water or roasted barley tea is served with meals. Sweet or carbonated drinks are not taken with Korean meals. Teas include five-grain, citrus, persimmon leaf, ginger, ginseng, green, and wild sesame. *Sikhye* is a lightly fermented rice drink.

Cooking

Kanjang, dwenjang, and kochujang are the three basic sauces of Korean cooking. Basic seasonings include garlic, green onions, red pepper flakes, fresh ginger, toasted sesame seeds, toasted sesame oil, and rice wine vinegar. Sweeteners include sugar, honey, malt barley, and malt syrup. White beef stock and sun-dried anchovy or kelp broth are the most common foundations for soups and stocks. Home cooks often use bouillon granules as a shortcut.

Contemporary cooking evolved from agrarian kitchens. Until the early 1970s, many households still used charcoal-fueled stoves, and poorer families often struggled with fuel shortages, especially during the winter. Large cylinders of charcoal were burned in an *agungi* (firebox) built into a stone table. One agungi heated at least two burners. The stone tables retained ambient heat and functioned to keep prepared foods warm before they were served.

The fireboxes also functioned to heat adjoining rooms, which were built slightly higher than the kitchen on raised masonry frames covered with clay. Agungi had vents in the back that were opened on chilly days. Smoke from the firebox was directed through flues underneath the rooms. The flues were insulated with layers of organic materials: shale, straw, stone, and clay. A vertical chimney at the other end of the house provided a draft. *Ondol* (underfloor heating systems) are still very popular in Korea. High-tech versions are utilized in homes, spas, and hotels.

Modern Korean kitchens are tiny by North American standards. They have gas-fueled stoves with at least four burners. Oven cooking is virtually unknown outside of European-style bakeries. Refrigerators are also very small by North American standards. Traditional rice pots are made from cast iron; some are made from stone for specialty dishes. Almost all households have electric rice cookers with different heat settings for cooking rice

Red peppers on display in a market in South Korea, Busan Jagalchi Street. (Firststar | Dreamstime.com)

and then keeping it warm. Rice is always served piping hot.

Soups and stews are served boiling hot. Basic soups or stews are made daily. Soybean-sprout, spinach, and seaweed *guk* (soup) are commonly prepared at home. Dwenjang, the fermented soybean paste, is a reliable source of protein and is used to flavor soups and stews. Dwenjang *chigae* (stew) is a convenient way to use leftover vegetables, beef, or fish cakes.

Pickled vegetables are served cold. Most households specialize in just a few kimchi preparations. *Baechu* kimchi (napa cabbage kimchi), *ggakdugi* kimchi (pickled daikon radish kimchi), and cucumber kimchi are probably the ones most commonly prepared at home. Other vegetable preparations are served at room temperature or slightly chilled. Besides pickling, vegetables are also blanched and lightly dressed with sesame oil, toasted sesame seeds, and minced garlic. Salad-type kimchi preparations are becoming increasingly common. Tender, uncooked greens are dressed in a kimchi vinaigrette of red pepper flakes, garlic, rice wine vinegar, toasted sesame oil, and sugar.

Since vegetables are a major component of the Korean diet, a great deal of emphasis is placed on precise vegetable preparations. Texture and color are of paramount importance. Each component of *japchae,* a dish of cellophane noodles tossed with a mixture of vegetables, is cooked individually even though all the ingredients are tossed together before plating: Spinach is blanched, then sautéed. Carrots are cut into matchsticks and sautéed until just tender but still a bit crunchy. Onions are thinly sliced and cooked until translucent. Mushrooms are lightly cooked, just enough to release their juices. Everything is seasoned with salt, toasted sesame oil, and garlic.

Koreans love fruit and tend to take great care in its presentation. Fruit is eaten as a snack and almost automatically offered to guests. Carefully peeled and neatly cut platters of fruit are served for dessert on special occasions. Otherwise, Koreans do not eat dessert of any kind on a regular basis. There is a cultural tendency to dislike very sweet foods. The Korean language has several words for gradations of sweetness; a light, natural sweetness is considered the most pleasing.

Typical Meals

Since industrialization, South Koreans, especially women, have been abandoning the agrarian life in droves. The population of the greater Seoul region is 24.5 million, about half the total population of South Korea. Extensive transportation systems throughout the country have made domestic travel very accessible. The country's smaller cities, such as the port city of Pusan and Taejon, have fewer Western food options. Eating habits tend to differ more according to generation than by region. Younger Koreans tend to eat more white bread, beef, and sugar. Older Koreans tend to remain faithful to rice, kimchi, and soup as the trinity of the Korean meal.

Korean cuisine has been extensively cataloged and documented in historical texts, museums, cultural organizations, and cookbooks. The royal court of the Chosun dynasty delighted in gathering regional specialties. Today, regional tourist centers heavily promote local agriculture and dishes. South Korea is dotted with living museums, called folk villages, where visitors get glimpses of daily life in rural villages as they existed 50 to 100 years ago. Regardless of industrialization, Korean people are not in danger of losing their food culture.

Traditionally, Koreans sit on the floor for meals, usually on cushions. Many families now have Western-style tables. Food is eaten with steel or silver chopsticks and spoons. Rice is the focal point of the meal, kimchi is a constant companion, and at least one soup is eaten every day. Korean meals prepared at home expand on these basic components to include additional side dishes. Restaurant food varies widely. South Korea is a very entrepreneurial country, and new dishes and styles of eating are created frequently.

Koreans tend to be early risers. Breakfast is eaten before work, anytime between 5:30 and 7 A.M. Breakfast tends to be a simple but hearty meal of rice, kimchi, and soup. Koreans do not have separate breakfast foods. Younger Koreans might have some bread purchased at a European-style bakery for breakfast.

Eating out for lunch is common and can be very inexpensive. Street food, food stalls, small snack shops, fast food, and food courts tend to be popular with students and young people, who are more likely to have noodles or bread for lunch than older Koreans. *Kimbap* (rice and vegetables wrapped in seaweed), *ddukbokki* (rice cakes and fish cakes in a spicy chili sauce), instant ramen, sandwiches, and burgers are common lunch items for students.

The Korean table is communal; all side dishes are shared. Koreans are very social eaters and love eating with family, friends, or coworkers. It's very common to go out for lunch and dinner with coworkers. Since Koreans also have a strong work ethic, lunch tends to be a bit rushed, and restaurants serve orders at astonishing speed. Again, there are no separate foods for lunch per se. Lunch meals tend to be lighter than dinner, but many of the same foods are served.

Dinner is the biggest meal of the day and is eaten at a more relaxed pace. Family mealtime is still honored. Unlike at lunch, rice is a must for dinner. Soups or stews tend to be heavier or more extravagant than those served for breakfast. Larger portions of protein are usually served, such as panfried fish, short ribs braised in soy sauce, barbecued beef, or barbecued pork marinated in chili sauce. More kimchi and vegetable dishes are also served.

Koreans cook a variety of dishes at the table. *Chongol,* one-pot stews of meat, poultry, or seafood and vegetables, with noodles sometimes added, are cooked in electric casseroles. Barbecue is cooked on aluminum grills or stone griddles over portable propane burners.

Eating Out

Dining-out options are ample, almost all Korean food or Koreanized food. The Chinese are the largest minority group in Korea. For most of Korea's history, the peninsula did not share a border with China. Chinese began moving into the frontier between Manchuria and Korea in the 19th century, and some Chinese immigrated to Korea. Chinese restaurants were the first non-Korean dining options in the country. Common and special occasions are still punctuated with meals at Chinese restaurants.

Seafood and soybean products such as dubu (tofu) are the most common source of protein. Raw-seafood restaurants serve sashimi and sushi in the traditional Korean manner or in the Japanese style. Koreans who were educated abroad introduced Americanized sushi. Korean *hwe* (raw fish) is served with a vinegar-chili condiment (*cho kochujang*) and salad greens for wrapping (*ssam*).

Korea was never colonized by a Western power, nor does it have a history of Western immigration. European influences in food were filtered through Japan, where the British introduced curry. Packaged curry sauce is a mixture of spices, mostly turmeric, in a solidified suspension of oil and flour. The Portuguese introduced breaded cutlets (*tonkatsu*) and croquettes to Japan. Curry and tonkatsu are popular light meals in Korea. Croquettes are purchased at Korean-European fusion bakeries and eaten as snacks.

American influences entered Korea during the Korean War and continued with the U.S. military presence in South Korea. (South Korea is dotted with more than two dozen U.S. military installations.) American influences were limited to products such as instant coffee, powdered milk, Spam, and hard liquor until the industrialization process reached the level of globalization.

During Japanese occupation, British and American missionaries taught English in schools, and Korean elites began sending their children abroad for higher education. Middle-class Koreans view English-language acquisition as a marketable skill and American education as a window into modernity, necessary to be active participants in globalization. Koreans who had left for educational and economic opportunities in other countries began returning to take advantage of a growing domestic economy hungry for foreign products. Domestic and foreign corporations began responding to an increasing demand for convenience foods and international flavors. Processed foods and American-style fast food began rapidly proliferating. Ketchup, mayonnaise, bottled dressing, canned tuna, and sausages are now fairly common ingredients.

Snacks are purchased from sidewalk vendors or at food courts. *Pochang matcha* (outdoor food stalls) specialize in a specific dish or a small group of related dishes, which can be eaten on the spot or more commonly as takeout. In the evening tented pochang matcha serve as casual drinking spots.

Korea has an extensive drinking culture; *anju,* food eaten with drinks, includes almost all variations from light snacks to elaborate platters. Mom-and-pop businesses serve *soju* (grain alcohol) and *makuli* (unfiltered rice wine) with dried squid. *Hofs* (pubs) serve beer and fried chicken. Western-style restaurants and clubs serve wine, cocktails, and hard liquor with expensive platters of anju. Male-dominated corporate drinking is usually conducted in restaurants with private rooms. Traditional holidays and special occasions include ceremonial drinking.

Restaurants are highly specialized. Noodle shops serve specific noodles. *Kalguksu* (literally, "knife noodles," or noodles cut with a knife) are thick, soft wheat noodles served in meat or seafood stock with onions and sliced beef or shellfish. *Nengymyun* (literally meaning "cold noodles"), a North Korean cold buckwheat noodle dish, is a traditional winter dish that is now a summertime favorite. Restaurants serving *chajang-myun* (Chinese noodles in black bean sauce) often have front-window stations to show hand-pulled noodles being made.

Korean barbecue restaurants use lump charcoal or gas-fired grills built into tabletops. A few places still use large charcoal cylinders that are brought to the table in portable grills. Diners are served banchan (small shared dishes) and rice, as well as marinated beef, pork, or poultry that is cooked at the table. Marinades are based on either soy sauce or chili paste, to which garlic, sugar, and toasted sesame oil are added. Chili-paste marinades usually include rice wine vinegar.

A food market in the Dongmyo district of Seoul, South Korea. (Sebastian Czapnik | Dreamstime.com)

Ssam, a style of eating, is not limited to raw seafood. Grilled meat or steamed pork belly is wrapped in lettuce leaves with slivers of raw garlic and thinly sliced raw green peppers, and served with *ssamjang,* literally, "wrap sauce."

Koreans eat soup almost every day with breakfast, lunch, or dinner. White beef stock, anchovy broth, or dried seaweed broth serves as the basis for light soups or noodle broths. Restaurants don't just serve soup; they serve specific types of *tang,* meat- or poultry-based soups. *Samgyetang,* game hens stuffed with sweet rice and cooked in a stock of ginseng, jujubes, and garlic, is considered a medicinal food. Ginseng is valued for its purported health benefits.

Bibimbap literally means "mixed rice." Many restaurants serve this dish, but restaurants that specialize in it tend to offer more elaborate versions. *Dolsot bibimbap* is almost exclusively a restaurant dish. It is served in a hot stone pot (*dolsot*) that creates a delicious crust at the bottom of the bowl.

On weekends, younger Koreans frequently go bar and restaurant hopping, with predinner drinks at a club, an appetizer at a trendy restaurant, and a main course at another restaurant, followed by a night of drinking and partying.

Hanjeongsik is a multicourse meal based on royal and aristocratic ways of eating. Contemporary interpretations are often presented as tourist attractions;

Bibimbap. (Courtesy of the Korea Tourism Organization)

dishes can vary widely, but the general idea is to serve a dozen or two regional preparations that also represent a range of ingredients and cooking methods. A meal might begin with a cold appetizer and abalone *juk* (rice porridge), followed by one or more of the following dishes: braised beef, grilled whole fish, *sinseollo* (hot pot made with meatballs, mushrooms, and vegetables), *chongol* (casserole-type hot pots), *gulchupan* (nine varieties of vegetables served with minicrepes and dipping sauces), marinated raw blue crab, cold seafood salads, stuffed mussels, steamed clams, crispy fried whole prawns, raw seafood plates, seaweed salad, stuffed peppers, battered and fried vegetables, and savory crepes. Various soups, kimchis, and salad-type preparations fill in the courses. Desserts include sweet-rice punch, cinnamon persimmon punch, or *omija* tea (five-flavored tea), fresh and dried fruit, and a selection of rice cakes and Korean cookies.

Special Occasions

Shamanism (known in Korea as Muism; the shaman is called a *mudang*) is the oldest religion in Korea, and a shaman might be consulted regarding marital or financial decisions, as an intercessor with the gods. Missionaries from Central Asia and China introduced Buddhism to Korea in the fourth century during the Three Kingdoms period of the Goguryeo, Baekje, and Silla dynasties; it became the official religion of all three states. The tradition continued when the three kingdoms were unified as the Koryo dynasty (917–935). The Chosun dynasty (1392–1910) adhered to the sociopolitical tenets of Korean neo-Confucianism and took a policy of tolerating Buddhism and relegating shamanism to rural areas. Figures vary widely, but it is estimated that approximately half of all Koreans who profess religious affiliation are Buddhists; the other half are Christians. Shamanism has declined rapidly during the past few decades.

Catholic missionaries first arrived in the 17th century. Koreans living in Manchuria first met Protestant missionaries from Scotland in 1884. Presbyterian Reverend John Ross helped translate the first Korean-language version of the Bible. In the

1880s, Methodists and Presbyterians from America came to Korea and worked as teachers and doctors. Medical missionaries helped build Korea's first Western hospital. The majority of Christians are Protestant, 70 percent of whom are Presbyterian. Christmas foods include barbecued *kalbi* (ribs), cellophane noodles with mixed vegetables, savory crepes, battered and fried vegetables, special pickles, and beef soup and rice.

Buddha's birthday is the most important holiday for Korean Buddhists. Weeklong festivities include lighting strings of colorful lanterns, lantern parades, and eating special foods. Many temples provide tea and *sanchae bibimbap,* rice mixed with wild greens.

Major cultural holidays shared by all Koreans include the lunar New Year (*seollal*) and harvest moon festival (*chuseok*). Dumpling and rice cake soup is the traditional New Year's dish. *Songpyeon* are crescent-shaped rice cakes that represent the moon for the harvest moon festival. Regional stuffing variations include pumpkin, chestnut paste, sesame seeds, and acorns. Five-colored songpyeon are a specialty of Seoul. Ingredients such as cinnamon powder, strawberry syrup, and gardenia seeds are used to tint the dough. White, pink, green, brown, and yellow represent the harmony of nature. In Pyongyang they make clam-shaped songpyeon. The ability to make aesthetically pleasing songpyeon is an auspicious sign of beautiful babies to come, especially lovely daughters.

Many families with a deceased parent or parents integrate memorial services into seollal and chuseok. These services are typically held at the eldest son's home. *Charye,* a ritualized system of presenting and consuming food, includes symbolic and seasonal dishes. The foods are placed on the table in a specific order following an east–west orientation. A variety of whole fruits is a must, as are ceremonial wine, rice cakes and cookies, whole fish, and seasonal vegetable dishes. Fresh vegetables are sliced, dipped in batter, and panfried to make *jun.* Vegetables are also chosen for color; spinach, mung bean sprouts, and fern brake (a kind of fiddlehead) are blanched and lightly seasoned. Kimchi is served freshly prepared, never fermented. Some families include whole dried cuttlefish and whole chicken.

Dried fruits include persimmon, jujubes, and apricots. At the head of the table are bowls of rice and rice cake soup; at the opposite end on a smaller table is the ceremonial wine.

Baekil is celebrated to mark the first 100 days of a baby's life. A variety of symbolic rice cakes are served, such as songpyeon for a healthy mind and white rice cakes for purity and longevity. For first-birthday celebrations, babies are dressed in *tolbok,* traditional clothes made of silk tied with a long silk belt representing longevity. A ceremonial table is prepared with the child at the head of the table. Towers of rice cakes and mounds of fresh whole fruit are served with soup and rice. Various objects including a book, needle and thread, and a ruler are placed in front of the child; whichever one he or she grabs first is considered a sign of the life to come. Books represent a scholarly life, a toy weapon represents warriorship, and thread represents longevity. Neighbors and friends give 24-carat gold rings. Children's Day is celebrated on May 5. Children are given presents, taken on field trips, given their favorite treats, and generally doted on.

South Korean wedding ceremonies have changed dramatically over the past few decades and continue to evolve and adapt to changing social structures. Contemporary weddings typically incorporate elements of Korean and Western-style ceremonies in varying degrees. Many couples have their *hanbok* (traditional clothes) custom made, as they will be worn again on traditional holidays. Western-style dresses and tuxedoes are available for rent at bridal shops. Wedding halls cater to both markets with turnkey packages. Noodles are served to represent hopes for a long and happy life together.

Diet and Health

Taoism was introduced into Korea in the seventh century. The first Taoist temple was built in the 12th century and was occupied by 11 Korean Taoist monks. However, Taoism never developed into an organization of believers or as a distinct branch of thought on the peninsula. Evidence indicates that elements of Taoism were integrated into shamanism and Buddhism. The national flag of South

Korea has the yin-yang symbol in the center and an I Ching trigram at each corner.

Traditional Korean medicine, *hanbang,* is based on the concepts of *chi, eum-yang* (yin and yang), and the five elements: wood, fire, earth, metal, and water. Concepts borrowed from Taoism were translated into Korean ethnomedicine and continue to evolve. Hanbang has a long contiguous history on the peninsula going back thousands of years.

Historically, hanbang had support from various royal dynasties and continued support from postwar governments. Aspects of it permeate Korean culture and persist even in diaspora societies, including among foreign-born Koreans, regardless of educational level and understanding of modern medicine. It is not considered an alternative medicine. Koreans tend to use hanbang remedies for preventative care, for strengthening the immune system, and for detoxification, general weakness, or chronic conditions, while they use Western medicine for acute problems. There is a cultural tendency toward syncretism; the two approaches are viewed as complementary, not contradictory. Hanbang also places importance on proper eating habits. Orally ingested remedies are not just in the form of herbal teas and tonics; food is also medicine.

Modernization has only made hanbang even more popular. It was always a part of Korean spa culture with hot herbal dips, aromatherapy rooms, and salt-bed treatments. More recently, hanbang herbs have been integrated into toiletries and expensive skin-care products. Marketing campaigns incorporate themes of nostalgia as the "natural approach of our ancestors."

Buddhism influenced virtually every aspect of Korean culture. Wonhyo (617–686), a Buddhist monk and great scholar, took Buddhism out of the exclusive realm of the ruling elites and aristocracy. He chose to travel the countryside, spreading Buddhism as penance after siring a son with a Silla princess. Pure-land Buddhism and meditative Buddhism had the greatest impact on Korean religious beliefs. Chinese Ch'an Buddhism was introduced into Korea in the seventh century, where it became interpreted as Son; almost 500 years later it would become Zen in Japan. Son Buddhism is the dominant form of Buddhism in Korea today.

Mahayana monks developed strictly vegetarian temple food. Temple cooking utilizes vegetables and herbs harvested in the mountains. This aspect of temple cooking probably influenced the Korean tendency to make kimchi out of virtually any vegetable. "Hot" vegetables such as garlic, green onion, rocambole (a kind of garlic), and leeks are not used. Temple kimchis do not include salted or fermented fish. The main seasonings are salt, soy sauce, red chili powder, ginger, and sesame seeds. Pine nuts and perilla leaves are used as thickeners. Some temples are renowned for specific types of kimchi.

Susan Ji-Young Park

Further Reading

Hepinstall, Hi Soo Shin. *Growing Up in a Korean Kitchen.* Berkeley, CA: Ten Speed Press, 2001.

Lee, Cecilia Hae-Jin. *Quick and Easy Korean Cooking.* San Francisco: Chronicle Books, 2009.

Lee, Chun Ja, Hye Won Park, and Kwi Young Kim. *The Book of Kimchi.* Seoul, Korea: Korean Overseas Culture and Information Service, 1998.

Pettid, Michael J. *Korean Cuisine: An Illustrated History.* London: Reaktion Books, 2008.

Lao People's Democratic Republic

Overview

The Lao People's Democratic Republic (Lao PDR), a landlocked country in Southeast Asia, is classified as a low-income food-deficit country. After decades of war, including fighting for independence from French colonial control and surviving the bombing inflicted by the American secret war, the country remains food insecure. The Communist Pathet Lao took over the country in 1975, ending the royal rule and feudal governance. The persistent poverty is reflected in the nutritional status of its population, with nearly half its children under five underweight, and many stunted and wasted. The government has been struggling to improve food security in the country.

The ethnic Lao in the Lao PDR represent 68 percent of the population. In addition, the Lao government recognizes 65 distinct ethnic groups but stresses "unity in diversity" among all ethnic groups. Ethnic minorities such as the Akha and Hmong cross national borders, while other groups occupy marginal lands such as dense upland forests. Most ethnic minorities are adapted to upland mountain ecologies. Theravada Buddhism is the dominant religion of the Lao in the Lao PDR; however, the Pathet Lao discouraged religious practice, and only recently have young men returned to the practice of being ordained as monks in their local temples.

🍽 Food Culture Snapshot

Khamla and Manivong live in a small village close to the old royal capital of Luang Prabang. They own a small farm and work it with Manivong's brother. They have four school-age children, three girls and one boy, but Manivong remembers her son who died at six months of age. Each morning, they steam glutinous rice, and they generally eat two rice meals a day, at dawn and dusk. Their children carry sticky rice in a basket along with some leftover fish with them to school to eat at midday. Their son watches for frogs and lizards he can capture and grill for lunch, but if his sisters see him, he must bring all the food home to share with the family. Like other families in their village, they might sit down in the evening to a basket of steamed sticky rice; a bowl of *padek* (fermented fish paste); a plate of fresh greens including cilantro, mint, basil, watercress, lettuce, and wild greens from the forest with a chili-based dipping sauce; and a pot of fish soup with bamboo shoots.

The rice comes from their own fields, along with beans and garlic that Manivong tends in their household garden. Most days, they are able to catch small fish at the edge of their fields. They gather bamboo shoots and mushrooms in the forest, where Manivong knows the location of wild foods. Manivong has been trying to teach her daughters how to recognize wild forest foods and process them to remove the toxins, but her daughters don't like the taste of wild foods and want to be taken into Luang Prabang where they can eat more refined foods and even French baguettes.

Major Foodstuffs

The Lao PDR is primarily agricultural. The key marker of the collective identity of lowland Lao is the use of glutinous or sticky rice as their daily staple. More recent arrivals to the Lao PDR such as the Yao and Hmong prefer to use nonglutinous rice. The Lao appreciate the qualities of glutinous rice and believe that glutinous rice is more nutritious and more aromatic than any other kind of rice. Rice adapts to local conditions, and rice surveys in the country have found over 3,000 distinct rice varieties, most of them glutinous. Glutinous rice is generally hardier and survives drought, salinity, and floods better than its nonglutinous relatives. Most glutinous rice is consumed close to its place of production. It is eaten by hand; a ball is formed by hand with a thumb-size indentation and then is used to scoop up some sauce or side dish.

In the forests of the Lao PDR, wild yams, cassava, and taro are collected by women who know where to find them and how to process them to remove poisons, if necessary, by soaking, cooking, and drying the roots. They also collect mushrooms, bamboo products, wild greens, and herbs. Greens, vegetables, and aromatic herbs are available from household gardens and collected from forests; they are particularly valued for their freshness and texture. Recent development projects on home gardens in rural areas have dramatically increased the amount of fresh vegetables available to households. Wild greens and herbs are often available free or at very low cost to rural households. Vegetables are used in soups and in quick stir-fries.

Fish and fermented fish products are important parts of Lao diets. The Mekong River supplies people from the Lao PDR with an abundant supply of river fish. The favorite, the giant Mekong catfish, whose properties have reached mythical proportions, is near extinction. Lao make use of fermented fish products made in the household to suit the taste of family members. Accompanying most rice

An old woman in ethnic clothing works in a rice paddy. (Shutterstock)

meals is a sauce or paste made from fermented fish or shellfish. The salted, dried fish are pounded and packed with toasted rice and rice husks in ceramic jars for a month or more. Rice husks along with salt break down the fish, and special ceramic jars absorb the odor. Fish products that are fermented become "cooked" and are no longer considered "raw." In its thicker form, called padek, fermented fish is served as a dish with rice. Many poor households may have only padek to eat with rice.

Roasted glutinous rice powder adds texture and taste to Lao dishes. It is made by dry-roasting glutinous rice in a dry pan until brown and fragrant. It is then cooled and ground to a powder. It can be stored for several weeks.

Cooking

Cooking for the Lao means to prepare food for consumption, not just to apply heat. Thus fermenting, sun-drying, and preparing raw dishes are important parts of the cooking process. Lao meals require the freshest possible ingredients, prepared simply by steaming, boiling, or grilling. Grilling of meats is most often done by men. However, everyday food preparation and cooking of rice are usually done by women and young girls.

Fermenting is one of the most important food-processing techniques in the Lao PDR. Fermented fish products are processed in rural households or purchased ready prepared at the market in towns and cities where modern neighbors might not appreciate the smell emitted by jars of fermenting fish. Other items such as bamboo shoots and bean curd can be fermented as well. Often, the water used for washing rice or the initial cooking of rice is used in the fermenting process. Sun-drying is another useful food-processing technique in communities without refrigeration. Vegetables can be sun-dried, as well as beef, water buffalo, and leftover glutinous rice. Vegetables may also be salted or pickled in vinegar to form the basis for sour salads or side dishes.

Glutinous rice must be soaked in water for several hours or overnight before it is steamed in a conical bamboo steamer. The cooked rice is then turned out, patted with a paddle or wooden spoon to remove lumps, and packed in rice baskets until ready to eat.

Soups are boiled and vary from the simplest flavored water to more complex fish broths. Grilling food over wood or charcoal has a long tradition in the Lao PDR. Grilled vegetables also add texture to many different recipes. When the cooking is done over an open fire, children emulate the technique by grilling frogs, fish, and insects over small fires. A variety of wrapped foods (*mok*) are roasted on hot embers. Fish and chicken pieces are easily turned on a grill when they are wedged between strips of split bamboo. The following Lao version of barbecued chicken traveled from the Lao PDR through northeastern Thailand into the specialty shops of Bangkok and around the world.

Gai yang being sold at an open air market in Laos. (Shutterstock)

Gai Yang (Lao-Style Barbecue Chicken)

1 chicken, split open (or use legs and thighs)

Marinade

1 stalk lemongrass, sliced

3 tbsp coriander roots, minced

Pinch salt

1 tbsp fish sauce

2 tsp white pepper

5 cloves garlic

(Coconut milk to moisten paste if necessary)

Grind marinade ingredients in a small food processor. Rub into the chicken pieces, and marinate at least 3 hours or overnight in the refrigerator. Grill until bottom side is brown; turn over and grill until juices run clear. Serve with steamed glutinous rice and papaya salad.

Typical Meals

In rural and urban communities, glutinous rice with side dishes of soup, vegetables, and fresh or fermented fish may be prepared for breakfast, with the leftover dishes and rice eaten at noon and evening meals. Towns and cities provide the opportunity to purchase fresh baguettes, which are consumed with relishes for breakfast or snacks. Fruit is also a common snack, often dipped in a mixture of sugar, salt, and dried chilies. When rural children take a basket of glutinous rice to school for a midday meal, they may pick up edible leaves, herbs, insects, fish, or frogs to go with their rice.

Most rural meals are served and consumed on woven floor mats or at low bamboo tables. Lao households and restaurants provide places for hand washing, since they use small balls of sticky rice as scoops for side dishes. Leaves, herbs, and greens can also be used as wrappers to carry food to the mouth. Side dishes are served all at once with baskets of sticky rice. *Jeaw,* the Lao version of a hot chili sauce, accompanies most meals. It is common for people to offer the best pieces from a side dish to others at the table. A choice piece of fish or meat, for example, might be picked up and placed on the plate of a favored relative or guest.

The best-known Lao dish is *laap,* a spicy minced fish or meat dish served primarily on festive occasions in villages but widely available in restaurants in the country and overseas. This dish condenses many significant contrasts; real men eat *laap dip* (raw laap), while women and those concerned about the health risks associated with eating raw meat prefer *laap suk,* or cooked laap. The following version is cooked lightly, but it could be modified for other taste preferences.

Beef Laap

1 lb lean ground beef

1 green onion, finely chopped

2 chilies, chopped

1-in. piece galangal, finely chopped

2 stalks lemongrass, finely chopped

1 tbsp fish sauce

2 tbsp lime juice

1½ tbsp roasted rice powder

½ c chopped mint

½ c chopped cilantro

Cook beef lightly in a nonstick pan, and let cool. Mix with all other ingredients. Adjust seasonings to taste, and serve on a bed of lettuce with extra cilantro and mint.

A legacy of French colonialism, baguettes have made their way into Lao meals at breakfast and in the form of baguette sandwiches that blend French and Vietnamese food items. In the cities and towns of the Lao PDR, these baguettes replace rice-based meals.

Eating Out

In a country that is food insecure like the Lao PDR, one might not expect great restaurants. But in cities like Vientiane and Luang Prabang wonderful

French restaurants are to be found, with Lao chefs trained in the French culinary arts. Restaurants are relatively new and cater to the newly developed tourist market in the country. Young tourists are often attracted to eating sticky rice with their hands. But Lao cuisine is not as well known as Thai or Vietnamese. Lao cuisine is often considered crude and rustic compared with Thai or Vietnamese cuisine. Lao cuisine is harder to replicate in overseas restaurants because of its reliance on aromatic and bitter herbs that are rarely imported or grown outside of the country. Many greens and herbs are wild forest foods gathered by villagers and consumed immediately.

In all areas of the Lao PDR, noodle or rice soup is available at small stands, served with platters of fresh vegetables and greens to be eaten on the side or submerged in the hot soup. Fried grasshoppers sold in street stalls in Lao towns provide protein for poor rural migrants and get rid of pesky grasshoppers that could damage crops.

Special Occasions

Lao people love parties and share food generously on any occasion. When people recover from an illness, move away, or change status, their souls may wander and need to be called back through a *sukhwan* ritual to entice their souls to reside firmly in their bodies, held in place with strings tied around their wrists. Spirit souls are attracted back through these household and community rituals, centered around a treelike structure draped with white strings, surrounded by dishes of cooked rice, boiled eggs, fruit, and whiskey. Following the ritual blessings, food and drink are shared among all participants.

Theravada Buddhist rituals of food sharing were discouraged by the Pathet Lao but are reemerging in many towns. Transplanting rice in particular is marked by ritual; during transplanting, the spirits of the rice fields are fed and honored with blessings. Community-wide feasts of merit are held in the uplands of the Lao PDR, when a buffalo might be sacrificed. In the uplands, people give feasts to gain political and spiritual potency. Fermented rice liquor plays a key role in many Lao celebrations, as consumption of alcohol creates links between the living and the dead, humans and spirits, and guests and hosts.

Diet and Health

Years of war reduced the formerly self-sufficient country to conditions that threatened the diet and health of much of the population. The Lao PDR is now a food-insecure country with high malnutrition rates. Insufficient food consumption, in addition to infection and poor health, is the primary cause of malnutrition. Poor diets can also contribute to other problems such as iron deficiency, vitamin A deficiency (resulting in night blindness), and iodine deficiency (resulting in goiter), a common problem in some regions of the country.

The Lao government, along with United Nations partners, is working toward reducing the high infant and under-five mortality rates, as well as maternal mortality rates and malnutrition. The national prevalence of critical food poverty was around 18 percent, indicating that nearly one in five people did not have enough income to buy the food necessary to meet their daily minimum energy requirements. The upland peoples depend more on natural resources than food purchases, but their wild food sources are increasingly threatened as forests are eroded.

Communities depend on traditional herbal medicines, since few people outside of cities have access to primary health care. Herbal medicines are part of health-maintenance systems, not simply treatments for specific diseases. Herbal medicines can be taken orally in alcohol, water, or rice water; swallowed in pill form; or rubbed on the body. They can also be used for a steam "sauna." Herbal saunas are particularly popular with women. Most striking is the number of products used in each concoction; common ingredients include chilies, red ginger, sesame oil, cottonseed, opium, bark, leaves, roots, and ground snail shells. Spirit doctors and shamans practice in some minority communities.

Penny Van Esterik

Further Reading

Davidson, Alan. *Fish and Fish Dishes of Laos.* Rutland, VT: Charles Tuttle, 1975.

Du Pont De Bie, Natacha. *Ant Egg Soup: The Adventures of a Food Tourist in Laos.* London: Hodder and Stoughton, 2004.

Hongthong, Penn. *Simple Laotian Cooking.* New York: Hippocrene Books, 2003.

Hongthong, Penn. *Taking Refuge: Lao Buddhists in North America.* Tempe: Program for Southeast Asian Studies, Arizona State University, 2003.

Lao Cuisine. http://laocuisine.la/.

Sing, Phia. *Traditional Recipes of Laos.* London: Prospect Books, 1981.

Van Esterik, Penny. *Food Culture in Southeast Asia.* Westport, CT: Greenwood Press, 2008.

Van Esterik, Penny. "From Hunger Foods to Heritage Foods: Challenges to Food Localization in Lao PDR." In *Fast Food/Slow Food: The Cultural Economy of the Global Food System,* edited by R. Wilk, 83–96. Lanham, MD: Altimira Press, 2006.

Macau

Overview

Macau (also spelled Macao) and its two associated islands of Coloane and Taipa is a tiny enclave located at the mouth of the Pearl River Estuary. Originally a small village populated by southern Chinese fisherman, Macau is the site of the earliest—and longest—European settlement in Asia. Portuguese merchants were the first to stop in Macau, which happened to be located on their Asian trade route, halfway between Japan and Melaka. The Chinese, being highly suspicious of foreigners, at first granted them only the right to drop anchor. Eventually they grew to tolerate the Portuguese traders who brought silver from Japan and were so eager to purchase Chinese silks, ceramics, and tea. Over four centuries, the Portuguese gradually extended their presence to erecting onshore storage for their warehouses and later establishing a permanent settlement and self-administration rights. Ultimately the Chinese lost all control of the enclave after the Opium War, when Macau was formally ceded to the Portuguese.

Macau was returned to China in 1999, but 500 years of exposure to Portuguese ways left an indelible impression on all aspects of life. Today, the local population is 95 percent Chinese, mostly of Cantonese or Fujianese descent, with Portuguese (both expatriates and local-born), as well as those of mixed Chinese Portuguese descent—the Macanese—making up the remainder. A contemporary visitor to Macau looking to experience the cuisine would find that most restaurants offer either Cantonese or Portuguese cuisine, with a small minority offering international alternatives such as Thai, Japanese, French, and fusion. Few restaurants serve only Macanese cuisine, and until recently Macanese dishes were usually found in Chinese or Portuguese restaurants as part of the larger menu or were prepared in private homes. This is perhaps reflective of the tiny Macanese demographic. Traditional Macanese recipes were thus prepared by only a small number of people, mostly female homemakers who tended to guard their recipes jealously. This has raised concerns that Macanese food culture is in danger of disappearing. The 1999 handover, however, has caused many local and expatriate Macanese to reexamine their unique identity, and happily this has resulted in a resurgent interest in Macanese foodways.

🍽 Food Culture Snapshot

Evelyn and Rick Lopes are a middle-class Macanese couple. Evelyn, who speaks both Cantonese and English, is of Chinese descent, but her family has lived in Macau for generations and consider themselves to be *ngo mun yan,* or "Macau people." Her husband, Rick, is of mixed Portuguese-Chinese descent. His primary languages are Cantonese and English, although he knows a smattering of Portuguese as well. Both work in one of the large casinos, Evelyn in marketing and Rick as security. Their food habits are typical of the local population's, which are very similar to those of Hong Kong. Breakfast either is a quick meal of toast and coffee at home or is eaten in one of the many *cha chaan teng* cafés before work. Ham and macaroni in chicken broth, preserved mustard greens with minced pork in soup noodles, or pineapple buns (sweet rolls with a cracked cookie-like crust on top) sliced and filled with a wedge of butter are typical choices. Rick eats lunch at the casino cafeteria, but Evelyn packs a hot thermos full of rice and leftovers from the night before. This may contain a chicken curry and some boiled green vegetables, *minchi* (a dish of ground meat and potatoes dish), or some salted fish. If she does not bring her lunch, she might go back to the cha chaan teng to order three-treasures rice (a selection of three different roasted meats over rice with some Chinese broccoli), *ma kai yau* (a local dish of fried potatoes with *bacalhau*—salted preserved fish), or fried fish croquettes. Similar to their neighbors in Hong Kong, dinner usually consists of rice, a soup, and two to three dishes that include vegetables and meat. If Rick is working late, he might go out after his shift for an additional meal of *siu yeh* with his friends. Favorite foods at this time include a sweet egg tea made with medicinal herbs, *cha cha* (pronounced *tsa tsa;* a Malaysian dessert of shaved coconut, taro, cream, sugar, and coconut milk), or long fried dough sticks called *yeow tsa gwai*, dunked in plain white congee (rice porridge).

There are only three "fresh" markets in Macau, and these are open twice a day—once in the morning at around 10 A.M. and again at 5 P.M., to catch office workers on their way home. Most Macanese will shop for their staples in these markets almost daily; freshness of ingredients is valued, and, in any case, homes and kitchens are small, limiting the amount of bulk purchases that can be made. There are well-stocked supermarkets in Macau, but these are frequented more for household items, frozen foods, snacks, and imported foods. There are generational differences in shopping preferences, too—the younger generation will do more shopping in supermarkets, while the older generation will purchase almost all their foods in the open markets and traditional specialty stores.

Minchi

Pronounced "meen tse" in Cantonese, this is probably a corruption of the English word *minced*. Minchi is a homey dish that does not usually appear on restaurant menus, but every Macanese family nonetheless has their own unique recipe for making it. The general formula consists of minced meat sau-

téed with fried diced potatoes and onions, flavored with soy sauce. Worcestershire sauce and molasses also appear in some versions—a reminder of the influence the British had on some groups of Macanese. The dish is quite salty, which makes it an ideal accompaniment over a mound of white rice. Minchi may also be topped with a fried egg, a flourish often assumed to derive from the Portuguese habit of topping steak with a fried egg. Combining meat with a variety of vegetables makes this an inexpensive, quick, and balanced one-pot meal (except for the rice, of course, which cooks in a rice cooker while this dish is prepared).

3 tbsp olive oil

2 medium russet potatoes, diced

3 cloves garlic, smashed and minced

1 onion, chopped into small dice

1 bay leaf

1 c fresh or frozen peas

1 lb minced pork, not too lean (at most 80% lean)

2 tsp sugar

1½ tbsp light soy sauce

3 tbsp dark soy sauce

1 tsp salt

2 tsp white pepper

½ tsp sesame oil

1. Heat 1 tablespoon olive oil in a wok or frying pan until shimmering. Sauté potatoes until golden and beginning to crisp at edges. Set aside.

2. Heat second tablespoon of olive oil in pan. Add garlic and sauté until fragrant, being careful not to burn it. Add onion and bay leaf, and stir-fry 3–4 minutes, then add peas. Continue to cook until onion is translucent and peas are tender. Set aside.

3. Place minced pork in a bowl. Add sugar, both soy sauces, salt, white pepper, and sesame oil.

4. Heat third tablespoon of oil. Add minced pork and stir-fry over high heat, alternately pressing down flat with a spatula and "slicing" the pork with the edge of the spatula to break down the meat into small bits, about 5 minutes.

5. Return onion, bay leaf, and peas to pan with pork, and continue to cook another 3–4 minutes, and taste. The minchi should be quite salty as it will be accompanying plain white rice, which can be sweet. Add more light and/or dark soy sauce as necessary.

6. Serve over white rice, with fried potatoes if desired.

Major Foodstuffs

The Macanese pantry is an edible lineup representing Portugal's colonial empire. When viewed together one might wonder how such an eclectic mix of ingredients could ever work together. In fact, they do so spectacularly, composing what has been referred to as the original East–West fusion cuisine.

As one of the most densely populated places in the world, Macau does not have a lot of arable land so food must be imported, mainly via Hong Kong and southern China. The foodstuffs may not originate from Hong Kong and China, but those places have a much more robust infrastructure (airports, container terminals, warehouses, etc.), and it is easier for little Macau to leverage these resources rather than build its own.

Dark and light soy sauces, Shaoxing rice wine for cooking, and *lap cheong* (sweet pork sausages) make up the local contingent of ingredients, while olive oil and olives, *morcela* (Portuguese blood sausage), bacalhau (salt-preserved codfish), and milk are the Portuguese contributions. Southeast Asian staples such as coconut milk, cinnamon, bay leaf, turmeric, curry mixes, bird's-eye chilies, saffron, tamarind, and fragrant jasmine rice round out the team to add depth and complexity to Macanese recipes.

Balichão is perhaps the most defining ingredient in Macanese cuisine. Usually described as a fermented fish sauce, it is actually made of shrimp, unlike the Vietnamese or Thai fish sauces that are often suggested as substitutions. Those are made from anchovies. The name is believed to be derived from Malaysian *balachan,* a krill-based paste that is sold in blocks, and balichão is believed to be the precursor of the very pungent Cantonese shrimp paste.

Bacalhau, a type of fish, cooked in Portuguese style. (Tim Martin | Dreamstime.com)

Balichão is used to flavor soups and stews, stir-fries, and casseroles. Sadly, there are few balichão producers today, and those who remain tend to be elderly. Since it may be difficult to purchase authentic balichão, fish sauces may be used or cooks may prepare their own.

Cooking

As in neighboring Hong Kong, basic cooking equipment found in every kitchen includes a rice cooker, Chinese cleaver, wok, and chopping block. Macanese households are more likely to use ovens than their Chinese counterparts to prepare Portuguese-style dishes such as casseroles, roasts, baked desserts, and such. Kitchens and homes are still very small, though, so not every household has a full stove and oven. Chinese households vastly outnumber Macanese ones in any case, which means that the cooking habits for most of Macau's population are similar to those of Hong Kong households.

Typical Meals

Macau is a complicated hybrid of so many cultures absorbed over time that food historians have had difficulty identifying what recipes should be considered "typical" or "traditional" to Macau. How dishes are prepared can vary according to preferences, identity, and economic status. For example, Portuguese Chinese cuisine was fused in Portuguese or mixed Portuguese-Chinese households that would hire Chinese cooks to prepare their daily meals. When certain ingredients were too expensive or not available, these cooks would find local substitutes. They would also prepare specialties from their home regions for their employers, resulting in a very eclectic combination of dishes at the table. In Chinese households on Macau the picture would have been very different. The food budget might not have been as large, and the preference might have been to prepare Chinese cuisine from inexpensive local ingredients. Later, when groups of Cristang (people of mixed Portuguese-Melakan heritage, a result of Portuguese settlement in the 16th century) migrated to Macau, they brought with them their foodways as well, which were in turn influenced by the Portuguese, Indians, Malays, and others. These differences have created a variety of possible Macanese culinary norms that have been passed along in families and communities. Additionally, truly Macanese households—those of mixed Portuguese-Chinese descent—are in the extreme minority. All these factors make it difficult to describe a typical meal in Macau.

Generally speaking, most Macanese tend to eat just one or two Macanese dishes a day. A Macanese meal at home today may include one Macanese dish—a meat-based casserole or curry, accompanied by several dishes that are more readily considered Chinese, such as a slow-simmered soup or simply cooked vegetables, and rice.

Contrary to what might be expected, collections of Macanese recipes contain few that seem to be of Chinese origin. However, there are also relatively few Macanese recipes for preparing vegetables. Green salads are popular instead and stand out in stark contrast to the usual Chinese abhorrence of raw vegetables. Otherwise, cooked vegetables are usually prepared in the simple Cantonese style by boiling and dressing them with oyster sauce or stir-frying them with garlic.

There is a well-established wine culture in Macau that is unusual for an Asian city. The earliest merchants and missionaries brought casks of wine and spirits with them. Over time locals grew to enjoy glasses of *vinho verde* (light green–tinted white wine) with their meals as well, which, incidentally, pairs well with the seafood-rich Macanese cuisine. Today, wine is preferred over soft drinks at the dinner table and is available at even the most humble hole-in-the-wall café. Indeed, Macau imports the best selection of Portuguese wines anywhere in the world outside of Portugal.

Eating Out

Macanese cuisine has a reputation for being tasty but not elegant, and the enclave is often considered Mediterranean-like in its pace. These characteristics are reflected by the fact that locals generally favor smaller, less formal dining establishments, such as cha chaan teng (literally, "tea diner"), noodle shops, or small mom-and-pop restaurants, and these types of restaurants make up the majority in Macau. There are international fast-food chains in Macau, but only a handful.

Surprisingly, there used to be few authentic Portuguese restaurants in the enclave. In the mid-1980s this began to change, and now there are a variety of well-respected Portuguese restaurants on Macau that have been written up in guidebooks and are a draw for gourmets and tourists alike.

The waterfront in Macau has seen quite a transformation in the early years of this century, with large and impressive new casinos being built on reclaimed land. It used to be that there were only a couple of restaurants located in the old casinos. They catered to tourists, day-trippers from Hong Kong trying their luck upstairs, and diners looking for a nostalgic experience. The food was mediocre,

Luxury casino and restaurant on the waterfront in Macau. (Leung Cho Pan | Dreamstime.com)

and by the late 1990s the once-grand decor—all-red carpeting, brass railings, large staircases, and crystal chandeliers—was just loud and shabby. With the arrival of the new casinos there are other options now, but food habits are hard to change, and the locals rarely visit casinos for their restaurants.

Special Occasions

The Macanese preference for laid-back, informal dining extends to special occasions. Birthdays, new years, and other events are best celebrated by having a feast known as *cha gorda* (literally, "fat tea") at home with the extended family. Cha gorda is the quintessential Macanese meal, a smorgasbord of favorite foods held at home and never at a restaurant. Roasted meats, soups, curries, rice, potatoes, bread, desserts, and a hot-pot dish of pig's feet and sausage known as *tacho*—all are piled onto a groaning table to feed the extended family and friends who are invited over.

Some favorite Macanese dishes at a cha gorda are Portuguese curried chicken (which paradoxically cannot be found in Portugal), African chicken, curried crab, and *vaca estufada* (braised beef loin). These are also occasions where a more expensive or time-consuming dish such as duck *bafassa* (*bafa* means "to simmer," and *assar*, "to roast"—the duck is first simmered in a vinegar-based mixture, then roasted) might make an appearance.

Diet and Health

Macanese cuisine, while heavily Portuguese in nature and not very vegetable-centric, includes many more vegetables in its repertoire than Portuguese cuisine does. This is probably due to influence from Chinese foodways, in which vegetables play a key role in maintenance of a healthy diet. Indeed, no meal is considered complete unless accompanied by at least one vegetable-centric dish. The local Chinese in turn have taken a cue from the Portuguese table and embraced olive oil in their cooking for its healthful properties.

Cholesterol might be a concern for those who consume Macanese specialties on a regular basis.

Lard is still a popular choice for cooking and pastry making. Local desserts such as Portuguese egg tarts (the pastry shell is best made with lard), flans, and custards are derived from Portuguese recipes, which tend to rely on egg yolks. The Macanese love their seafood, and seafood in general can be high in cholesterol, but crab—which is the featured ingredient in Macau's famous curried crab dish—is also picked clean of its greenish hepatopancreas (commonly referred to as the "mustard"). The mustard is considered a delicacy, but toxins such as mercury can accumulate here if the crab is raised in polluted waters and therefore it should be consumed with caution.

One of the more unhealthy Macanese dietary habits—the heavy consumption of carbohydrates—can be considered a curious side effect of being influenced by so many cuisines. Minchi, for example, is a popular home-style dish of minced meat with fried diced potatoes that is eaten over rice, often served with a side of bread.

In terms of how the general Macanese population eats, whether Chinese, Portuguese, Macanese, or expatriate, Macau has its share of dietary concerns arising from the increased consumption of processed, junk, and fast foods. Local public health authorities are trying to raise awareness of the risks associated with overconsumption of these foods and promote healthier alternatives.

Karen Lau Taylor

Further Reading

Cheung, Sidney C. H., and Chee Beng Tan, eds. *Food and Foodways in Asia: Resource, Tradition, and Cooking.* London: Routledge, 2007.

Doling, Annabel. *Macau on a Plate.* Hong Kong: Hong Kong University Press, 1996.

Jackson, Annabel. *Taste of Macau: Portuguese Cuisine on the China Coast.* New York: Hippocrene Books, 2004.

Malaysia

Overview

Malaysia, a country located in Southeast Asia, is surrounded by the South China Sea in the east and the Strait of Melaka in the west. This country consists of two parts, East Malaysia and West Malaysia. East Malaysia is made up of two states called Sabah and Sarawak, which are located on the island of Borneo. It faces the South China Sea and is bordered by the Philippine archipelago in the north. The more populated and more advanced part is West Malaysia, where the capital city, Kuala Lumpur, is located. West Malaysia, or Peninsular Malaysia, also shares a border with Thailand in the north and Singapore in the south.

The country gained its independence from the British in 1957. Before that Malaysia was colonized by several world powers for many decades, namely, the Portuguese, the Dutch, the English, and the Japanese. However, after World War II, the colonizers relinquished their power to the local people. Now, after 52 years of independence, Malaysia has developed from a commodity-based economy to an industrial one and is slowly progressing toward a service economy. By 2020, Malaysia is expected to reach the status of a fully developed country.

Much of Malaysia's current economic and political system was influenced by the British. For example, Malaysia's parliament was adopted from the English parliamentary system. Additionally, the education system, from primary school to higher levels, also was typically based on the British educational system.

The country's population is reaching 30 million people. It includes Malay as the majority of the population, followed by Chinese and Indians. Malaysia also has many indigenous tribes in Peninsular and East Malaysia, mainly found in rural and rain forest parts of the country. Today, these people still practice their traditional lifestyles; however, they have begun to adopt modern lifestyles while still maintaining their roots. The government is striving to provide better housing, medical care, and education for these groups. These days most of them have basic access to education and lifestyles that will reduce their dependence on local resources.

🍽 Food Culture Snapshot

In the rural village of Mersing, Johor, a married couple named Mustapha Omar and Fatimah Ramli own several acres of paddy fields and live next to one. Mustapha works as a farmer, growing paddy and some vegetables for personal consumption. His wife is a full-time housekeeper. She usually performs household chores and sometimes helps Mustapha during the harvesting season. They have five children, who live in different cities in Malaysia. Normally, Mustapha wakes up very early in the morning to pray and then prepares himself for the paddy fields. His wife also wakes up as early as 5:30 A.M. to prepare breakfast for her husband. It will be a heavy breakfast to make sure that her husband will have enough energy to perform his work. Sometimes she will cook *nasi lemak* (coconut steamed rice) served with fried or hard-boiled eggs, *sambal ikan bilis* (a hot and spicy sauce made from chilies cooked with anchovies), nuts, cucumbers, and sometimes fried chicken or fish as accompaniments. Besides nasi lemak, other breakfast items in her repertoire are *nasi goreng* (fried rice), *mee goreng* (fried noodles), *lontong* (compressed rice cakes in a stew of coconut and vegetables), *roti jala* (a lacy pancake, served with chicken curry), *roti canai* (a flaky thin bread), and some *kueh-mueh* (traditional cakes) like *popia* (spring rolls) and doughnuts. Hot coffee or hot tea is served during breakfast.

Mustapha eats breakfast at 6:30 so he can be at the paddy field by 7 A.M. He will return home at 12:30 P.M. for lunch. His wife will prepare a simple lunch for him that she cooks by herself. She will pick some vegetables such as bird's-eye chili, eggplant, and okra from her backyard and use them in her daily cooking. She and her husband plant herbs and vegetables in the garden. She usually cooks plain white rice with several dishes. The structure of the lunch includes steamed white rice with fish, chicken, or meat stew; stir-fried vegetables; *sambal belachan* (chili pounded with shrimp paste); and fried salted fish. She buys fresh produce and other ingredients from a nearby wet market. Some of the dishes that she normally prepares are *ikan masak asam pedas* (fish cooked with tamarind) and sambal or hot chili paste cooked with lots of onion and seafood or chicken. Besides that, she prepares *nangka masak lemak* (young jackfruit cooked in coconut milk and turmeric), *daging masak kicap* (beef cooked in soy sauce), and *kangkung masak belachan* (stir-fried water convolvulus—a kind of bindweed vine). Coconut milk is added to many dishes, especially in preparing stews and desserts. All of the dishes are usually consumed with *ulam* (local culinary herbs that are eaten fresh) and sambal belachan. At lunch, they normally drink plain water or homemade pandanus syrup (pandanus is a screw pine, also called *kewra*). In the afternoon, she will prepare *cucur* (onion fritters), *pengat pisang* (sweet banana porridge dessert), or *bubur pulut hitam* (black glutinous rice porridge), which are accompanied by hot tea or coffee during teatime. Sometimes, she will get some fried bananas from the stall nearby. Both of them will have their dinner at 8 P.M. Usually, she will reheat the leftovers from lunch and sometimes will cook a vegetable dish. By 10 P.M. both of them are already in bed.

Major Foodstuffs

Rice is the staple diet in this country for all peoples, of Malay, Chinese, or Indian origin. Rice is typically served at breakfast, lunch, and dinner. Besides rice, noodles also are very important in the Malaysian diet. Normally, Malaysians will have three meals a day. Noodles are prepared in various methods such as noodle soup or curry noodles, which are stir-fried according to Malay, Chinese, or Indian styles. It is very unique in Malaysia that foods such as nasi lemak (steamed coconut rice) are served throughout the day, from breakfast to supper, and are savored by Malaysians from different races. Similarly, different types of noodles also can be served throughout the whole day. Noodles are flavored with different ingredients such as chicken, curry, seafood, and vegetables.

Another important food item in Malaysia is roti canai (flaky thin bread), known as *paratha* in India. This particular dish was introduced by the Indians in Malaysia, who brought this flaky bread when they immigrated from Chennai, India, about 70 to 80 years ago. However, this bread has become one of the most popular foods, served at breakfast or any time of the day. Different types of roti canai have different types of fillings, which include onions, eggs, sardines, and bananas. Many authentic Malay dishes are served during breakfast; some of them are *soto ayam* (chicken soup served with compressed rice), lontong (a spicy stew of coconut and vegetables with compressed rice and condiments), *mee rebus* (curried noodles), and varieties of local *kueh* (sweets). Sometimes, in the village, onion and anchovy fritters are freshly made at home. Since

Nasi lemak, a traditional Malaysian spicy rice dish. (Shutterstock)

Malaysia is also home to many different species of bananas, not surprisingly banana fritters are sold at stalls by the roadside or at some restaurants. Banana fritters are also another favorite, served during the day, especially at breakfast and teatime. Other types of fritters such as sweet potato and yam are also well known. *Cha kueh* (Chinese deep-fried bread) is popular among Malaysians.

Typical Malaysian cakes include savories and sweets. Examples of savories are curry puffs (a savory pastry filled with curried potatoes and chicken), *pulut panggang* (glutinous rice wrapped in banana leaves and stuffed with spicy coconut and dried shrimp), fried spring rolls, a lacy pancake served with chicken curry, *kueh badak* (sweet potatoes filled with a spicy coconut filling), and *murtabak* (chicken- or meat-filled layered bread). Sweet cakes are made from rice flour, glutinous rice flour, or whole glutinous rice. Examples are *seri muka* (glutinous rice topped with pandanus custards), *kosui* (a brown sugar custard served with freshly grated coconut), *kueh lapis* (steamed layered red and white cake made from glutinous rice flour and coconut milk flavored with rose syrup), and *kueh koci* (glutinous rice stuffed with sweet coconut and wrapped in banana leaf). All these local cakes have been adopted by other races in the country; the method of making them remains the same, but the color and presentation of the cake could be based on individual style.

Cooking

Typical Malaysian cooking styles are divided into three major ethnicities: Malay, Chinese, and Indian. Malay cooking styles are typically influenced by the neighboring countries; for example, the northern states are mainly influenced by Thai cuisines. The cooking styles there resemble foods from the southern part of Thailand. The flavor of the food is dominated by sweet, sour, and salty flavors, which are the major flavors in Thai food.

In Penang, the food reflects a combination of Malay and Indian influences. A lot of curries and Indian cooking originated from the southern part of India. Indian traders who came to Malaysia brought their food culture. Marriages between Indians and local women also contributed to enriching the flavor and style of the local food. Penang is well known for its hawker (street) foods ranging from simple appetizers, snacks, and main dishes to succulent desserts. Popular food items include *nasi kandar* (rice served with various curry dishes), *mee goreng mamak* (fried noodles Indian style), and *cendol* (pandanus dessert with coconut milk). When eating nasi kandar, one picks dishes from a wide selection of items. The price of the food depends on what you pick at the food counter.

The Chinese settlers have also greatly influenced the cuisine. Various Chinese dishes such as *char kuay teow* (stir-fried flat noodles) and *lee chee kang* (sweet soup served with dried fruits and black fungus) have become national favorites among all Malaysians. Nyonya food was derived from the marriage of Chinese dishes and local dishes. The food is mostly enriched with coconut milk, local spices, and Chinese ingredients. Cooking methods for Nyonya dishes vary from stir-frying to stewing to steaming. *Kari kapitan* (chicken curry), *terong belachan* (stir-fried eggplant and shrimp paste), and *itik tim* (duck soup) are some of the dishes that can be found in Nyonya restaurants.

States in the middle region such as Perak and Pahang are mostly influenced by Chinese traders. The Chinese foods from these states are known to be the best because they are heavily populated by Chinese. This provides a wide range of Chinese cuisines since there are more Chinese settlements here. Perak offers some of the greatest *pan mee* (hand-kneaded noodles, cooked and served to the customer in a hot frying pan), while Pahang offers many varieties of noodles such as *wan tan mee* (noodles served in soup with prawn dumplings) and *loh mee* (fresh thick yellow noodles cooked with thick soy sauce, egg, prawns, and chicken).

For those states in the southern part, the Malay cooking is influenced by the various Indonesian ethnicities, for example, Minangkabau, Bugis, and Javanese. All these people were traders, and they traveled to Malaysia and finally settled there. They brought with them their cultures and lifestyles, which determine the daily food culture. Basically, Minangkabau food is popular in Negeri Sembilan. Coconut is used in most of the main dishes. For example, beef or chicken *rendang* (spicy beef or chicken simmered in coconut milk) is the most popular food during major celebrations. The meat is cooked with coconut milk, spices, and other fresh ingredients and stewed for several hours. A delicate and full-flavored dish is produced, and this is eaten with steamed white rice or rice pilaf, accompanied by other dishes.

Food influenced by the Bugis can be found in the state of Johor, which is located at the southern tip of Malaysia. The food in Johor is a blend of Middle Eastern, Indonesian, and traditional Malay food. The ancestors of the people here originated from the Arab countries and several parts of Indonesia. The food as such is flavored by various spices and ingredients that produce a unique flavor. For example, the famous *biryani* rice (mixed with meats and vegetables) is an influence of Arabs and Indian settlers. Several dishes brought by the Indonesians in the past have become local traditional dishes, such as lontong. Although these dishes have been influenced by other cultures, the flavor of these foods is unique and authentically represents the cuisine of Malaysia. The taste of these foods in Indonesia or India is totally different, and they have become truly Malaysian dishes.

In East Malaysia, cooking is made up of indigenous dishes that vary according to ethnic group. These states are heavily populated by indigenous peoples such as the Dayak, Tekun, Iban, Temiang, and Umai, who reside in many interior parts of

Spices, such as curry, are popular in Malaysian cooking. (Shutterstock)

Sarawak. Some of the local dishes that are well known in Sarawak are *midin, nasi aruk, linut,* and *bubur pedas.* Midin is a kind of fern that is typically stir-fried with plenty of garlic. It is usually served with white rice along with other dishes. Nasi aruk is Sarawakian fried rice, which is similar to the fried rice found on the peninsula. The ingredients are anchovies, garlic, onion, and egg. Linut is a finger food made of sago flour that is fried in deep oil and dipped into chili sauce. It is usually served with tea or coffee. Finally, bubur pedas is the Sarawak version of savory porridge, which is usually cooked in the fasting month of Ramadan. Its main ingredients are turmeric, lemongrass, galangal, chili, ginger, coconut, and shallots, which are boiled with the rice.

As for Sabah, which has an equally large number of ethnic groups that settled in the interior of the state, the largest known groups are the Murut and the Dusun. Their cuisine predominates compared to the lesser-known groups. Among the frequently served dishes are *jaruk, hinava tongii,* and *bambangan.* Jaruk is a dish made by packing chunks of uncooked wild boar or river fish into a wide bamboo tube together with salt and cooked rice. The bamboo tube is filled with leaves, and the contents are fermented for months and are normally served in small portions with rice or tapioca starch. Hinava tongii is a type of pickled Spanish mackerel (*ikan tenggiri*). It is a delicious combination of fresh fish, red chilies, shredded ginger, and sliced shallots, drenched in a lot of lime juice, which "cooks" the fish. Also incorporated into the dish is the grated seed of several mangoes found in Sabah, called the *bambangan.* It is a perfect complement for white rice. Bambangan is a variety of mango that is not eaten as fruit but rather as a pickle or cooked with fish to provide a distinctive flavor.

Dishes from both Sabah and Sarawak are commonly found in homes and during festivals nowadays. Many restaurants are serving fewer ethnic foods and opting for more popular dishes that have already been mentioned (Chinese, Malay, and Indian cuisines) and Western foods.

Malay cooking methods comprise frying, sautéing, steaming, stewing, and boiling. Frying usually is used to cook fish, chicken, and snacks such as *keropok lekor* (fish crackers). Sautéing is used to cook vegetable dishes. Most of the time herbs and spices are sautéed until aromatic to produce well-flavored dishes. Steaming is used to prepare traditional steamed cakes and desserts such as kueh koci (glutinous rice with coconut wrapped in banana leaf), *kueh talam beras* (steamed rice cake), kueh lapis (layered steamed cake), and *seri muka* (steamed glutinous rice topped with egg custard). Stewing is mainly used to prepare soups and rendang, an authentic hot and spicy dish that can be made from various types of meats such as chicken, beef, mutton, and seafood. It can also be made from certain types of vegetables. The most popular rendang is made from beef, cooked with fresh and dried spices, coconut milk, and chili and stewed for four to five hours. It is served with white rice or compressed rice during major celebrations. There are many varieties of rendang originating from different areas in Malaysia. The color of the dish also varies from dark brown and dark green to red, depending on the types of ingredients being used.

Malay cooking does not really require an extensive array of cooking utensils. The traditional utensils are the mortar and pestle, *kuali* (wok), pot, steamer, and coconut grater. In certain celebrations such as at wedding ceremonies, meals are prepared in a big wok known as a *kawah* and large pots that can fit the meat from a whole cow. Additionally, other utensils used together with the kawah are long wooden spatulas or stainless steel ladles. In the past, most ingredients were pounded manually; however, today, machines are used to grind the ingredients for everyday cooking. However, some families are still using the traditional methods because they give a better flavor to the food.

Typical Meals

Malaysian cuisine is known for its unique range of flavors and culinary styles that provide an endless gastronomic adventure. Malay food is known for being hot and spicy. It contains rich flavors from many herbs and spices like galangal (*lengkuas*), turmeric (*kunyit*), kaffir lime leaves, torch ginger (*bunga kantan*), and screw-pine leaves (pandanus leaves). Typical food items for Malay cuisine are nasi lemak, *satay* (skewered strips of meat), beef rendang, mutton soup, *karipap* (a small flaky pie of curried chicken), roti canai, *teh tarik* ("pulled" tea with condensed milk; i.e., it is poured back and forth between two glasses), and *air bandung* (rose-flavored milk). There is no distinct difference between the eating cultures of rural and urban Malays. The only difference is in the eating style because some Malays eat with their hands and some eat with a fork and spoon. The former mix the rice with curry, meats, or vegetables with their fingers and scoop the food into their mouths. Most Malays in the cities eat with forks and spoons as this is more convenient because they do not have to wash their hands before and after eating.

Beef Rendang

This is one of the most popular dishes in Malaysia. It can be made from other meats such as chicken and mutton. However, the most popular are beef and chicken rendang. It has to be simmered for several hours until it becomes thick and well flavored.

Ingredients

2.2 lb beef, preferably top side—stew meat or round, cubed

15 shallots, ground

5 garlic cloves, ground

1 in. fresh ginger, ground

½ in. fresh turmeric root, ground

3 tbsp ground dried chili

3 stalks lemongrass, thinly sliced

A handful of kaffir lime leaves

2 tbsp ground coriander

½ tbsp ground black pepper

4 c coconut milk

Salt to taste

Mix all ingredients except the coconut milk with the meat, and place the mixture in a saucepan. Bring to a boil, and simmer for 30 to 45 minutes. Stir occasionally until the meat and the other ingredients are thoroughly cooked. Add the coconut milk, and stir for another 15 to 20 minutes. Lower the heat and stir continuously to prevent from sticking. Season with salt. Remove from the heat, and serve with steamed white rice.

Chinese cuisines consist of a variety of cooking styles like Cantonese, Hokkien, Hakka, and Szechuan. Normally, Chinese cuisines are mild in flavor, but Chinese dishes in Malaysia are slightly spicier due to the influences of Malay and Indian food cultures. Chinese cuisines often use garlic and ginger to enhance the flavor of dishes. Typical meals for Chinese cuisines are dim sum, *bak kut teh* (meat bone tea), char kuay teow, Hainanese chicken rice, chili crab, wan tan mee (noodles and pork), and fried *mee hoon* (fried rice noodles). Usually Chinese in rural places have their meals at stalls or hawkers, while Chinese in the city have their meals at restaurants.

Indian cuisines can be divided into two types: northern and southern cuisines. Bread is always the main item for both North and South Indian cuisines. Typical dishes for Indians in Malaysia are *nan* (leavened bread with poppy seeds), paratha (flaky bread flavored with ghee), chapati (wheat-flour pancakes), *putu mayam* (Indian steamed noodles, normally as a snack or for breakfast), mutton curry, *thosai* (sourdough flatbread), *rasam* (Indian soup, prepared with tamarind juice, pepper, and other spices), and *raita* (Indian yogurt containing spices like curry leaves, onion, and dry chilies). Spices are the heart and soul of Indian cooking. They use spices in their food and rice and even in drinks. There is not much difference in food culture between rural and city areas. Many Indian restaurants or Mamak stalls (*Mamak* refers to Tamil Muslims from India) stalls can be found everywhere.

Nowadays, Malaysians' eating habits in cities have been influenced by Western food habits. People living in big cities are always in a hurry compared to people living in the rural areas. There is one common phenomenon among the Malay, Chinese, and Indian food cultures in the cities. They spend more on eating out compared to rural citizens because urban life is more hectic and challenging than rural life. Therefore, they try to save time by having meals outside the home. In contrast, rural life is more peaceful and less hectic, and this allows rural people to prepare home-cooked meals.

Eating Out

In Malaysia, eating out is becoming more popular. This is due to smaller family sizes, so that parents feel that it is not worth it to cook. Most Chinese families choose Chinese restaurants to dine in. Sometimes, Chinese families will eat out when there is a special occasion such as family member's birthday or anniversary. During this time, they will probably choose Western restaurants because the ambiance is better than in Chinese restaurants, which are always very noisy. Another place for Malaysians to eat out is the *pasar malam* (night market), *pasar tani* (farmers' market), and outdoor stalls.

Malays tend to eat at home more or to love home-cooked food, but sometimes for special occasions or ceremonies, Malays prefer dining at restaurants, hotels, fast-food restaurants, coffee-concept restaurants, food stalls, and Mamak restaurants serving Indian food and local delicacies. This habit actually varies according to the age range. For example, teenagers and students prefer to dine at fast-food and Mamak restaurants due to their financial constraints. During the month of fasting, Malays will go to the Ramadan bazaar to buy their food for breaking the fast. Chinese and Indians will also go to Ramadan bazaar to savor traditional Malay food. Nowadays, in a Malay family, working parents will just buy *nasi campur* (rice served with several dishes) at lunch for their children and will perhaps take their children to a local restaurant for dinner. Working people in Malaysia prefer having "economical" rice for lunch. This is a plate of rice served with a variety of vegetables and meats. The price is calculated according to the amount and the type of food chosen.

Street vendor offers a dazzling variety of delicious Indian foods on Lebuh Penang in the Little India district of George-town on Penang Island, Malaysia. (Lee Snider | Dreamstime.com)

Special Occasions

Eid al-Fitr (Hari Raya Aidilfitri) is the biggest celebration in the country. Muslims from around the world celebrate this event. After successfully going through the fasting period in the month of Ramadan, Muslims feast. Normally, many types of authentic and traditional dishes will be prepared. Throughout the country, maintaining an open house is very popular during this time; people visit from house to house. Another important celebration observed by Muslims in Malaysia is Eid al-Adha (Hari Raya Aidil Adha, also known as Hari Raya Korban or Hari Raya Haji). Normally, it is celebrated two months after Eid al-Fitr, usually on the 10th day of Zulhijah, the 12th month of the Muslim calendar, which marks the end of the hajj pilgrimage period (about two weeks), and hence it is sometimes called

Hari Raya Haji (festival of the pilgrimage). Eid al-Adha also commemorates the sacrifices made by the prophet Abraham (hence the word *korban,* which means sacrifice), who fully accepted the command from Allah to sacrifice his own son when Allah tested him. Eid al-Adha is celebrated among family members only, and it is mainly observed for just two to three days. Popular dishes during these two celebrations are rendang, curries, *ketupat* (rice wrapped in coconut leaves and boiled for several hours), *lemang* (glutinous rice cooked in bamboo), and other dishes. Some of these dishes are quite similar to those served during Eid al-Fitr, and different regions in Malaysia will prepare different types of food during the celebration.

The Chinese in Malaysia celebrate festivals that are similar to those in China. The festivals include Chinese New Year, Chap Go Meh (the last day of the Chinese New Year), the Moon Cake Festival, the Dumpling Festival, and also the Hungry Ghost Festival. The biggest celebration for Chinese is the Chinese New Year. Chinese New Year is the first day in the lunar calendar. On the Chinese New Year's Eve, Chinese will have their reunion dinner whereby the whole family will have their meal together and all the foods prepared have their own meaning so that the family will have a good beginning for the next year. For example, the chicken must be presented with a head, tail, and feet to symbolize completeness so that the family members will do their jobs with a good beginning and perfect results; fish is served but should not be finished during the meal so that the family will always have some savings at the end of the year. During Chinese New Year, *nian gao,* a sweet steamed sticky rice pudding, is served, and it means wishes for the children to grow well. The *fa gao* cake is made from wheat flour and is a symbol of prosperity.

The Chinese Moon Cake Festival falls on the 15th day of the eighth month in the Chinese lunar calendar. It can be considered as a historical festival rather than a religious festival, since it marks the successful rebellion against the Mongol rulers during the 14th century in China. The Mongols had established the Yuan dynasty, which was very oppressive. During that time, the Mongols did not eat moon cakes, so they were used as a medium for the Ming revolutionaries to distribute letters secretly in the conspiracy to overthrow the Mongolian rulers. This idea was conceived by Zhu Yuan Zhang and his advisor Liu Bo Wen, who circulated a rumor that a fatal plague was spreading and the only way to prevent it was to eat moon cakes. Then, this prompted quick distribution of moon cakes with a hidden secret message coordinating the Han Chinese revolt on the 15th day of the eighth lunar month. Besides hiding the message in the filling, the other method was printing the message on the surface of the moon cakes as a simple puzzle or mosaic. To read the encrypted message, each of the four moon cakes packed together had to be cut into four parts and the total 16 pieces of moon cake then had to be fixed together in such a pattern that the secret message

could be read. The moon cakes were then eaten to destroy the message.

During this festival, foods that are often consumed are moon cakes, tea, and *pamelo* (or pomelo, a kind of citrus). Since moon cakes are considered a sweet dish, they are usually consumed with tea to revive the taste buds. Traditionally, the filling of the moon cakes includes lotus seed paste, sweet bean paste, jujube paste, taro paste, and five kernels from among the following: walnuts, pumpkin seeds, watermelon seeds, peanuts, sesame, or almonds. Nowadays, there is more variety in the filling, such as cream cheese, ginseng, bird's nests, chicken floss (shredded dried chicken), tiramisu, green tea, durian, chocolate, coffee, and others.

Malaysian Indians celebrate many occasions throughout the year. The three biggest festivals are Deepavali, Thaipusam, and Thaiponggol. During these festivals, a lot of different foodstuffs are served. Deepavali, or the Festival of Lights, is celebrated by Indians in Malaysia around late October and November. On the morning of Deepavali, Indians will light their homes with oil lamps. This custom is practiced to thank the gods for bringing happiness, health, and wealth into their life. Two to three weeks before the festivals, most Indians will be busy preparing for the big celebration. Indians clean their houses before the festival, and buying new clothes and accessories is necessary in their culture. During Deepavali, a variety of scrumptious food can be found in Indian homes. Popular sweets in Indian families are *muruku* (also called *chakkali*), *halwa* (made from flour, oil, and some nuts), *burfi* (made from condensed milk and sugar), *athirasam* (a sweet made by mixing flour, sugar, jaggery, and spices and then frying it before it is served), and *laddu* (made from flour and formed into a ball shape, also called *nei urundai*).

Hindus love eating spicy food and indulge in favorites like mutton curry, prawn sambal, and fish-head curry. During Deepavali, Indian homes normally serve sweet *pongal* (cooked rice mixed with cashew nuts and ghee) when praying. Sweet pongal symbolizes planting new crops and thanking the gods for all the prosperity in the previous year. A typical Deepavali spread includes Indian foods such as rice and curries for the main course; savory snacks such as muruku, made of rice flour; and sweet coconut candy. *Gulab jamun* is also one of the special foods served. It is made with milk, cream, and ghee and is then rolled into balls and fried.

During Thaipusam, buttermilk and free meals, or *annathanam,* are served to devotees who throng the temples. Only vegetarian food is served during this festival. Additionally, at the Thaiponggol celebration, freshly harvested rice is cooked in a new pot outside the home with milk and sugar at dawn. As the rice boils over, the members of the family often shout "pongalo pongal," and then all family members have their vegetarian breakfast.

Besides the three major festivals, weddings are also a big celebration for Indians where a lot of foodstuffs are served to the guests. The types of food prepared are steamed white rice, biryani rice, tomato rice, sambal roasted chicken, lamb *korma* (stewed with yogurt), vegetable curry, cabbage *pakora* (deep-fried cabbage with chickpea flour), mango *pacheri* (in sweet and sour sauce), and the like. Drinks such as mango *lassi* (a mango and yogurt drink) and syrup are also served. Vegetarian foods are also served at weddings.

Diet and Health

Malaysian cooking uses numerous local herbs and spices. These herbs have been used for generations, and they contribute to a healthier diet. For example, kaffir lime leaves provide a refreshing taste that is crucial in many local dishes such as soups, curries, and stews. This leaf can act as a digestive aid and cleanses the blood while helping to maintain healthy teeth and gums. Turmeric root is also another important ingredient in food preparation. It has been used for preparing special dishes such as rendang, *gulai lemak* (beef and coconut stew), and *pais ikan* (fish cooked in banana leaves) to provide an exotic taste to the food. Like the root, the leaf also has many health benefits like aiding digestion, fighting bacteria, and cleansing the system. Another

important leaf in Malaysian cooking is *daun kesum,* used in making *laksa* (a noodle soup using fish as the base for the soup). At some places in Malaysia, daun kesum is referred to as *daun laksa* or *laksa* leaves. Daun kesum is a member of the mint family. And, finally, screw-pine leaves are long, narrow, dark green leaves from the screw pine, or pandanus tree. The leaves have a sweet perfume and flavor and are often used in Southeast Asian cooking to flavor rice, puddings, and other desserts. The green color from the leaves is extracted and used as a natural food coloring.

The Chinese in Malaysia use a lot of garlic in their cooking. It can be used to treat high cholesterol, parasites, respiratory problems, poor digestion, and low energy. Studies have found that eating garlic regularly helps lower blood pressure, controls blood sugar and blood cholesterol, and boosts the immune system. It has also been found to reduce the risk of esophageal, stomach, and colon cancer.

In Indian cooking, they use a lot of spices that have medical properties and are good for health. Mostly dried herbs such as cumin, coriander, cinnamon, aniseed, and curry leaves are used. The different cooking styles and ingredients used reflect the demographic variation in the land of origin, which is mainly divided into the northern and southern regions. In addition, Indian cuisines are also influenced by religious beliefs as many dishes are meant to be served to the gods.

M. Shahrim Al-Karim and Che Ann Abdul Ghani

Further Reading

"Chinese Food." Marimari.com. http://www.marimari.com/cOnTENT/malaysia/food/chinese/chinese.html.

"Chinese Mid Autumn Festival or Moon Cake Festival." Regit.com. http://www.regit.com/hongkong/festival/mooncake.htm.

"Cultures of Sabah." SabahTravelGuide.com. http://www.sabahtravelguide.com/culture/.

"Food of Sarawak." Travour.com. http://www.travour.com/travel-to-malaysia/food-of-sarawak.html.

"Indian Food." Marimari.com. http://www.marimari.com/cOnTENT/malaysia/food/indian/indian.html.

"Kuala Lumpur Culture & Heritage." Asia Web Direct. http://www.kuala-lumpur.ws/culture-traditions/.

"Malay Food." Marimari.com. http://www.marimari.com/cOnTENT/malaysia/food/malay/malay.html.

"What Is Malay Food?" Malaysian Food.net. http://www.malaysianfood.net/Malayfood.html.

"What Is Malaysian Chinese Food?" Malaysian Food.net. http://www.malaysianfood.net/Chinesefood.html.

"What Is Malaysian Indian Food?" Malaysian Food.net. http://www.malaysianfood.net/Indianfood.html.

Māori

Overview

Aotearoa, or New Zealand, is an island nation located in the southwestern Pacific Ocean, separated from Australia by the Tasman Sea. Aotearoa is usually taken to means "land of the long white cloud" in Māori, the language of Aotearoa's indigenous inhabitants. Aotearoa consists of two large islands, Te Ika A Maui in the north and Te Waipounamu, sometimes called Te Waka A Maui, in the south, as well as numerous small coastal islands. Māori legends claim that Aotearoa was originally inhabited by the mythical Moriori, but there is no archaeological evidence for the existence of the Moriori of Aotearoa. The Moriori of Aotearoa should not be confused with the Moriori of Rekohu, known as the Chatham Islands in English and Wharekauri in Māori, who were very much real until relatively recently. It is generally accepted that the Māori initially settled in Aotearoa over 1,000 years ago.

Aotearoa was largely isolated until Western contact in 1642. The Treaty of Waitangi, still a controversial document, was signed in 1840, at which point the British claimed Aotearoa for the Crown. Aotearoa experienced a great influx of immigrants, while disease and warfare took a toll on the Māori population. Only 15 percent of New Zealanders now identify themselves as Māori. Māori culture has, however, experienced a revival and is a source of national character and pride. Māori food, although not as common as it once was, is still eaten today. *Kai,* or food, is central to Māori life.

🍴 Food Culture Snapshot

Rachel Rawiri lives in Grey Lynn, a suburb of Auckland, Aotearoa's largest city, located on Te Ika A Maui. She is a postgraduate student at the University of Auckland and lives in an apartment she shares with two other students. Rachel is of mixed Māori, Scottish, and English ancestry but identifies herself as Māori. Although Rachel is originally from Wellington, she is a member of the Ngāpuhi iwi of Northland. Like many Māori, Rachel's family moved to an urban area for the better economic opportunities it offered.

Rachel's eating and shopping habits mirror those of mainstream New Zealand. She does most of her food shopping at one of the large supermarkets located near her home, and occasionally picks up items at convenience stores, known as dairies. Rachel's student allowance keeps her on a tight budget. She will occasionally visit a greengrocer or a discount butcher shop to cut costs. Rachel does not cook frequently, and cutting back on grocery expenses allows her to eat out more often. Rachel prefers convenience foods to prepare at home, such as canned baked beans, bread, cold cereal, and packaged pasta.

Rachel almost always eats a simple breakfast at home. Lunch is eaten either at home or at the university, where Rachel picks up something inexpensive from a cafeteria or nearby café. Likewise, dinner is sometimes eaten in the home but is often purchased from a restaurant, café, take-out shop, or pub. She rarely eats dinner alone, usually sharing the meal with her roommates or friends from the university. Rachel's eating habits mirror those of most university students in New Zealand. Distinctly Māori foods are rarely consumed, although special family occasions will sometimes feature traditional Māori fare.

Major Foodstuffs

Polynesian voyagers carried a suite of domesticated plants and animals with them throughout the Pacific to ensure successful settlements. Many of these plants were of tropical origin and poorly suited to Aotearoa's temperate climate. Agriculture was more important in Aotearoa's warmer northern reaches, while hunting and gathering were prominent in the south. Māori everywhere, however, relied largely on the forest and sea for daily subsistence.

The only introduced animals to survive were the *kuri,* the Māori dog, and the *kiore,* the Polynesian rat. Both animals were important sources of meat and supplemented the protein provided through hunting and fishing native game. Kuri were kept among Māori society, while kiore lived in the wild and were hunted and trapped when desired, like indigenous food animals. Aotearoa's only native mammals are bats. With a lack of large game animals Māori hunting focused on birds and aquatic resources.

Aotearoa has been home to thousands of bird species, many of which were endemic. Some of these have played, and in some cases continue to play, a significant role in the Māori diet. Moa, gigantic flightless birds, once inhabited Aotearoa and provided early Māori with large amounts of meat. These docile birds were quickly hunted to extinction. Kiwi, small flightless birds revered by the Māori, were also eaten in the past. Kiwi, which have become a national emblem of New Zealand, are now endangered and under federal protection. This is due largely to the introduction of dogs and cats from Europe. Like the kiwi, many of the native birds that the Māori once relied on are now endangered and are no longer considered suitable for food. Once exception is the *tītī,* a type of petrel commonly called muttonbird for its lamblike flavor. Tītī chicks are harvested from April 1 to May 31 by the Rakiura Māori, who have maintained gathering

rights for the Tītī Islands. Tītī, either fresh or preserved in fat, can be found for sale in specialty shops throughout New Zealand and are considered a special treat.

Seafood, including fish and shellfish, made up a large portion of the traditional Māori diet, and it is still extremely popular and widely available in New Zealand today. Snapper was the dominant catch in the north, whereas red cod was the most commonly consumed fish in the south. Both fishes are commercially fished today, and snapper is now New Zealand's most popular fish. Many of the shellfish varieties the Māori consumed prior to contact have fallen out of use today, but others not only are popular with Māori but have also been adopted into New Zealand's national cuisine. *Kōura,* known commonly as crayfish in New Zealand and rock lobster

The Moa bird, from W. Rothschild's *Extinct Birds* published in 1907. (Getty Images)

abroad, has become an expensive luxury food. Green-lipped mussels, *pipi* (a type of small clam), and *tuangi* (commonly known as cockles) are inexpensive in New Zealand but are exported at higher prices as luxury items. There are a number of shellfishes that are still collected for consumption but are rarely available for purchase. *Tuatua,* a larger clam, and *pūpū,* an aquatic snail, are still gathered by hand. *Kina,* a local variety of sea urchin, are very popular in Māori communities and are gaining in popularity with the general population. As demand has increased, so has the price. *Pāua,* the black-footed abalone, has also gained favor outside of the Māori communities, and they are commonly offered in fritter form at fish and chip shops. Bluff oysters and small rock oysters, which were part of the traditional Māori diet, are now widespread favorites throughout New Zealand and beyond. Seaweeds, such as *karengo,* provided important nutrients and held ceremonial importance. Freshwater foods also hold a place of prominence in the Māori diet. Freshwater eels, called *tuna* but known by a number of Māori names according to color and skin types, can be found dried, smoked, and live in many fish markets today. They are popular steamed, roasted, and especially grilled. Whitebait are the juveniles of the *īnanga, kōaro,* and *kōkopu* fishes. These delicate fish are collected seasonally in screens or nets and can be found at supermarkets and fish shops, but prices are exorbitant. Once making up a large part of the Māori diet, fish and shellfish are now relegated to the category of special-occasion foods because of their high price tags.

Other once-common foods have become less popular for other reasons. *Huhu* is a type of native beetle whose large, whitish larva, called a grub, is still sometimes eaten as a delicacy. Once a common snack for some Māori, huhu are now enjoyed only by those who are more traditional or more adventurous. The European aversion to bug eating has become widespread in Aotearoa, where most people consider eating bugs disgusting.

Some of the traditional Māori plant foods have remained popular, while others have declined or disappeared altogether. It is believed that prior to contact *aruhe,* the bracken fern, was an important staple food. The rhizomes of the plant were pounded, separating the inedible fiber from the starch, which was made into versatile cakes. Although aruhe itself is not especially palatable, it could be sweetened or flavored and served alongside nearly anything. The practice of eating aruhe has largely been abandoned in favor of introduced starches. Other fern foods, however, have remained more popular. The young fern shoots, called *koru* or fiddleheads, of a variety of ferns were commonly eaten. Koru have a delicate flavor and pleasing texture, commonly being likened to young asparagus. The koru of the *kiokio* and *pikopiko* are still enjoyed today, when in season, and are sometimes showcased on fine-dining menus.

Taro, *kūmara* (sweet potatoes in English), and *uwhi* (a type of small yam) were brought to Aotearoa by Polynesian settlers. Taro, a tropical plant, was established only in the northern reaches of Te Ika A Maui, while the more rugged uwhi did slightly better. Kūmara had the largest range and quickly became the most important cultivated food. The importance of kūmara can be seen in Māori religion and ceremonial life. Kūmara is associated with Rongo, the god of peace, and the kūmara-planting cycle dictated much of the Māori year.

Māori potatoes are another important source of starch. Although there are traditions that claim potatoes were present in precontact Aotearoa, it is generally accepted that early contact with European explorers resulted in the introduction of the potato, a South American cultivar. Nevertheless, the potato, which is well adapted to New Zealand's cool climate, quickly became one of the Māori's most important food sources. Adapting Māori cultivation to potatoes was easy, as they are produced in much the same way as kūmara. Because they were an outside food source, potatoes were also considered *noa,* meaning unlike kūmara there were no religious restrictions on their production. Māori potatoes range in size and color but tend to be small, thin-skinned, and pinkish, purplish, or swirled. They more closely resemble a number of South American varieties than they do their European counterparts, which is most likely due to their early introduction, as potatoes were not well established in Europe at that time.

Potatoes have become a major component of the wider New Zealand diet, following the modern British tradition. Māori potato consumption has paralleled this, and they are widely available today. Their lovely coloring and waxy texture have earned them a place at many gourmet shops and restaurants. *Rewena paraoa* is a sourdough potato bread specific to the Māori, known in English as Māori bread. Rewena paraoa is commonly served alongside many modern Māori dishes, such as boil-up, or *hāngi.*

Cooking

Traditional Māori cooking methods include fire roasting, hot stone grilling, and steam roasting in a *hāngi.* In addition to cooking, there is also a tradition of eating many seafoods, such as kina and pūpū, raw. Modern Western cooking implements and techniques have replaced traditional cooking styles with the exceptions of the hāngi and fire roasting, which are still sometimes done at beaches or while camping. Hāngi are underground ovens, similar to the Hawaiian *imu* or Fijian *lovo.* Parcels of food are placed in a hole with hot rocks from a wood fire and then covered with earth to steam roast for several hours before being dug up and enjoyed. Fish, pork, lamb, chicken, potatoes, corn, pumpkins, kūmara, onions, carrots, stuffing, and cabbage are all common hāngi foods. Hāngi are traditionally prepared by men, although women may prepare some of the foods that will be cooked in the hāngi. Because hāngi is labor-intensive, it is now often reserved for celebrations and special occasions, although it is now sometimes offered for purchase at cultural festivals and outdoor markets. Hāngi is also offered as part of a package at some Māori cultural showcases, where traditional Māori song and dance are performed for tourists. Many of these outfits have built permanent hāngi out of concrete or brick, resulting in a significant loss of flavor.

Typical Meals

Māori meal patterns are generally the same as those of mainstream New Zealand. There are, however, a number of Māori meals that are eaten regularly in addition to the famous hāngi. One of the most common is called boil-up. Boil-up is a dish made from pork bones and watercress or *puha,* sometimes known as prickly sow thistle, boiled together with various vegetables to make a hearty soup. The pork bones are often smoked. Vegetables added to boil-up often include carrots, kūmara, potatoes, and pieces of pumpkin. Boil-up is often served with rewena bread or doughboys, which are large flour-and-water dumplings. There are also a number of Māori sweet dishes. *Kaanga piro* or *kanga wai,* commonly known as rotten corn, is a dish made from fermented maize. A basket of corn is placed in running water, such as a stream, or in a barrel of water that is changed daily, and allowed to ferment. This produces a sweet but strong-smelling mush that can then be eaten or made into other dishes, such as rotten corn custard. Kūmara is also featured in many sweet dishes, such as *roroi.* Roroi is a pudding made from grated kūmara and sugar, which is then steamed or baked.

Roroi Kūmara

5 kūmara (sweet potatoes), peeled and grated

¼ c brown sugar

¼ c sugar

2 tbsp butter, melted

I kūmara (sweet potato), sliced

Mix grated kūmara, brown sugar, sugar, and melted butter in a bowl. Place in a lightly greased baking dish and cover with sliced kūmara. Cover with aluminum foil, and bake at 350°F for I hour. Serve warm or cold with whipped cream.

Boil-Up

5 lb meaty pork bones

10 potatoes, halved

3 kūmara, quartered

I small pumpkin, seeded and cut into pieces

2 large onions, quartered

I large bunch watercress (or puha), cleaned and trimmed

Salt to taste

Pepper to taste

Place the pork bones in a large pot, and cover with water. Bring to a boil, and allow to simmer for 2 hours, adding more water as needed. Add the potatoes, kūmara, pumpkin, and onion, and simmer for 20 minutes. Add the watercress, and simmer for an additional 15 minutes. Add salt and pepper to taste. Serve hot with fresh bread.

Eating Out

Although most Māori do eat out, Māori food is not commonly found in restaurants. Māori foods, especially hāngi and rewena paraoa, are offered at cultural festivals and outdoor markets. Māori food is also offered at cultural showcases, as already mentioned, and many *marae,* Māori meeting grounds, take pride in offering Māori food at marae gatherings. With the rise of local and regional cuisine, many native ingredients that have been consumed by Māori for generations have begun to be showcased in New Zealand's finest restaurants.

Special Occasions

The day-to-day eating habits of most Māori are similar to those of New Zealanders of predominantly European descent. Many traditional Māori foods have become expensive or are difficult to obtain or prepare. Special occasions have become a time when the extra expense and effort are made and traditional foods are prepared. Events such as weddings, birthdays, and anniversaries are celebrated by laying down a hāngi or purchasing or gathering fresh seafood. Funerals, or *tangihanga,* are important events within Māori communities. Ceremonial feasts follow these *tangi.* When leaving the graveyard, or *urupa,* Māori wash to break the *tapu* (i.e.,

taboo associated with death), especially before eating. Rewena bread can be crumbled and used to restore noa in place of water.

Diet and Health

Prior to Western contact Māori enjoyed relatively good health. A physically active lifestyle, coupled with a nutritious diet, resulted in a strong and vigorous community. Warfare among Māori was common and was a much greater threat to Māori health than famine or disease. Western contact introduced new diseases that became epidemics in Māori communities, and the Māori Wars increased Māori attrition rates and land confiscations. The Māori were relegated to the lower classes during the colonial period, which has had lasting effects on the Māori peoples.

Poor health and diet continue to plague Māori communities. Māori are among the poorest New Zealanders, which directly affects the modern Māori diet. Like the urban poor in most counties, Māori are plied with inexpensive packaged food that offers little nutritional value. Poor diet is then coupled with poor health care. Although health care in New Zealand is free, Māori remain among the most underserviced, especially in rural areas. The traditional Māori diet would be a far wiser choice than the industrialized diet of today.

Kelila Jaffe

Further Reading

Duffie, Mary Katharine. *Through the Eye of a Needle: A Māori Elder Remembers.* New York: Wordsworth, 2000.

Fuller, David. *Māori Food and Cookery.* Auckland, New Zealand: A. H. and A. W. Reed, 1978.

Ministry for Culture and Heritage/Te Manatū Taonga. *Te Ara: The Encyclopaedia of New Zealand.* 2010. http://www.teara.govt.nz.

Mongolia

Overview

Mongolia is the world's largest landlocked nation, sandwiched between China and Russia's Siberia in northern Asia. At approximately 604,000 square miles, Mongolia is slightly larger than Alaska and more than three times as large as France. With a population of only about 2.9 million, it is among the most sparsely populated countries in the world. Called Mongol Uls in Mongolian, it is also known as Outer Mongolia, to differentiate it from the Mongol-inhabited region of China known as Inner Mongolia.

The image people generally have of Mongolia—the vast, sweeping steppe that was once home to the great armies of Chinggis Khaan (the Mongolian spelling of Genghis Khan)—is close to being the whole story in Mongolia. Almost 80 percent of the land is steppe pastureland, which supports huge herds of grazing livestock. The remaining 20 percent of the country is divided almost equally between barren desert and forested mountains. Less than 1 percent of the land is arable, and of that, only about 840 square miles is irrigated. The climate is extreme continental, with hot summers, tremendously cold winters, and little precipitation.

Despite dramatic political changes during the 20th century, Mongolians retain most of their traditions and cultural identity. Early in the century, Mongolia escaped Chinese control, only to find itself taken over by the Soviet Union. The Soviet machine worked to force urbanization on the previously nomadic population and built the kind of hideously polluting industrial installations and blocky worker housing for which the Soviets became so well known, and they replaced Mongolian script with Russia's Cyrillic alphabet. Then, with the dissolution of the Soviet Union in 1990, Mongolia regained its independence. It reverted to being called Mongolia after nearly 60 years as the Mongolian People's Republic; adopted a multiparty, democratic form of government, with free elections; and started on the road to becoming a participant on the world stage. Russian architecture, Cyrillic signage, and a few introduced foods are lingering reminders of the Soviet era, but today, Mongolia balances between the joyous return to traditions by many and the equally joyous rush toward modernization by others.

Even now, with more opportunities available in the cities, half of the country's population still pursues the traditional life of the nomadic herder. Millions of grazing sheep, goats, yaks, horses, and camels spread out across the vast, open grasslands of the steppe. However, even among urban Mongolians, many traditions are observed, including living in *gers* (the round felt-covered tents of the nomads—called yurts by the Russians; *ger* is pronounced more or less like *gair*). Even Ulaanbaatar, the capital and largest city, has large neighborhoods of gers. Along with habitation, food customs have also been preserved.

The population of Mongolia is almost entirely Mongol (about 95%). However, geography and history have dictated that, while religion and housing may differ among the minorities, lifestyle and foodways are very similar nationwide. Education is compulsory for nine years, and the literacy rate is 98 percent. The dominant religion is Tibetan

A local man herds goats in the Mongolian countryside. Most of Mongolia's people live the pastoral life of animal herders in the country's harsh climate. (Travel-Images.com)

Buddhism, usually blended with traditional shamanistic/spiritist beliefs. The Kazakh minority is primarily Muslim. Due to the Soviets' concerted efforts to eradicate religion, about 40 percent of Mongolians now identify themselves as not being part of any religion, though they carry on some of the traditions. Most religious activities involve food at some level, and they often revolve around food and the hope of having enough.

The half of the population that remains nomadic raises livestock, including sheep, goats, horses, yaks, and camels. The makeup of herds varies by region, with more yaks in the north and more camels in the south. The Dukha, a small minority living in the far north, raise reindeer instead and live in tepees rather than gers, but they are nomadic herders like other Mongolians. Livestock raising makes up about

70 percent of the value of agricultural production in Mongolia, and most of the industry that has grown up revolves around processing related to herding, from processing and knitting cashmere to tanning leather to producing meat and milk products. Mongolia does have mineral reserves that have more recently become a factor in the country's economy, but it is still the herds that rule.

Food Culture Snapshot

Batbayar sits on the edge of the small, metal-framed bed that was placed against the back wall of the ger. The felt at the base of the ger is turned up to allow whatever breeze there might be to pass through. July in the Gobi is hot, but the white of the felt reflects the heat and, with the breeze, makes the ger relatively comfortable. Soon, the neighbors will arrive, to both help with and celebrate the first milking of the mares. Batbayar watches as his wife, Sarangerel, fills a huge bowl with boiled mutton, scoops soft blobs of camel-milk cheese into another bowl, and stacks dried curd (called *aaruul*) and fried dough (*boortsog*) on a metal plate.

Batbayar and Sarangerel have already started preparing for the winter, as the summer is so short. Strips of drying meat—mutton and horse—hang from the ger framework along one wall. Blocks of aaruul dry on the roof. Large jars along another wall hold various fermented milk products—milk vodka (*arkhi*) from the sheep, yogurt from the camels, *airag* (a fermented milk) from the horses (better known in the West by its Russian name, kumiss). Outside, their herds prepare, too, grazing on coarse golden grass, recovering from the harsh winter and putting on fat for the winter to come—and, more important, having babies and making milk.

Batbayar and Sarangerel's four children play outside among the camels until the guests begin to arrive, and then they enter the ger, too, not wishing to miss any of the celebratory food. As the guests enter, the men begin to pass around their snuff bottles, as the custom of hospitality dictates. Everyone politely reaches around the outside of the two ger poles, never between. Sarangerel opens a large metal container and ladles camel-milk yogurt into bowls, which are passed around the room. Lumps of dried camel milk are passed next.

After eating, everyone goes outdoors—it is time to go to work. First, the foals have to be captured. About half of the men are on horseback. Those on foot help guide the stampeding horses away from the children and toward the riders. One rider has a long pole with a lasso at the end—a device called an *uurga*. This permits the rider to slip a loop of rope over the neck of a horse more easily. As the foals are captured, they are tethered nearby. The foals have to be captured because, unlike cows, mares won't give milk if their foals are not beside them. The mares are captured next and tethered near their foals.

After all this effort, it is time for some refreshment. In the ger, Batbayar pours sheep-milk vodka into a glass, and the glass is handed to one neighbor. After he drinks all he wants, the glass is handed back, refilled, and passed to the next guest. This continues until all have had a drink. Then this is repeated with the camel-milk vodka. A *morin khuur*—the traditional horse-headed fiddle of Mongolia—is produced, and the men sing songs about the earth. Then, at the time appointed by tradition, everyone goes back outside for the milking of the mares. Women are expected to milk sheep, goats, yaks, and camels, but milking horses is men's work. Mare's milk is made into cheese and vodka, like other milks, but most of it is made into airag, a slightly alcoholic, yogurtlike beverage that is the national drink of Mongolia.

Mares milked, the crowd returns to the ger for more food. Sarangerel passes around bowls of mutton soup with noodles while the men fall on the mound of boiled mutton. Soon everyone—men, women, children—are gnawing bones and downing blood sausage and lumps of fat. The meal ends with bowls of tea with camel milk and salt.

Batbayar mounts his horse. The first pail of mare's milk is handed to him, and he threads it onto the uurga pole. Two riders join him, one on either side, holding the pole, while Batbayar holds a ladle. The three then gallop around the camp three times in a clockwise direction, with Batbayar ladling milk into the air, as a gift to the sky. This is to ensure that the mares will continue to give milk.

Guriltai Shol (Mutton Soup with Noodles)

Traditional Mongolians would make the noodles from scratch as well—simply flat noodles made of wheat flour, water, and a little salt, kneaded, rolled thin, and cut by hand, but in the cities, packets of noodles are available for busy urbanites who no longer have the luxury of time but still long for familiar dishes.

1 lb fatty mutton (beef may be substituted)

1 tsp salt

8 c cold water

Meaty soup bones (optional)

2 medium onions, thinly sliced

4 oz packaged noodles (¾ in. wide)

Cut the meat into strips, as if you were preparing it for a stir-fry dish. Put the meat and 1 tsp salt into the water. (If using soup bones, to create a heartier broth, add them to the water, too.) Boil until the meat is thoroughly cooked and water has become a light broth (about 45 minutes), skimming if scum forms. If you used bones, remove them from the broth after the meat is cooked. Then add the onion and noodles, and continue to boil until noodles are done. Taste for seasoning, and add salt if necessary. Soup is ready to serve once the noodles are cooked.

Major Foodstuffs

For about half of the population, the "grocery store" is grazing outside, and the "pantry" is any available space in the ger. Grazing animals—sheep, goats, horses, camels, yaks, and, for one ethnic minority, reindeer—provide almost the entire diet, in the form of both meat and milk products, for the half of Mongolia's population that still live as nomad herders. Even those who live in the city often rely on these same provisions, begging relatives for carafes of airag and going to the meat market to buy whole butchered sheep or goats.

Hunting supplements the meat supply, with marmot season of particular importance to those who have developed a taste for this large squirrel relative. Mongolian gazelles and wild sheep are also hunted for their meat. Interestingly, though Mongolia's lakes and rivers team with fish, supporting a small fishing industry, most of the fish that are caught are canned and shipped overseas. While some fish may be served in the cities, it is not part of the traditional Mongolian diet.

Meat and dairy, though occasionally consumed fresh, are usually processed into a wide range of products that will last without refrigeration. Thanks to the dry air (the humidity averages about 10 percent), even milk and meat can be dried safely. Dried meat is called *borts*. The rock-hard borts can be easily stored or transported until needed, at which time it is pounded to powder and put in boiling water. Milk may be fermented, distilled, made into cheese or yogurt, churned into butter, or dried. When fresh milk is available, milk tea, or *suutei tsai,* is the favorite way to consume it. Milk and hot tea are combined in equal parts, and then salt and sometimes butter are added. This beverage makes sense in an arid country where life depends on water, salt, and getting enough calories.

These dining traditions have remained unchanged for 1,000 years or more. When Marco Polo visited this land 700 years ago, his report on the diet was virtually identical to what can be seen today—meat, milk (including mare's milk, which startled the explorer), and game (including marmot, which Polo described as being abundant). He even described the methods of producing dried milk, which are the same methods used by Mongolian nomads today.

Mongolia has one major crop, wheat, though a small amount of barley and millet is also grown. With so little arable land and such a short summer, Mongolia is not a major grain producer, but that hasn't kept Mongolians from utilizing wheat flour, in particular, in traditional cuisine. Bread, boortsog (fried dough strips that are also sometimes called "nomad biscuits"), noodles, and dumplings are the main outlet for wheat. Meat-filled dumplings are much loved, and there are those who believe that the reason every culture from Korea through to eastern Europe has meat-filled dumplings is that that was the extent of the Mongolian Empire. There are three types of dumplings: *buuz, bansh,* and *huushuur* (*buuz* is pronounced *boats,* but the other two are pronounced pretty much as they appear).

Mongolians will sometimes eat fruit and vegetables when they are available, though fruit is the rarer option. As some of the population has adopted a more settled lifestyle, small garden farms have begun to appear around the countryside, making vegetables more readily available. Not too surprisingly, because of both climate and history, the hardy and hearty vegetables valued by the Russians are the ones most commonly found in Mongolia. Beets, carrots, cabbage, potatoes, onions, and turnips are generally the available options. Any and all may appear in soups or stews. The beets, carrots,

A Chinese man selling his fresh produce on a street in HoHot, Inner Mongolia, northern China. (Nico Smit | Dreamstime.com)

and cabbage are most regularly seen shredded and served as salads (even at breakfast), simply tossed with chopped garlic and a little mayonnaise or oil and vinegar.

A few indigenous plants are collected, but they are not a major source of calories. Some imported goods, such as rice and sugar, make their way into the diet in even remote settlements, and a fairly wide range of imports are coming into the cities now. However, the main diet is still meat, milk, and flour. It is this diet that has seen the population not only through centuries of history but also, in recent years, through the severe economic upheaval when the Soviets pulled out.

Even in the cities, while local vegetables are readily available, the foods on offer are heavily weighted toward meat, dairy, flour, and vodka. More convenience foods and imports are appearing in the few grocery stores, but these mostly draw foreigners, while locals get their food at the huge outdoor markets.

Cooking

A lot of the traditional fare of the Mongolians is not cooked. Meat and curd are dried. Milk is fermented, distilled, or made into cheese. However, Mongolia has some delicious and much-loved fare that is cooked. If an animal is killed for food during the summer, it must be processed immediately. If it is not torn in strips and dried, it must be cooked. Out on the steppe, there are essentially two recipes for cooking a whole animal: You make *horhog* or *boodog*. Both dishes involve hot rocks.

First, two or three dozen medium-sized, water-smoothed stones are collected. The stones are placed in an open fire and heated until almost red hot. For horhog, a sheep is cut into pieces, with the bones still in. A few quarts of water are poured into a large metal container (a 40-quart container for a medium sheep) with a tight-fitting lid, and then the pieces of meat are added, alternating layers of meat and hot stones. The lid is tightly closed, and the meat is left to cook for an hour or two. This renders a fabulously moist meat that falls off the bone.

Boodog is a dish made of goat or marmot. There is no metal container, as the animal becomes the cooking vessel. The goat or marmot is cleaned out, the entrails being removed through the neck, in order to leave the skin whole, and then the body is filled with the red-hot rocks. It is then sealed tightly. While the meat cooks from the inside out, a torch or gas burner is used to burn off all the hair on the outside.

For both boodog and horhog, when the dishes are cooked, the greasy, still-warm stones are removed first and passed around to the diners, who move the rocks from hand to hand, holding them long enough to warm the hands. This is considered to be healthful; it is definitely relaxing.

While firewood is burned to heat stones for boodog and horhog, for other more common cooking, especially in the steppe, the primary fuel is dried dung, which is abundant and is almost all plant matter. Soups—all with meat—are boiled in pots over open fires, as is the water for suutei tsai (milk tea). Boortsog, a traditional "biscuit," is fried in the oil rendered when soup is made. All these dishes are prepared over the dung fires.

The only other traditional cooked foods are dumplings, and while their recipes are all quite similar, their sizes and the methods for cooking them are quite different. The dough is a simple one of flour and water, and the filling is chopped meat (usually mutton) with onion, garlic, and seasonings. Buuz (pronounced "boats") are two-bite dumplings that are similar to, though fatter than, pot stickers. Buuz are steamed. Bansh are much smaller and are boiled. They commonly appear bobbing around in soup or milk tea. Huushuur are much larger, about five or six inches on its longest side. Huushuur are fried, which makes it more portable than the other two dumplings. In fact, huushuur often appear at outdoor venues and festivals, where they are eaten out of hand.

Huushuur (Mongolian Fried Meat-Filled Pastries)

Makes 8 pastries

Dough

2¼ c flour

¼ tsp salt

About 1 c water

Filling

1 lb chopped or ground fatty beef or mutton

1½ tsp salt

¼ tsp ground black pepper

½ tsp marjoram

½ onion, finely chopped

1–2 cloves garlic, finely chopped

Oil for frying the filled pastries (mutton fat is traditional, but cooking oil works)

Combine flour and salt. Add half a cup of water to the flour, and then continue to add water a little at a time, mixing it thoroughly, until you have a rough, dry dough, about the texture of that for pie crust.

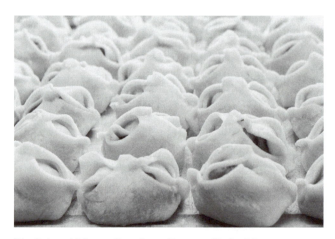

Traditional Mongolian dumplings stuffed with meat. (Shutterstock)

Knead until dough is smooth and elastic. Cover and let rest for 5 to 10 minutes.

Combine all filling ingredients, mixing thoroughly. If dry, add a few drops of water to moisten.

Divide the dough into quarters. Roll each quarter into a cylinder, and cut in half. Roll each half cylinder into a circle about 5–6 inches across. Place about 2 to 2½ tablespoons of the filling on one side of the circle, leaving space around the outside edge. Fold the other side over, creating a half-moon. Pinch the edges closed, squeezing out air and flattening the filling as you work. Repeat the process with the rest of the filling and dough pieces.

Pour oil into a frying pan to a depth of about ½ inch. Heat oil until hot. Fry two or three pastries at a time for 2 minutes per side, until they are golden to brown and the meat is cooked. The huushuur can be eaten hot or cold.

Typical Meals

Among the nomad population, the amount and types of food vary with the seasons. In summer, the consumption of dairy products is heaviest, while meat is more heavily consumed during the rest of the year. Cooking is generally done once a day, unless there are guests. Breakfast and lunch are the biggest meals of the day and generally consist of boortsog (fried bread), salty milk tea, boiled mutton, broth with noodles or another starch, and dairy products, depending on what is available—fresh milk, sour clotted milk, yogurt, cheese, curds, or airag. In summer, an entire meal can be made of dairy, or "white food," as the Mongolians call it.

Minor variations exist across the country. In the north, the high-fat milk of yaks is more common, while camels and goats are more numerous in desert regions, so a more common source of milk there. In the far north, around Lake Khuvsgul, the Dukha rely on their reindeer. But everyone is still mixing the milk with tea and salt, making yogurt and cheese, and drying curd. The Muslim Kazakhs of Mongolia's west find nothing to object to in the Mongolian diet, but they tend to eat more horse meat than other Mongolians do. Throughout Mongolia, however, meat and milk are still the foundations of the meal.

In an urban setting, meals vary only slightly. A meal will usually consist of broth with noodles, or possibly borscht, a relic of the longtime Russian presence; a salad of shredded beet, carrot, and/or cabbage; and a meat dish. Desserts are uncommon.

Eating Out

Eating out for the majority of Mongolians pretty much means either dining outdoors or visiting the neighbors, even for those living in urban areas. The only real exception for many is if one makes the trek to the annual Naadam Festival, and even then, most of the food on offer is fairly traditional, with fresh fruit and ice cream being among the most exotic items offered, amid a sea of grilled meat and huushuur.

However, not every meal is eaten at home. The rural population in particular is very mobile, moving with the herds or making regular, if infrequent, runs to town or distant farms for supplies, and the urban population is increasingly too busy to make familiar dishes. Almost ubiquitous in Mongolia is an eatery called a *guanz*. These generally modest dining establishments can be found in abundance in every town or city, as well as along roads that have regular traffic. A guanz may be located in a building, a ger, a small hut, or even a railway car. These little shops offer basic Mongolian comfort food, including soup, salty milk tea, and either buuz or huushuur. There are also nicer restaurants that serve traditional specialties, including some that offer traditional Mongolian entertainment. However, the average Mongolian is more likely to stop at a guanz to fill up on cheap, familiar favorites.

The real advent of varied cuisine came after the Soviets pulled out. Mongolia is now able to have business and political ties with other countries, there has been an influx of foreign workers and entrepreneurs, more young Mongolians are traveling overseas for advanced education, and tourism is an increasingly important part of the nation's income. All these factors have contributed to growing

A Chinese Mongolian elder offers traditional sweets blessed by Buddhist Lamas at a ceremony on a shrine on top of a hill, during the Naadam festival on the grassland of Gegental Steppe in China's Inner Mongolia region. (Getty Images)

opened in Ulaanbaatar and has found an amused but appreciative audience. Cafés have become popular, with outdoor seating cherished during the short summer, and there are a few brewpubs, primarily serving local beers, such as Altan gobi, Khan brau, and Chinggis. Pizza has put in an appearance, as have submarine sandwiches (Sub-Baatar), catering primarily to the younger generation. It is unlikely that a major portion of the population will be giving up milk tea and dumplings anytime soon, but for those who wish to explore, or those who have fond memories of food consumed during their travels, there are now several options besides traditional Mongolian food.

Special Occasions

The biggest event in Mongolia is the Naadam Festival (*naadam* means "games"), held every year on July 11–13. Founded more than 800 years ago by Chinggis Khaan, the Naadam Festival has come to be a celebration of both the great Khaan's birth and Mongolia's independence. This three-day event features the "three manly sports" of horse racing, archery, and wrestling (though women may compete in archery, and children ride in some races). A few remote areas hold their own naadam events, but the big event is in Ulaanbaatar. Temporary villages of gers crowd fields and hillsides around the city. Herds of horses clog the roadways, slowing motor traffic. Everyone who is able comes to Ulaanbaatar for this event, and those who can't come are usually glued to their televisions, to see which horse, archer, or massive, powerful wrestler will be victorious. The president, top officials, and visiting dignitaries attend.

interest in what the rest of the world is eating—and a growing number of immigrants able to bring the cuisines of the world to Mongolia's cities.

Many of the restaurants that are not specifically Mongolian focus on cuisines that value meat, from Korean barbecue to Turkish kebabs. In recent years, French, Italian, German, Mexican, and Indian foods have become available in Ulaanbaatar, as well as in other large cities. A few cities even have vegetarian restaurants. While the cooking style identified as "Mongolian barbecue" in the United States was invented by the Chinese and bears no resemblance to any cooking method in Mongolia, an American Mongolian barbecue restaurant has

As much fun as watching the sports is the fairway, for those attending. This is the one opportunity many nomadic or rural Mongolians have to eat fruit or buy new clothes, and the fairway is lined with vendors selling everything from huushuur to infant's shoes, and from ice cream to cooking pots—every necessity, as well as a number of luxuries. Even so, many of the vendors are selling familiar foods, and grilled meat is more common than the modest stacks of fresh fruit.

The most important holiday on the Mongolian calendar is Tsagaan Sar, or "White Moon"—the lunar new year. This holiday, which follows lunar cycles, can fall anywhere from late January to early March. It symbolizes new beginnings and is considered to be the day when spring begins to return. Food is a key component of the holiday, as a full belly during Tsagaan Sar is said to represent prosperity in the year ahead. Tsagaan Sar is a family holiday, and much of urban Mongolia shuts down, as people travel to be with their families. Everyone dresses in their best clothes and goes from ger to ger, visiting neighbors. The festivities last for several days. Every family will cook a saddle of mutton and prepare mountains of buuz for family and visitors, and there is even more feasting on the night of the new moon.

Mongolians happily celebrate anything that marks a milestone in life or the year. Birthdays, the first cutting of a child's hair (at age three), weddings, the first milking of mares, and gatherings to shear sheep and make felt for gers at the end of summer are all reasons for eating and drinking. For special events, white foods (dairy products) are served first; these are considered pure and noble. Then red foods (meat) are served.

Mongolian nomads have a strict code of hospitality. Anyone can approach a ger and ask for food and drink. However, there are elaborate rules and ceremonies surrounding both giving and accepting hospitality—including the cry of "hold the dogs" on approaching a ger—which is both good manners and an important safety measure. When the traveler leaves, the host will dip his finger in milk and flick it into the air, in the general direction the traveler will be taking. Like the larger milk-sprinkling ceremony that follows the first milking of the mares, this is done to honor the gods of sky and nature and ask for protection for the traveler.

Diet and Health

On the whole, Mongolians, particularly those living a traditional lifestyle, are a robust people. However, conflicting reports and incomplete research that started only after Soviet withdrawal make it difficult to know precisely how healthy the Mongolian diet is. The traditional Mongolian diet is not well balanced, and some deficiencies have been detected in some groups but not as many as one might expect. Mare's milk is high in vitamin C, which compensates largely for the lack of fruits and vegetables in the diet. The vigorous lifestyle, especially in winter, requires a high calorie intake, and only the meat and dairy diet can supply all the calories needed, especially in a country where people are generally too poor to seek other calorie sources. Some research seems to suggest that, after more than 1,000 years of eating the same thing, Mongolians have either adapted or are genetically predisposed to digesting large amounts of protein.

While the traditional diet may not be perfect, the urban diet has introduced a number of new problems. Dental health has worsened. Children in Ulaanbaatar, where sugar is readily available, have far more cavities and dental problems than nomad children, for whom the consumption of hard cheese offers generally good dental health. The World Health Organization notes that cancer, heart disease, and other problems associated with lifestyle change are increasing. While urban diets have more variety, increasing urbanization also leads to a generally more sedentary lifestyle and greater consumption of refined carbohydrates and highly processed foods, including a switch to sugared soft drinks in place of milk. While vegetables are more available, it remains to be seen whether the added vegetables compensate for the loss of vitamin C and calcium from the consumption of abundant mare's milk. The sedentary lifestyle has, not too surprisingly, led to an increase in obesity in urban settings.

As more people are living in close proximity to one another, there is also the issue of safe water and sanitation. Mongolia is turning to its allies and trade partners for aid in establishing water-safety and sanitation practices that aren't necessary when one's nearest neighbor is a few dozen miles away.

The biggest threats to health for those who eat the traditional diet are external. Foremost is the *zud* (also occasionally spelled *dzud*). About every 10 years, Mongolia experiences a zud, or dangerously colder winter than usual. The long winter is normally cold, with January temperatures averaging minus 20 degrees Fahrenheit (minus 30 degrees Celsius). Mongolians and their animals easily survive these ordinary freezes, but a zud takes the temperature much lower or brings a combination of factors, such as heavy snow or a layer of ice, which keep the animals from eating. During the winters of 1999/2000 and 2000/2001, approximately six million head of Mongolian livestock (sheep, goats, horses, camels, yaks) perished in record zuds. When animals die, people often perish as well, for lack of food. These last two disastrous cold spells threatened the health and food security of approximately 40 percent of Mongolia's population.

Another external threat is marmot hunting. Marmots may be a favored food, but they are rodents—flea-bearing rodents that often have bubonic plague. As a result, there are a few deaths from the plague each summer, usually after marmot-hunting season.

Cynthia Clampitt

Further Reading

Blundun, Jane, *Mongolia.* 2nd ed. Guilford, CT: Globe Pequot, 2008.

Byambadalai. "Mongolian Cooking Recipes." Best of Mongolia. http://www.e-mongol.com/mongolia_culture_cooking-recipes.htm.

Fox, Susan. "Mongolia Monday." March 2, 2009. Susan Fox's Web site. http://foxstudio.wordpress.com/2009/03/02/mongolia-monday-tsagaan-sargreat-food/.

Hudgins, Sharon. "Raw Liver, Singed Sheep's Head, and Boiled Stomach Pudding: Encounters with Traditional Buriat Cuisine." *Sibirica* 3, No. 2 (2003): 131–52.

Mischler, Georg, and Chuluun-Erdene Sosorbaram. All Mongolian Recipes: The Food of the Nomads. http://www.mongolfood.info/en/.

"Mongolian Food: Meat Milk and Mongolia." Mongol Uls.net. http://www.mongoluls.net/ger/meatmilk.shtml.

Mongolia Culture Blog. http://mongolculture.blogspot.com/.

Naadam. http://naadam.viahistoria.com/.

Thayer, Helen. *Walking the Gobi.* Seattle: Mountaineers Books, 2007.

Nepal

Overview

The Federal Democratic Republic of Nepal (until December 2008 the Kingdom of Nepal) is a landlocked country bordered to the north by Tibet and to the south, east, and west by India. It has an area of 57,000 square miles and a population of approximately 30 million. Unlike the rest of South Asia (except Afghanistan) Nepal was never occupied by a foreign power. It was virtually isolated from the rest of the world until the 1950s. The country thereafter became a magnet for tourists, including trekkers, mountain climbers, and young people from Western countries. Nepal is an extremely poor country, with an average per-capita gross national product of $1,200.

Nepal is divided into three geographic regions: the lowlands, or Terai (an extension of India's Ganges Plain); the central *pahar* (foothills), which range from 1,000 feet to nearly 15,000 feet with many valleys, including the populous and cultivated Kathmandu Valley; and the Himalayan region with many of the world's highest peaks, including Mount Everest. These east–west regions are intersected by many rivers and streams. Until the 1950s transportation was poor, so that many ethnic groups and tribes lived in isolation from each other for centuries and retained their own customs and foodways.

The original inhabitants of Nepal were probably Mongoloid people speaking Tibeto-Burman languages who came from the Tibetan Plateau. In more recent times, Tibetan refugees came to Nepal. Starting around 2000 B.C. people speaking Indo-European languages came to the region from the plains of India and the western Himalayas and between the 12th and 6th century B.C. established small kingdoms in the Himalayan foothills. Siddhartha Gautama, who became the Buddha, was born in one of these kingdoms in 624 B.C., and Buddhism became the dominant religion of Nepal. The region later came under the cultural influence of various Indian empires, which led to the spread of Hinduism and the entrenchment of the caste system. From 1846 to 1953 the country was ruled by the Ranas, who were originally Rajputs from India. This reinforced the cultural and culinary ties with India.

Nepal is one of the world's most ethnically diverse countries. The 2001 census identified 92 languages belonging to four major linguistic groups (Indo-European, Dravidian, Sino-Tibetan, and Austro-Asiatic) and 103 distinct caste and ethnic groups. More than 80 percent of the population is Hindu, nearly 11 percent are Buddhist, 4 percent are Muslim, and 5 percent are Christian and animists.

The northern region is inhabited by Buddhist ethnic groups of Tibetan origin, including the Sherpas, famous as mountain guides, and the Gurkhas, who once ruled the area and later made their mark as intrepid soldiers in the British army. Other groups include the Gurungs, Magars, and Chetris in the west and the Rais and Limbus in the east. The pahar (meaning "mountain regions") is home to the Parbatiya, the name given to Nepali-speaking Hindus, and the Newars, who live mainly in the Kathmandu Valley. Although numbering only one million they have retained their cultural and culinary identity and have made important contributions to the art, architecture, and cuisine of the country. The Terai region, once nearly deserted because of malaria, became home to many immigrants from India after the discovery of DDT. The residents have close ethnic and culinary ties with people in the adjacent Indian states of Bihar and Uttar Pradesh.

This diversity means that it is extremely difficult to generalize about Nepali cuisine. Although a national cuisine is developing, or at least certain national dishes, there is still reliance on local ingredients, especially in remote mountain areas.

🍽 Food Culture Snapshot

Uttam Karki is a senior civil servant in the Nepali government. He and his wife, Rajani; their 13-year-old son, Devendra; and their 10-year-old daughter, Uma, live on the outskirts of Kathmandu. After taking their baths, the family has a meal at 9:30 A.M. consisting of dal, rice, and a vegetable stew (a meal known as *dal-bhat-tarkari*), with a little spicy pickle (*achaar*) on the side. The adults drink strong black tea with milk and sugar; the children have a glass of cow or water buffalo milk.

The father and children enjoy a light lunch at their office or school canteens. When Devendra and Uma return from school around 4:00, they join their mother for a light meal called tea or *tiffin*. It includes savory dishes such as pressed rice flakes (*chiura*) with spices and nuts, sautéed potatoes, and samosas (pastries filled with spiced vegetables or meat) as well as sweets (*mithai*) bought from an outside vendor. Like most Nepalis, the Karkis have dinner at 9 or 9:30 P.M. Dinner is the same as the morning meal but with an additional dish, such as a goat curry or sautéed greens.

The Karkis are Hindus belonging to the *chhetri* (warrior) caste (*kshatriya* in India), which means that they eat goat, lamb, and chicken but not beef. Like many Hindus Rajani fasts twice a month. On these days she avoids meat and spicy food and eats only rice, dal, and boiled vegetables. During the festival Dashain the Karkis go to the Dakshinkali temple in Kathmandu, where they purchase a goat for sacrifice. They leave behind the head, neck, and tail at the temple as an offering and take the rest home to prepare.

Major Foodstuffs

Nepal is a predominantly rural country. The largest crop and the dietary staple for most Nepalis is rice, which is grown mainly in the central region. At higher, drier altitudes, people cultivate wheat, corn, barley, millet, buckwheat, amaranth, and root vegetables as the staples. According to the United Nations' Food and Agriculture Organization, in 2005 Nepalis consumed an average of 180 pounds (82 kilograms) of rice, 86 pounds (39 kilograms) of wheat, and 77 pounds (35 kilograms) of corn per capita per year.

Other important crops are vegetables such as potatoes, okra, taro, radishes, cauliflower, kohlrabi, bitter gourds, snake gourds, *iskus* (a squashlike vegetable with a delicate skin), eggplants, and many vegetables that have no English equivalents, including local greens known collectively as *saag*. Bamboo grows in profusion in Nepal, and the tender shoots are used in many different ways for making pickles and in curries.

Tama ko Tarkari (Bamboo-Shoot Curry)

1 medium onion, finely sliced

2 tbsp mustard oil or corn oil

1 tbsp ginger, finely minced

½ tsp turmeric

½ tsp ground coriander

½ tsp chili powder

1 tsp salt, or to taste

1 c potatoes, cut into 1-in. pieces

1 c black-eyed peas, soaked overnight

A Sherpa woman uses a flat basket to winnow barley in Nepal. (Christine Kolisch | Corbis)

1 ripe tomato, cut in pieces

1½ c water

½ c bamboo shoots (canned or fermented)

Sauté the onion in the oil in a heavy pan until it is golden brown. Add the spices and salt, and fry until they separate from the oil. Add the potatoes, black-eyed peas, and tomato. Cook until tender. Add the water. When it begins to boil, add the bamboo shoots, and cook for a few minutes until they are hot. Serve with rice.

Locally grown spices include ginger, mustard seed (of which Nepal is the world's largest exporter), nutmeg, mace, cardamom, and chilies. Hotness also comes from *timur*, a berry similar to Sichuan pepper. *Jimbu*, an aromatic grass with a shallot-like flavor, is a popular seasoning, as is *chhyapi*, a member of the *Allium* genus that resembles chives. Oranges and tangerines grow in the hilly regions, mangoes in the Terai, and pineapple in eastern Nepal.

Although most Nepalis practice Hinduism or Buddhism, which have restrictions on meat consumption, all except the most orthodox Brahmins and Vaishnavs (worshippers of Vishnu) eat meat. However, each ethnic group has its own preferences and prohibitions. Virtually no one eats beef (cows are the national animal of Nepal, and killing a cow used to be a capital offense). Some people avoid yak and water buffalo, because they are similar to cows, and chicken, which is considered unclean, although they may eat wild jungle fowl. Venison and wild boar are popular, although their populations in the wild are declining. Some ethnic groups domesticate and eat pigs. Goat meat is eaten by almost everyone and is the preferred animal in sacrifices, which play an important role in Hindu rituals. Fish consumption is not common in central Nepal, but fish is eaten in the Himalayas where carp, trout, and catfish are caught in local streams. Often, fish are smoked or sun-dried.

Tea is grown in eastern Nepal in the region adjacent to Darjeeling in India. Production is small and mainly for domestic consumption. Cow and yak milk are common beverages and are turned into yogurt and *ghiu* (clarified butter).

Cooking

Traditionally, most utensils and dishes were made of copper or brass. As in India, the main cooking devices are a *karahi*, a woklike pan with two handles used for deep-frying, and a *tawa*, a flat iron pan for sautéing breads. Meat and vegetables are cut on a *chules*, a slanting footlong blade fixed on a piece of wood. The user sits on the ground, presses the end of the wooden block with her foot, holds the item to be cut in both hands, and cuts it by pushing it against the blade. Spices are traditionally ground on a stone slab with a stone roller, but middle-class homes have electric spice grinders and pressure cookers. Standard cooking mediums are ghiu, vegetable oil, and pungent mustard oil. Traditional meals are served on a *thali*, a round tray made of stainless steel or brass with a rim. The rice is placed on the thali, and the other dishes are served in small metal bowls or directly on the thali.

Two popular techniques in Nepal are fermentation and drying. A dish called *gundruk* is made by drying green leafy vegetables in the sun, shredding and crushing them, and then storing them in an earthen jar lined with banana leaves. The vegetables ferment for 10 days, after which they are again dried in the sun. Gundruk is used as an ingredient in curries, soups, or pickles. Meat, especially venison, is cut into long, thin strips and marinated in garlic, turmeric, ginger, and other spices; it is then slowly dried in the air and sun or over a slow fire, a process that may take several days, to make a dish called *sukuti*.

Typical Meals

Middle-class people in central and southern Nepal eat two main meals a day, one in midmorning and the second in the evening. The meals are basically the same, except that the evening meal may have one or two more dishes since there is more time for preparation. A typical meal consists of a starch—rice among those who can afford it, or corn, wheat, or millet in the hillier regions and among poorer people—accompanied by boiled lentils (dal), two or three sautéed or curried vegetables, and a small serving of hot pickles (achaar), chutney, or salad. This meal, known as dal-bhat-tarkari, is identical to that eaten throughout northern and eastern India.

Most Nepalis eat rice at every meal. A common greeting is the equivalent of "Have you eaten your rice?" Both long-grain and short-grain white rice are used, and there are many varieties, some of which are boiled and fermented to make alcoholic drinks. A popular rice product is *chiura,* which is made by soaking rice in water, drying and roasting it, and then beating it into flat flakes that are mixed with spices, nuts, or raisins and eaten as a snack. Rice can be sautéed with spices and cooked with meat or vegetables to make *pulaos,* as in North India.

Bread, called roti, is made from wheat, corn, millet, soybeans, legumes, rice, and potatoes. Typically, breads are sautéed in a little oil on a tawa or are deep-fried. Wheat breads similar to those in North India include puri (deep-fried puffy disks), *parathas* (a flaky sautéed flatbread), and flat chapatis. Bread made from corn flour is popular in the hilly regions. In the harsh climate of northeastern Nepal, bread is made from sweet potatoes.

The second major dietary component is legumes, known collectively as *dal,* a word that refers to both the raw material and the boiled dish. They include a wide variety of beans: yellow, green (*moong*), orange (*masur*), black, horse gram, split peas, pigeon peas, and chickpeas. Combined with grains, dal provides most of the amino acids needed to maintain health. The most common method of preparation is boiling the dal in water and adding spices sautéed in ghee or oil at the end. Nepali dal tends to be thinner than dal in India. Soybeans are extensively grown and consumed in Nepal (unlike in India where they have never caught on) and are an ingredient in salads and soups. One of the most famous Nepali lentil dishes that is of Newari origin is *kwaati,* made by sprouting nine or more varieties of lentils and beans, sautéing them with spices, and cooking them to make a thick soup.

Vegetables are eaten at every meal. A standard method of cooking is to sauté spices, ginger, garlic, onions, chilies, and herbs in mustard oil, vegetable oil, or clarified butter, and then add vegetables or greens, cover, and cook slowly, adding water if necessary.

Most families eat meat and fish only occasionally, since they are expensive. Poor people consume meat only on special occasions and at festivals. The most common meat is a freshly slaughtered goat. The Nepali word for goat is the same as the word for meat—*khas* or *boka.* Lamb and pork are eaten less frequently.

A standard way of preparing meat is to marinate it in yogurt, spices, onions, and garlic, then cook it slowly until it is done and the gravy has thickened. The spice mixture often contains fenugreek and *ajowan* seeds and is generally milder than in Indian dishes. The meat is always cooked with the bones since this adds flavor. *Bhutuwa* is a method of preparing boneless goat, pork, or water buffalo by cooking the meat in oil and spices over high heat until it browns. Meat can be cooked very slowly in water and spices to make a thin souplike dish called *suruwa.* Pieces of goat or chicken are marinated in yogurt and spices and grilled to make kebabs, called *sekuwa.*

Achaars (pickles) are an essential component of a Nepali meal since they provide vitamins that may otherwise be lacking as well as variety of flavor. Mustard oil and chilies give hotness and pungency. Almost any fruit or vegetable or even meat can be used to make an achaar, although tomato is the most common ingredient. Chutneys made from fruit, vegetables, dried fish, or mint are usually prepared fresh for each meal and can range from mild to fiery hot.

Achaar (Tomato Pickle)

2 lb tomatoes

6 cloves garlic, finely chopped

4 green chilies

½ in. piece of ginger, finely chopped

½ tsp salt

⅛ tsp timur (or Sichuan pepper)

¼ c finely chopped cilantro

Bake the tomatoes in the oven at 450°F for 30 minutes or on a grill until the skin darkens. Let cool and remove the skin. Roast the garlic and the green chilies in the oven or on the grill. Grind the garlic, chilies, ginger, salt, and timur in a blender, then add the tomatoes and mix well. Transfer to a bowl and add the chopped cilantro.

A meal may end with fruit but does not generally include a prepared dessert.

In the midafternoon, a light afternoon meal (sometimes called tiffin or tea) consisting of snacks and sweets is served. Typical teatime snacks are chiura (flattened rice), *pakoras* (vegetable fritters), and samosas (baked or fried pastries filled with meat or vegetables). Many sweets are identical to those of North India, including *halwa* (a grain or vegetable pudding), *gulab jaman* (sugar and milk balls in a sugar syrup), *jilebis* (pretzel-like coils of chickpea batter fried in oil and soaked in sugar syrup), and *barfi* (a fudge made from flour, lentils, nut, fruits or vegetables, and thickened milk). A distinctly Nepali sweet dish is *juju dhau,* a sweetened yogurt traditionally made from buffalo milk and fermented in red clay pots. Tea drinking is an important part of Nepali social life; tea is served throughout the day, usually with milk and sugar.

The 1.2 million Newars, who live mainly in the Kathmandu Valley, have an extremely rich culture and cuisine based on the wide variety of vegetables that grow in their fertile habitat. Newars are one of the few ethnic groups who eat the meat of water buffalo, which may be fried, grilled, dried to make a kind of jerky, boiled into a broth, or cooked in curries. A delicacy is *cho-hi,* steamed buffalo blood eaten with marrow and spices.

Wo, a patty made of ground lentils with a meat or egg topping, is eaten as a snack. Two distinctive rice-flour breads are *chatamari,* a flat, round bread eaten plain or topped with minced meat, egg, or sugar, and *yomari,* a steamed conch-shaped dumpling filled with roasted sesame seeds and brown sugar.

The Newaris are famous for their alcohol drinks made from rice and other grains. *Jaand* is a mild rice beer made by fermenting cooked rice for 24 hours and adding water. *Raksi,* sometimes called Nepali whiskey, is a stronger drink distilled from fermented rice, millet, and barley.

Rice will not grow at high altitudes, so in the Himalayas the main starches are barley, millet, and potatoes, made into bread or noodles. A traditional Sherpa meal consists of boiled potatoes rubbed in a thick paste of hot chilies with a few slivers of yak meat dried above the fire. Another staple is roasted barley flour or millet flour boiled in water to make a thick paste (*tsampa*) eaten with chilies. The standard drink is tea with yak butter and salt.

The Tibetan population has made important contributions to the cuisine of Nepal. The most famous Tibetan dish is *momos,* small steamed or fried dumplings made from wheat flour and filled with meat, vegetables, and onion. Other ingredients used in the region are bamboo shoots, soy sauce, salted and pickled radish, and sun-dried fish from the mountain streams. *Thupka* is a traditional Sherpa soup made with noodles and meat. A local alcoholic drink is *chhang,* made from boiled millet fermented in a bamboo container and then in an earthen jar.

Traditional fried Nepalese dumplings, or momos. (Shariff Che' Lah | Dreamstime.com)

Momos

4 c white flour

2–3 c water

I lb minced beef, lamb, pork, or chicken

I medium onion, minced

I clove garlic, minced

½ tsp salt, or to taste

½ tsp chili pepper

Knead the flour into a soft, fine dough, adding water as needed. Combine the other ingredients in a bowl and mix well. Pinch off balls of dough the size of an egg and flatten them on a floured surface. Hold a ball in your palm and place I tablespoon of filling in the center. Fold over the sides and use the other hand to squeeze the edges tightly to seal and make a little bite-sized bag.

Grease a steamer tray, place momos in it, and steam for 10 minutes. Serve with a mint or tomato chutney.

The foodways in the Terai are very similar to those of the neighboring Indian states of Bihar and Uttar Pradesh, since many of the residents migrated from there. The standard meal consists of dals, wheat bread or rice, and one or two seasonal vegetable dishes. A typical food of the poor is *sattu,* roasted chickpea flour. Laborers carry it in a towel to their jobs and eat it mixed with salt and green chilies.

Eating Out

Traditionally Nepalis did not eat meals outside the home, although snack and sweet shops have always existed, but the influx of Western tourists into Kathmandu starting in the 1950s led to a proliferation of restaurants of all kinds, including German, Russian, Indian, Chinese, Italian, French, Japanese, and now American fast food. Kathmandu is famous for its pastry shops that sell Western-style pies and cakes. Tibetan restaurants serving momos are especially popular.

Special Occasions

Nepali festivals and the foods and food rituals associated with them are numerous. The Newars in particular are known for their festivals, especially during the three harvest months from August to October. The biggest festival is Dashain (the equivalent of Dussehara in North India), which is celebrated for 15 days in September/October. Worshippers celebrate the victory of the goddess Durga over a demon, and the belief is that she must be appeased with blood to prevent her from doing further harm. During this festival, tens of thousands of animals are sacrificed to the goddess, especially goats and black water buffalo, and the courtyards of the temples are literally filled with blood from the sacrifices. People also sacrifice animals at home.

After the animals are killed, every part is consumed, including the liver, intestines, lungs, heart, testicles, and blood. At important temples, braziers are kept burning all day so that the worshippers can cook and consume their meat on the spot. Congealed blood (*ragati*) is considered a delicacy and prepared in different ways. It can be mixed with cumin, garlic, ginger, chili, and turmeric, boiled to a solid mass, and then cut into strips and fried for use in curries. It can be steamed and then cooked with vegetables or be boiled, cut into chunks, flavored with lime juice, and served as a salad. In one version of a dish called *bhutuwa,* intestines and other organs are boiled until done, then cut into small pieces and fried with turmeric, cumin, and chili powder.

Paradoxically, many Hindus fast on certain days of the month, especially on the 11th day after the full moon and the 11th day after the new moon and during festivals associated with the god Vishnu. Fasting can mean many things: abstaining from meat; eliminating cooked food, salted food, or rice; or avoiding food altogether.

Second in importance among Hindus is Tihar, a five-day festival dedicated to the goddess Laxmi and celebrated in October. It is the equivalent of Deepavali/Diwali in northern India. People present each other with sweets during this period. On the first day, food is offered to crows, on the second day people honor dogs, and on the third day cows.

Diet and Health

Because medical resources are limited, especially in remote areas, many Nepalis have recourse to traditional systems of medicine, including Ayurveda, the ancient Indian system of medicine, and Amchi, a Tibetan healing practice. There are an estimated 400,000 practitioners of traditional medicine in Nepal. Both systems rely on the use of local herbs (*jadibuti*) to treat illnesses, and the harvesting of these herbs is a source of income for farmers. In Ayurveda food plays an essential role in preventing and curing illnesses. It is based on the principle that disease is caused by an imbalance of humors (*doshas*) in the body that can be restored by eating the appropriate foods prescribed by an Ayurvedic physician.

Colleen Taylor Sen

Further Reading

Majupuria, Indra. *Joys of Nepalese Cooking.* Gwalior, India: S. Devi, 1982.

Nepal Food. http://www.food-nepal.com.

Pathak, Jyoti. *Taste of Nepal.* New York: Hippocrene Books, 2007.

Pakistan

Overview

The Islamic Republic of Pakistan has a land area of around 308,881 square miles (800,000 square kilometers) and a population of more than 130 million. It has borders with Iran, Afghanistan, China, and India and 650 miles of coastline on the Arabian Sea. There are three major geographic areas: the towering Hindu Kush Mountains in the north, the green valleys and fertile plains of the Indus River valley, and barren desert in the south. The climate ranges from extreme heat to cold, and the soil varies from rich to barren.

A separate Muslim state on the subcontinent was first proposed in 1930 by the poet-philosopher Muhammad Iqbal, who suggested that the four northwestern provinces of India (Sindh, Balochistan, Punjab, and the North-West Frontier Province) be united to form such a state. His vision became reality in 1947 when India gained independence from the British Empire and was partitioned into two countries: India, a secular republic with a Hindu majority, and Pakistan, with a Muslim majority. Pakistan initially comprised two parts, West Pakistan and East Pakistan, separated by about 1,000 miles (1,600 kilometers) of Indian territory.

During the partitioning, more than 14 million people crossed the new borders. Some 7 million non-Muslims (Sikhs, Hindus, Parsis, Christians) moved to India, while around the same number of Indian Muslims, many from northern India, moved to Pakistan. In 1971 East Pakistan gained its independence following a short war and became the Republic of Bangladesh. Although Pakistan is an Islamic state, the constitution guarantees freedom of religion. According to the 1998 census, 96 percent of the population is Muslim, 1.6 percent Hindu, and 1.5 percent Christian, plus tiny communities of Sikhs and Parsis.

Modern Pakistan consists of four states: Punjab, Sindh, the Northwest Frontier Province, and Balochistan plus several small federally administered tribal areas. Urdu, an Indo-European language written in a Persian script, is the official language of Pakistan; the national language (used in government documents) is English. Around 66 percent of the population speak Punjabi as their first language; 13 percent Sindhi; 9 percent Pashtu; and 3 percent Balochi. The remaining 8 percent are immigrants from India called Muhajirs (Arabic for "immigrants") or their descendants. Their first language is Urdu. The capital is Islamabad, a city built in the 1960s to replace Karachi as the capital.

Speakers of these languages belong to the major ethnic groups in Pakistan, a term we define as a community of persons, related to each other by origin and language, and close to each other by mode of life and culture. These ethnic groups have their distinctive cuisines and dishes, but these are not uniquely theirs since they share the culinary traditions of their co-ethnics in adjacent countries. For example, the food of Punjabis in Pakistan is very similar to that of Punjabis on the Indian side of the border, subject to religious dietary restrictions. Pork is forbidden to Muslims, while most Hindus and Sikhs do not eat beef and many are vegetarian. Balochis and Pashtuns share dishes with their co-ethnics in Afghanistan and Iran. The cuisine of the Muhajirs, with its rich, aromatic *biryanis* (mixed rice dishes), *pulaos* (rice pilafs), and *kormas* (made with yogurt and nuts), is essentially identical to that eaten by Muslims in Indian cities like Lucknow or New Delhi. There are very few, if any, dishes that are exclusively Pakistani.

One of the very few cookbooks in English with the word *Pakistan* in the title is K. G. Saiyidain's *Muslim Cooking of Pakistan.* Much of it is a verbatim transcription Balbir Singh's superb *Indian Cookery,* first published in the United Kingdom in 1961. The recipes for bread, meat, and rice dishes in the two books are identical except that the publishers of Saiyidain's book substitute the word *Islamic* or *Pakistani* for *Indian* in Singh's text. A significant difference is that whereas *Indian Cookery* has 25 vegetarian recipes, the so-called Pakistani cookbook has only 12, indicative of the important role meat plays in Pakistani cuisine.

🍽 Food Culture Snapshot

Sayeed Ali and his wife, Anita, are a young married couple who live in Lahore, the capital of the province of Punjab. The couple runs a computer consulting business. Their typical breakfast consists of *paratha,* a thick sautéed bread, sometimes stuffed with potatoes, onions, or radish; pickle; and any leftovers from the previous night's dinner, accompanied by a glass of sweet lassi, a drink of beaten yogurt, water, salt or sugar, and mango. Sometimes they have an "American breakfast" consisting of toast and jam and perhaps eggs.

Lunch, eaten around 1 P.M., consists of a chapati, a round wheat bread cooked on a grill; dal (boiled spiced lentils); a couple of vegetable dishes—perhaps carrots or okra sautéed in spices or a potato curry; and just a little meat, since meat is very expensive. Goat meat costs the equivalent of a dollar a pound, the daily salary of an average workingman. Dinner consists of chapati, a *salan* (a goat or lamb curry in a thin gravy) or kebabs, and a vegetable. The Alis eat rice once or twice a week. When guests come they may prepare a more elaborate biryani, a rice and meat dish (see the following). Dessert is not a standard part of their meals, but sometimes they may have fruit in season, a *kheer* (rice pudding), or *firni,* a custard.

Major Foodstuffs

Pakistan is a predominantly rural country, where more than half the population is involved in agriculture. The dietary staple is wheat, the country's largest cash crop. According to data from the United Nations' Food and Agriculture Organization, in 2003 per-capita consumption of wheat in Pakistan was 240 pounds (109 kilograms), compared with 136 pounds (63 kilograms) for India. Although rice is the country's second-largest crop, per-capita consumption is only 35 pounds (16 kilograms) per year compared with 136 pounds (63 kilograms) in India and 352 pounds (160 kilograms) in Bangladesh (where rice is the staple). Much of the rice, especially basmati and other high-end varieties, is exported to the Middle East. Other food grains are millet, sorghum, corn, and barley. Chickpeas are the main nongrain food crop in area and production. Pakistan is an important producer of apricots, oranges, mangoes, and other citrus fruits. Livestock, mainly cattle, buffalo, and goats, contributes about half the value added in the agricultural sector, amounting to nearly 11 percent of Pakistan's gross domestic product.

Farmers harvest wheat by hand in Pakistan's Punjab region. (Ric Ergenbright | Corbis)

Cooking

As in other parts of the subcontinent, most domestic cooking is done in a pot on top of a simple burner traditionally fueled by charcoal, twigs, and dried cow patties. Today, middle-class households use a small cooktop fueled by bottled propane gas. Sautéing and deep-frying are done in a wok-shaped pot made of stainless steel or cast iron, called a *kadhai.* Many urban households own a pressure cooker, which considerably shortens the time needed to cook meat until tender. A heavy flat iron griddle with a wooden handle, called a *tawa,* is used for roasting spices and sautéing breads.

Spices, onions, garlic, and herbs are crushed using a small rolling pin on a stone slab or, in more modern households, in an electric spice grinder. Spices can be dry-roasted and ground into a powder, called *garam masala,* or "warm seasonings"; this is stored in airtight bottles. A few pinches are added to a dish just before serving. Powdered or whole spices may be sautéed and added to a dish at the end of the cooking process to add flavor. Spices can also be ground into a wet paste with onions, garlic, ginger, yogurt, coconut milk, or some other liquid and used to make a sauce or gravy.

A standard method for preparing meat starts with frying spices, garlic, onions, ginger, and perhaps tomatoes in a little oil, then sautéing the meat in the mixture and adding small amounts of water, yogurt, or other liquid a little at a time, stirring constantly. Since most households do not have ovens, roasted and grilled foods, such as kebabs (pieces of meat impaled on a stick and grilled over hot coals or in a tandoor, a large clay oven), are either purchased from outside vendors or sent to a local bakery for cooking. Some villages have communal tandoors for baking bread and roasting meat.

Typical Meals

One of the most characteristic features of Pakistani foodways is the consumption of meat (at least by those who can afford it), which is two to three times higher on a per-capita basis than in India, even though Pakistan's gross national product and per-capita income is lower. There are very few vegetarians in Pakistan, although there is a tradition of vegetarianism among Sufi saints, who are revered in Pakistan.

Meat is the centerpiece of all feasts and celebrations, including religious holidays and weddings: The greater the number of meat dishes, the higher the status and wealth of the host. The most popular meats are goat, lamb, and chicken; beef is considered somewhat inferior. All parts of the animal are eaten, including the feet, kidneys, livers, brains, and other organs. Pork is never eaten by Muslims.

The most popular meat dishes in Pakistan were brought by the Muhajir immigrants from northern India. This style of cooking is often called Mogul, after the Mogul emperors who ruled much of the subcontinent from 1526 to 1857, but this is a misnomer popularized by restaurateurs and food writers. This cuisine developed over centuries in the kitchens of the Central Asian and Afghan dynasties who ruled northern India from Delhi from the early 12th to the 15th century. Their wealthy courts were magnets for travelers and scholars from the entire Islamic world—the Middle East, Persia, Afghanistan, Central Asia, even North Africa—who brought rose water, saffron, almonds, pistachios, dried fruit, and sweet dishes and pastries. Characteristic ingredients of this cuisine include onions and garlic (shunned by some Hindus); aromatic spices such as cloves, brown and green cardamom, nutmeg, mace, black pepper, and cinnamon; yogurt, cream, and butter; other aromatic flavorings; and nuts, raisins, and other dried fruits.

Meat Dishes with a Gravy

The most popular are *roghan josh,* an aromatic, red-colored curry (stew) marinated in yogurt; korma (also spelled *qorma*), a mildly aromatic braised whitish-colored curry made with yogurt; *dopiaza,* a curry made with a large proportion of onions; and *kalia* (*qalia*), a hot preparation with a sauce made with a paste of ground ginger and onion.

A standard method of preparing meat curries starts with sautéing onions, garlic, and ginger in clarified butter or cooking oil until they are brown; adding the

Roghan josh made with lamb and served with basmati rice. (Monkey Business Images | Dreamstime.com)

spices (both ground and whole); sautéing the meat, which may have been marinated in spices, yogurt, or both; and then adding a small amount of liquid, covering the pot, and simmering slowly. The dish may be flavored with rose water and decorated with fried onions, slivered almonds, and silver or gold foil on special occasions.

Korma (Lamb Stew with Yogurt)

3 medium onions, sliced

2 whole green cardamom pods

½ c oil or ghee

½ c yogurt

2–3 cloves garlic

1-in. piece fresh ginger

1 tsp black pepper

1 tsp black cardamom seeds

2 lb boneless lean lamb, cut into 1-in. cubes

½–1 tsp red chili powder (to taste)

1–2 tsp salt (to taste)

Several drops of rose water

15 roasted almonds

Sauté the onions and the cardamom pods in the oil or ghee in a medium pot. When they start to brown, remove them with a slotted spoon and drain as much oil as possible back into the pot. Grind the onions, cardamom seeds, and yogurt into a paste in a food processor or blender, and set aside. Grind the garlic, ginger, pepper, and cardamom pods with a little water until smooth. Heat the oil again, and add the meat, the garlic mixture, and the chili powder. Cook over medium heat for 10 minutes, stirring so that the meat is well coated. Add the onion/yogurt mixture, 2 cups water, and salt. Simmer, partly covered, for an hour or until the meat is tender. Pour into a bowl and sprinkle with rose water, and garnish with the roasted almonds. Serve with paratha or rice.

Meat and Grain Dishes

The most popular dishes are pulao (also spelled pilau, pilaf) and biryani, both originally Persian words. The distinction between these two dishes is blurred and a subject of controversy. Some people claim that a pulao (which can be made with vegetables and seafood as well as meat) is more refined than a biryani; others say the opposite. Both involve cooking the meat with spices, boiling the rice, and combining the two, but the order and manner in which this is done vary.

One way of making a biryani is to boil the meat with spices, cook the rice in the meat water, and then layer the rice and meat in a pan and bake them in an oven. Alternatively, the meat may be marinated in yogurt, spices, and crushed onions while the rice is half-cooked in water. The meat is spread at the bottom of a pot and covered with saffron-flavored milk, the rice water, fried onions, and spices. A layer of rice is spread over the meat and sprinkled with the remaining saffron milk, ground cardamom, and lime juice. The pot is sealed with dough and cooked very slowly so that the contents have a soft texture. On special occasions, biryanis and pulaos are garnished with fried nuts, raisins, or other dried fruits and decorated with gold and silver foil. *Kabuli (qabuli) pulao,* a popular rice dish that originated in Afghanistan, is made with lamb or chicken, vegetables such as cauliflower or carrots, and sometimes raisins.

Haleem (halim), a popular winter breakfast dish, probably came from Iran or Afghanistan and resembles *harissa* in the Arab countries. It is a thick porridge-like stew made from whole and cracked wheat, lentils, sometimes other grains, spices, and beef or lamb; it is garnished with sliced green chilies, fried onions, and coriander and is eaten with nan. It is cooked overnight and stirred constantly to ensure the right consistency. It is used to break the fast during Ramadan and is also eaten during the festival Muharram if it falls during the winter.

Kebabs

These grilled meats originated in Central Asia and the Middle East and are typically made of lamb or beef. Usually they are purchased from restaurants or roadside stalls and either eaten on the spot or taken home. Some popular kebabs are

- *Seekh* kebab: ground spiced meat rolled into long cylinders and grilled on skewers
- *Shami* kebab: a lightly sautéed small patty made of minced meat and ground chickpeas
- *Chapli* kebab: a spicy flattened meat patty (a specialty of the Northwest Frontier Province)
- *Bihari* kebab: long, thin strips of meat, usually beef, marinated in yogurt, papaya, and spices and roasted on skewers
- *Boti* kebab: whole chunks of meat marinated in yogurt and/or spices and grilled on skewers (also called *tikka* kebab).
- Tandoori chicken: chicken marinated in yogurt and spices and baked in a clay oven (tandoor)
- *Shawarma,* unspiced lamb, beef, or chicken roasted on a spit and served with pita bread or baguette (this dish was brought to Pakistan by workers from the Mideast)

Sweet Dishes

Pakistan has a rich tradition of desserts. They include *halwa,* a kind of pudding made from ground vegetables (such as carrot and green squash) cooked in ghee; kheer, a thick rice or vermicelli pudding made from boiled-down milk (*khoya*); *zarda,* a kind of pulao made from rice, raisins, sugar, nuts, and saffron; *kulfi,* cream flavored with mango, cardamom, or saffron and frozen in small cylinders; *jalebis,* funnel cake–like coils of chickpea batter and sugar deep-fried and soaked in sugar syrup; *sewian,* very thin strands of vermicelli fried in ghee, then cooked slowly in milk until it thickens and flavored with rose water; and *sheer korma,* a sweet pudding made from vermicelli, milk, saffron, sugar, spices, and ghee.

Sewian

2 oz fine vermicelli

¾ c ghee

6 crushed green cardamom pods

3 cloves

¾ c sugar

1 qt milk

2 oz dried coconut

10 drops of rose water or *kewra* (screw pine) water

Break the vermicelli into small pieces, and roast them in a heavy frying pan until they are pink. Heat the ghee in a frying pan, and brown the cardamom pods and cloves, then add the sugar and milk. When the milk is reduced to half its volume, add the fried vermicelli and dried coconut. Cook until done. Sprinkle with rose water or kewra water, and serve hot or cold.

Breads

The major staple in Pakistan is bread, usually made from *atta,* a whole wheat flour that has much of the bran and husk left in it. Probably no other region of the world has such a variety of breads as North India and Pakistan. They may be leavened, semileavened, or unleavened; flat, disk-shaped, round, or oblong; soft, crispy, flaky, or spongy; small, medium, or large; austere or opulent; plain or stuffed; and dry-roasted, sautéed, deep-fried, or baked.

Table 22.1

Name of Bread	Ingredients	Method of Cooking	Comments
Chapati/Roti	Atta	Dry roasted on a tawa	Unleavened. Saucer-shaped; puffs up slightly, then flattens
Phulka	Atta	Dry roasted on a tawa, then held with tongs over an open flame	Unleavened. Puffs up to a round ball, then deflates
Paratha	Atta, ghee	Fried in a little ghee or oil	Unleavened. May be round, square, or triangular. Ghee is added during rolling to create a layered, flaky texture. May be stuffed with vegetables, eggs, or meat
Puri	Atta or a mixture of atta and white flour; ghee	Deep-fried	Round, 4–5 inches in diameter; puffs up, then flattens. May have a vegetable filling. Often eaten with halwa
Bhatura	White flour, semolina, sugar, yogurt, baking powder	Deep-fried	Semileavened. Round, slightly puffy. Served with chickpeas. A typical Punjabi dish
Khameeri	Atta and white flour, milk, ghee, yeast, sugar, aniseed, yogurt	Roasted in tandoor or deep-fried	Leavened, sweetened bread
Nan or tandoori roti	Atta or white flour, ghee, sometimes baking powder, eggs, yogurt, milk, sugar	Baked on the wall of a tandoor	Slightly leavened. Round or cylindrical. Rather thick, slightly puffy in places. Served sprinkled with poppy seeds and nigella
Bakarkhani	White flour, milk, sugar, yeast, ghee, almonds, raisins	Baked	
Barqi paratha	White flour, milk, sugar, ghee	Sautéed in ghee on tawa	Rolled several times, adding ghee to layers. Very flaky and rich
Missi roti	Atta and chickpea flour, onion, ghee, spices, fenugreek leaves	Cooked on hot tawa, then roasted over fire	Served with fresh butter and yogurt
Kulcha	Atta, yeast, milk, yogurt, ghee	Baked in tandoor	Semifermented, circular or square shape. Often eaten with chickpeas
Sheermal	White flour, ghee, milk, sugar, egg	Baked	Leavened. After baking, bread is moistened with milk flavored with cardamom and saffron
Double roti	White flour	Oven	Name for Western-style bread
Makki ki roti	Corn flour	Dry roasted or sautéed in a little ghee	Eaten with mustard greens and spinach in the Punjab
Taftan	Atta, saffron, cardamom	Baked in tandoor	Leavened. Served with *nihari*

Typically a Pakistani breakfast consists of parathas, perhaps stuffed with potatoes, cauliflower, or grated radish, or chapatis, sometimes accompanied by halwa. More westernized families start the day with toast and eggs or cereal and milk.

The midday meal, eaten around 1:30 or 2:00, typically consists of a vegetable dish, a salan (a curry with a thin gravy), korma, or some other meat curry; dal; pickles or chutney; and yogurt (especially in the summer), accompanied by bread or perhaps a rice pulao. Most people have a light afternoon meal, called a tea, featuring salty items such as *pakora,* vegetables coated with chickpea batter and deep-fried; *aloo bhaji,* potatoes sautéed in spices; or kebabs purchased from a street vendor.

Dinner is eaten around 7:30 or 8 P.M. In some families, dinner is lighter than the midday meal and consists largely of leftovers from lunch. In others, dinner is the main meal of the day and features dishes that involve more preparation, such as haleem, pulao, *kofte* (meatballs), or kebabs, served with rice or bread or both along with yogurt, pickles, and salad.

Desserts are not a standard part of a Pakistani meal, but sometimes fruit (such as mangoes in season) or kheer is served, especially if guests are present.

Punjab, the nation's largest state with 25 percent of the land area and 48 percent of the population, shares a border and a culinary tradition with the adjacent Indian states of Punjab and Haryana. This region is the breadbasket of Pakistan, and the food is closely linked to the land. Typical meat dishes include *keema matar,* a rich, dry stew of minced mutton, beans, tomatoes, onions, garlic, and spices, and *mutton rarha,* cooked with yogurt, tomatoes, and spices until the gravy dries up and the meat is well browned.

The region's thick, rich dals are famous all over the subcontinent. *Dal makhani* is made from black lentils, chickpeas, black-eyed peas, or kidney beans simmered for a long time over a slow fire until they become thick and then flavored with spices and cream. Another well-known Punjabi dish is mustard greens, *sarson ka saag,* served with cornbread that is very similar to corn tortillas.

The second-largest state is Sindh, whose capital, the port of Karachi, is Pakistan's largest city. Since the province has a long coastline, fish and seafood are important parts of the diet. A local delicacy is *bunda palais,* fish stuffed with a paste of red pepper, garlic, ginger, and dried pomegranate seeds, then wrapped in cloth and buried three feet deep in hot sand in the sun for several hours. Other characteristic

View of traditional Pakistani dishes. Much of Pakistani cuisine includes pickles, lentils, chutneys, and a variety of spices. (Shutterstock)

Sindhi dishes are *palo kok,* lotus stems cooked in earthenware pots, and *kori gosht,* saddle of mutton marinated in salt, tamarind, and yogurt and roasted slowly over a low flame. A popular drink is *thandal,* made from milk and ground almonds, sometimes with rose petals, cardamom, and other spices.

Many of the residents of Karachi are Muhajirs, who brought with them the food traditions of Lucknow and Delhi. A traditional breakfast dish is *nihari,* beef shank cooked slowly overnight with ginger, fried onions, green chilies, and aromatic spices until a dark, rich gravy is formed. It is garnished with coriander, sliced ginger, and chilies and served with nan. Nihari became so popular that it is now served in special restaurants all day long. *Paya* are goat trotters slowly cooked in a spicy dark brown gravy that becomes gelatinous.

Nihari (Beef Stew with Ginger)

2 large onions, sliced

1 tbsp oil

1 lb boneless beef, cut into 1½-in. cubes

1-in. piece fresh ginger

3 cloves garlic

1 tsp chili powder

1 tsp salt

2 tsp flour

Garam Masala (Spice Mixture)

6 cloves

1 tsp cumin seeds

8 black cardamom seeds, removed from pods

8 black peppercorns

1 2-in. piece cinnamon stick

Garnish

Sliced ginger, sliced green chilies, chopped fresh cilantro leaves

Cook the onions in the oil in a medium-size pot for 5 or 6 minutes until they become golden brown. Add the meat, and cook over medium heat for 30 minutes, stirring frequently. Grind the ginger and garlic in a food processor or blender with a little water until they are smooth. Add to the meat and cook 10 minutes more. Add the chili powder and salt, and cook another 30 minutes. Meanwhile, grind the spices for the garam masala in a spice or coffee grinder to make a fine powder. Mix the flour and spices with a little water, stir into the beef mixture, and add 4 cups water. Mix well, and cook, tightly covered, over very low heat for about an hour or until the meat is tender. Before serving, add the garnishes, and serve with parathas.

The state of Baluchistan borders on Iran and Afghanistan, and Baluchis live on both sides of the border. Traditionally nomads, they cook many of their dishes over an open fire or in a tandoor. Spicing is much milder than in other parts of the subcontinent. Kebabs are very popular. The best-known Baluchi dish is *sajji,* a whole lamb with all the fat intact, marinated in salt and sometimes papaya paste (for tenderizing), stuffed with rice, and roasted over coals or in a tandoor. It is accompanied by *kaak,* a rock-hard bread made by rolling the dough over a stone and baking it in a tandoor.

Eating Out

Large cities such as Karachi and Lahore have a thriving restaurant culture that encompasses many kinds of establishments, ranging from little roadside stands serving snacks and kebabs to modern Western fast-food chains and pricey Thai, French, Italian, and even Indian restaurants in five-star hotels. The most popular "ethnic" food by far is Chinese food. Chinese restaurants are everywhere, and chicken corn soup is a standard item on the menus of most restaurants, even those serving Pakistani food.

The country's most famous food district is Gowal Mandi (Food Street) in Lahore, which is lined with restaurants serving traditional dishes like nihari, paya, sajji, kebabs, and biryani at reasonable prices. In Karachi, the main restaurant district is Burns Road, but a newly fashionable area is Zam Zama market, where Thai, French, Japanese, Italian, pizza, steak,

Mediterranean, Lebanese, and traditional restaurants are found. During Ramadan, people break their fast by flocking to restaurants and food stalls, which do a booming business at this time.

Special Occasions

Ramadan, or Ramazan, the ninth month in the Islamic lunar calendar, is a period of prayers and fasting. Fasting, one of the five pillars of Islam, commemorates the revelation of the Quran to Muhammad and is a means of physical and spiritual purification. The fast is strictly observed: No food or water can be taken between dawn and dusk, although special dispensations are given for pregnant women, children, sick people, and travelers.

Muslims begin the day with a predawn meal of porridge, bread, or fruit. The fast is broken every day at sunset with a sip of water, dates, and perhaps a little fruit, a custom called *iftar.* People then enjoy sumptuous feasts with their friends and families, centered around meat dishes such as biryanis, kormas, and haleem. The end of Ramadan, called Eid al-Fitr, is marked by the sighting of the new moon and is celebrated with great fanfare. People put on new clothes, visit the mosque, and give food and alms to the poor. Special sweet dishes are prepared, such as sewian and sheer korma.

The second major festival of Muslims is Eid al-Adha (Eid-ul-Zuha or Bakrid), which commemorates Abraham's offering of his son to God, who at the last moment replaced him with a ram (an event also described in the Old Testament). On this day Muslims are expected to sacrifice a ram or goat if they can afford it and to distribute one-third of the meat to friends, one-third to family, and one-third to the poor. Every meal will include meat dishes until the animal is eaten. Another holiday is Shab-i-Barat, the night when God registers men's deeds and determines their fates. People distribute sweets in the name of their ancestors and offer flowers.

A Muslim wedding banquet is a lavish affair featuring as many meat dishes as the bride's family can afford. Traditionally it includes at least one biryani, a korma, mixed vegetables, shami kebab, fish curry or fried fish, yogurt and cucumber salad, bread, and many desserts.

Pakistani Muslim men eat a predawn meal before beginning their fast at a restaurant in Islamabad on the second week of the Muslim holy month of Ramadan. (AFP | Getty Images)

Diet and Health

The Unani system of medicine (Unani tibbia) was introduced into the subcontinent by the Muslim conquerors in the 14th century and is adhered to by many Pakistanis. The theoretical framework is derived from the writings of the Greek physicians Hippocrates (460–377 B.C.) and Galen (died ca. 200 A.D.) via the Muslim physician ibn Sina (Avicenna, ca. 980–1037). The Arabic word *Unan* derives from Ionian, the west coast of Turkey, which was at the time part of the Greek world. Unani practitioners are called *hakims*.

Unani medicine is based on the humoral theory of Greek medicine, which assumes the presence of four humors in the body: blood, phlegm, yellow bile, and black bile. Every person is born with a unique humoral constitution, which represents his healthy state and determines his personality. When the amounts of the humors are changed and thrown out of balance

with each other, it leads to disease. Restoring the quality and balance of humors is the goal of treatment, using the body's natural power of self-preservation and adjustment.

Digestion plays a central role in the Unani system. Certain foods can cause indigestion and are to be avoided: those that putrefy quickly (milk and fresh fish), those that take time to digest (such as beef), stale foods, spices and chilies, alcohol, strong tea, coffee, and oily food. However, any food is acceptable in moderation. Aids to digestion include drinks made from *ajwain* seeds, mint, and fennel and coriander seeds; pomegranate juice; and other herbs and spices.

When a disease is advanced, treatment often begins with a total fast, which gives the patient's system a chance to rest, or with the restriction of food. A liquid diet consisting of fruit juices or soups made from meat or vegetables is prescribed for digestive failure. A semisolid diet comprising yogurt or *khichri* (boiled rice and lentils) is recommended in the case of poor or incomplete digestion.

People are also advised to eat foods that have the opposite quality to their distemper. A person who has too much of the sanguine humor, which leads to increased heat, should eat cold food such as barley water or fish and take cooling herbs; if there is a thinning of the sanguine humor, warm and dry foods are prescribed. For diabetes, bitter and astringent foods are prescribed, such as bitter gourd juice. Weaknesses of specific organs are corrected by eating the same organ of an animal.

Colleen Taylor Sen

Further Reading

Nicholson, Louise. *The Festive Food of India and Pakistan.* London: Kyle Cathie, 2006.

"Pakistan." Asia Recipe. http://asiarecipe.com/pakfood.html.

"Pakistan Recipes." KhanaPakana.com. http://www.khanapakana.com/pakistani-recipes/pakistani-recipes.html.

Saiyidain, K. G. *Muslim Cooking of Pakistan.* Lahore, Pakistan: Sheikh Muhammad Ashraf, 2001.

Papua New Guinea

Including Bariai, West New Britain Province

Overview

Papua New Guinea (PNG), an independent nation-state (since 1975) and member of the commonwealth of former British colonies, is perhaps the most culturally and linguistically diverse area of the world (800–900 languages). Geographically, PNG varies from the high mountains and lush valleys of the highlands, to sea coasts and reefs, to the verdant volcanic islands off its coast. This cultural, linguistic, and geographic diversity makes it impossible to generalize about anything pertaining to PNG. Foodways in PNG share many commonalities, and more specific examples will be given from West New Britain Province, in particular for the 1,500 speakers of Bariai, one of the approximately 25 cultural groups on the northwestern coast of West New Britain. The island of New Britain (population 405,000) lies off the east coast of PNG in the Bismarck Sea, oriented east and west, between 4° and 5° south of the equator. New Britain is a large island, about 373 miles (600 kilometers) in length and between 31 and 62 miles (50 and 100 kilometers) across. The island's spine is comprised of active volcanic mountains, which are reminders of its geomorphic origins, dense tropical rain forests, narrow coastal plains, and, in many areas, beaches protected from the ocean by a fringe of magnificent coral reefs. Given the ecological features of the environment, different foods take on a central role in people's diet, but food is never just about nutrition; food also carries a huge symbolic load in terms of cosmology, gender relations, exchange value, and identity.

More than 85 percent of the population of PNG is rural, with a self-sufficient, subsistence-based system of horticulture and accessing of resources from land, forest, rivers, and ocean. Food production—planting, weeding, harvesting, preparation, and distribution—is primarily a female task. Men help create gardens by cutting down the biggest trees and slashing the low growth, all of which is burned to clear the way for planting and to add needed nutrients to the thin tropical soils. Men also build fences to keep out marauding pigs and perform garden magic to make crops grow well, to keep out various pests that destroy taro and sweet potatoes, and to keep the food from wandering away into a competitor's garden. In addition to its nutritional value, food throughout PNG has social and cultural meaning and is a key ingredient for creating and maintaining social relationships, as well as earning and manipulating power and prestige.

Major Foodstuffs

Since their introduction to PNG 200 years ago, and as recently as 60 years ago in some areas (see Ballard et al. 2005), sweet potatoes (*Ipomoea batatas*) have become the nutritional basis for people and for pig husbandry. Other sources of carbohydrates, such as sago (*Metroxylon sagu*), taro (*Colocasia esculenta*), cassava (*Manihot esculenta*), and numerous varieties of yams, are preferred foods and items of symbolic value and exchange. Crops such as *pit-pit* (*Saccharum edule*) and many varieties of bananas, plantains, leafy greens, and the omnipresent coconut (*Cocos nucifera*) round out the daily fare throughout much of PNG. Gardens also contain imported food crops, such as pineapples, tomatoes, cucumbers, squash, and onions and, in highlands environments, the "Irish" potato, cabbages, and carrots. Where conditions allow, people utilize and semicultivate tropical fruits and nuts such as breadfruit, the Malay apple (*Syzygium malaccense*), mangoes, papayas, various citrus fruits, the Polynesian chestnut (*Inocarpus fagifer*), and the *galip* nut (*Canarium indicum*). Although knowledge of bush foods and medicines is declining throughout PNG, the Bariai access a wide range of seasonal, wild, uncultivated, or "famine" foods (Bariai: *baginga*) gathered when gardens are not mature or not producing due to too much or too little rain or pest infestations.

Pigs are raised primarily for exchange and consumption during ceremonials. Animal protein is obtained from the sea or rivers, and hunting in the tropical forests provides other sources of meat including wild pigs, birds, fruit bats (*Megachiroptera* spp.), the dwarf cassowary (*Casuarius bennetti*), lizards, possum, and wallaby. For the Bariai and other PNG coastal dwellers and fisherfolk, the sea and its bounty figure large in people's diets. The Bariai seafood repertoire includes all kinds of reef and deepsea fish, shark, sea turtles, octopus, squid, spiny lobster, crabs, numerous shellfish, and *bêche-demer* (sea cucumber) species. Seaweeds, a salty treat in a largely salt-free diet, are eaten raw or cooked with boiled and baked food as a seasoning and salty garnish.

Every culture has a range of foods considered edible or nonedible, preferred or less preferred. Famine foods are not preferred foods but are accessed as necessary, but knowledge of their seasonality and processing is fast disappearing. The sweet potato, although an introduced crop, is a staple food eaten every day; however, sweet potatoes are also considered pig fodder and take third place to the most important and savored of foods: taro (B: *moi*) and the flour processed from the sago palm (B: *mama*), or, in the highlands, yams. Originally planted as a cash crop (copra) for export, the coconut palm has a number of uses, but, most important, just about everything is cooked in coconut cream or with grated coconut meat. All Papua New Guineans, including the Bariai, are able to purchase imported and processed foods, some of which are just treats (e.g., cookies, soft drinks, potato chips, candy) but others of which, such as rice, flour, salt, sugar, and tea (and in some instances alcoholic beverages), have become indispensable to daily and ceremonial life. Clearly, the Bariai and most people in PNG have an abundance of foods, whether cultivated in gardens and groves; collected or hunted from the tropical forest, the sea, and the coral reefs along their coast and the rivers they navigate; or purchased from shops in towns.

Typical Meals

Most Papua New Guineans eat two meals a day, one in the morning and one in late afternoon, and in most villages (and towns) meal preparation is heralded by a familiar "scrape, scrape, pause . . . scrape, scrape, pause," the rhythmic sounds of women scraping coconut meat from the shell. The grated coconut is squeezed with water to produce coconut cream. The "scrape, scrape, pause" is accompanied by the thump of axes as women chop wood for the fire, the swish of rakes as women and girls sweep up the debris from around their houses, and the incessant noise of roosters crowing, pigs squealing, dogs barking, and babies crying. Taro is seasonal, vulnerable to pests and drought, and not always available. For both meals, sweet potatoes, cassava (*tapiok*), sweet bananas, or plantains are peeled, cut into aluminum pots, covered with coconut cream, and set on the wood fire to cook. Sometimes tubers are laid on the open fire to roast for snacking later in the day or for children's school lunches. Both the potato peelings and the used grated coconut meat are fed to the pigs. Breakfast is very often accompanied by fish caught in the nets set overnight or by octopus, squid, and lobster caught at night using burning coconut fronds, kerosene lamps, or flashlights. Large fish are cut up and boiled in coconut cream with curry powder and onions if available; smaller fish are roasted on the open fire.

Men often fish at night in preparation for an upcoming church feast day or a traditional ceremony. The fish is slow-smoked over an open fire and keeps for two to four days without rotting. Smoked fish is quite dried out and is eaten cold; only occasionally will it be put on the fire to warm it up. An ideal meal is taro (but more often sweet potatoes and cassava) accompanied by fish, shellfish, or pork and greens. To eat only sweet potatoes or even taro without a fish or meat accompaniment is not a satisfactory meal.

In Bariai villages, eating is a private act, and families do not sit together to eat; indeed, there is no such thing as a dining table or dining space. In the not-so-distant past, children delivered cooked food to their fathers and elder brothers, who lived and slept in the men's ceremonial house where men ate together, away from their wives and young children. Now, men's houses are not being built, so husbands and sons usually retreat to individual private areas on the house veranda, in the cookhouse, or on the beachfront, where they eat with their backs turned to everyone. During ceremonial feasts, men still eat together in small kinship groups, as do women with their small children and unmarried daughters. At mealtimes, small children run around with a boiled tuber or roasted tapiok root or piece of fish or pork in their hands. Women and their daughters eat last.

After their morning meal, people head off to their gardens and daily chores. Schoolchildren start out on their typically five-mile (eight-kilometer) walk to school, eating their breakfast of roasted tubers or boiled sweet potatoes as they go. No midday meal is prepared, but schoolchildren carry food to school, usually tubers cooked that morning, or grated tapiok that was wrapped in banana leaves and cooked overnight in a stone oven. If available, they carry a roasted fish as well. Women prepare enough food in the morning so that children and elders who stay in the village can help themselves during the day. On returning from their gardens in late afternoon, women haul water, rebuild their cooking fires, and

Bosco, Francis, Tony, and John smoking fish for a feast the next day. (N. McPherson, 2003)

prepare the evening meal following the same routine as for the morning meal.

Eating Out

Only those who live in towns and cities have an opportunity to eat out at restaurants, which are becoming very popular. Villagers visiting town go to fast-food, take-out vendors who offer roasted cuts of pork and chicken and deep-fried, battered fish with French fried and boiled sweet potatoes as sides. Ice cream cones are a favorite with adults and children alike, and juice boxes and carbonated soft drinks of all varieties are the beverages of choice. Some shops also offer lamb flaps, a very fatty cheap meat that Papua New Guineans, traditionally used to a low-fat diet, find satisfying and tasty. Many women who market subsistence foods as a source of cash income in towns and cities purchase boxes of frozen lamb flaps from supermarkets and cut them into pieces to barbecue at the markets for people to buy as a snack on the go (Gewertz and Errington 2009). Besides basic foods such as taro, sweet potatoes, fruits, and vegetables, market foods also include hard-boiled eggs, rice balls cooked with meat in them, smoked fish, and popsicle-like frozen treats.

Special Occasions

Even when people's gardens are plentiful with sweet potatoes, tapiok, and bananas, Bariai still crave taro, their "real" food. Taro is so important that it is the focus of three ceremonies that honor a mother and her firstborn child. On the occasion of the appearance of their firstborn's first tooth, parents send bundles of taro stalks, areca (betel) nut, and sprouting coconuts to be distributed in each village to every newly married couple who has not yet conceived or given birth to their first child. The taro corms are immediate food, and the stalks can be planted for future consumption. Thus, taro here is symbolic of plenitude, well-being, and reproduction. The sprouting coconut is also associated with temporal reproduction; planting the nut means a producing coconut tree in the future. The red saliva created when

chewing betel nut with betel pepper and lime powder symbolizes blood, not only that of the child's sore gums but also the blood of menstruation and childbirth. A second ceremony requires taro production and a distribution to the firstborn's lineage members and to the married couple who oversee the child's entire ceremonial cycle and the firstborn's decorative finery. Finally, a taro distribution called *otnga dadanga* (clearing or stripping the garden) entails the firstborn's mother preparing and planting five or more taro gardens, thus displaying her strength and ability to work hard, to plan into the future, and to provide sustenance. The firstborn, as her exemplar and in whose name these gardens are made and the taro distributed, is seen as a provider of food. Thus, the Bariai say, "We eat from the hand of the firstborn." The mother, the firstborn, and the taro are decorated and paraded through the village.

Taro decorated for *otnga dadanga* distribution. (N. McPherson, 2005)

Nutritionally, taro is high in fiber and carbohydrates, but it has no fat (until it is boiled in coconut cream) and contains vitamin C, niacin, calcium, and iron. Eaten with fish or pork and leafy greens it is a nutritious meal. Sago flour is not very nutritious at all, being about 90 percent carbohydrates, but, cooked with coconut cream and served with leafy greens and fish or meat protein, sago is a palatable and healthy meal. During the rainy season or times of famine, when sago flour might be eaten everyday in various guises but without the garnish of vegetables and fish, it is merely a carbohydrate filler and over long periods not nutritious at all. Both taro and sago are such important foods, ripe with symbolic and cultural meaning, that their origins are given in mythology, presented here in truncated form.

The Origin of Taro

Galiki, the firstborn, and her grandmother huddled together as the sun set on their fifth day without food. Galiki asked Grandmother to cut her hair, prepare a fire, and make some coconut oil, half of which should be tinted with red pigment and the other half with black pigment. When ready, Grandmother decorated Galiki with red oil on the left side of her head and body and black pigment on the right side.

Then Galiki asked Grandmother to heat a stone oven (*eamo*) even though they had no food to cook. When the stones were blinking with heat, Grandmother removed the big rocks and spread banana leaves on the hot stones lining the oven bed. Galiki sat down in the middle of the leaves on the bed of hot stones. "Replace the hot stones" she said, "and cook me. You will hear me sizzling, like this, SSSSeeeee. When the sizzling stops, I will be done and you can remove the stones. Then you will understand."

When the sizzling stopped, frantic and weeping, Grandmother removed the cool stones. There on the banana-leaf bed, Galiki had been transformed into the many different colors of taro, red, black, white, purple. "Eat, Grandmother, taste me! Collect all the taro stalks you see lying around," said Galiki's voice, "and in five days I will sprout and grow into more taro." Grandmother gathered up and planted the stalks and tended them until the taro matured. She heard Galiki's voice: "All is well again, the taro has matured. We will always have taro and never be hungry again. Taro will sustain us."

Siko Pore, who told this myth in 1985, commented that

taro is our primary food, ahead of all other foods. Taro is number one, sago is number two and all bush foods are last. Other foods, such as yam and sweet potato, we depend on, but the true basis of subsistence is taro. Taro is significant to us because it was once a human being. If you don't look after taro the pigs will eat it, the sun will scorch it. In times of drought, soak taro stalks in the river and they will germinate for you. Take good care of it and taro will always be with you.

The relationship between food and gender is important here. Taro is the sine qua non of human sustenance and was produced by a process of cooking—transforming the inedible to the edible—in this instance, the female body is transformed by fire into taro. Like the female body, which is symbolically moist, plump, and cool, taro grows well in a cool, moist environment to produce rounded, well-formed corms. Women also create food through the transformation of their labor, the sweat of their brows; and, as already noted, taro, like one's wife, needs to be treated well so that its/her beneficence will not run away, leaving people without any true sustenance. These symbolic meanings appear again when two families reach an agreement concerning a daughter's marriage and her bridewealth amount, and the future groom's family provides a gift of taro and wealth (B: *murannga*) to the bride's parents. The taro corms, complete with stalks, are tied in bundles of four, decorated, and presented in a carved ironwood bowl (B: *tabla*) with two lengths of the highest value of "gold" shell wealth (B: *bula misi*) and five lengths of lesser valued black shell wealth (B: *bula kasuksuk*) to seal the betrothal. The role of taro as the sine qua non of foodstuffs, and its association with the human female body, with women's bridewealth and their future productivity as taro gardeners, with their reproductive promise of many children, as well as its central role in ceremonies, underscore how important this food is to the Bariai.

Taro gardens were ideally created in quadrants, with each color of taro—red, yellow, white, and purple flesh, the colors the mythic Galiki is adorned in—planted in its own quadrant. While the color quadrants are rarely created today, taro gardens usually have no other foodstuffs grown in them. Garden magic is performed by knowledgeable men who say spells over the red leaves of the blood banana plant (B: *bonbone*), probably *Musa zebrina*. The bespelled banana plants are planted throughout the garden to protect the taro from pests and disease and to make the corms grow large. Before a woman has completed the *otnga dadanga,* both she and her firstborn are unable to wear red in their clothing, decorations, and paint. Red, here represented in the red banana plant, is symbolic of energy, strength, production, reproduction, and the blood of generations of females. To wear red communicates a woman's having achieved high status for having completed the massive taro garden distribution (otnga dadanga).

Taro is cooked by boiling it in coconut cream, roasting it on top of the fire, or baking it in the stone oven. Taro cooked in a clay pot (B: *ulo*) with coconut cream, sweet bananas, and greens is the most relished everyday dish, as clay cooking pots

Rambo and Gena placing grated tapiok wrapped in banana leaves, sweet potato, and taro on banana leaves to bake in the stone oven. (N. McPherson, 2009)

add flavor that is absent from foods cooked in aluminum pots. The most favored and the most important taro dish, always served at ceremonies, is *sapala*. Sapala is prepared by first peeling and cutting the taro into small pieces, then wrapping the chopped taro in banana leaves and baking it in the stone oven. While the cooked taro is still hot, it is placed in a large ironwood bowl (B: *tabla*) or a specially carved mortar (B: *nagalgal*) held between the knees. Coconut cream is added to the hot taro, a little at a time, while pounding with a pestle (B: *iut*) to combine the taro and coconut milk. When done, the taro is a chunky, creamy, and oily mixture that is very sweet, a favored dish with everyone. When taro is unavailable, this same dish can be prepared by substituting ground cassava. For the final firstborn ceremony (of 17), the child's parents prepare sapala in a very large ironwood bowl, top it with 20 to 30 lengths of gold and black shell wealth, and present it to their ceremonial partners to compensate them and mark the completion of their work for the firstborn.

Taro is symbolically female, women are the gardeners (producers) and child bearers (reproducers), and taro ceremonies focus on the mother and her child (fathers are not decorated or celebrated in any firstborn ceremonies). The Bariai do have a gendered division of labor. Men fish at sea, hunt, and do the heavy work of garden preparation and building houses, canoes, and fences. Women also collect

Andrew tipping sago pith into the trough for washing; the flour settles to the bottom of the canoe/container below the trough. Eventually all the water is displaced as the container fills with flour. (N. McPherson, 2009)

shellfish, seaweeds, lobster, crabs, octopus, and squid. Men may help plant new gardens, but after that the labor of weeding, harvesting, and preparing foods is women's work. As is the case throughout PNG, the production of food is primarily a female responsibility, which girls learn from a very early age. Sago processing, however, is often the exception to the rule, and, in many PNG cultures, it is an exclusively male activity. Processing sago flour from the pith of the palm is arduous work. The palm, often 33 feet (10 meters) high or more, is felled. The outer bark is then split and peeled back to expose the inner pith, which must be pounded to loosen the fibers, which are then drenched in water and squeezed to separate the flour from the pith.

Sago work parties leave the village before dawn and rarely return before dusk with the fruits of their labor. Although it is primarily men who chop down the palm and pound the pith, Bariai men and women often share the work involved in washing the sago flour from the pith. But this was not always the case.

The Story of Sago Processing

In the past, the story goes, women dressed in their traditional finery and went off in groups to process the sago palms growing near river banks. They did this for several days, cutting, pounding, and washing sago while their menfolk stayed behind in the village. Each day the women, who should have been hot, tired, and dirty from their efforts to process the sago flour, returned looking rested and happy, with large amounts of sago flour. One day, the men decided to spy on the women as they washed sago. Instead of seeing the women hard at work along the riverbank, the men found them, still beautifully outfitted in their best finery, obviously enjoying themselves talking, laughing, and singing together. Unobserved by the women, the men sneaked back to the village, intent on chastising their wives when they returned that evening without sago flour. Instead of returning empty-handed, the women came home with an abundance of sago flour. The men concluded that the women were meeting their lovers in the bush, and these men were processing the

sago flour in exchange for sexual favors. Henceforth, the men proclaimed, women would not leave the village to process sago; this work would be a male responsibility. Of course, the women were not meeting their lovers in the bush. The sago was processed for them by powerful spirit beings, who, insulted and angered by the men's jealousy, refused to perform this same service for the men. It is due to the jealous behavior of men that sago processing is now backbreaking men's work.

Since this mythic event, sago processing among the Bariai has been and continues to be a female activity performed by males. Men express this state of affairs in the idiom *tikado tue,* "they use clam shells," the traditional female all-purpose tool (*tue*) made from the sharpened half-shell of the mangrove oyster bivalve (B: *kina*). Sago processing is a time when men "use women's tools" and do women's work, and Bariai men rue the day that masculine foolishness saddled them with this tedious, hard work.

The Bariai process two types of sago: a wild variety (*Metroxylon amicarum*) called *mama gigi* that is dangerously spiny, grows in swamps, has whitish flour, and is less productive than the cultivated variety (*Metroxylon sagu*), which has no spines. The Bariai cultivate the palm by cutting the suckers it produces and transplanting them where the palm will be more accessible for processing. *Mamatau*, the thornless sago, produces a pale pink flour. The sago palm matures in about 15 years, when it sends up a single flower indicating that starch content is at its maximum before going to seed. Sago palms (and other food-bearing trees) are owned by individuals, who keep close watch on them in order to process them at peak starch production when the flowering begins. The tools used to process the sago flour are all made on the spot from the sago palm itself. Fronds are also used for thatch; and the newly sprouted pale yellow-green leaf spear is shredded lengthwise, dried, and dyed for women's grass skirts and used fresh and undyed for skirts worn by spirit beings. The narrow end of the midrib is trimmed and lashed together to make house walls; the wide end of the midrib is used for carrying containers or to hold down roof thatch.

Sago is the only food in this tropical environment that can be stored for months at a time without refrigerating or processing it, usually as a solid piece of hard-packed flour wrapped in banana leaves. Sago is eaten daily when available, and it is a required ceremonial food as well as a famine food. The sago palm is so plentiful in Bariai that, during lean times, neighboring coastal and island groups come to Bariai to trade or purchase processed sago flour or the entire palm, which they then process themselves on the spot. About 90 percent carbohydrates, the nutritional value of sago is very low. An important by-product of the sago palm is the sago grub (B: *aoatol*), the larval form of the Capricorn beetle (B: *tangguri*), which lays its eggs in a felled or damaged sago palm. Sago grubs are a tasty delicacy, eaten raw (minus the head), roasted on an open fire, or wrapped in leaves and baked in a stone oven. The grubs are high in fat and protein, as well as trace elements such as iron and zinc, and are a welcome accompaniment to the bland sago-flour carbohydrates, or simply as a treat.

Perhaps because it is such a bland food, sago recipes abound. *Salnga* is made by dry-frying sago flour until it is very crumbly and warmed through. Then coconut cream is stirred into the dry flour to make a thick paste. The sago coconut paste is wrapped in banana-leaf packages and baked in the stone oven. When done, the sago is gelatinous and solid, often a red-purple color. This makes a great take-out meal when traveling by canoe or spending a day in the gardens or on the reefs. *Mama krokrok* is sago flour mixed with grated coconut meat, wrapped in a banana leaf, and roasted on top of the open fire. As the banana leaf dries and burns, it is scraped off. The bundle is repeatedly turned and scraped until it is cooked and the leaf wrapping is all removed. The toasted outside of the bundle of sago has a thin rind of gelled grated coconut, and the inside is dry and floury. For *didnga*, plain sago flour is wrapped in a banana leaf and cooked on top of the open fire. When done, the sago flour is cut in small bits, placed in a pot of boiling water, and cooked until the sago pieces begin to dissolve slightly around the edges. The boiled sago cubes are removed from the water onto a banana leaf, covered with co-

Aisiga and Giarob offer aoatol, sago grubs. (N. McPherson, 2003)

conut cream, wrapped, and baked in the stone oven. Similar to this recipe is *kapokapo*. When left uncovered, sago flour turns a deep orange color; kapokapo uses this orange flour pressed into small balls and put in a pot of boiling coconut cream. When the sago-flour balls have absorbed all the coconut cream, they are ready to eat. Both sago and taro are ideally eaten with a fish or meat accompaniment and leafy greens. To eat them without a protein or vegetable garnish is unpalatable, and people complain they have had less than a proper meal.

Diet and Health

Papua New Guineans have been interacting with outsiders—missionaries, colonialists, and anthropologists—from as early as 200 years ago to as recently as 60 years ago, but it is only in the last

Katrin's daughters watch her prepare sapala in an ironwood bowl. Note the empty coconut shells, the fresh banana leaves ready to wrap food or use as plates, and the cooked taro and tapiok in the brown banana leaves. (N. McPherson, 2003)

30 years that most rural villagers have had easier access to imported processed foods. In the past decade, these foods have become an integral part of the PNG diet, with some imported foodstuffs eaten on almost a daily basis. Canned tuna and mackerel, corned beef, and other meat products are now processed in PNG, while other protein sources, such as lamb flaps or turkey tails (Gewertz and Errington 2009), are imported from Australia and New Zealand. Processed imported foods most desired by villagers include white rice, white flour, white sugar, cooking oil, tea, coffee, various biscuits, cookies, and sweet treats. Children in particular desire candy, potato chips, puffed cheese treats, and carbonated soft drinks. None of these foods is particularly nutritious, most are empty calories, and all must be purchased; thus, people need to find a way to make money.

Most recently, the Bariai have exploited the various species of echinoderms, or bêche-de-mer or sea cucumber (B: *anwe*), a traditional foodstuff that was boiled for a long time to make them soft enough to get one's teeth into. For the past few years, women have been collecting and drying bêche-de-mer on a daily basis for sale to visiting buyers, who sell the product to buyers from China, Japan, Hong Kong, and Indonesia. By 2009, bêche-de-mer species had become quite scarce. Bariai women expressed concern that the supply would soon be gone; however, they are reluctant to curtail collecting sea cucumbers as these are an exceptionally lucrative income source. Women use money earned from bêche-de-mer sales to pay school and medical fees and buy the imported foods and other goods that were once considered luxury items but have become necessities.

Many villagers in West New Britain, if offered the choice, would prefer canned fish or meat to fresh fish from the sea. Indeed, rice, fried flour, tea or coffee overly sweetened with sugar, canned corned beef, and fish have become especially necessary ingredients for ceremonial feasts. Even with the availability of taro, sweet potatoes, cassava, and sago flour, ceremonies are often put off because no one has money to buy rice, sugar, and tea. The growing need for and consumption of processed foods throughout PNG is beginning to create health problems. When the local Bariai aid-post attendant traveled from village to village for his well-baby clinic, he also lectured the women about diseases associated with eating processed foods (obesity, diabetes, heart disease). He tried to impress on the women the importance of growing and eating traditional foods and the sustainability of their lifestyle based on subsistence horticulture. As the need for a cash economy increases and people live off money rather than their gardens and environment, the need to purchase processed and imported foods will increase. The many imported foods that have become an increasingly central part of their diet are an important issue in food and nutrition studies since these are foods with empty calories and an unhealthy source of sugar, fat, and salt. Obesity, heart disease, and diabetes have become critical health issues in PNG, and there is a movement to encourage people to eat local foods grown in their gardens.

Naomi M. McPherson

Further Reading

Ballard, Chris, Paula Brown, R. Michael Bourke, and Tracy Howard. *The Sweet Potato in Oceania: A Reappraisal.* Oceania Monograph 56. Sydney, Australia: University of Sydney. 2005

Gewertz, Deborah, and Fred Errington. *Cheap Meat: The Global Omnivore's Dilemma in the Pacific Islands.* Berkeley: University of California Press, 2009.

McPherson, Naomi M. *Galiki the Firstborn: Mythic Female and Feminine Ideal in Bariai, West New Britain, Papua New Guinea.* Nouméa, New Caledonia: Le Rocher-à-la-Voile, 2008.

Scaletta, Naomi M. (McPherson). "Firstborn Child and Mortuary Traditions in Kabana (Bariai), West New Britain, Papua New Guinea." PhD diss., McMaster University, 1985.

Whitehead, Harriet. *Food Rules: Hunting, Sharing, and Tabooing Game in Papua New Guinea.* Ann Arbor: University of Michigan Press, 2000.

Philippines

Overview

The Republic of the Philippines consists of 7,107 islands located in Southeast Asia. Its long, broken coastline is surrounded by three major bodies of water—the Pacific Ocean on the east, the South China Sea on the north and west, and the Celebes Sea on the south. The country is divided into three major island groups—Luzon, Visayas, and Mindanao—with 17 regions, 81 provinces, and 136 cities. It has 120 ethnic groups and over 180 languages and dialects. Filipino, the national language, and English are the official languages. The Philippines is the 12th most populous country in the world, with over 90 million people. Over 80 percent of the population is Roman Catholic, followed by Muslims (5%), who live mainly on the island of Mindanao. Manila, situated on the island of Luzon, is the nation's capital.

Geography has largely shaped what Filipinos eat. The country's closeness to water sources, its forests and fields, and a tropical climate marked by dry and rainy seasons account for the Filipinos' dependence on rice, fish, and vegetables as diet staples. Other cultures—from the 300-plus years of Spanish rule that started in the 16th century, the presence of Chinese traders and immigrants dating back to the precolonial and Spanish colonial periods, and the 20th-century American occupation—have had a lasting impact on the country's foodways. Filipinos have adapted ("Filipinized") these cultures' dishes to native tastes and the use of local ingredients. In addition, regional differences have resulted in food variations as well as the emergence of trademark dishes.

Food Culture Snapshot

Ramon and Malou Fernandez live with their two children and a housemaid in a housing development in metropolitan Manila. Ramon is a purchasing manager for a multinational company, and Malou is an administrative assistant to the vice president of a big Filipino corporation. They are a typical two-income middle-class Filipino family who can afford the luxury of a full-time housemaid.

Malou starts every weekend by going to a nearby wet market early Saturday morning with her maid's help. At the market, she buys fresh meats such as chicken, beef sirloin, brisket, and pork loin, as well as shrimp and fish like tilapia, grouper, sole, and milkfish. She also purchases fruits like bananas, apples, pears, papayas, and oranges.

Most Saturday afternoons, the whole family goes to the big supermarket in an upscale mall for grocery shopping. Here, Malou buys pantry staples including corn and olive oils, soy sauce, vinegar, fish sauce, and spices. She also gets rice, pasta, canned fish (tuna and sardines), canned meats (corned beef, Spam, chorizos—spicy sausages), sliced white bread, cereals, low-fat milk, and fruit juices in cartons. In the fresh vegetables section, she often gets potatoes, onions, garlic, tomatoes, lettuce, squash, cauliflower, and swamp cabbage. Occasionally, she also purchases packaged fresh Vigan *longanisas* (specialty sausages from Ilocos Sur, a province north of Manila) and *tocino* (sweet cured pork), which are both popular breakfast foods. She replenishes her stash of snack foods by buying cookies, potato chips, crackers, and ice cream.

Malou writes down a weekly menu for the housemaid, indicating what to serve for breakfast and dinner every weekday (the couple has lunch at work and the kids eat at school). The family starts their day early, having a quick breakfast around 6:30 A.M., usually consisting of rice, corned beef or sardines, and fried or scrambled eggs. On occasion, they would have cereal with milk and sliced fruit. Dinner is a more leisurely affair. They convene at around 7 P.M. and dine on typical fare like rice, barbecue chicken or grilled fish, fresh green salad, and/or sautéed vegetables like mung beans or shredded cabbage. Dessert is usually fruit such as sliced mangoes, watermelon, or bananas.

Their meals during weekends are more special or elaborate. The family goes out for lunch on Saturdays, usually for Chinese, Italian, or Japanese food. Malou usually cooks dinner Saturday nights, making her husband's and kids' favorite dishes like pasta with pesto, tempura, sukiyaki, and Caesar salad. Sundays are usually spent having lunch with the in-laws.

Many Filipino families still eat home-cooked meals, although some of the meals may come from or include packaged sources, on which there is a heavy reliance (flavoring packets, instant noodles, canned soups). Filipino families, particularly in the urban areas, now also rely heavily on supermarkets for many of their meals, eschewing the wet markets that used to be the primary source for fresh meats, fish, and produce. Although the Fernandez family orders the occasional pizza from Domino's for an afternoon snack, Filipinos in general have not totally embraced the concept of take-out food. They prefer to eat out and, for the middle and upper classes, experiment with other cuisines, as evidenced by the burgeoning growth of ethnic restaurants in many cities around the country. Overall, restaurants serving Filipino food and cheap fast food are still very popular go-to places especially for the middle and lower classes.

Major Foodstuffs

The Philippines is an agricultural country. Its lands are most conducive to rice growing because of excess rainfall brought about by the monsoon season as well as the year-round warm climate. Rice is the primary staple food of Filipinos, who eat it for lunch and dinner and, frequently, for breakfast. It serves as a base for other foods or viands they eat—from foods as basic as dried fish and vegetables to richer meat and seafood dishes. Steamed rice with its inherent blandness is an excellent foil for the salty, sour, spicy, and bitter foods that Filipinos eat.

Rice is also made into dessert or snack cakes, such as *suman* (a rice cake made from glutinous rice and coconut milk), *puto* (a steamed rice cake), and *sapin-sapin* (a layered multicolored rice cake made with coconut milk). Popular afternoon snacks include rice-based savory dishes like *arroz caldo*, which is rice gruel with chicken and ginger, and the stir-fried rice noodle dish called *pancit bihon*.

Fish and other seafood figure prominently in the Filipino diet. The surrounding ocean and seas, and the country's numerous rivers, lakes, and interior waterways, spawn a wide variety and abundance of seafood. One of the more popular varieties of fish is *bangus*, or milkfish, the national fish, which can be stuffed with onions and tomatoes and grilled, or be salted and dried and then fried. The latter is often eaten for breakfast with garlic rice. Other widely consumed fish varieties are tilapia, swordfish, blue marlin, grouper, catfish, and tuna. Shrimp, prawns, squid, mussels, oysters, and clams are also abundant. Dried fish, called *tuyo*, which could be any salted and dried small fish, is common fare for the country's poor. Fish sauce, or *patis*, made from salted or fermented tiny fish or shrimp, is typically used in Filipino cooking to flavor food or as a dipping sauce. A fermented fish or shrimp paste, *bagoong*, is often paired with certain foods like *kare-kare* (oxtail stew) and used as an ingredient in many dishes.

The coconut is another important land-based crop in the Philippines. Its meat in varying stages of maturity is used for different purposes. The juice of the young coconut, or *buko*, makes a refreshing drink, and its white tender meat can be eaten fresh or used for making sweets, salads, or savory dishes. The mature coconut's (*niyog*) meat is used in sweets and can be grated to make coconut milk. Filipinos also consume coconut-based liquor called *tuba* and *lambanog* as well as coconut vinegar, which is used in cooking and in dipping sauces.

The fertile lands yield a bountiful variety of vegetables. Most vegetables are either steamed, cooked in soups, or sautéed with other vegetables. There are root crops like cassava (*kamoteng kahoy*), purple yam (*ube*), sweet potato (*camote*), taro (*gabi*), and yam bean (*singkamas*). Other commonly eaten vegetables include swamp cabbage (*kangkong*—water convolvulus, sometimes called water spinach), mustard greens (*mustasa*), banana hearts (*puso ng saging*—actually the blossom of the banana plant), eggplants, and mung beans (*munggo*), as well as gourds like bottle gourds (*upo*), sponge gourds, and bitter melons (*ampalaya*). Garlic is an indispensable flavoring ingredient in everyday Filipino cooking. Tomatoes were introduced to the country by way of the Spanish galleons that plied the route between Manila and Acapulco during the mid-16th to 18th centuries. They are widely used in salads, dipping sauces, and many Spanish-influenced Filipino stews and, when sautéed with garlic and onions, make up the principal flavor base of Filipino cuisine.

Chicken, pork, and beef are the meat staples in the Filipino diet (with the exception of the Muslims on Mindanao, who do not eat pork). Chinese traders are believed to have introduced pork in the precolonial period, which accounts for the Chinese names of many cuts like *liempo* (pork belly) and *kasim* (lean pork). Filipinos use almost every part of the pig in cooking, including its blood and intestines. Beef is said to have been introduced during the Spaniard colonial period, with popular cuts named in Spanish like *solomillo* (tenderloin) and *punta y pecho* (brisket). Many Spanish-influenced dishes use beef as a main ingredient.

Pancit (also spelled *pansit*), or noodles, is a mainstay ingredient that has undergone significant adaptations in the preparation process. Filipinos use different types of noodles, such as those made from rice, egg, wheat, and mung beans, to make various pancit dishes. Introduced by the Chinese during the Spanish period, the dish has been Filipinized, and various regions have come up with their own versions as well. These include *pancit Malabon* from the coastal town of Malabon, which is noodles topped with shrimp, oysters, and squid, and *pancit habhab* from the town of Lukban in Quezon Province, which is brown wheat noodles prepared with chayote and pork and eaten without utensils from a banana leaf that serves as the plate.

Filipinos use an assortment of herbs and spices in everyday cooking such as ginger, galangal, lemongrass, coriander, turmeric, bay leaves, screw pine (*pandan*), and black pepper. Different varieties of chili peppers are also common, but the spiciest ones, like the small, very hot pepper called *siling labuyo,* are mainstay ingredients of the Bicol and Lanao regions, where foods tend to be on the very spicy side. Annatto, or *atsuete,* introduced by Mexicans by way of the Spanish galleon trade, is typically used as a food coloring. Tamarind and *kamias* (bilimbi) are used as souring agents, mostly in soups, but they are also made into sweets.

The locally grown *calamansi* or calamondin, a small, tart, green citrus fruit, is a very popular ingredient. It is made into juice, is used to accent foods, and is squeezed into dipping sauces (*sawsawan*) containing soy or fish sauce to complement roasted or grilled meats, seafood, and noodles.

Fruits, just like vegetables, are plentiful in the Philippines. Many of the popular tropical fruits enjoyed by Filipinos such as guavas, pineapples, papayas, avocados, and sugar apples were brought over from Mexico via the Spanish galleon trade. The yellow Philippine mango, *mangga,* is the favorite and most famous fruit, known for its signature succulent sweetness. It is typically eaten fresh and frequently made into desserts. These mangoes are also dried, mostly for export. The province of Davao on the island of Mindanao is the country's fruit capital—it has many plantations growing pineapples, bananas, pomelos, and mangosteens for export.

Water is always served with meals. Juices from fruits like the calamansi, pomelo, watermelon, and *dalandan* (a type of green citrus) are widely drunk. Soda drinks are heavily consumed everywhere in the country. Coffee is grown in the Batangas region on the island of Luzon as well as in certain areas in Mindanao. Filipinos typically drink instant coffee and, increasingly, with the advent of popular chains such as Starbucks and local ones like Figaro, freshly brewed coffee in the metropolitan areas.

Cooking

In the Filipino household, it is usually the head female—in most instances the wife and mother—who shops for and prepares the meals. More affluent households have househelp who do the food preparation, which may include the shopping and, in most cases, the cooking. The most affluent households employ cooks whose sole job is to run the kitchen and prepare the family meals.

It used to be that Filipino kitchens were small and basic, with food cooked in earthenware pots on clay burners (*kalan*) over coal or wood fires. But the American occupation in the early 20th century changed all that as Americans introduced technology for cooking and food preservation and Western-style kitchens to Filipinos. Now, many households have gas or electric stoves and burners, refrigerators, microwaves, rice cookers, and other modern conveniences. Cookware such as aluminum and nonstick pots and pans is commonly used. During big feasts or fiestas, however, some of the old cooking implements resurface, such as clay pots (*palayok*) and big metal vats (*kawa*), typically used for cooking food for large numbers of people.

Many middle- and upper-class homes, particularly in the urban areas, have "dirty kitchens," second kitchens where the dirty work involved in food preparation is done. This can include activities like cleaning chicken and fish, chopping vegetables, and peeling shrimp. Some dirty kitchens are still equipped with traditional native cooking implements such as the *kawali*, a multipurpose wok-like cast iron pan, or the mortar and pestle used to pound garlic and spices. The main kitchen houses the modern appliances and is where much of the actual cooking is done.

The most common cooking methods are boiling, grilling, stewing, steaming, and frying—all but frying are indigenous and were used prior to the arrival of the Spaniards. Many of the most popular Filipino dishes are boiled, or *nilaga,* including *bulalo,* a soup made from boiling and simmering beef kneecaps and vegetables that is coveted for its marrow. Grilling, particularly on coals, is widely used for meats and fish.

Stewing is a favored cooking method for chicken and other meats. The country's national dish, adobo, is a stew of fowl, pork, or vegetables (or a combination) typically prepared with garlic, vinegar, and soy sauce. From Spain come tomato-based stews, such as *callos* (tripe with chickpeas) and *apritada* (chicken or pork simmered in tomatoes).

Frying and sautéing in oil are not indigenous cooking methods but are commonly used techniques. Filipinos adapted sautéing, or *guisa* (*guisa* derives from the Spanish word *guisar,* meaning "to sauté"), from the Spanish; it involves sautéing garlic, tomatoes, and onions together.

Many Filipinos, especially those who live close to the water, often make fresh fish and seafood (or meats) into *kinilaw.* This involves putting the raw seafood or meat in vinegar, at times with other ingredients like lime juice and onions. The acidity of the vinegar (as well as the lime, if used) "cooks" the food, even if no heat is involved in the process.

Chicken adobo with egg, a traditional Filipino dish. (Rolen Facundo | Dreamstime.com)

Kinilaw is popular as *pulutan,* which are finger foods typically consumed with alcoholic drinks.

Salting is another common method used for fish, a way to preserve an abundant catch for later consumption. Salted fish—tuyo for small fish and *daing* for bigger fish—is a breakfast mainstay in the Filipino diet. Meat, fish, and vegetable dishes, as well as fruits, that are cooked in rich coconut milk or cream are called *ginataan,* a cooking method particularly popular in the Bicol region in the southern part of the country.

Typical Meals

Most Filipinos eat five times a day: breakfast, lunch, and dinner, plus two snacks in between—one in midmorning and one in midafternoon, called *merienda.* The food courses in a Filipino meal are served almost all at once on the table, including the soup course if one has been prepared. Typically, the soup is not just eaten on its own but also enjoyed with the food—the diner often ladles some soup broth onto the rice to flavor and moisten it. Communal platters or bowls containing rice and viands (one or two or several) are placed at the center of the table; small sauce plates containing sawsawan, or dipping sauces, are placed on the table as well.

The typical implements in a Filipino meal are a fork and spoon. The spoon is used primarily to scoop the rice and other foods from the plate. In many rural areas, people still eat the traditional *kamayan* way—using their hands. Filipinos from all classes who attend fiestas or feast days in the provinces also get an opportunity to eat celebration food kamayan style.

Steamed white rice is the basis of every major Filipino meal. A main dish consisting of fish, chicken, or some other form of protein is always served with the rice. A vegetable dish usually rounds out the meal. Soup is served on occasion and can also stand in for the main viand if it contains seafood, chicken, or meats. The Filipino table is not complete without a small dish or two containing sawsawan, or dipping sauce. The sauce helps tailor the dish to the diner's individual taste. Grilled fish is often served with a sauce of patis (fish sauce) and a squeeze of the local lime calamansi, while deep-fried pork knuckles are often accompanied by a sauce of soy sauce, vinegar, and crushed garlic. Desserts are not elaborate in an everyday Filipino meal. It can be as simple as a piece or slice of fruit or a serving of ice cream.

Economic status and regional differences and preferences are factors that influence variations in the typical Filipino meal. Poor Filipinos typically subsist on rice and salted, dried, or canned fish and, for the very poor, rice mixed with fermented fish or shrimp paste. Affluent Filipinos may eat rice with two or three kinds of meat on the table.

The regional variations in the typical Filipino meal were primarily shaped by the regions' natural resources—the people used ingredients they were able to readily source from their surroundings—as well as their collective taste preferences. In the Ilocos region north of Manila, known for its harsh climate and limited arable lands, the natives eat a diet heavy in rice, vegetables, and bagoong (fermented fish or shrimp paste), which they use to flavor vegetables and as a dipping sauce. The hardy and thrifty Ilokanos, as the people are called, also have a preference for bitter foods, including ampalaya (bitter melon) and for dishes called *pinapaitan,* where bitter bile from a goat or cow is added to a dish as a flavoring ingredient.

There are many regional versions of the national dish adobo—an everyday dish usually of chicken or pork (or both) stewed in vinegar, garlic, peppercorns, bay leaves, and, often, soy sauce. Manila has the version with soy sauce and vinegar, Cavite in the south puts mashed pork liver in it to thicken the sauce, and Zamboanga adds coconut cream. Other ingredients such as vegetables, seafood, and various fowl (such as duck or snipe) can also be prepared into adobo.

Chicken Adobo

Serves 4

Ingredients

8 chicken thighs

Cloves from a head of garlic, crushed and peeled

2 bay leaves

1 tsp whole black peppercorns, lightly crushed

1 c palm or cane vinegar (or apple cider vinegar)

½ c soy sauce

1 c water

1. In a large pot, combine the chicken, garlic, bay leaves, peppercorns, vinegar, soy sauce, and water, and bring to a boil. Reduce the heat, cover, and simmer for about 25 minutes. Discard bay leaves.

2. Remove the chicken pieces, and broil them in a pan on each side until golden brown, about 10 minutes total (alternatively, you can fry the chicken in a skillet in 2 tablespoons olive oil). Transfer chicken to a platter, and set aside.

3. Meanwhile, boil the sauce until about 1½ cups remain, about 15–20 minutes. Pour the sauce over the broiled chicken. Serve with steamed white rice.

A typical Filipino breakfast consists of *sinangag* (garlic fried rice), fried eggs, and any of the following: fried *tapa* (dried salted sliced beef), fried longanisa (native sausage), sautéed (canned) corned beef, and fried salted dried fish. A dipping sauce of vinegar with salt, crushed garlic, or chilies is typically served with the fried beef, sausage, or fish. At times, Filipinos skip rice and eat the traditional breakfast bread called *pan de sal* (meaning "bread of salt"), which are small, oval-shaped buns that pair well with eggs and popular fillings like *kesong puti* (white fresh carabao-milk cheese), peanut butter, corned beef, and ham. Instant or brewed coffee is often consumed at breakfast.

Lunch usually consists of rice and a dish such as fried or grilled fish like tilapia or pompano, or local dishes like *bistek* (fried sliced beef marinated in soy sauce and calamansi) or *binagoongang baboy* (pork with shrimp or fish paste). Popular vegetable dishes are *munggo guisado* (sautéed mung beans with diced pork and bitter melon), *pinakbet* (a popular dish from the Ilocos region, made of sliced eggplant, okra, squash, and other vegetables flavored with fermented fish or shrimp paste), or *laing* (taro leaves in coconut milk, a specialty of the Bicol region, which is known for its spicy dishes).

A typical dinner features dishes similar to lunch, with rice and perhaps a vegetable side dish. It may also include soup, and among the more typical ones are the classic Filipino soup *sinigang* (fish, meat, or shrimp in broth made with a souring ingredient like tamarind), *tinolang manok* (boiled chicken with ginger), or *suam na tulya* (corn and clam soup from the province of Pampanga, a region acclaimed for its culinary excellence).

Popular merienda (midafternoon) snacks include noodle dishes like *sotanghon* (stir-fried mung bean noodles with chicken and vegetables) and *pancit molo* (soup with stuffed pork and shrimp dumplings that originated from the town of Molo in Iloilo Province). Other favorite merienda foods include *dinuguan* (stew made with pork blood), which is often served with steamed rice cakes, and *tokwa't baboy* (fried tofu cubes and boiled pork in a sauce of vinegar, soy sauce, and garlic).

Filipino food is characterized by four dominant flavors: salty, sour, sweet, and bitter. All these flavors complement rice. There are many food pairings in Filipino cuisine that allow combinations of contrasting flavors to meld pleasingly on the native palate, such as sour green mangoes dipped in salty fermented fish or shrimp paste.

Eating Out

During the Spanish colonial period, ambulant vendors walked the streets selling foods to natives, sometimes setting up makeshift tables from where they would sell their food to lure passersby. These vendors, called *chow-chow* (from stir-frying or "chow") vendors and known for their noodle dishes, were Chinese and are credited for introducing street-food culture in the country.

In the early 19th century, Chinese immigrants began setting up places for public eating, located mostly in Manila, where the Spaniards allowed them to live in a designated area. These places, called *panciterias* (from *pancit,* or noodles), served Chinese foods with Spanish names on their menus like *morisqueta tostada* (fried rice), *camaron rebozado* (shrimp croquettes), and *torta de cangrejo* (crab omelet). The Spanish nomenclature benefited the patrons, many of whom were from the Spanish-speaking class. To this day, some restaurants in Manila's Chinatown and other parts of the country still list dishes with Spanish names on their menus.

Cooking and entertaining at home were the norm until a restaurant culture emerged around the 1950s, post American rule. During this period, restaurants offering American food, Spanish food, Continental cuisine from countries like France and Germany, and Asian food sprouted in urban areas, particularly in Manila. Filipinos were finally opening up their palates to other cuisines. But at that time, only a few restaurants offered Filipino food, including two that are still around today, the Aristocrat (founded in 1936) and Barrio Fiesta (founded in 1958).

In the 1960s, more restaurants in the cities started serving Filipino food—the kind typically cooked only at home, such as adobo and *caldereta* (beef stew). With urbanization and industrialization came the need for more restaurants as people became busier and had less time to cook at home. Tourism was starting to climb, too, and an opportunity arose in the form of Filipino restaurants that would cater primarily to tourists. Urbanites also started hankering for the foods they ate growing up. It became very trendy to open all-Filipino food restaurants—from gourmet-type places, to those offering only regional specialties, to those serving only one type of food (such as bangus, or milkfish, restaurants). This became more than just a passing trend, as Filipino restaurants are still very much around today.

Chinese cuisine has remained very popular in the country, and Spanish restaurants serving upscale dishes that Filipinos still associate with special celebrations have stayed around. But globalization has also had a very strong impact on the thriving local restaurant scene. Many urban restaurants offer the world's most prominent cuisines, including Japanese, Indian, Italian, and French. Local and foreign chefs alike are offering fusion-style food marrying Filipino ingredients or traditional dishes with Asian or European ingredients, particularly in the country's major cities.

The United States has made its culinary mark on the country most significantly in the area of fast foods. American fast-food and drink companies such as McDonald's, Kentucky Fried Chicken, Dunkin' Donuts, and Coca-Cola are ubiquitous in many cities and towns all over the country. McDonald's is a big favorite, luring the Filipino palate with their offerings of local dishes such as the McSpaghetti, spaghetti topped with sweet Filipino-style tomato sauce, and dishes like their longanisa breakfast value meal composed of fried garlic rice, fried egg, and fried native sausage. Many Filipino rivals to this food giant, most notably the highly successful and very popular local chain Jollibee, are giving McDonald's and its ilk stiff competition with their Filipino-influenced burgers and other fast-food dishes.

The Filipino masses also patronize fare served in *carinderias,* or open-air food stalls—places where people sit communally to eat home-style food. Then there are the *turo-turo* ("point-point") establishments, downscale places where one can order from a buffet-style arrangement by pointing to the food one wants to consume. Most of these eateries are found close to offices, public markets, and transportation hubs, catering mostly to low-income workers and families in search of quick, cheap, but satisfying meals.

Ambulant vendors are still very much part of the street landscape today. Popular offerings consist of *balut* (a local boiled delicacy of fertilized duck's egg), *taho* (soybean curd topped with sugar syrup), and fish balls on sticks dipped in sweet or spicy sauce. There are vendors with stationary stalls offering snack fare such as *banana-cue* and

Buying fried bananas from a street vendor in the Philippines. (Mtkang | Dreamstime.com)

camote-cue—syrup-coated plantain bananas and sweet potatoes on sticks—and barbecued pork and chicken parts, including entrails. Some of these parts were baptized by Filipinos with descriptive colloquial names such as "Adidas" for chicken feet and "Walkman" for pig's ears. Other popular street foods include fried *ukoy* (fritters made from rice dough or flour topped with small unshelled shrimp) and *halo-halo* (cut-up fruit, beans, and tubers in crushed ice with milk).

Special Occasions

The introduction of Catholicism during the Spanish colonial period paved the way for the annual celebration of feasts, or fiestas, honoring various towns' patron saints, a ritual that became deeply ingrained in Filipino community life; to this day these are celebrated with much anticipation, fanfare, and local color. Now more than just a saint's feast day, the celebration can also be a thanksgiving for a successful harvest as well as for God's benevolence.

Today's fiestas are a mixture of the religious and the secular—the parish church organizes mass, processions for the honored saint, and prayer sessions, while the townfolk in turn organize events like beauty contests, sporting matches, dances, and other activities intended to bring not just communal enjoyment but also extra funding to the town's coffers. All these activities set the stage for private gatherings that bring friends, families, and even strangers back to townspeople's homes to share the typically extravagant fiesta meal.

The fiestas in the Spanish colonial period were led by the Spanish friar, the head of the church, so the foods that became widely associated with the town celebration tended to showcase Spanish cuisine, as is still the case today. The fare includes the quintessential fiesta food and table centerpiece, the *lechon,* a whole roasted pig, often stuffed with aromatic leaves like lemongrass or tamarind. Spanish-influenced dishes such as paella (rice with meats and/or seafood), *galantina* (stuffed deboned chicken), and *morcon* (stuffed beef roll) remain fiesta mainstays. Some Filipino fare is served as well, such as kare-kare (oxtail stew) and various kinds of steamed or grilled local fish and seafood. The popular Chinese-influenced *pancit* (noodles with meats or seafood and vegetables), typically in one of its more sumptuous regional variations, is usually offered. There are also Spanish-style desserts such as *leche flan* (steamed or baked egg custard) and *brazo de mercedes* (meringue roll filled with custard), as well as American-style cakes and native sweets.

Among the popular fiestas in the Philippines is the Pahiyas, a highly colorful town celebration held in Lukban, in Quezon Province, every May 15 to honor their patron saint San Isidro de Labrador. Here, homeowners decorate the facades of their houses with colorful and edible rice wafers, together with various fruits and vegetables. The wafers are usually fried and eaten after the celebration. In the town of Balayan in Batangas, the Parada ng Lechon, or Parade of Roasted Pigs, is held in honor of the patron saint St. John the Baptist. The pigs are dressed according to the sponsoring team's theme, blessed by the priest in church, and then consumed by the townspeople afterward.

Another highly anticipated event for Filipinos is the Christmas season. Like the fiesta, it has become more than just a religious celebration. One of the highlights of the season is the family meal served during Noche Buena (meaning "night of goodness," that is, Christmas Eve), a meal eaten after attending the midnight mass celebrated in honor of the birth of Jesus Christ. Filipinos celebrate with their families by eating foods like Chinese ham, *queso de bola* (Edam cheese), roast turkey or chicken, fruit salad, and the requisite Spanish-influenced foods like *cocido* (boiled meats and vegetables with broth), *chicken pastel* (chicken topped with a savory crust), *ensaimada* (a brioche-like bun topped with butter and cheese), and hot chocolate (also introduced during the Spanish period). Grapes, apples, and roasted chestnuts are often served.

The season also includes the traditional Misa de Gallo (Rooster's Mass), a 4 A.M. dawn mass held for nine consecutive mornings leading up to Christmas Day. Here, native delicacies—freshly made *bibingka* (a steamed rice pancake topped with butter, cheese, and grated coconut) and *puto bumbong* (a steamed cylindrical sticky purple rice cake served with butter, sugar, and grated coconut)—are served from stalls outside churches to churchgoers after the dawn mass. Hot ginger tea, or *salabat,* the typical drink accompaniment, helps ward off the early-morning chill.

Diet and Health

The basic Filipino diet conforms to the tenets of what is universally recognized as healthy eating—rice and tubers are high in carbohydrates, fish is an excellent source of protein and omega-3 oils, and vegetables provide necessary vitamins and minerals. While these food groups remain the basis of the Filipino diet, there have been significant changes in dietary patterns over the years, resulting in obesity and increased incidences of serious diseases.

Filipinos are now eating copious amounts of processed foods (including meats, instant noodles, chips, and baked goods) and drinking more soda. Prices of some processed foods have become even more affordable to the average Filipino than prices of fruits and vegetables. The consumption of fruits and vegetables including roots and tubers has decreased, while consumption of animal-based foods, as well as foods high in sugar, fats, and oils, has increased. Instant noodles are overwhelmingly popular, a major source of empty calories. Many Filipinos are increasingly dependent on street food not just for snacking but for their major meals as well. Most street foods are full of calories, fat, and cholesterol but are highly patronized because of their accessibility, low cost, and ability to fill one up. Restaurant fast foods are now a fixture in the everyday Filipino diet. The incidence of coronary diseases has vastly increased and is associated with the changes in dietary trends in the country. Heart disease is now among the leading causes of adult mortality in the country, alongside tuberculosis, pneumonia, and cancer. Adult obesity continues to rise.

Widespread and fast-growing urbanization, globalization (as evident in the rise of food imports and preference for fast foods), and easier access to technology (cell phones, computers, videos) have all contributed to the significant changes in the Filipino's food-consumption habits. The increased preference for Western foods is a development that has reached even the remotest areas in the country.

With all these changes in the Filipino diet, some things have remained constant. Many Filipinos still turn to the practice of alternative folk medicine by using plants, herbs, vegetables, and other foods to cure common ailments and diseases. Some of these plants and herbs are being manufactured commercially into capsules, powders, and other easily digestible forms. The ampalaya, or bitter melon, widely eaten in the country, is now available in teabag form, and it is being promoted as a treatment for a certain type of diabetes. It is also used for treating cough, liver problems, and sterility. The roots of the *banaba,* a flowering tree, are used for various stomach ailments, and its leaves and flowers for fevers and as a diuretic.

Maria "Ging" Gutierrez Steinberg

Further Reading

Alvina, Corazon S. "Regional Dishes." In *The Food of the Philippines: Authentic Recipes from the Pearl of the Orient,* edited by Reynaldo Alejandro, 10–13. Boston: Periplus, 1998.

Besa, Amy, and Romy Dorotan. *Memories of Philippine Kitchens: Stories and Recipes from Far and Near.* New York: Stewart, Tabori & Chang, 2006.

Fernandez, Doreen G. "Culture Ingested: Notes on the Indigenization of Philippine Food." *Gastronomica—The Journal of Food and Culture* 3, No. 1 (2003): 61–71.

Fernandez, Doreen G. *Palayok: Philippine Food through Time, on Site, in the Pot.* Makati, Philippines: Bookmark, 2000.

Rodell, Paul. *Culture and Customs of the Philippines.* Westport, CT: Greenwood Press, 2002.

Portuguese in Asia

Overview

At the end of the 15th century Portuguese navigators sailed around the southern tip of Africa and opened a new sea route to the spice-growing regions of India and the Far East. For the next 150 years, Portugal's monopoly of the European spice trade and profits from slave trading in Africa and sugar plantations in Brazil made 16th-century Lisbon the richest capital in Europe. Merchants from all corners of the globe mingled in the Estado da India (the Asian portion of the Portuguese Empire). Mixed marriages between Roman Catholic Portuguese men and indigenous women from Malacca, Indonesia, the Philippines, India, Africa, Japan, and China gave rise to a richly multicultural Portuguese Eurasian community and a unique cuisine that combined Iberian ingredients and techniques with the great culinary traditions of Asia.

The Portuguese colonies in Asia were Goa (now a state of India), Malacca (the modern Malaysian city of Melaka), Macau (now a special administrative region of the People's Republic of China), and East Timor (independent Timor Leste). Smaller Portuguese enclaves were located elsewhere in India and Ceylon (Sri Lanka), in trading ports scattered around the Indian Ocean, throughout Southeast Asia, and as far east as Japan. Malacca was lost to the Dutch in 1641, but the other colonies remained Portuguese possessions until the 20th century, when they achieved independence and many Portuguese Eurasians dispersed to other parts of the world. Descendants of the Portuguese traders, with family names such as DeMello, DeSousa, Rodrigues, Monteiro, and Fernandes, still reside in the former colonies and territories, in enclaves throughout Asia, and in a global diaspora. Wherever they live and regardless of their ethnic origins, Portuguese Eurasians are united by the Catholic faith and an Iberian heritage that celebrates hospitality, a *sossegado* (relaxed) attitude toward life, and the Latin love of a convivial and generous table.

Food Culture Snapshot

Sérgio Rui de Pina and Josefina A. do Rosário are Macanese expatriates residing in greater Vancouver, Canada. Sérgio is a retired businessman and a well-known member of the Macanese community. His wife, Josefina, is the current president of the Macau Cultural Association (Casa de Macau) of Western Canada, a cultural and social-networking organization linked to other Casas de Macau and Macanese communities around the world.

Throughout the four and a half centuries of their history, the people of Macau dispersed throughout South Asia and the Far East, primarily as traders. The last significant wave of emigration took place in the mid-20th century when many Macanese left Macau for the United States, Canada, Australia, Brazil, Portugal, and other European countries. Since the return of Macau to Chinese administration in December 1999, Macanese in the diaspora have had to make adjustments to their political, financial, social, and cultural outlook, changes that have come with some costs and sacrifices. Despite this, the Macanese have managed to retain many aspects of their traditional culture, customs, language, and culinary heritage.

Afternoon tea is a time-honored tradition among the Macanese. (D2xed | Dreamstime.com)

Like all Macanese in the diaspora, Sérgio and Josefina have adjusted their traditional eating habits and methods of food preparation in response to their new environment and the availability of ingredients. But their Portuguese Chinese identity still shapes their tastes and the way they cook and eat.

Their day typically begins around 9:00 with a light breakfast of strong, dark brewed coffee and warm bread buns with butter. At around noon they take a very light lunch. Because of Josefina's tight work schedule, it's usually a fairly quick meal in one of Vancouver's many Chinese restaurants. Sometimes, they'll go to a place serving westernized or fusion food for a change. Like most busy people living in large urban centers, Sérgio and Josefina sometimes eat on the run and have learned to accept and enjoy North American fast foods, like burgers with fries, and fish and chips. Afternoon tea is a time-honored tradition among the Macanese. For Sérgio and Josefina, a short afternoon tea break usually means more coffee, accompanied by some biscuits or home-baked cookies or cakes.

Their evening meal is eaten at around 8:00 or a bit later. There isn't as much time for "proper" home cooking and shopping for fresh ingredients every day, but it will still be a fairly traditional Macanese meal, starting with *caldo verde* or another vegetable soup, based on tomatoes, potatoes, or cabbage, with some soup bones in the pot or a few slices of *chouriço* (a spicy sausage) added as a garnish, along with the signature Portuguese finishing touch of olive oil. One or two main dishes and a side dish of vegetables follow. *Pork bafassa*, a joint of pork butt or fresh ham cooked with the skin on and flavored with garlic, green onions, and saffron, is a favorite, although Sérgio and Josefina sometimes use turmeric, which is cheaper than saffron and more readily available in North America. Plain steamed rice, rather than potatoes or bread, accompanies most evening meals, along with a glass or two of red wine. Dessert might be fresh fruit, or a slice of cake or flan, and to finish off the meal, they have a cup of good strong coffee.

Major Foodstuffs

Luso-Asian cuisine evolved through Iberian contact with Indian, Malay, and Chinese culinary cultures, enhanced by trading links with Southeast Asia, Indonesia, Sri Lanka, Africa, and the Arabian Gulf. The traffic of people and ingredients along the Portuguese trade routes provided an enormously varied pantry. Rice paddies, coconut groves, the bountiful harvest of the sea, and the cornucopia of Asian fruits, vegetables, and herbs provided the staples. Supply fleets from Lisbon brought wine, olive oil, vinegar, olives, figs, marmalade, jams, and fruits. Merchants from Arabia offered dried fruit, almonds, plums, conserves, saffron, rose water, and dates. From Malacca came spices, Chinese tea, and rhubarb.

Vasco da Gama enjoyed his first meal of fish curry with rice and ghee in India, and the adaptable Portuguese quickly adjusted to a rice-based diet. But their Roman Catholic religion and love of bread, wine, and pork distinguished them from their Asian neighbors, many of whom abstained from alcohol and meat.

Pork is the favorite meat of the Portuguese Eurasians. Roast suckling pig is their classic celebratory dish, and pork is the basis of European-style stews and Asian curries. Pork charcuterie, including chouriço and *linguiça* sausages, *presunto* (Iberian ham), and *morçela* (blood sausage) are enjoyed on their own or used to add flavor to other dishes. Goa's spicy *chourissam* sausages and Cantonese *lap cheong* are local substitutes. Traditionally, lard was used as a frying medium and as a fat for baking.

Bolo de carne, a bacon-studded tea cake, is still made in Goa.

Portuguese Eurasians are fond of offal, which is used in dishes such as Goa's *sarapatel* (a vinegary stew), Malacca's *curry feng,* and Macanese *sarrabulho.* They also enjoy beef tripe, liver, and tongue. They are thrifty cooks who traditionally utilized ears, snouts, tails, intestines, hooves, and trotters, as well as the meat of rabbits, horses, frogs, wild game, and fowl.

Fish and shellfish are central to the diet of the Portuguese and the Portuguese Eurasians. *Bacalhau* (salt cod) is prepared in many ways and is much loved, although it's now getting harder to come by. Sea and river fish, rays, octopus, squid, shellfish, prawns, crabs, eels, turtles, crayfish, and lobsters are curried, fried, or steamed in the Asian manner or prepared Portuguese-style, stuffed, grilled, marinated, or included in hearty soups and stews.

The Cristang ("Christian people") of Malacca were specialists in making the pungent fermented shrimp paste called *belacan,* and they use it in a wide variety of dishes. *Balichão* is a Goan adaptation, made with prawns, vinegar, chilies, and garlic. It is eaten as a condiment or used to flavor dishes of meat or fish also called *balchãos.* The Macanese version of belacan is called *balichão* or *balichang.*

Bread is a signature of Luso-Asian cuisine. Soft white rolls—called *pão* in Portugal, *pav* in Goa, *pau* or *bau* in Macau, and *pang* in Malacca—are often served in addition to rice. Bread is used to thicken soups called *açordas,* and breadcrumbs are made into a stuffing-like dish called *migas.* A variety of Asian snacks, such as *epuk-epuk* (Malaysia), *pastel* (Indonesia), *chilicotes* (Macau), and *empadinhas* (Goa), are descendants of Iberian pies traditionally encased in bread, called empanadas.

Fresh cheeses, olives, olive oil, fresh cilantro, and plenty of onions and garlic are other Iberian elements of Luso-Asian cuisine. Olive oil is used for frying and vinaigrettes and is drizzled over finished dishes. Black and green olives are eaten as an accompaniment to wine and used as an ingredient or garnish.

The Portuguese carried many new plants from the Americas to Asia, including tobacco, papayas, guavas, cashew nuts, pineapples, jicamas, squashes, peanuts, custard apples, avocados, passion fruit, sapodillas, tomatoes, capsicums, maize, sweet potatoes, and cassava. New starch crops, in particular sweet potatoes and cassava, helped to reduce the region's dependence on rice and susceptibility to famine. New World fruits and vegetables play an important role in Luso-Asian cuisine.

Cashew trees now grow all over Goa. The nuts are served as snacks, baked into cakes and biscuits, added to meat and vegetable dishes, and used to enrich curries. Another hugely successful import was the chili pepper, which was enthusiastically adopted by the peoples of Asia, including the Portuguese Eurasians. In Goa, mild Kashmiri chilies are used in great quantities to give dishes a distinctive red color. Much more potent *piri-piri* peppers are added for heat. Cristang meals typically include a range of chili-based *sambals.* The Macanese are not so liberal in their use of chilies but enjoy piri-piri sauce and a table condiment of chilies in oil.

The Portuguese had plenty of Brazilian sugar when it was a rare and expensive commodity for the rest of the world. Sweet preserves and conserves, sugar-glazed pastries, fritters and donuts cooked in sugar syrup, candied fruits and vegetables, and versions of the Portuguese quince paste called *marmelada,* using local fruits such as bananas, mangoes, and guavas, make up the Luso-Asian sweet repertoire. The Portuguese also brought the techniques for making marzipans, caramels, and hard candy to Asia and developed fudges (*alua* and *dodol*) and other sweetmeats using local ingredients such as rice flour, jaggery (unrefined cane sugar or palm-sap sugar), and coconut.

European wine, brandies, and liqueurs and exotic local blends made from palm toddy, hibiscus flowers, fruits, spices, ginger, and other aromatics are drunk for pleasure and used in cooking. Portuguese monks introduced the technique of double distillation that made *arak* (palm wine) more potent and produced Goa's infamous *feni,* a brandy made from coconut toddy or cashew-fruit juice. Portuguese Eurasians in India, Malacca, and Macau traditionally chewed areca nut and betel leaf, but this habit has now largely gone out of style.

Modern Portuguese Eurasian cooks have access to ready-made spice pastes and other convenient foods such as canned frankfurters, coconut powder, evaporated milk, mayonnaise, bottled sauces, and instant noodles. They are acquiring international palates, shopping in supermarkets, and using more manufactured foods. Inevitably, some traditional foodways are being lost, but adaptation and innovation lie at the heart of Luso-Asian cuisine, and it continues to evolve.

Cooking

Luso-Asian cooking is characterized by complex flavors and generous use of spices and aromatics. Common ingredients include European herbs such as bay leaf, thyme, rosemary, and fresh cilantro; Middle Eastern saffron; Indian spices including turmeric, cumin, cinnamon, coriander, and ginger; and Southeast Asian flavorings such as tamarind, lemongrass, galangal, candlenuts, and belacan (shrimp paste). Chinese ingredients such as soy sauce and star anise are also used, along with Indonesian pepper, cloves, nutmeg, and mace.

Historically, many Portuguese Eurasians were economically challenged. They are thrifty cooks who excel at producing richly flavored and nourishing dishes from humble ingredients. Stir-frying and clay pot cooking, which conserve fuel, are common cooking methods. Portuguese techniques such as roasting (*assado*), stuffing (*recheado*), stewing (*guisado*), and steaming (*bafado*) are also used. Braising meats and then finishing them by frying is a Portuguese technique used in dishes such as Malay/Indonesian *rendang*. The class of Indonesian dishes called *balado* ("with chilies") probably also originated with the Portuguese.

Luso-Asian cuisine relies heavily on meat, which is often marinated in vinegar or cooked with it. *Vinho d'alhos,* a marinade of wine, vinegar, and garlic that improves the keeping quality of foods and imparts a distinctive tangy taste, gave rise to dishes such as Goa's famous *vindalho.* Local souring agents such as lime, tamarind, and *belimbing* (star fruit or carambola) are also used to give dishes an acidic zing.

Vinho d'alhos, a marinade of wine, vinegar, and garlic that improves the keeping quality of foods and imparts a distinctive tangy taste, gave rise to dishes such as Goa's famous vindalho. (iStockPhoto)

Goan Vindalho

Vindaloo served in Indian restaurants in the West has a reputation for being fiercely hot, but the amount of chili or cayenne can be adjusted to suit your taste. The Portuguese favor pork, but the recipe works just as well with beef. Vindalho tastes best when made a day or two ahead so the flavors can develop.

Ingredients

8 tbsp olive oil, divided

6 medium onions, peeled and sliced into half-moons

2 tsp cumin seeds

2 dried, hot red chilies, or 1 tsp cayenne

1 tsp black peppercorns

1 tsp cardamom seeds

3-in. cinnamon stick

2 tsp black mustard seeds

1 tsp fenugreek seeds

5 tbsp red wine vinegar

2 tsp salt

1 tsp brown sugar

6 tbsp water, divided

2 lb boneless pork shoulder or loin, cubed

8 cloves garlic, peeled

1-in. piece fresh ginger, peeled

1 tbsp ground coriander

1 tsp ground turmeric

1 c red wine

Heat 4 tablespoons of the olive oil, and fry the onions, stirring occasionally, until deep brown, about 20 minutes. While they are cooking, grind the cumin, red chilies, peppercorns, cardamom, cinnamon, black mustard, and fenugreek seeds in a coffee grinder. Put in a blender with the vinegar, salt, brown sugar, and 3 tablespoons of the water. Add the browned onions, and blend to a paste. Scrape out into a large bowl, and mix with the pork cubes until they are well coated. Set aside for 1 hour (or up to 24 hours in the fridge).

Roughly chop the garlic and ginger, and put into the blender (or a mortar and pestle) with 3 tablespoons water. Blend to a coarse paste. Heat the remaining 4 tablespoons olive oil, and fry the paste for 1 or 2 minutes until fragrant. Add the coriander and turmeric. Fry for another 30 seconds. Add the pork cubes, scraping in all the spice paste, and add the wine. Bring to a boil, cover, turn down the heat, and simmer very gently for 2 hours, stirring occasionally, until the pork is very tender.

Traditionally, every Portuguese Eurasian household had a kitchen garden (*horta*), and sourcing the freshest produce is very important. The Cristang, who endured centuries of economic deprivation after the loss of Malacca to the Dutch, developed a wide range of vegetable and meat-stretching dishes. Like Macanese cooks, they cut vegetables on the bias and stir-fry them in the Chinese manner. Many Goan vegetable dishes reflect the influence of the indigenous Saraswati Hindus, whose meatless curries and dals were adopted for Catholic fasting days. Dishes made with fresh palm toddy, salted buttermilk, curd, yogurt, and ghee, as well as fruit desserts and sweets made with rice, coconut, and jaggery (palm sugar loaves, also made from sugarcane), crossed over from the Hindu kitchen.

The Portuguese Eurasians are masters of preserving fruits and vegetables using salt, vinegar, and sugar. In India, they developed tangy-sweet chutneys that inspired Anglo-Indian classics like Major Grey's. They also adopted the Indian vinegared vegetable pickles called *achars* and Southeast Asian sambals (chili sauces).

Many dishes start with the classic Portuguese *refogado* of garlic and onions slowly caramelized in olive oil. In Malacca, traditional Iberian pot roasting combined with the Chinese *lu* technique gave rise to the method known as "flavor-potting." It is widely believed that the Portuguese popularized deep-frying in Asia, inspiring many of the region's snack foods and Japanese tempura.

Kitchen tools include the Portuguese *tacho* and *panela* (a terra-cotta baking dish and iron soup kettle), the Malay *batu giling* (grinding stone) and *pilung tek-tek* (mortar and pestle), Indian-style *tezalers* (curry pots) and *kadais* (miniwoks), and a Chinese wok and cleaver.

Herbs and spices are usually ground fresh in the Indian manner. Goans make South Indian–style curries thickened with freshly grated coconut. Cristang cooks use the Malay technique of frying spice pastes in coconut cream.

At the village level in Asia, traditional cooking methods are still used in simple kitchens equipped with propane cooktops and/or a charcoal brazier. European-style cakes were traditionally cooked in a makeshift oven made by putting a tray of hot coals on top of the brazier. Today, broilers or toaster ovens are often used to achieve a characteristic browned top on baked cakes. Full-size Western ovens, which are expensive to run and heat up the kitchen, are mostly used in Western-style homes or apartments with air-conditioning.

Many Asian cakes and sweets are of Portuguese origin, with rice flour, tapioca, cassava, and other starches replacing wheat flour. Seventeenth-century Portuguese nuns were famous for confections made from egg yolks and sugar. Thai temple sweets such as *foy thong* (golden threads), Malaysia's *serikaya* (a curd made from coconut, sugar, and eggs), and Chinese egg tarts are believed to have descended from these traditional Portuguese sweets. Cakes such as *bolu, molho, koku,* and *putugal* appear in all the former Portuguese territories in Asia, along with the wafers known as *love letters,* sweet fritters called *sonhos* ("dreams"), and various interpretations of *bebinca,* a rich layer cake made from reduced coconut milk and jaggery.

Modernization is changing the way foods are procured, prepared, and consumed. Families are smaller; many women have jobs and rely on convenience foods and cooking methods. Fewer Portuguese Eurasian households hire domestic help, and there isn't enough time to prepare the labor-intensive dishes of the past. Refrigerators do away with the need for preserving, and well-stocked supermarkets mean there is no need to stockpile food for the monsoon. But Portuguese Eurasian cooks still recognize that the best flavors come from coconut, chilies, herbs, and spices ground fresh every day and the traditional cooking methods of their grandmothers.

Typical Meals

The wealthy colonial Portuguese lived in grand style. A huge staff of slaves and servants supervised by the *dona de casa* (lady of the house) dealt with the daily tasks of purchasing and preparing food. The main meal in a Catholic Goan country mansion, served in the evening or as a leisurely lunch, was an elaborate affair. A soup course came first, with crusty bread, cocktails or sangria, and cashews and other snacks such as salt cod balls, turnovers, or shrimp rissoles. Main dishes might include

grilled prawns, a pork balchão, fish curries, roasted pomfret (a popular white fish in Goa) stuffed with chili paste, or chouriço or Goan chourissam sausages fried with potatoes and onions, accompanied by European breads and Indian chapatis, boiled rice and an elaborate pilaf, salads, vegetable dishes, and an array of pickles and condiments. The repast would be washed down with Portuguese wines and Indian or Chinese tea, followed by digestifs, port, and desserts such as pudding, flan, or bebinca and fresh fruit. These excessive meals were never wasted—leftovers were distributed to household staff and less-well-off members of the Portuguese community.

Except for the bread and wine of Holy Communion and the very occasional feast of roast pig, the poorer Portuguese and *mestiços* (children of mixed marriages) largely followed indigenous foodways, often at a subsistence level. Modern Luso-Asian cuisine is far more egalitarian, the main dichotomy existing between rural (more traditional) and urban (more westernized) foodways. In both groups the dining table, chairs, and tablecloth are likely to be European, but dishes are served all at once, Asian-style.

Fish curry and rice is the staple dish of Hindu and Catholic Goans and is eaten at any time of day. Many Portuguese Eurasians now start the day with tea and toast, but breakfast might also be leftover fish curry for a Goan or a bowl of congee (rice porridge with tasty toppings) for a Macanese. Lunch and dinner are similar meals, centered on rice and a mixture of meat, fish, and vegetable preparations served with condiments and Asian or European breads. Traditionally, a wide variety of dishes were brought to the table, even at lunchtime, but nowadays meals tend to be simpler, with one or two principal dishes, such as *caldeirada* (fish stew), *guisado* (pot roast), or *xacuti* (a fiery Hindu curry of vegetables with chicken or pork). Some traditional Muslim dishes, including rice-based pilafs and *biryanis,* kebabs, mutton dishes, rich *kormas* (food cooked in a yogurt and nut sauce), and desserts such as sweet rice and *kheer* (rice pudding) also appear on Portuguese Eurasian tables. A wide array of chutneys, pickles, and condiments typically accompany a Luso-Asian meal. Portuguese kale soup (caldo verde), made with local Asian greens, is a Luso-Asian soul food that often appears as a first course.

A Cristang meal will typically consist of rice, two or more curries, sambals, and vegetable dishes. Diners help themselves and traditionally eat with the fingers of the right hand in the Malay fashion, or with a spoon and fork. *Bife assado* (beef pot roast), *debal* (devil curry), and curry feng are Cristang specialties. Rice dishes are either European-style (*arroz*) or Malay-style (*nasi*).

The Dutch and British who followed the Portuguese into Asia also influenced Luso-Asian cooking. Stews containing carrots, cabbage, onions, and potatoes; meatballs called *frikkerdel* or *pikkadel;* yeasted sweet breads; and cakes baked in fancy brass molds and cakes with dried fruit reflect the Dutch influence. The British popularized hams, roast beef, dishes served on toast, and afternoon-tea treats such as filled cakes, sandwiches, and scones.

Along with the Portuguese, Chinese, Arab, and Indian settlers influenced Timorese cuisine. *Seu mai* (dumplings) and *chau min* (noodles) are local renditions of Chinese dishes. Arab-inspired kebabs (*sassate*) are made with goat meat or chicken. Frugal, one-bowl meals called *agua e sal* (water and salt), made from meat, poultry, fish, or vegetables served over rice and eaten with a fork and spoon, are enjoyed in every household. The mountain people's traditional stew (*seduk*) is also widely consumed.

The final course of a Luso-Asian meal is likely to consist of fresh fruit or a European-style dessert. Mango pudding is a tropical version of the Portuguese *pudim,* and there are various Asian interpretations of Iberian flan. There might also be a European butter cake, Chinese mung bean porridge, or Peranakan pineapple tarts. Pastes made from guavas and lime juice (*perada*) or mangoes (*mangada*) are served with coffee or a glass of port.

Eating Out

"Goa is crying for her lost cuisine," reads a billboard advertisement for a restaurant in the state capital, Panjim. When Portuguese Eurasians eat out, it will rarely be at a restaurant serving their own, homey cuisine. Many people outside the Portuguese Eurasian community find their traditional foods too spicy or strange or think them unrefined.

Few traditional restaurants survived Macau's transformation into a Chinese tourist resort with Vegas-style casinos and hotels. A few token "Portuguese" and "Macanese" restaurants cater to foreign visitors with an interest in cultural tourism. When the overseas Macanese eat out, which they love to do, they'll often head for the local Chinatown. There are only a handful of Cristang living in Malacca today and even fewer traditional cooks. Some Cristang dishes may be found at Peranakan restaurants.

Although restaurants are not a feature of traditional Luso-Asian culture, eating foods prepared outside the home has always been popular. In Asia, hawker stands, bakeries, and the "merenda man" (vendor of teatime treats) traditionally provided a wide range of inexpensive cooked foods at any time of the day or night—curries and bread in Goa; noodles, steamed buns, and barbecued pork and ducks in Macau; sticks of chicken *satay* and entire meals of rice, meat, and vegetables wrapped in banana leaves in Malacca. The cry of street vendors and the steam whistles, bells, and clacking bamboo that announced the arrival of a hawker pushing a cart or balancing a shoulder yoke are nostalgic memories for Portuguese Eurasians in the diaspora. The familiar street foods of their childhood are often the first thing they seek out when they go home for a visit.

Lightened and modernized by chefs who have studied contemporary cooking in the West, Luso-Asian cuisine is starting to be recognized for its eclectic, exotic flavors and unique multicultural style and may begin to appear more often on restaurant menus.

Special Occasions

Easter and Christmas are the biggest celebrations of the Luso-Asian year and are associated with traditional Portuguese foods. Yeasted cakes and breads, some decorated with colored eggs, are popular at Easter. Most Catholics fast to some degree during Lent, even if it just means giving up a favorite indulgence such as chocolate or steak. A whole roast lamb or kid on Easter Sunday is the traditional reward.

The 12 days of Christmas are the high point of the culinary year, bringing forth a multitude of marzipans, halwas, breads, cakes, and confections with evocative names such as nun's bellies, pope's ears, sighs, dreams, and pillows for Baby Jesus, as well as a super-rich egg custard called *toucinho de ceu* (heavenly bacon). Christmas Eve calls for *consoada* (bacalhau and potatoes) or *galinhia pai* (chicken pie), eaten after midnight mass. The Cristang serve a brandied pig-trotter soup, called *teem,* and debal, a spicy curry of Christmas leftovers. Sarapatel, traditionally served with *sanna* (puffy breads made from rice and palm toddy), is mandatory at Goan feasts.

The Portuguese Eurasians also participate in some indigenous Asian holidays, such as Chinese New Year and the Mid-Autumn Festival, which are celebrated by the Macanese. Catholic Goans take part in the Hindu carnival called Holi, buy or make special sweets for Diwali, and celebrate Pongal, the South Indian harvest festival, with the traditional dish of sweetened rice. Cristang cooks will prepare special treats for their Muslim friends and neighbors at the close of Ramadan.

Luso-Asian weddings combine a Catholic ceremony (blessed with bread and wine and followed by wedding cake) with local nuptial customs. Cristang brides traditionally dress in Malay sarong and *kebaya,* while Catholic Goan and Macanese brides may appear first in a European bridal gown and then in Asian costume. Portuguese folk dances and music accompany the wedding feast, which in Timor may include the sacrifice of a buffalo.

The Feast of St. Francis Xavier, patron saint of the Portuguese Eurasians, draws Catholics from all over the world to the Basilica of Bom Jesus in Old Goa, where the Jesuit missionary's body is preserved. In Mumbai, the Bandra Feast celebrating the birthday of Mary attracts pilgrims from throughout India. In Malacca, the Festa de San Pedro involves a blessing of the fishing fleet, carnival competitions, and a traditional parade.

Among the Macanese, birthdays, weddings, important business meetings, and other community celebrations call for *cha gordo,* which literally means "fat tea." Community cooks band together to create a banquet featuring the dishes that connect the Macanese with their heritage. There will be *chamuças* (like samosas), *bolos de bacalhau* (codfish cakes), *pão recheado* (small, deep-fried stuffed buns), and other finger foods. Chafing dishes will display *chicken cafreal* (spicy African chicken), *tacho* (a hearty pork and offal stew), *porco balichang tamarinho* (pork belly with tamarind and shrimp paste), chili prawns, Goan vindalho, and steaming mounds of white rice, *arroz chau-chau* (Portuguese fried rice), and stir-fried noodles. There may be *empada* (an exotic fish pie enclosed in sweet pastry) or *capela* (meatloaf baked in the shape of a crown), and there will definitely be the much-loved *minchi* (ground beef and/or pork with soy sauce and other Asian flavorings, onions, and cubes of fried potato).

Sarapatel, a vinegary stew often served on Christmas Eve by Portuguese Eurasians. (iStockPhoto)

Minchi (Macanese Ground Meat)

All Macanese cooks have their own (often secret) recipe for minchi, the Macanese version of "mince." It's a comforting and homely dish that can be served at any time of day, by itself or with rice, noodles, bread, or just about anything else.

2 potatoes, peeled and cut into small cubes
Oil for frying

1 lb ground beef

½ lb ground pork

1 tsp light soy sauce

4 tsp dark soy sauce

1 tsp sugar

1 tsp salt

½ tsp pepper

1 onion, finely chopped

2 cloves garlic, chopped

Deep-fry the potato cubes, and set aside. Mix the ground beef and pork with the soy sauces, sugar, salt, and pepper. Sauté the onions and garlic in a little oil until softened. Add the seasoned meat, and stir-fry until cooked but not dry. Mix in the fried potatoes. Taste and adjust the seasoning before serving. Some cooks like to add a dash of Worcestershire sauce, toasted sesame oil, or *tau cheo* (fermented yellow soybean paste).

At the dessert end of the table, choices might include *baji* (glutinous rice pudding), *bebinga de leite* (a coconut custard), *pastéis de nata* (Portuguese custard tarts), and *cabelo de noiva* (a tart topped with sweet egg threads called angel's hair). There will be *bolos* (sponge cakes and pound cakes rich with eggs and butter), *batatada* (a delicious sweet-potato cake), cornstarch cookies called *genetes,* cupcakes, and *malassadas,* which are little donuts.

And, if the guests are lucky, one of the older Macanese cooks will still remember how to make *alua* (a fudge containing lard) and *ladu,* another very traditional confection. Otherwise, they will have to be brought back from Macau, where one or two artisan confectioners may still make these treasured heritage sweets.

Diet and Health

The Roman Catholic calendar of fast and feast days laid the framework of the Portuguese diet. Fasting, either total or partial abstention from meat and rich foods, was associated with spiritual purity and undertaken by most of the population. At the basic level, Portuguese Catholics abstained from eating meat on Fridays and the eve of feast days, ate sparingly during the week, and enjoyed a more elaborate meal on Sundays after church.

The 16th-century Portuguese relied on humoral theory, herbal potions, bloodletting, superstitions, and religious interventions to ensure good health. Antidotes against poisoning by one's enemies were particularly important, and when long-distance voyaging revealed the scourge of scurvy, the diet of seamen became another concern. Vasco da Gama noted that citrus fruits cured scurvy, a fact unknown to British mariners until the 18th century, but a huge number of lives were lost on Portuguese ships sailing to the East, and unfamiliar tropical diseases claimed many more.

The Portuguese studied indigenous Asian healing systems, dietary principles, and folk medicine. They adopted aspects of holistic Indian Ayurvedic practice as well as the Chinese theory of hot and cold, and wet and dry, foods. In Malacca, they learned about *jamu* (Javanese herbal medicine) and the Malay spiritual healers called *dukun.*

The physician Garcia de Orta established a garden for medicinal plants in Goa and wrote Europe's first treatise on tropical medicine. Christoforas Acosta, born in Portuguese Mozambique, published another of the Western world's earliest pharmacological manuals. Jesuit doctors in Macau studied Chinese medicines and used them in their hospital. The Portuguese also studied the effects of local intoxicants and poisons, including palm wine, marijuana, betel leaf, and datura (which contains atropine, both hallucinogenic and poisonous). Goan Catholic women were reputedly notorious for drugging their husbands with heady-scented datura in order to facilitate amorous liaisons with other men. The Portuguese captain Rui Freyre de Andrada escaped from British capture in the Persian Gulf by lacing his enemies' food with the drug.

Some elements of the Portuguese Eurasians' traditional diet are falling from favor in modern times. Animal fats, once an important source of calories, are now thought to encourage arteriosclerosis, and eating food from communal platters with chopsticks is thought to encourage transmission of disease.

Factory-farmed pigs are regarded as "cleaner" than the pigs that root around in village garbage heaps. A generation accustomed to supermarkets is put off by the sights and smells of traditional wet markets. Homely dishes containing offal and animal "parts" are increasingly seen as fodder of the lower classes, while the cuisine of the modernized West is synonymous with social and economic advancement.

Like everyone else living in industrialized countries, the modern Portuguese Eurasians are now falling victim to illnesses caused by urban lifestyles and stress. Most use Western medicine, but traditional folk remedies still have their place. The Cristang protect their health by avoiding eating too much meat. A Macanese with a sore throat may brew up a restorative herbal soup or a traditional cure called *mui-garganta,* made from salted plums. Goan housewives still know that the juice from the cashew apple helps the digestion and that sour belimbi fruits cleanse the blood.

Janet Boileau

Further Reading

Disney, A. R. *A History of Portugal and the Portuguese Empire.* 2 vols. New York: Cambridge University Press, 2009.

Hamilton, Cherie Y. *Cuisines of Portuguese Encounters.* New York: Hippocrene Books, 2008.

Hutton, Wendy. *The Food of Love.* New York: Singapore Marshall Cavendish, 2007.

Jorge, Cecília. *Macanese Cooking: A Journey across Generations.* Translated by Carole Garton and Raquel Magalhães. Macau: Associação Promotora da Instrução dos Macaenses, 2004.

Marbeck, Celine J. *Cuzinhia Cristang: A Malacca-Portuguese Cookbook.* Kuala Lumpur, Malaysia: Tropical Press, 1998.

Menezes, Maria Teresa. *The Essential Goa Cookbook.* London: Penguin, 2000.

Singapore

Overview

Singapore is a small island nation in Southeast Asia, whose geographic size belies its international and culinary significance. It is the third-largest port in the world and commands a standing disproportionate to its population, particularly with regard to technology and regional leadership. Singapore, unique in many ways, is politically and geographically unique in being a city-state. It is an entirely urban nation, with no agricultural hinterland.

Historically, Singapore was a sporadically occupied trading site before its establishment as a British Crown Colony in 1819. Between the 7th and 10th centuries it is thought that the Sumatran Buddhist Srivijaya kingdom used Singapore as a trading outpost. Likewise, between the 13th and 15th centuries there is archaeological evidence to suggest that the island was used by Muslim traders based in Melaka. During the period of Portuguese rule in Melaka (in the past spelled Malacca), a sultanate was established in Johor—just across the causeway from Singapore, and again there is some limited archaeological evidence of trade activities. There was no permanent indigenous population or local food culture.

Today, however, with a Chinese majority population (76%) coexisting with Malay (15%), Indian (8%), and other (1%) minority communities, Singapore forms a uniquely Chinese society in a predominantly Muslim and Malay region. This Chinese population has diverse origins, and although officially Mandarin-speaking, many can trace their origins to dialect-speaking southern China.

In terms of religion the Singaporean Chinese population is quite diverse, with many people incorporating a mixture of Taoist and Buddhist practices and Christianity—both Catholic and Protestant. The Malay population is largely Muslim, and the Singaporean Indian population Hindu, though there are also some Christian Indians—both Catholic and Protestant.

Singapore's population of only four million includes one million migrants. Foreign workers present a wide spectrum—both by class and by occupation—including day workers who sleep in Malaysia and work in Singapore; Western and Chinese "foreign talent" who work in Singapore for high salaries for a limited period; domestic workers on five-year maid contracts; and construction workers on one-year limited visas. Migration has thus historically promoted, and to an extent continues to promote, diversity and cosmopolitanism in Singapore.

The island has a land area of only 247 square miles, and no land boundaries, other than the causeway to Johor in Malaysia; its total coastline is 120 miles. The foundation of Singapore's geographic constraints thus lies in its small size. Size aside, Singapore has other geographic challenges. Although the rivers were one of the factors that led to the original settlement, Singapore no longer has sufficient water to supply its needs. Recently, Singapore has been buying dirty water from Malaysia, cleaning it, keeping half, and selling half back; this "new water," however, still leaves them dependent on another nation-state for an essential resource. In attempts to rid itself of this dependency, Singapore is emerging as a world leader in water conservation, reclamation, and desalination.

Singapore's unusual path to nationhood (a reluctant expulsion from the Malaysian Federation in 1965) and its remarkable economic success give it some unique characteristics. Singapore has no lengthy history, no farmland, and only limited water. That is, without the port, Singapore cannot exist. Historically, the status of the port as entrepôt was critical, and while economic policies have shifted with global economic changes, the port remains critical to Singapore's economy and character. The port is the breadbasket of Singapore. The port feeds the nation in multiple ways: bringing in the goods that fill the population's bowls; providing the money that allows people to buy food; and fundamentally shaping how Singaporeans think about their country.

Though culturally and geographically distinct, Singapore has much in common with its Asian neighbors, including the experiences of colonialism and Japanese occupation. Like Hong Kong and Taiwan, it is an island-state with a predominantly Chinese population. Like Malaysia, it is a former British colony with strong political leadership. And like many Asian nations, it has pursued capitalist economic development, evolving from export-oriented industrialization to high-tech industrialization and more recently to information technology and notably successful value-added service industries.

🍽 Food Culture Snapshot

The Chan family conforms exactly to the Singaporean archetype—a husband, a wife, and three children. Husband Jason is two years older than his wife, a product, in part, of the two-year national service requirement, which meant that when Jason and Siew Mae met in their first year at the university, Jason was older than Siew Mae. They married after they had both graduated and accumulated substantial savings for their married life. Both adults work full-time. The children, Kevin (nine), Lily (six), and Timothy (four), are the major focus of the family.

Living with the Chan family is a maid, Wulandari. She is from Indonesia, although many of her colleagues are from the Philippines and increasingly from Bangladesh. Wulandari is employed largely to care for the children, but her duties also include some food preparation, especially for the children, and breakfast for the family.

Breakfast is an early meal; with school starting at 7:30, everyone in the household is up by 6:00. All the children eat cereal. In some households congee, or Chinese porridge, would be more common. Toast is also a popular breakfast choice, often served with *kaya,* a coconut jam. Many Singaporeans eat breakfast out, but a large number still eat this meal in their homes.

Having spent time overseas, Jason and Siew Mae developed Western breakfast habits for weekdays. But on the weekends, holidays, or special occasions they are more likely to eat the foods of their childhoods. For Siew Mae this might be congee, a savory Chinese rice porridge. She knows how to make this dish herself but is more likely to go out and buy congee than cook it at home.

The two older children take small snack foods with them to school—a packet of dried raisins or rice crackers. They will eat lunch at the school canteen. The food at school is generally healthy, and options are provided to meet dietary restrictions, especially those that are religious in nature. As in all canteens, separate trays are used for halal food and utensils. Children are taught to respect religious and ethnic practices in a practical everyday manner by following respectful food practices, such as keeping halal and nonhalal plates separate.

Jason and Siew Mae will both eat out for lunch as well. For Jason this will be a meal at his workplace canteen. Small food stalls are given very low-cost leases in the workplace canteen, and each stall makes only one or two dishes, further keeping prices low. His employer is, thus, effectively subsidizing Jason's meal. The food provided will range from snack foods to elaborate meals. At his workplace there are more than a dozen food stalls, including an Indian food stall (which sells only vegetarian foods), a Muslim Indian stall (which has both vegetarian and meat dishes), a halal Malay stall (which sells rice and vegetable and meat dishes), a Western stall (which sells dishes such as fried eggs, sausages, and chops), a stall that sells steamed dumplings, a fresh fruit and juice stall, a stall that sells fried *kway teah* (a noodle dish), and a Malay noodle stall (which sells *mee rebus* and *mee siam,* spicy noodle dishes with peanuts and shrimp), as well as hot-drink stalls that sell tea and coffee (available sweetened with condensed milk). The canteen is simple and utilitarian, with washable surfaces, attention to ventilation, and reusable plastic or metal tableware. The food is good, fast, and cheap. Jason eats *Hokien prawn mee* today—noodles cooked with prawns.

There is also a stall that specializes in a dish called carrot cake. It is in fact neither a cake (in the sense of a sweet baked dish) nor made with carrots. Rather it is a savory dish made with grated white radish and eggs, flavored with spring onions, soy sauce, and chili. It is a snack food. Jason comes back to the canteen in the midafternoon for a cup of coffee and a serving of carrot cake.

Siew Mae eats in a hawker center (like a food court) for lunch. It is similar to the canteen where her husband eats lunch, though not subsidized. Prices, however, are still low. She selects a dish of roasted pork, rice, and steamed Chinese green vegetables. The vegetables are served with oyster sauce and deep-fried shallots. Siew Mae does not have time for a formal snack like Jason's, but she has tea and a small cake when she gets home from work. She buys the cakes on her way home and shares them with the children and the maid.

Wulandari does most of the food shopping. Buying food takes her to a variety of places. Fruits, vegetables, and meats come from the local wet market, and specialty markets may be visited for other items. In addition, she visits several different supermarkets—the local supermarket run by the National Trade Union for staple foods and ColdStorage, a competing supermarket, for other items, especially school snack items.

Sometimes Wulandari does the shopping for the evening meal—chicken, vegetables, and rice. Depending on the needs of the children, she will occasionally cook this meal and eat it with the family. Sometimes Jason cooks, and sometimes Siew Mae cooks. On a school night these are simple meals—a chicken curry thickened with potatoes and served with rice and a green vegetable. For a special occasion much more elaborate meals would be cooked.

After a long day, when no one is cooking, the family might get take-out food. At the bottom of their apartment complex is a small hawker center, less elaborate than where Siew Mae ate lunch. This is an indoor/outdoor space with open sides for the breeze; meals can be eaten here or taken out. The Chan family orders steamed fish, fried chicken, stir-fried *kang kong* (water spinach), a dish of Chinese flat noodles with soup and dumplings, and ostrich in black pepper sauce, as well as rice. Items are purchased from a variety of stalls—noodles from one stall, meat from another, and vegetables from a third. The dishes will be shared, although all the children have specific favorites. The meal concludes with fresh fruit.

With the children in bed and the work of home and office caught up on, Jason and Siew Mae will have a light supper (as the latest evening meal is called) at 10 or 11 P.M. This may be no more than a cup of tea and perhaps a leftover cake. If there is lots of work still to be done, they might instead step downstairs for a more substantial snack—perhaps sharing a piece of *prata* (fried bread) dipped in curry gravy.

Major Foodstuffs

With the exception of hydroponic bean sprouts, there is basically no agriculture in Singapore. There is very limited landmass and an inadequate water supply. Public spaces devoted to parks and the botanical gardens preserve some of the early attempts at agriculture in Singapore, but housing, business, and public services take priority over agriculture for land use.

The island-state relies entirely on imported food and, consequently, on the port. Fresh milk, meats, and other perishables also arrive by plane. Many of these goods come from Australia and New Zealand (milk and meat), but foods are also imported from China, Britain, North America, and Europe. Goods from Southeast Asia arrive by ship or by bus.

Despite, or perhaps because of, these agricultural limitations, Singapore has developed a very varied national cuisine. The foods of the ethnic groups—Chinese, Malay, and Indian—dominate, but the port has provided ingredients from all over the world, and this is evident in the cuisine. Among other influences, there is a sustained tradition of British food, a product of colonial rule. The culinary evidence of this can be seen in both food adaptations and food traditions, including high tea, sandwiches, and pies.

Rojak, a Malay-influenced salad, is a tremendously important and commonly eaten dish that illustrates the breadth of Singaporean foodstuffs. It consists of both fruit and vegetables such as pineapple, cucumber, onions, and bean sprouts and may include fried tofu. It is dressed with *belacan* (a dried shrimp paste), sugar, chilies, and lime juice. The ingredients are cut into bite-sized pieces, tossed in a bowl with the dressing, and topped with chopped peanuts. This dish has also come to have a social meaning—the term *rojak* literally means "mixture" in Malay. Rojak has colloquially come to be an expression for any kind of mix and in particular is often used to describe the multiethnic character of Singaporean society. That is, all the pieces in the salad are separate and remain distinct rather than being mixed, but they are bound together by the dressing. Singapore describes its ethnic policy as one of multiracialism rather than multiculturalism—the salad bowl, not the mixing bowl—and rojak exemplifies that. A delicious salad, the metaphor of rojak is a potent national symbol that simultaneously speaks to diversity and unity.

Cooking

Much of the cooking in Singapore is done by professionals or paid help. Even a lot of "home cooking" in middle-class homes is done by a domestic worker. In hawker stalls where food is cooked over open flames and intense heat, the physicality of the work has somewhat gendered it; much of the commercial cooking is done by men. There certainly is some domestic cooking, but it is difficult to categorize. In some families, the majority of meals are eaten at home, cooked by an older woman, perhaps. In others the work of cooking is shared by members

Street food vendor preparing a spring roll in Singapore. (Shutterstock)

of the family. In others still, cooking at home is for a special occasion or event.

A lot of Singaporean food requires cooking at high heat, so it is a noisy, messy affair. Singaporean kitchens are architecturally distinct, being largely indoor-outdoor spaces—even in high-rise apartment buildings. Many kitchens back onto a balcony for better ventilation. There is nearly always a door between the kitchen and the living room—to protect the living space from the heat and fumes from the kitchen.

Rice is an important staple for all the ethnic groups in Singapore, and many kitchens have a rice cooker. Likewise, refrigerators are essential for the safe preservation of food in hot and humid temperatures. Kitchens will have a stovetop, often gas, but ovens are rare, since they generate too much heat in the tropical climate. Wealthy Singaporeans, however, may have ovens, and baking has become something of a class symbol.

Kaya

Kaya is a jam made with coconut and egg. Its method and qualities are similar to that of lemon curd, only with coconut and *pandan* (screw pine)-leaf flavoring. As with other jams, kaya is typically spread on toast and is eaten both at breakfast and as a snack. Traditionally kaya is made only with fresh coconuts, but it is possible to make a version with strained coconut milk. To make strained coconut milk, place a piece of muslin in a large sieve, pour a can of coconut cream into the sieve, and leave to drain for an hour.

Ingredients

2 c granulated sugar, if possible caster sugar

4 eggs, lightly beaten

½ c thick coconut flesh and milk, from 1 grated coconut

2 pandan (screw pine) leaves, fresh if possible

Place the sugar in a wok (or large saucepan), and slowly heat it, stirring regularly, until the sugar is golden brown. (Do not try to substitute brown sugar!) When it has become golden, remove the pan from the heat. Once the sugar has cooled a little, transfer it to a large bowl, and add the eggs, one at a time, stirring as you go, and then add the coconut. Beat until the sugar has dissolved. Pour into a pan, and add pandan leaves. On low heat, stir the mixture until it starts to thicken (to test for thickness, place some of the mixture on the back of your spoon and run your finger through it—if it stays separate, then it is ready). Allow the kaya to cool a little before you put it in jars—this gives the pandan leaves extra time to flavor the jam. Remove the leaves just before sealing the jars. Traditionally, this mixture is not refrigerated, but it can be stored in the fridge.

Typical Meals

Breakfast, like all meals in Singapore, varies depending on the ethnicity and social position of the person consuming it. For many Singaporeans rushing to get to work, breakfast is a quick meal—cereal with milk, toast, and so forth. Breakfast is also a meal that might be consumed on the way to work, purchased at a hawker center; this kind of meal might be *nasi lemak*—rice cooked in coconut milk, served with a rich curry gravy, peanuts, a cold hard-boiled egg, and *ikan bilis* (air-dried and salted fish). Congee is another common breakfast food, especially for Chinese Singaporeans. *Tong ho choy,* "tea" made from pork ribs, various herbs, and soy sauce, might also be drunk. Tea and coffee are popular beverages, and a wide range of fresh juices—watermelon, papaya, star fruit, pineapple—are readily available.

Like breakfast, lunch could include food from a wide variety of ethnic backgrounds. Of all the meals it is the one at which people are most likely to eat food outside of their cultural background. This could be because they are eating with a group of colleagues or because they are grabbing a quick and self-contained meal. Noodles and rice form a staple of lunch offerings. Popular noodle dishes could be either Chinese or Malay.

Typical Malay noodle dishes are mee rebus and mee siam. The noodles in mee rebus are yellow egg noodles, and these are served in a thick and spicy gravy. The gravy is thickened with potatoes and flavored with salted soybeans, dried shrimp, and peanuts. Mee rebus may be garnished with hard-boiled egg, limes, spring onions, fried shallots, and bean sprouts. Mee siam can be served "wet" (with a lot of gravy) or "dry" (with less gravy). The noodles in this dish are thin, and the gravy, while spiced, is sour and tangy in taste and has a tamarind base. The dish can be garnished quite similarly to mee rebus and is likely to be topped with dried bean curd.

The Chinese-influenced noodle dishes that might be eaten at lunch vary from indulgent and rich dishes to austere and healthy ones. *Char koay teow* is made from flat rice noodles stir-fried with soy sauce, chili, *belachan* (shrimp paste), tamarind juice, bean sprouts, and spring onions. Other additions might include prawns, cockles, Chinese sausage, beef, and fish cakes. Traditionally, the dish is cooked in pork lard, but many stalls now offer healthier oils. *Lor mee* is another

Fish-ball soup with noodles, a very common soup in Singapore. (Yew Wah Kok | Dreamstime.com)

popular noodle dish in which a gravy of spiced corn-starch is used. Fish-ball soup and plain soups with rice noodles, a little cooked meat, and green vegetables are common choices.

Dishes served with rice are popular in Chinese, Malay, and Indian lunch choices. A very popular option is fish-head curry, in which the head of a fish is stewed in a curried gravy with vegetables such as okra and eggplant. The dish is usually served with rice, but some people will order it with bread. *Biryani,* or, as it is sometimes referred to, *nasi biryani,* is an Indian spiced rice dish. It is served both as a meal, when made with meat or fish, and as an accompaniment to wet curried dishes for special occasions. Plain white rice served with curried meat and vegetables is very popular at both lunch and dinner, especially, but not exclusively, among the Indian community. An Indian lunch meal, especially one purchased from a hawker stall, will generally include rice, dal, and two or more other dishes such as a bitter melon curry, curried mutton, curried chicken, a dish of spiced and shredded carrots and cabbage, or a green vegetable.

Snacks are a very important part of eating in Singapore and may be had at most times of the day and night. They are multiethnic and widely available. *Tahu goreng* (fried tofu) is one such snack food. The tofu is deep-fried, then cut into triangles and served with bean sprouts, cucumber, spring onions, and a dark, spiced sauce enriched with tamarind, chili, and shrimp paste. Indian snacks might include *murtabak,* a folded and fried bread filled with ground mutton, eggs, and onions and served with a dipping gravy. A less filling version of this dish—*roti prata*—is very popular: unfilled fried bread served with a dipping gravy. *Popiah,* a local variant of a fresh spring roll, is also a popular snack. The exterior is made of a flour-based crepe, and it is filled with a sweet hoisin-based sauce and a mixture of white turnip or jicama, grated carrots, chopped lettuce, tofu, and bean sprouts. It can be topped with fried shallots and peanuts. Curry puffs are a very common snack food. These are small pies made of a puff pastry, filled with curry—vegetarian or chicken and vegetables—and deep-fried. All these snacks can be purchased at small stalls or coffee shops and at hawker markets.

A wide variety of drinks are available in Singapore, and many will be consumed with snacks or instead of a snack. Cold drinks include fresh fruit juices; fresh lime juice diluted with water and sugar is another popular fruit drink. Milk-based drinks—such as Milo Dinosaurs (a chocolate-malt drink with an extra scoop of powder on top)—are quite popular as are bubble teas. India-style tea and *teh tarik* (a pulled tea in which condensed milk is rapidly poured to create both texture and foam) are very popular. Coffee is widely consumed, both in the commercial form produced by international chains and in local variants, often sweetened with condensed milk. Alcoholic beverages, including the locally produced Tiger beer, are available but high priced.

Dinner might include many of the aforementioned items eaten for lunch. It is a meal that is likely to be shared and to include many more dishes—but perhaps only a few mouthfuls of each dish. Some dishes are less likely to be shared—such as *laksa,* a coconut-based noodle soup—but many families will order or cook a range of dishes, which might include meats, fish, vegetables, tofu, rice, and noodles. Many families will purchase some or all of the dishes for an evening meal at a local hawker center but may well eat at home. Singapore's signature dish, chili crab, while not eaten every day, may make an appearance even in hawker fare. The dish is made with soft-shell crabs, such as a mud crab, and the sauce has a base of chili and tomato, flavored with garlic and rice vinegar and thickened with flour and ribbons of egg. It is often served with *mantou*—steamed bread rolls.

If eaten out, especially if eaten in a hawker center, dinner is more likely to include dessert. There is a wide range of Singaporean desserts. One of the most popular is *ice kacang,* a mixture of shaved ice, sweet syrup, and beans. Fruit is often included, and the syrup is brightly colored so the dessert forms a large cone of multicolored ice. Variations are also common in the toppings, including grass jelly, palm seeds, coconut milk, corn, and red beans. Tropical fruits are often served for dessert and are used in other desserts, too, such as mango pudding, which is made with mango, evaporated milk, sugar, and agar.

A typical meal in Singapore is shared. That could be both in the sense of not eating alone and in the

Dessert kebabs made with fruit and glazed being sold in an all-night market. (Kelvintt | Dreamstime.com)

sense of sharing dishes. One particularly notable Singaporean dish is chicken rice. It is a dish that can be enjoyed by Singaporean of all religious groups. The dish relies on a master stock, identifying it as Chinese in origin, but also includes ingredients from Southeast Asia, such as sweet Indonesian-style soy sauce—*kecap manis* (from which the word *ketchup* is derived).

Chicken Rice

Ingredients

For the Master Stock

2 chicken carcasses with meat removed

4–6 chicken wings

3 pieces ginger

2 shallots, or 1 red onion

For the Chicken

1 chicken (as fresh as possible)

6 thick slices fresh ginger

2–3 cloves garlic, peeled and crushed

4 shallots, sliced in a few pieces

1 tbsp Chinese rice wine

2 tbsp soy sauce, divided

1 tsp sesame oil

½ tsp salt

For the Rice

3 c rice, preferably long-grain

2 tbsp chicken fat or vegetable oil

1 small piece ginger, finely grated

3–4 cloves garlic, finely chopped

1 tsp salt

3½ c chicken stock

For the Chili Sauce

10 small red chili peppers, seeds removed

3 cloves garlic

1 large piece ginger

2 tsp chicken stock

1 lime, juiced (kaffir limes or regular limes)

Salt to taste

For the Ginger Sauce for Dipping

1 large piece ginger

6 cloves garlic

½ tsp salt

2 tsp lime juice

2 tbsp chicken stock

For the Chicken Soup

Chicken stock (from the boiled chicken)

Chopped shallots and a little bit of cabbage, chopped

As a Garnish or Condiment

Sliced cucumbers, sesame oil, and fresh cilantro

A large stockpot is required for this dish. Begin by making the master stock. Place the chicken carcasses and wings in a large stockpot. Add the ginger and shallots. Cover generously with water. Bring to a boil. Skim the foam from the surface. Turn the temperature down, and let the mixture cook for at least 90 minutes, stirring occasionally. The stock will now need to be strained. Using a large sieve pour the liquid into a large bowl. Discard the bones and other flavorings. The stock can be left to cool. If left overnight a layer of chicken fat will form on top; this can be discarded (not traditional) or used to cook the rice.

When you are ready to cook the chicken, heat the stock; you will need a pot large enough to fit a whole chicken and sufficient liquid to cover it. Make a paste of the ginger, garlic, and shallot. Rub the chicken inside with rice wine and a little soy sauce, and place the paste inside. Bring the stock to a boil, turn off the heat, and put the chicken into the stock with more pieces of ginger and shallot. Every 5 minutes lift the chicken out of the stock and let the liquid drain. Then put it back into the pot. Repeat several times to make sure the chicken cooks through. After half an hour turn the heat back on, but be sure not to let the stock boil. Then turn the heat off again, and let it sit for another half an hour undisturbed. Then remove the chicken from the pot and rub with more soy sauce, sesame oil, and salt. Let cool, and then cut directly through the bones with a heavy cleaver into bite-sized pieces.

To make the rice, begin by washing the rice and draining it. Next, put the chicken fat or oil in a hot wok, and fry the chopped ginger and garlic. Remove them, and add rice and toss for about a minute or two. Remove the rice, place in a pot, and add chicken stock. Bring to a boil, then lower the heat and cook gently, covered, for about 20 minutes.

The chili sauce is made by chopping the chilies with the garlic and ginger and either pounding it into a fine paste with a mortar and pestle or pureeing it in a food processor. Add some stock, lime juice, and salt. The ginger sauce is made the same way. These are both served on the side.

For the chicken soup, reheat the master stock and ladle a small amount into serving bowls. Add finely chopped shallot. Blanch the cabbage and add to the bowls.

To serve, the sauces should be placed on the table, so people can add them to suit their taste. The kecap manis should also be placed on the table. The chopped chicken can be placed on a platter, and the rice is served individually. Slices of cucumber, dressed with sesame oil and topped with cilantro, can be placed either on a separate platter or under the chopped chicken.

Eating Out

Singapore is a nation of eaters, and much of this eating takes place outside the home. In part, this is a product of geography. The island of Singapore is very small, and the housing is largely high-rise apartments, so that a variety of public spaces are vitally important to Singaporean food culture and socializing. The coffee shop is not just a place where people eat and drink, it is a social space in which Singaporeans "talk-cock," that is, talk hyperbolically, voice conspiracy theories, and gossip.

The hawker center is likewise a vital part of the fabric of Singaporean society—a space where the quality of the food is far more important than the decor. While eating is a universal human experience, for Singaporeans it takes on a preeminent position in definitions of both the national and the everyday lived experience. The popular Singlish phrase, "die die must try," is not so much an exaggeration as it is a reflection of the lengths that Singaporeans will go to find great dishes.

A huge array of food is available in Singapore. Singaporean cuisine is certainly worthy of celebration, but it is also a city in which foods from all over the world can be sampled. There are, of course, the ubiquitous chains—KFC, Deli-France, Starbucks—but there is far more than this; there are European, Australian, and Asian restaurants, there are casual places and glamorous places, there is terrible pizza and delicious pizza, there are Vietnamese delicacies and Sri Lankan curries, and there is spaghetti cooked in a wok.

Food provides Singaporeans with a memory of home, with comfort and nostalgia, as it does elsewhere; but in a society that has undergone substantial change in a relatively short amount of time, food serves as a poignant connection to the ever-changing past. Eating—the how and the what—has provided a unifying experience for a diverse society, a metaphor for multiracialism and recognizable national symbols for a fledgling state.

Special Occasions

Chinese New Year is an important event for Chinese communities around the world, including Singapore. For Chinese Singaporeans the reunion meal (New Year's Eve meal) is highly significant and may be eaten at home or out. If eaten out, it is a very expensive affair, with many restaurants charging by the table rather than by the number of diners. The menus, at home or out, incorporate a range of specific foods associated with key concepts of good fortune in Chinese ideology.

In Singapore, *lo hei,* a fish salad, is commonly eaten at the start of a celebratory meal on the seventh day of the Chinese New Year. The dish is said to have the capacity to raise good luck. The dish has a clearly performative aspect—all the ingredients are chopped, perhaps including the fish, shredded white radish, carrots, red peppers, and shrimp crackers. A family, or gathering of friends, will crowd around the platter that it is being served in, and using their chopsticks they will toss the salad ingredients in the air, calling as they do "Jíxiáng Huà"—auspicious wishes and greetings. The higher you toss, the greater your fortunes are reputed to be.

The dish is a crucial part of Singaporean Chinese New Year celebrations, but it would not be recognizable to a mainland Chinese person. Although the origins of the dish are Chinese—a raw fish salad tossed by the diners—the dish as eaten in Singapore originated in 1964 at the Lai Wah Restaurant and was invented as a symbol of prosperity and good health among the Chinese.

Moon cakes, eaten at the Mid-August (or Zhongqiu) Festival, are another traditional celebratory food for Chinese Singaporeans. Moon cakes are

Fish salad, traditional cuisine eaten during Chinese New Year. (Wai Chung Tang | Dreamstime.com)

made of a light dough and a sweet, dense filling. The cakes contain one or more whole salted egg yolks in their center to symbolize the full moon.

For Indian and Malay Singaporeans, festival foods are also important. For Malay Singaporeans the Islamic calendar determines many of these, with Ramadan being the most significant. During Ramadan, Singaporean Muslims fast during the day and break their fast in the evening with quite luscious foods—a practice more common in Southeast Asia than in the Middle East. The end of Ramadan (or Hari Raya Puasa) is marked with especially delicious foods, generally in the form of a family feast. As this is a time marked by openness of heart and mind, non-Muslim friends and colleagues are often invited to share the meal.

Deepavali, the Festival of Lights, is celebrated by Hindus and Sikhs in Singapore; from a culinary perspective it is a time of small snacks, especially sweets. The festival is a public holiday in Singapore and a time when people visit friends and family and receive guests, with ensuing hospitality.

Aside from religious festivals, weddings are considered one of the most special of occasions in Singapore, underscored in Singapore by anxiety about falling birth rates, associated in the public mind with delays in marriage. Wedding food varies by ethnicity and social class. A midrange Chinese wedding banquet, for example, might include eight or nine dishes. Only one to two of these would be sweet—perhaps red bean cakes with lotus seeds—and the majority would be savory. Dishes would be intended to be shared by the table rather than plated individually. The shared dishes would likely include a shark's-fin dish and a range of other seafood dishes, such as scallops with celery or steamed sea bass. There would be meat dishes, perhaps roast pork or a golden fried chicken dish. There would also be a vegetable dish and a noodle dish, like braised *ee-fun* noodles.

A more elaborate and expensive Chinese-style wedding banquet would offer a greater number of dishes, probably 10, and more elaborate dishes. One distinction is exemplified by the different ways shark's fin might be presented on a wedding catering menu. A basic affair might list "Braised Shark's Fin with Crabmeat in Thick Sauce," while a midrange menu might include "Shark's-Fin Soup with Crabmeat and Golden Mushrooms in Lotus Leaf." The most expensive menu would have more elaborate preparations and more expensive ingredients, such as "Double-Boiled Superior Shark's Fin in Thick Sauce." The 10-course version would tend to include more seafood (maybe abalone and dishes of whole fish), more poultry (especially roasted duck), and more meat (generally more pork dishes).

The menus at Malay and Indian weddings would be equally elaborate, although in the typical Malay wedding banquet, rules of halal food preparation exclude pork. Items in a Malay wedding banquet might include a spicy mutton soup, fried or baked chicken, *ikan asam manis* (a sweet and sour fish dish), some kind of *satay* dish (meat or seafood grilled on a skewer), a curried vegetable dish, and a rice dish (*nasi goreng*—fried rice—or *nasi padang*—a pilaf-style dish). Again, a simple dessert course would be served—maybe coconut and pandan-leaf flavored sweets or bean curd served with fruit.

Some families serve buffet-style wedding banquets—generally a more expensive option. Such a buffet might include up to 20 savory dishes and a notably more elaborate dessert menu, including perhaps 5 to 10 different sweets and a wide range of fresh fruit. The buffet would certainly include a range of beef dishes—like beef *rendang* (a slow-cooked beef curry)—and far more side dishes, such as *bawang sambal telur* (an egg and onion dish).

Singaporean Indian weddings are both Indian and Singaporean in character. In form, the Indian wedding banquet is structured more like a Western meal, with a clearer distinction between appetizers and the main course. Appetizers might include *allo chaat* (a potato dish) and grilled chicken dishes. Like the Malay menu, a soup would be included. There would be a range of meat dishes, probably a chicken dish, a mutton curry of some variety, and a dish like *machchi* curry (a Goan-style fish dish). The banquet would also include a range of vegetable dishes such as *aloo gobhi* (potato and cauliflower curry) and *mattar paneer* (pea and cheese curry), as well as curries made from okra and eggplant. There would be plain basmati rice, *biryani* rice (basmati rice cooked with spices and meat), and condiments such as a fresh chutney made with cilantro. To finish the meal there might be *gajar halwa* (a sweet carrot dish) or *gulab jamun* (a sweet dairy-based dessert served in a sugar syrup).

Diet and Health

Singapore has an enviable world-class health care system. Despite the culinary focus of the culture, the population has not been beset by the problems of widespread obesity, diabetes, heart disease, and so forth. That said, the government takes an active role in preventative campaigning. In the "Healthy Choices" campaign, for example, Singaporeans are encouraged to select foods that are less rich and lower in fat and to eat coconut-based dishes in moderation because of the high levels of saturated fat. Stalls at hawker markets will display government signs about types of oils, indicating that a "healthy choice" can be made at their stall. Largely, Singaporeans are quite health conscious.

While traditional medical practitioners play a role in Singaporean health care, people are more likely to consult these specialists for minor matters, especially relating to the skin and stress. Additionally, the medicinal properties of food are widely respected by members of the three major ethnic groups, and people will alter their food choices in line with, for example, Chinese medical practices. There are a range of restaurants that cater to these needs. It is possible, for example, to order soups with specific herbs or ones that are prescribed for specific conditions.

All three major ethnic groups in Singapore follow specific dietary practices for pregnancy and the period following birth. The month or so after birth is referred to as the confinement period, which was traditionally characterized by a specific diet and the assistance of a confinement specialist who would cook the required foods and help the mother with the new baby. During this period the mother would not leave the home, hence confinement. Confinement diets are continually evolving and will both prohibit some foods and prescribe others. Today, many Singaporean women follow some of the practices of confinement, especially the confinement diet, and middle-class women still often employ a confinement specialist.

There are significant similarities between Chinese, Malay, and Indian confinement practices, but there are also some important variations. The Chinese confinement diet aims to enhance immunity and to help women regain physical strength. Restrictions include discouraging eating cold food. Cold in this context means both temperature and temperament. It is believed that cold foods can harm the spleen because they retard the discharge of toxins. Foods that are considered cold include some meats and seafoods (especially snails, clams, and oysters), certain fruits (including pomelo, star fruit, and watermelon), a range of vegetables (mushrooms, bitter gourd, water spinach, bamboo shoots), and other items such as seaweed and soy sauce.

Malay mothers in confinement are discouraged from eating spicy food, foods cooked with coconut milk, shellfish, and eggs. Their confinement diet emphasizes soft food, especially soups, often served with rice, as well as noodle dishes. Indian confinement diets also have restrictions and a focus on the role of food as medicinal. Additionally, certain foods are encouraged as aiding bodily functions—for example, brown sugar to expel blood from the uterus or toasted garlic to increase lactation. In all three traditions, women are encouraged to drink warm rather than cold water.

Nicole Tarulevicz

Further Reading

Hawkins, Kathryn, and Deh-Ta Hsiung. *The Singapore Cookbook: Over 200 Tantalizing Recipes.* London: Salamander Press, 1999.

Hutton, Wendy. *The Food of Singapore: Authentic Recipes from the Manhattan of the East.* Singapore: Periplus, 1994.

Lee, Chin Koon. *The New Mrs. Lee's Cookbook: Nonya Recipes and Other Favourite Recipes.* New York and Singapore: Marshall Cavendish, 2004.

Oon, Violet. *A Singapore Family Cookbook.* Singapore: Pen International, 1998.

Oon, Violet. *Timeless Recipes: Tasty Singapore.* Singapore: International Enterprise Singapore, 2007.

Tan, Terry. *Shiok! Exciting Tropical Asian Flavors.* Singapore: Periplus, 2003.

Sri Lanka

Overview

Known as Ceylon until 1972, Sri Lanka ("resplendent isle") is a teardrop-shaped island located in the Indian Ocean approximately 30 miles south of India. Sri Lanka is considered part of the Indian Subcontinent, which also includes India, Pakistan, Bangladesh, Nepal, and Bhutan. The country is made up of nine provinces and 25 districts. Besides being Sri Lanka's capital and largest city, Colombo has served as a major seaport since the fifth century. During the 15th and 16th centuries, foreign traders from the Netherlands, Portugal, and Great Britain brought spices and cooking styles from all over the world to Sri Lanka. As a result, Sri Lankan cuisine reflects these influences, along with aspects of Arab, Malay, and Indian food and cooking techniques.

Language and religion shape Sri Lanka's ethnic groups. Among the population of 20 million, 73 percent are Sinhalese, 18 percent are Tamils, and 9 percent are Muslims. There are also smaller communities of Veddas, Burghers, Moors, and other ethnic groups. The majority of Sri Lankans follow Buddhism. Hinduism, Islam, Christianity, and other religions are also practiced. The common perception is that the prevalence of vegetarian dishes in Sri Lankan cuisine is due to religious reasons. While vegetarianism is more prevalent among Hindus, Sri Lanka's tropical climate and long history as an agricultural society, along with the rising price of meat, also play a major role in the population's preference for vegetables.

 Food Culture Snapshot

Padma Vaas is a high school student who lives in Colombo with her parents and younger brother. Her family is considered middle class, with both parents employed professionally. On weekdays, Padma eats a quick breakfast of *hoppers* (little bowl-shaped rice-flour pancakes), fruit, and hot tea before heading off to classes. For lunch, her mother packs her rice and curry, or she purchases a lunch packet from the street vendor by her school. Padma occasionally picks up a pastry or roti (flatbread) from a short-eats stand after school. Dinner, the most substantial meal of the day, provides an opportunity for the family to catch up and is always eaten together. Padma's mother starts cooking around 6 P.M., with the family sitting down to eat by 8 P.M. A typical weekday-night dinner for the Vaas family is steamed rice, a fish or chicken curry dish, and two or three vegetable or lentil curry side dishes.

However, it is on the weekends that Padma and her mother really have the opportunity to cook together and talk. The urban home garden they started last year has now flourished, yielding abundant eggplant (*brinjal*) and chili harvests. The day's menu is planned the night before, followed by an early-morning trip to Pettah Market, an open-air market in Colombo with a dizzying array of wares, spices, vegetables, dried fish, and fruits. Dried shrimp, *goraka* (dried fruit for curry dishes), *Maldive fish* (dried fish), and coconut meat are frequently on the Vaas's shopping list. Once home, Padma and her mother spend the remainder of the day preparing the dinner meal—which includes a lengthy process of roasting spices and simmering a multitude of curry dishes. On the weekends, up to 12 side dishes may be served, sometimes more if extended family members visit.

Major Foodstuffs

Despite the rise of the manufacturing sector, Sri Lanka remains mainly an agricultural society—tea, rubber, coconut, cacao, and spices are key exports. Tea estates can be found throughout the southern and central regions at altitudes between 3,000 and 8,000 feet. Tea was first commercially produced in Sri Lanka in 1867 by a Scot, James Taylor, and was largely controlled by British companies until 1971, when the Sri Lankan government assumed ownership through the Land Reform Act. The majority of the world's spices are also produced by Sri Lanka. These include cinnamon, cardamom, pepper, turmeric, and ginger. Two-thirds of the world's supply of cinnamon is grown in Sri Lanka.

Rice is a main staple of the Sri Lankan diet. Over 15 varieties are grown for local consumption, along with fruits and vegetables. Bowl-shaped, thin pancakes (hoppers) are considered native to Sri Lanka and eaten as a staple for breakfast and lunch. To make *stringhoppers,* rice flour and salt are formed into a paste and forced through a mortar with a circular opening (*ural*) onto a steaming tray. They are then steamed for 5–10 minutes and served with *sambal* (coconut-based chutney) and/or curries. Stringhoppers can also be purchased ready-made in restaurants and grocery stores. Other types of hoppers include egg, milk, and sweet varieties (*vandu-appa, paniappa*).

Sri Lanka's year-round tropical climate offers a fruit paradise with many varieties: mangoes, papayas, durians, bananas, passion fruit, mangosteens, and rambutans, among others. Besides being used for refreshing drinks, fruit is a central ingredient for producing chutneys, cordials, syrups, jams, and marmalades.

Seafood factors heavily into the Sri Lankan diet, with fishing connected to the country's two monsoon seasons. Cattle are mainly used for milk and farmwork. Though some Sri Lankan dishes incorporate beef as an ingredient, Hindus highly revere

Display of fruit in a Sri Lankan vendor's stall. Many tropical fruits are native to Sri Lanka, including durians, passion fruit, and woodapples. (Shutterstock)

cows and do not eat beef. Most Buddhists also refrain from beef consumption.

The most popular nonalcoholic beverage in Sri Lanka is tea sweetened with sugar or milk. Coffee is rarely drunk, though available in more upscale urban areas. Popular drinks on a hot tropical day are *tambili* (water from orange coconuts) and *kurumba* (water from young coconuts)—both are believed to bring health benefits. The most popular alcoholic drink is *arrack,* which is distilled from fermented coconut-palm or palmyra-tree sap (toddy). Toddy tappers travel between treetops using rope walkways high above ground to collect sap, "tapping" up to 100 trees a day.

Popular snacks include a deep-fried patty made of lentils and flour (*vadai*) and a soft tortilla filled with different mixtures such as meat, vegetables, and chili peppers (*rotty*). Two sweets commonly consumed in Sri Lanka are *kavun* and *wattalapan.* Made of rice flour and treacle, kavun is deep-fried until golden brown. Wattalapan, first introduced by the Malays, is a steamed pudding cake made of coconut milk, eggs, and jaggery (refined sugar from palm-tree sap). Most sweets are of South Indian (Tamil Nadu) origin and are served during New Year celebrations.

Cooking

Globalization has heralded an influx of fast-food options such as McDonald's and Pizza Hut in Sri Lanka. However, most meals are still traditionally cooked, though exact recipes are seldom followed and preparation can be labor-intensive. Cooking in middle- and upper-class families may be handled by cooks or servants. In households without servants, women are responsible for housework and meal preparation. However, gender roles are shifting, especially in urban households where both the husband and wife may be employed outside of the home.

Due to the smokiness associated with Sri Lankan cooking, the traditional kitchen is located either at the back of the main house or in a detached structure. An open fireplace (*lipa*) is common, with coconut-frond stems serving as fuel for the fire. A brick or iron oven with a door handle and fire pit is also frequently found in rural homes. However, since many aspects of the traditional kitchen are impractical, the two-burner propane stove has now replaced the lipa in most modern kitchens.

Many Sri Lankan dishes appear similar to those of South India, though two distinguishing hallmarks are the use of extremely hot spices and local ingredients. Sri Lankan dishes are considered among the spiciest in the world. Hot chilies, such as *amu miris, kochchii miris,* and *maalu miris* (capsicum), are frequently incorporated into dishes, along with coconut milk.

Unique fresh herb- and spice-preparation methods (roasting, pounding, tempering) also distinguish the cuisine from others. Traditional kitchens often have a chili stone (*mirisgala*) made of granite (or another hard stone) that serves as a hard surface for grinding chilies and whole spices. A mortar and pestle (*vangediya*) is used for ingredients that cannot be effectively pounded on the mirisgala. The cylinder-shaped mortar is also made of a hard stone and can reach heights and widths of up to 12 inches. Pestles may be up to five feet long and are generally made of *kitul* wood. In modern times, spice preparation involves heating spices in a dry pan until fragrant, then grinding them in an electric grinder once cool.

Regional availability of fresh ingredients largely defines the variances in dishes served. The north is known for the palmyra tree, while rice, fish, and jackfruit appear frequently in dishes from the south. In the central region, also hill country, vegetables and mutton are the mainstays, with fish and spices used

less intensely. Maldive fish (dried fish) is another local ingredient often used to thicken and flavor dishes, especially vegetable curries.

The two most prevalent frying techniques are tempering and sautéing, with the first being more common. Whereas sautéing is a gentler form of cooking ingredients in a flat-bottomed skillet until translucent, tempered ingredients are fried over very high heat until they are fragrant and golden brown. Following tempering, the ingredients are then simmered on low heat with a partially closed lid. Seasonings are adjusted just before the food is served. Clay pots are the preferred cooking vessel—older pots flavor food more intensely and function similar to cast iron skillets in Western cooking.

Typical Meals

A simple Sinhalese greeting literally translates into "Have you eaten rice?" The typical Sri Lankan meal (also called "rice and curry") is not divided into separate courses, such as appetizers and entrées. Instead, all dishes are served at the same time, with rice being the central mainstay, accompanied by curry-based side dishes. Lighter fare (called short eats) may be served first at social events, though.

After everyone has been served, meals are traditionally eaten using the fingertips of the right hand to form small balls of rice and curry. In rural homes, meals are consumed while seated on leaf mats on the floor; in urban settings, the dining room table is the site of social activity and meals. While multigenerational households are fairly common throughout Sri Lanka, the number of nuclear families is on the rise with the influences of westernization and urbanization. Most Sri Lankans consume three meals a day (breakfast, lunch, and dinner).

Traditional breakfasts, especially in rural homes, consist of tea and rice-based dishes, including hoppers, a steamed rice/coconut mixture (*pittu*), panfried soft bread (*rotis*), milk rice (*kiri buth*), and leftover rice, curries, and sambals. City dwellers may have bread, fruit, and eggs during weekdays and a more substantial, traditional breakfast on the weekends.

Steamed rice and curry form the staples of lunch and dinner meals and are consumed almost daily. Dinner, usually eaten around 8 P.M., is considered the

Egg hoppers, a crepelike hopper containing a fried egg. (Paul Cowan | Dreamstime.com)

heaviest meal of the day. The typical meal consists of a main curry, made with fish or meat, and several vegetable-, fruit-, or lentil-based curries (*dhal*). Depending on the spices and seasonings used, curries can be white, brown, black, or red. Coconut is frequently incorporated as a base in many dishes. Up to 12 side dishes can be served; these include pickles, chutneys, and spicy chili-based condiments or sauces (sambals).

Brinjal (Eggplant) Sambal

Sambals tend to be spicy hot and are served as a condiment or relish alongside rice and curry dishes. There are many variations of sambals—sugar (*seeni*) sambals are the most traditional. Typical sambals use different combinations of chilies, vegetables, and spices.

Serves 2

¼ lb eggplant, diced

¼ tsp ground turmeric (optional)

½ tsp salt

1½ tbsp canola or vegetable oil

1–2 chilies, chopped

¼ c yellow onions, chopped

½ lime, juiced

1½ tbsp coconut milk

Salt to taste

Wash and dice eggplant. Season with turmeric (if using) and salt. Heat oil and fry eggplant until browned. Remove from pan and drain on a paper towel. Mix chilies, onions, lime juice, and coconut milk. Combine with eggplant, and add salt as needed.

Most meals end with a serving of fruit, which is readily available on this tropical island. Desserts are reserved for special occasions and teatime.

Eating Out

Sri Lanka has been slow to cultivate a distinctive restaurant culture, since most authentic meals are served within the home. *Buth kadé* (a rice shop) and *kopi kadé* (a coffee shop) selling short eats are available in most towns and villages. As a result of globalization, American fast-food chains are becoming more prominent, though fast food is considered more of a snack than a meal. The impact of tourism can be observed, with at least one Chinese-style restaurant in each town, and restaurants serving local and international cuisines in most large urban cities. Lunch packets (rice, curry, curried vegetables, and sambal), typically sold between 11 A.M. and 2 P.M., are also immensely popular.

Special Occasions

Sri Lankans embrace a strong connection between food and festivities—food embodies much more than

The interior of a typical Sri Lankan restaurant. (StockPhotoPro)

just a means for survival. As a symbol of life and fertility, rice is frequently incorporated into celebrations. For example, milk rice (kiri buth) is served at almost all major ceremonial festivities, including as a baby's first solid food, the first food a new bride and groom serve each other, and a food eaten during the New Year. For the Sinhalese, milk rice boiling over the pot is considered to be a good-luck omen during New Year celebrations. Alcoholic beverages are not included as part of any formal ceremonial festivies.

There are over 30 public Buddhist, Hindu, Muslim, and Christian holidays celebrated annually—many which correspond to the full moon (*poya*) and lunar calendar. The Buddhist and Hindu Sri Lankan New Year (Aurudu) occurs on April 14, which aligns with the end of the harvest season and beginning of the southwestern monsoon season. Special foods enjoyed during these festivies include plantains, oil cake (*kaung*), and sweetmeat (*kokis*).

The beginning of the harvest (Thai Pongal) is celebrated by Hindus in January with boiled milk, rice, and jaggery (*pongal*) offered to the sun god. In honor of Ramadan, Muslims fast until Eid al-Fitr, when dates, steamed pudding (*vatalappan*), and rice porridge (congee) with a spicy meat-rice dish (*biryani*) are shared and eaten.

Diet and Health

Ayurveda, an ancient medicinal system that views the five elements (air, earth, light, water, ether) as connected with the five senses and an individual's biological, psychological, and physiological life forces (*doshas*), is popular in Sri Lanka. The premise is that when doshas are out of balance, disease and illness may prevail. Almost all foods are classified into a "hot" or "cold" framework, whereby over- or underconsumption may contribute to health issues.

Herbs, roots, spices, and dietary changes are often prescribed to address unbalanced doshas. For example, when consumed in moderation, tea is believed to have medicinal properties, ranging from improved digestion to prevention of heart disease. *Gotu kola,* another leafy green plant commonly used in Sri Lankan dishes (*mallung*), is also believed to possess health benefits as a diuretic and mild anti-inflammatory and antibacterial, among other functions.

Mary Gee

Further Reading

Barr-Kumarakulasinghe, Chandra, and Sereno Barr-Kumarakulasinghe. Recipes from Sri Lanka. http://www.infolanka.com/org/srilanka/food/recipes.html.

Dassanayaka, Channa. *Sri Lankan Flavours: A Journey through the Island's Food and Culture.* Prahran, Australia: Hardie Grant Books, 2003.

Kuruvita, Peter. *Serendip: My Sri Lankan Kitchen.* Sydney, Australia: Murdoch Books, 2009.

Seneviratne, Suharshini. *Exotic Tastes of Sri Lanka.* New York: Hippocrene Book, 2003.

Thailand

Overview

Thailand is a constitutional monarchy, headed by the longest-ruling monarch in the world, King Bhumibol Aduladej. Bangkok, the capital, dominates the economy and culture of the country. The Thai in Thailand make up the dominant ethnic majority in the country—about 75 percent of the population. Many other ethnic minorities including Chinese and Vietnamese live in towns and cities, and groups such as the Lisu, Chin, Kachin and Akha, and Hmong occupy more marginal lands, including upland forests. Theravada Buddhism is the dominant religion in Thailand. The upland peoples often practice shifting (swidden) cultivation; fields are cleared, burned for fertilizer, planted, harvested, and left to fallow; these subsistence farmers then shift to plant new fields. Rivers such as the Mekong and Chao Phraya create rich alluvial soils ideally suited for wet-rice agriculture. Between the uplands and the lowland river valleys, there are a variety of different agricultural niches. Rice, the dominant staple of Thailand, adapts to these different ecological niches.

🍽 Food Culture Snapshot

Thongchai and Lek live with their two school-age daughters in the suburbs of Bangkok. Thongchai is a Thai civil servant, and Lek works in a bank. Every morning, they set the electric rice cooker to have hot rice available by 6 A.M., when Lek's mother stands outside the door to offer rice to the orange-robed monks who pass by their laneway on their way back to the temple from their morning alms round. Thongchai and Lek make coffee and eat a quick meal of rice and leftover dishes from last night's dinner. Their daughters prefer toast and jam with a yogurt drink that they learned to like at school. Lek drops the girls at school after two hours in the congested Bangkok traffic.

Lunch is a formal Chinese restaurant meal with business associates for Thongchai, and a quick bowl of noodles from her favorite street vendor for Lek. She uses her lunch hour to pick up vegetables and condiments at a nearby supermarket and keeps them fresh in a cooler in her car. Like busy women everywhere, Lek does not have a great deal of time to devote to food preparation. Lek might be considered one of Bangkok's many plastic-bag housewives, who pick up bags of wonderful side dishes on the way home from work from street vendors. Leaving work at 5 P.M., Lek returns to her favorite street vendors and picks up plastic bags of freshly made beef curry, *tom yam kung* (tamarind-based shrimp soup), and some Thai desserts made from agar-agar and coconut, favorites of her girls.

Once home, electric rice cookers make monitoring the timing for cooked rice a thing of the past. Electric grinders and blenders shave hours from complex food-processing tasks such as making flavor pastes. Once a week, the family does a larger shopping trip at a supermarket near their home. Thongchai prefers buying fish and fresh vegetables at the open markets early on Saturday morning, but Lek enjoys the air-conditioned comfort of the supermarket where she can pick up vegetables and condiments from all over the world, as well as packages of precut vegetables, fresh herbs, and shrimp paste for making traditional Thai side dishes "from scratch."

Major Foodstuffs

In Thailand, rice is the dominant and preferred cereal crop; it is used for making noodles, rice flour, and rice wine, and it is valued far beyond its nutritional value. Rice needs constant attention from humans to grow, for rice has a soul that must be nurtured. The best-known Thai rice is the long-grain variety known as aromatic jasmine. High-yielding varieties of rice are widely grown in Thailand and exported to North America and elsewhere. Thailand is the world's largest exporter of rice, with around 10 million metric tons projected for the year 2010.

Since the 1960s, high-yielding varieties of irrigated wet rice produced by the green revolution increased rice yields dramatically in the country. However, the newer varieties rely on irrigation to flourish and require insecticides and fertilizers to produce high yields. They also damaged the delicate rice ecologies and encouraged a shift away from subsistence production. Nevertheless, most rice grown in Thailand comes from modern high-yielding varieties. Dry rice varieties are grown in the uplands. Rice is milled and polished in local rice mills. Thai in the north and northeast of the country use glutinous or sticky rice as their daily staple. In other areas of the country, glutinous rice is grown for making desserts, rice flour, and rice wine. Unpolished black and purple varieties are particularly popular for making special desserts.

Fish is also very important in the Thai diet. Freshwater fish, sea fish, and shellfish are the major sources of protein for most meals. Snapper, catfish, and mackerel are popular fish eaten in the country. The Thai enjoy a long coastline that gives them access to an abundance of fish plus lobsters, crabs, squids, and shrimp. Many rural Thai raise fish in ponds near their homes and rice fields. People seek out fresh fish

A food stall in an open air market in Bangkok, Thailand. (Jiri Kulhanek | Dreamstime.com)

in rivers, streams, or ponds late in the day to eat for the evening meal. Fish and other seafood are widely available in the open markets. Small sun-dried and salted fish are popular additions to meals throughout the year. Fish are most plentiful in the rice fields after the rainy season (October to December). Today, raw fish dishes are discouraged as public health officials consider them unhealthy.

Accompanying most Thai meals is a sauce or paste made from fermented fish or shellfish. The fish are salted, dried, pounded, and packed with toasted rice and rice husks in jars for a month or more. Fish sauce (in Thai, *nam plaa*) is a crucial ingredient in most Thai dishes. The Thai make a fermented salted shrimp mixture usually mixed with chili peppers, called *kapi*. Most often, fish sauce is mixed with chili peppers. The Thai term *nam prik* refers to a fish sauce mixed with ground roasted chilies and other local ingredients according to the region of the country to produce *nam prik plaa pon* (with the addition of ground dried fish), *nam prik plaa raa* (with the addition of fermented fish), *nam prik kapi* (with the addition of shrimp paste), or *nam prik ong* (with the addition of ground pork and tomatoes).

Side dishes including raw salads are made using a wide range of fresh greens and vegetables, including different varieties of onions, garlic, water spinach, eggplants (from long green or purple plants used for grilling or stir-fries to tiny bitter pealike plants flavoring Thai curries), banana blossoms, bitter melons, lotus, bok choy, rapini, napa cabbage, sweet potatoes, bean sprouts (from soy and mung beans), and a wide variety of local greens. Fruit is eaten as a snack between meals or incorporated into special desserts like mangoes and sticky rice.

Cooking

Thai cooks seek out the freshest possible ingredients and spend a great deal of time cutting and preparing them for cooking. But cooking times are usually short and make use of simple techniques like boiling, steaming, and grilling. Cooking techniques in Thai households are not learned through cookbooks, although Thai cookbooks authored by celebrities sell well in a market that is fascinated with elite cooks and royal meals. Professional chefs may read cookbooks to learn what is new in Hong Kong or Singapore, but chefs expect that books will not reveal all secrets about a dish, including a complete listing of all ingredients. The idea of recording favorite family recipes has a long history among the Thai elite. Since the late 1800s, cremation volumes, small books given away at funerals, often included cooking instructions and favorite recipes of the deceased.

Kitchens of the rural poor are sparse and may contain only an open fire or a closed ceramic or cement bucket-like stove, a mortar and pestle, cutting board, bamboo steamer, cleaver, wok, spatula, ladle, coconut graters, and baskets for storing rice, vegetables, and spices. The space is always clean and uncluttered, as the equipment is often hung vertically on hooks. Coconut-shell implements are rapidly being replaced by plastic in communities with markets and a cash economy. Dishes may be limited to a few enamel plates or bowls. Food may also be served in cucumbers, coconuts, and pineapples or wrapped in banana or pandanus leaves. Urban Thai households have kitchens as modern and elaborate as Euro-American kitchens, with electric refrigerators, stoves, rice cookers, microwave ovens, and a wide range of specialized appliances from local, Japanese, and European suppliers. But these modern urban homes may also have a simple village-style kitchen behind the house with a charcoal stove, grill, and mortar and pestle for preparing traditional dishes.

Supermarkets in the cities of Thailand provide precut ingredients to simplify cooking tasks in households no longer employing cooks. Many elements of a Thai meal can be prepared ahead in quantities and kept in jars or frozen for later use. For example, fried onions and garlic can be prepared in quantity and stored in jars; curry pastes can be ground in amounts sufficient for several meals; ground toasted rice for Thai-Lao dishes can be prepared and stored for later use; and canned coconut milk and rice paper make meal preparation easier for urban cooks and displaced Thai in North America. Canned bamboo shoots are acceptable substitutes in American kitchens.

The popularity of Thai food overseas has been reinforced by the availability and promotion of semiprepared Thai food in food kits (also for sale in the Bangkok airport). Outside of Thailand, flavor pastes have recently become available in powdered, canned, and frozen forms, lessening the burden for new immigrants to Australia, Europe, and North America who want to make the dishes they remember from home. To release the flavors, one fries the paste in oil or heats it in coconut milk.

The palace kitchens of the Indianized royal courts in Thailand and Cambodia always produced more elaborate recipes and meals. In the 1800s, Western cooks were hired to teach Western-style dishes to palace cooks. Culinary skills for women were particularly highly valued. The service of royal wives and concubines provided the extra effort necessary to make elaborate meals with theatrical garnishes; time-consuming carving of fruit and vegetables displayed royal power. Even a carved flower made from a green onion, a chili pepper, or a radish could turn a simple stir-fry into a dish fit for a king. The Thai royal tradition in palace food has been made public in a number of cookbooks, complete with instructions for vegetable carving and for making time-consuming difficult elements like egg nets.

Typical Meals

Both rural and urban Thai generally prepare rice with side dishes such as curries, soups, and stir-fried dishes for all meals. Western-style breakfasts with cereal and toast are recent urban innovations. Towns and cities provide more alternatives, such as noodle soups or lightly boiled eggs for early breakfasts and late-night snacks. Desserts are seldom included with meals, but fruit is a welcome snack any time of day.

Food acquisition in rural areas can be as simple as reaching out the back door to grab a handful of edible greens such as watercress or morning glory leaves. Throughout the country, in rural villages, direct patron-client relations distribute and redistribute food within the community. One household may regularly provide another with fresh vegetables, in return for emergency supplies of rice in the hungry season or for help with special occasions such as weddings or funerals. These food-based debts are never fully repaid, for to do so would be to end reciprocal relations basic to community survival.

Thai meals are always presented in aesthetically pleasing ways, even in poor households. Side dishes of food are garnished with fresh aromatic herbs, fried onions, or even edible flowers. Plates, rice bowls, or shallow rimmed bowls are in common use and vary from antique works of art, to products from local ceramic factories, to brightly colored plastic. Forks and spoons are the easiest, most efficient way to eat rice and side dishes, with chopsticks used primarily for noodles and Chinese dishes.

Rice is the central core of most Thai meals, and it is usually served from a common bowl. Rice has a soul and is a gift of the ancestors; its quantity and quality, taste and smell, are a matter of constant concern. Side dishes, literally referred to as "with-rice" dishes, accompany rice and are also served in common bowls for sharing. If rice is not served, then one is "eating for fun," often with drinks, rather than consuming a meal. Thai meals are served all at once rather than in courses. This simultaneous presentation of all parts of the meal provides the eater with maximum choices about what tastes go best together. Each meal served with rice tries to balance the tastes of hot, sour, salty, and sweet. The people eating the meal create the final balance as they serve themselves from the available side dishes in the order they prefer and fine-tune tastes with wet or dry condiments, reflecting individual needs and desires.

Side dishes usually include soup as a meal component along with rice and other side dishes, rather than as a separate course. Soups are served from a common bowl directly onto rice or into individual bowls. Most soups are fast-cooking, keeping vegetables crisp and nutrients readily available. Soup, either a rice congee or a noodle soup, can also be a meal in itself—often for breakfast or a late-night snack. Soups with a coconut base are more associated with palace cooking, as in this Thai favorite.

Tom Kha Gai (Coconut Chicken Soup)

4 c stock

4 chicken breasts, sliced

2 pieces galangal, 1 in. long, split or sliced

4 wild lime leaves, deveined and torn

2 pieces crushed lemongrass, about 2 in. long

4 c coconut milk

4 chilies, sliced

4 tbsp fish sauce

Bring the stock to a simmer, and add chicken, galangal, lime leaves, and lemongrass. Cook 10 minutes or until chicken is cooked through. Add coconut milk, chilies, and fish sauce; heat through and serve.

Eating Out

Bangkok provides the largest range of restaurants for dining out. But in the 1960s, there were very few Thai restaurants in the city. The best known include Jit Pochana, Seefah, and Sorng Daeng, where visitors and middle-class Thai ate classic dishes, many from the palace tradition. Sorng Daeng opened in 1957 in its present location near government offices in Bangkok and still operates today. Here, one could eat a very high-quality noodle dish served on a banana leaf, tasting very much like the dish served by street vendors in the back alleys but, of course, much pricier.

Eating out for lunch is particularly common in urban areas like Bangkok where the traffic can be very slow and the workplace very distant from home. Street vendors provide foods for early-morning travelers and late-night revelers. Night markets in the towns and cities of Thailand gather together a number of food vendors to facilitate late-night dining when the temperature is lower. Hawker or street foods are not always available in restaurants; they can best be enjoyed on the street. The preparation of some street foods may be too complex or labor-intensive for restaurants or may require special equipment.

Although McDonald's, Kentucky Fried Chicken, Dunkin' Donuts, and other Western fast-food outlets are common in Thai cities, they have not displaced local fast foods that offer better value for money. Today, food courts are available in shopping malls throughout the country and are popular with tourists and locals alike. The customer buys redeemable coupons and uses them as cash to purchase a wide range of dishes from a selection of food vendors. The vendors then redeem the coupons and pay a percentage to the owner of the food-court space.

Chinese restaurants are still the most popular locations for special meals consumed outside the house. Chinese restaurants have adapted to local tastes with the use of coriander root, tamarind paste, lemongrass, and chilies. But attempts have been made to distinguish between a Chinese and a local noodle dish for nationalistic purposes. For example, pad Thai (Thai fried noodles) is a dish invented in the 1940s in Bangkok in an attempt to distinguish Thai noodles from Chinese noodles and to encourage Thai civil servants to eat local. Pad Thai is one of the favorite Thai dishes of foreigners visiting Thailand, and it is popular in Thai restaurants overseas. But it is only one of many fried noodle dishes available in Thailand. Perhaps its popularity with foreigners is due to the fact that it can be ordered by name in restaurants and from street vendors without the need to speak Thai. Other Thai noodles involve a long dialogue: Do you want your noodles thin, medium, or wide? Wet or dry? With beef, shrimp, or chicken?

Pad Thai (Thai Fried Noodles)

A dry stir-fried noodle dish well known outside of Thailand, pad Thai is usually accompanied by bowls of chili-vinegar sauce, dried chili flakes, lime slices, chopped peanuts, sugar, bean sprouts, and sliced cucumbers and is decorated with cilantro.

Pad Thai, a dry stir-fried noodle dish well known outside of Thailand. (Shutterstock)

2 oz thinly sliced pork

1 tsp sugar

1 tbsp soy sauce

1 tbsp fish sauce

1 tbsp tamarind juice (or pulp squeezed from tamarinds soaked in 2–3 tbsp warm water)

2 eggs

3 tbsp oil

2–3 cloves minced garlic

2 oz thinly sliced tofu (a 2-in. cake)

½ lb dried rice noodles, soaked in warm water for 20 minutes

2 c rinsed bean sprouts

3 green onions, cut in 1-in. pieces

1 tbsp dried shrimp

Toss pork slices with sugar. In a small bowl, mix the soy sauce, fish sauce, and tamarind juice. Lightly beat eggs with a pinch of salt. Stir-fry the garlic, pork, and tofu in a tablespoon of oil. Pour in egg mixture until it starts to set, and remove to a plate. In the remaining oil, stir-fry the drained noodles until they are well heated and seared. Add to the center of the wok the bean sprouts, green onions, dried shrimp, and the soy sauce mixture. Mix in the egg and pork mixture. Turn out onto a platter or individual plates, and garnish with an assortment of the condiments listed.

Special Occasions

Food creates and maintains social relations between Thai, and between them and the spirit world. Feeding others occurs across all transitions in the life cycle and across the generations. Those who sponsor feasts gain status from feeding others appropriately and generously. It would be unthinkable to celebrate without food. Most celebrations have a religious or ritual component to them, but purely secular celebrations also involve food.

The predominant religious tradition in Thailand is Theravada Buddhism, a community-based religion practiced in rural and urban areas in varying intensities. Buddhism and food intertwine at the level of rituals and lay offerings but also at the level of ideology and text. Fasting and not feasting is the Buddhist pattern, recalling always the middle way, avoiding the extremes of asceticism. However, community-based rituals with lay participation are usually celebrated with elaborate shared meals.

Religious rituals are closely integrated with the seasonal agricultural cycle, primarily irrigated rice in mainland Southeast Asia. However, the adoption of high-yielding varieties of rice and other technologies that permit two or three crops a year alter the significance of Buddhist celebrations, since the cycle of planting, transplanting, and harvesting is no longer coordinated with Buddhist seasonal rituals. This results in differences in what Buddhist rituals are emphasized in rural and urban temples.

Everywhere in Southeast Asia, the spirit of rice is feminine and must be placated and carefully tended. Mother rice is the self-sacrificing mother who is given gifts and offerings of food to guarantee a bountiful rice harvest. She is treated like a pregnant woman whose every whim must be indulged. Known as *mae prasob* in Thai, she determines the auspicious days to plant, transplant, and harvest rice. The rice fields are protected by spirits who must be ritually fed for the land to produce the highest rice yields. Feeding spirits may involve simple practices such as leaving a small serving of rice and fruit in a spirit house in the northeastern corner of a Bangkok house, as the inhabitants leave for work.

Theravada Buddhism provides a structure for sharing the best dishes the household can prepare with monks on their early-morning alms round. After elderly household members place some of these dishes in the monks' bowls, the family consumes these special dishes or shares them with neighbors at the community temple. For the rural poor, these occasions may be the only days that rich coconut-based meat curries are made. Ordinations, weddings, and funerals are also occasions for special meals. On such occasions, households may provide elaborate wet and dry desserts that require time and skill to prepare. Some are shaped to resemble miniature fruits and vegetables.

Monks, like spirits, need to be fed. The Buddhist pattern of moderate asceticism is reflected in the practice of restricting the number of meals for monks and the timing of meals. Monks fast from noon on, accepting only tea or sweet drinks in the afternoon and evening. Buddhists accrue merit through *dana* (meritorious giving), including giving daily food to monks. This is one route to a better rebirth and to avoiding dangers in the present life. Most of those feeding monks and spirits are women. In all the Theravada countries, women are the most generous supporters of temples, providing the food for early-morning alms rounds, cooked dishes for the monks' noon meal, and uncooked rice for special ceremonies and community rituals at the temple. In a more commercial vein, women often sell food at temple fairs as a means of earning merit and money.

Ordinations of new monks, giving of gifts of robes to monks, and consecrations of religious buildings and Buddha images are all occasions for pilgrimages and festive meals. Food connects urban and rural communities on these occasions. Income differences may be apparent in the foods given to monks; however, any food given with a good intention is valued. Ethnic heritage may also be reflected in the food given to monks. For example, a rice-flour noodle known as *kanom jeen* mixed with a fish curry (*nam yaa plaa chon*) is often served at temple events in areas of Thailand where the Mon settled. It is made from snakehead fish, garlic, shallots, shrimp paste, galangal, and ginger and is served over coiled rice noodles.

After the food is given to monks, everyone who participated in the service shares the donated food. In Buddhist ceremonies, white thread is used to define sacred space and transfer the merit made by feeding monks and spirits to all who participated in the ritual. Merit made by feeding monks can also be transferred to ancestors in general or recently deceased relatives through a ritual known as *kluat nam;* water that has been blessed by the monks is slowly poured into another container or onto the ground, while monks chant appropriate Pali stanzas. Thus, both food and merit are widely shared with the living and the dead.

Theravada Buddhists are not generally vegetarian. In the Theravada tradition, meat dishes are given to monks in most communities. In Buddhist communities, it is more often the elderly who fast, meditate, and keep extra precepts all day, because they no longer have to worry about the work of food production and preparation. Women and the elderly are also more likely to enter into longer-term fasts. New Buddhist movements such as Santi Asoke require their adherents to be vegetarian. Recently, more Theravada Buddhists are taking on the Mahayana practice of fasting a few days a month.

Diet and Health

Thailand imported from India some of the ideas about the cooling and heating properties of food

Buddhist monks carry alms given in the street, Thailand. (StockPhotoPro)

and how food affects individuals at certain stages of their life cycle. But since Thailand did not import the South Asian system of castes and subcastes, the heating and cooling properties of food and people had no connotation of purity and pollution; as a result, everyone could eat together.

In the Theravada Buddhist communities of Thailand, some monks, particularly forest monks who reside alone and practice meditation, gain reputations for their skills in healing through herbal and spiritual methods. In the past when villagers might not have had access to any health services, monks were honored as valuable healers who helped reduce suffering out of loving-kindness, free of charge. Ritual speech, words spoken over medicinal mixtures, can be called on in cures. Whether efficacy can be attributed to the placebo effect, or the peace of mind that comes from practicing morality, is not of great concern, particularly in households where no other remedies are available. Spiritual healing is particularly important in palliative care, treating chronic diseases, and when illnesses have a mental health component. Midwives, specialists in traditional massage, herbalists, and shamans all contribute their expertise to the varied healing strategies in Thailand, in addition to the sophisticated and effective public health system in the country.

Food-secure countries like Thailand face a difficult set of problems, as their policy makers must deal with problems related to both under- and overnutrition. This double dilemma is a result of improvements in food supply combined with changes in food habits. Food security and good health care systems in Thailand are reflected in the low infant and under-five mortality rates in 2005: 18 per 1,000 and 21 per 1,000. A related challenge concerns the complex interactions between malnutrition and HIV/AIDS. For the many people living with HIV/AIDS in Thailand, adequate and healthy food is their most immediate and critical need, as antiretroviral therapy works effectively only for people who are well nourished.

Although Thailand has low rates of malnutrition, some families may still have to deal with both low-birth-weight infants and overweight schoolchildren.

In addition to an estimate of 9 percent low-birth-weight infants and 10–15 percent overweight children in primary schools in the country, about half the people in central Thailand and urban areas now have high cholesterol rates. Changes in food habits and food availability are responsible for this modern "toxic food environment," according to media reports in Thailand. Climbing obesity rates are blamed on Western fast-food chains. Problematic foods are identified as those high in salt, sugar, and fat, including instant noodles, deep-fried chicken, pizzas, hamburgers, French fries, doughnuts, cookies, and cakes. These mouth-watering edibles are found everywhere, leading to increasing rates of coronary heart disease, diabetes, hypertension, and, to some extent, cancer. Heart disease and cancer, diseases of the affluent, are now the primary causes of death in Thailand.

Penny Van Esterik

Further Reading

Bhumichitr, Vatcharin. *The Taste of Thailand.* London: Pavilion Books, 1988.

Brennan, Jennifer. *The Original Thai Cookbook.* New York: Coward, McCann and Geoghegan, 1981.

Brissenden, Rosemary. *Southeast Asian Food.* Singapore: Periplus, 2007.

Muntarbhorn, Kanit. *Gastronomy in Asia, Book I.* Bangkok, Thailand: M. T. Press, 2007.

Na Songkhla, Wandee. *The Royal Favourite Dishes.* Bangkok, Thailand, 1977.

Na Songkla, Wandee. *Royal Thai Cuisine, Book I.* Bangkok, Thailand, 1980.

Pinsuvana, Malulee. *Cooking Thai Food in American Kitchens.* 3rd ed. Bangkok, Thailand: Sahamitr Industrial Printing, 1979.

Thompson, David. *Thai Food.* Berkeley, CA: Ten Speed Press, 2002.

Van Esterik, Penny. "Anna and the King: Digesting Difference." *Southeast Asian Research* 14, No. 2 (2006): 289–307.

Van Esterik, Penny. *Food Culture in Southeast Asia.* Westport, CT: Greenwood Press, 2008.

Van Esterik, Penny. "From Marco Polo to McDonalds: Thai Cuisine in Transition." *Food and Foodways* 5, No. 2 (1992): 177–93.

Van Esterik, Penny. *Women of Southeast Asia.* DeKalb, IL: Southeast Asia Monograph Series, Northern Illinois University, 1996.

Warren, William, ed. *Thailand: The Beautiful Cookbook, Heritage Edition.* Bangkok, Thailand: Asia Books, 1992.

Tibet

Overview

Tibet is an autonomous region of southwestern China (since 1950) that borders the nations of India, Nepal, Burma, and Bhutan. With an area of 471,700 square miles, it occupies most of the landmass known as the Qinghai-Tibet Plateau—the highest region on earth—and sits at an average elevation of 14,000 feet above sea level. Tibet is virtually surrounded by mountains, including the renowned Himalayan range, where Mount Everest (Chomo Langma), the world's highest at over 29,000 feet, straddles the border with Nepal. Given its geographic position, the climate of Tibet is primarily cold and dry, although some parts of the south are mild and temperate. Many of Asia's largest rivers run through the plateau, including the Mekong (Zachu), the Yangtze (Drichu), and the Indus (Senge khabab). Tibet is divided into one municipality—the capital city of Lhasa—and six prefectures including Shigatse in the southwest, Ngari in the west, Lhaoka in the south (central), Chamdo in the east, Nakchu in the north, and Nyingtri in the southeast. The total population in 2008 was reported at approximately 2.8 million, mostly concentrated in Lhasa or other urban areas. This figure does not include any ethnic Tibetans living in surrounding Chinese provinces that belonged to Tibet prior to Chinese occupation. The total number of ethnic Tibetans living in and surrounding the autonomous region is around six million.

Before 1950, Tibet was an independent territory ruled by a theocratic government, with the Dalai Lama—a Buddhist high priest believed to be a reincarnated deity—acting as head of state. As the official public religion, Buddhism shaped all social values, norms, rituals, and institutions. Following a political rebellion in 1959, the Dalai Lama fled to India to establish a government-in-exile, triggering the exodus of numerous Tibetans into neighboring countries and beyond. Today, Tibetan Buddhism remains the leading religion in the area, with only a small number who practice the traditional Bön religion (an indigenous faith that some contend existed before Buddhism but that has nonetheless been strongly influenced by it), and even fewer Muslims.

Tibet's strategic location in Central Asia has made it vulnerable to invasion throughout its long history, particularly by the Mongolians and the Chinese. Nevertheless, the Tibetan people have remained relatively isolated from outside influences, resulting in a truly unique culture with its own ethnic group, language, social customs, and cuisine.

🍽 Food Culture Snapshot

Norbu Tsering and his wife, Rinchen Lhamo, live in a small house in the historic district of Lhasa—the largest city and the capital of Tibet—together with their seven-year-old daughter, Rabten Pema, and five-year-old son, Lobsong Tashi. Since Norbu and Rinchen were born after Chinese occupation at a time when Tibetan culture was undergoing a tremendous surge of development, they each had the opportunity to receive a formal education—a new phenomenon for many Tibetans. Both of them grew up in farming villages outside of Lhasa but moved into the city to attend Tibet University, where they first met as students of literature. While many ethnic Tibetans have greeted the Chinafication of their society with great resistance, Norbu

A Tibetan family has their meals in the wild field after working on their farm. (Gan Hui | Dreamstime.com)

and Rinchen believe they will have more ability to effect positive change as well as greater personal opportunity if they are compliant. They are both fluent in Tibetan and Mandarin Chinese, which serves as an important factor in finding and maintaining full-time employment, especially in a region where inequality is continually on the rise and the throngs of Han Chinese immigrants seem to be getting preferential treatment (most jobs require an understanding of Mandarin). Norbu is a teacher at a local elementary school, and Rinchen works as an editor at a Lhasa television station. Most of Norbu's colleagues are Han cadres, sent to the area by the central Chinese government to serve terms lasting between two and eight years. Similarly, Rinchen's coworkers are predominantly Chinese from neighboring provinces like Sichuan and Yunnan. The children attend the primary school where their father teaches and count language classes in both Tibetan and Mandarin as some of their favorite subjects. In socioeconomic terms, this

family is characteristic of the emerging urban middle class in contemporary Tibetan culture.

Norbu, Rinchen, and the children enjoy and are very thankful for all of the conveniences an urban life affords them. Their home is outfitted with electric power, providing them with heat during the harsh winter months and plenty of light throughout the year. Rinchen has a very modern kitchen by Tibetan standards, with appliances like a methane-fueled stove, a pressure cooker, an electric butter churner, a small refrigerator, and a host of plastic storage containers on hand. The family especially appreciates the color television they recently received from Rinchen's company. Watching televised programs has become a favorite family activity and a special time to spend together.

Among the many benefits of living in the city, Norbu and his family relish most the availability and variety of foods to be found. Lhasa has several daily food markets and street-side stalls selling everything from fresh vegetables and yak meat to yogurt (*sho*), yak butter (*mar*), barley (*ney*), and brick tea (compressed black tea). While fresh meat and produce were hard to come by in the past, they appear abundantly all over the city today. Greenhouse farming has become very popular throughout Tibet, leading to the cultivation of "exotic" foods such as strawberries and watermelons—fruits that Rabten and Lobsong find particularly enjoyable. Locally produced peaches, pears, apricots, and grapes are favorites for the whole family when in season. Additionally, Rinchen likes to keep dried fruit and nuts on hand for special occasions.

Enormous quantities of fresh produce are flown into the region from neighboring provinces on a daily basis. Therefore, it is not uncommon to find tomatoes, chili peppers, bok choy, carrots, bean sprouts, eggs, spices, cabbage, turnips, potatoes, radishes, garlic, ginger, and more lining market shelves. Wild herbs and mushrooms are abundant throughout the city, too, and the family likes to keep them on hand for medicinal purposes. Rinchen makes regular trips to the market because she likes to keep fresh items on hand but has little refrigerator space in which to store them.

In recent years, Lhasa has seen the opening of three supermarkets, making access to dietary staples and packaged foods all the more convenient. Rinchen purchases the bulk of her family's food from street markets because she believes the quality of the ingredients is far superior, but occasionally she visits the supermarket to purchase processed roasted barley flour (*tsampa*), wheat, rice, salt, cooking oil (canola), dried yak meat, instant noodles, candy, Pepsi, local barley beer (*chang*), and the like.

While Rinchen handles most of the cooking and shopping, Norbu and the children like to participate from time to time. They particularly enjoy going to the Tianhai Night Market on the west side of town because it is lined with all sorts of street foods, snacks, and sweets. In fact, the daytime market on Barkhor Street is closer to their home, but Rinchen's work schedule makes it difficult for her to shop during the day. Fortunately, Tianhai is open in the evenings, and the prices are much lower. Here, the family enjoys an inexpensive night out, making dinner out of the Sichuan food stalls. While numerous restaurants are popping up all over the city, many of them are too expensive for the whole family.

Rinchen keeps the family well stocked on Tibetan staples like barley, dairy products (yogurt, cheese, and butter), and yak meat, but on occasion she enjoys splurging on rare or unusual foodstuffs like eggs, seafood, pork, and chicken. The children have acquired a taste for these and other Sichuan foods, as they appear regularly during mealtime at school. Historically, Tibetans were forbidden to eat small animals according to Buddhist law. Yet following the Chinese occupation and the influx of Han ethnic groups, attitudes toward religious taboos relaxed; and poultry, pork, and seafood became increasingly available. Norbu and Rinchen still feel that it is best not to indulge in these foods, except on special occasions.

In contrast to the modern lifestyle led by Norbu and his family, the traditional ways of procuring food in Tibet were far more complex. In fact, this is still very much the case in most rural areas today. Prior to Chinese occupation, many of the foods used in Tibetan cooking were cultivated, prepared, and consumed directly in the home. Everything else was purchased at annual or biannual markets (*lotsong*). These markets were held following a harvest, usually during the ninth month of the year (Tibetans observe a lunar calendar), and were located in areas easily accessed by nomads and farmers alike. Lotsong typically took place over a period of two to three weeks to ensure enough time for exchanging goods and stocking up on important staples not readily available at home. Ordinarily, markets were regionally based, providing goods for up to five or six villages at once, but larger cities offered their own municipal markets. Nomads would bring with them an abundance of animal products in exchange for the agricultural harvests of village farmers. Vegetables and fruits were dried to ensure a long shelf life—because the growing season was very short—and to stand up to the demands of the nomadic lifestyle.

Major Foodstuffs

The high elevation and cold, dry climate of Tibet, serving as a natural boundary to the variety of foods grown in the region, have been instrumental in the development of a unique cuisine. Traditionally, very few agricultural crops could withstand such extreme weather conditions, making the use of animal products an essential means of subsistence. Limited international trade and religious dietary restrictions have been equally influential. Only a few items from surrounding countries such as brick tea, rice, and sugar appear with any regularity, and Buddhist law has forbidden the consumption of seafood, poultry, and other small animals. In recent years, Tibetan cuisine has begun to see major changes, yet food staples have remained relatively constant.

Perhaps more than any other factor, however, social diversification has shaped the production and specification of food in Tibetan homes. It is difficult to understand Tibetan culture at all apart from an understanding of its social structure—with farmers (*rongpa*), nomadic animal herders or pastoralists (*drokpa*), and religious clerics forming the basis of society. Until recently, social organization throughout Tibet remained largely unchanged, thanks to the region's relative geopolitical isolation. Farmers had permanent homes in villages and towns, where they cultivated their own crops and consumed a predominantly vegetable-based diet. Since most of them did not have their own livestock, they relied on pastoralists for meat and dairy products. Alternatively, animal herders lived as nomads, occupying tents and moving from place to place depending on the season. Most of the foods consumed by pastoralists came from their own herds, including meat, fat (*tsilu*), and dairy products. With little access to vegetables or grains, nomads depended on the agricultural harvest of farmers to supplement their diet. Occupying the highest social positions in Tibetan society were monks, priests (*lamas*), and nuns, who did not produce their own food—although they did cook—but depended on the provisions of farmers and herders for all their dietary needs including vegetables, grains, and dairy products (they were forbidden to eat meat).

A Tibetan monk shopping in Lhasa, Tibet. (iStockPhoto)

The most abundant and valuable crop in Tibet is barley (ney), which alone accounts for around 55 percent of all cultivated land and 56 percent of total food production. The average person consumes around 341 pounds (155 kilograms) of the grain per year. Most of the time, barley is ground into flour and toasted (tsampa), forming the basis of the Tibetan diet. A typical adult will consume at least 176 pounds (80 kilograms) of tsampa every year. And children will eat as much as 158.5 pounds (72 kilograms) in the same time period. No home is considered complete without tsampa. Other grains might be substituted including wheat, buckwheat, corn, millet, oats, or soybeans, but the most popular and respected tsampa is made with barley. Tibetan people believe that tsampa is pure only if barley is used and that it possesses healing, restorative properties. It is so highly revered that it is used as an offering in most religious ceremonies and is always present on special occasions. While it is mainly mixed with a little Tibetan butter tea and eaten as a sort of dough, tsampa is used in a multitude of recipes, from soups (*tsamtuk*) and dumplings to sweet and savory cakes (*sengong* and *pag*). In a typical Tibetan home, tsampa is eaten with every meal—three times a day—and is processed on-site. Each household is equipped with milling stones for grinding flour, and every village has a mill house, used to process large quantities. The grains are thoroughly cleaned, then toasted in sand prior to being ground, which cooks them evenly and reduces the threat of burning. A sieve is used to separate the barley from the sand. The whole grains of barley (ney) are also popular when toasted and eaten as a snack (*yoe*).

In addition, barley (ney) is used to make beer (chang), another staple of Tibetan cuisine. Like tsampa, other grains may be used such as rice, corn, oats, millet, and wheat, but the most traditional and popular chang is made with barley (ney). It appears at almost all religious events and festivals, although most monks and priests (lamas) are forbidden to drink alcohol. Chang is enjoyed by people of all ages either hot or cold, and it has an alcohol content of approximately 5 percent. In almost any home, chang is offered as a sign of courtesy to guests, who out of respect for the host must first take three sips and then drink the entire serving. Chang can be made into a distilled alcohol (*arag*) as well, appearing regularly at religious ceremonies and on special occasions.

The use of animal products in everyday cooking has been fundamental to the survival of the Tibetan people. As a result, meat, fats, and dairy products predominate in the local cuisine. Almost all foods consumed in Tibet are accompanied by something from an animal—be it meat, fat, butter, yogurt, or cheese. Ironically, Buddhism forbids the killing of animals, except in places where vegetables and grains are so scarce that meat is the only means of survival. Historically, it was only the nomads—animal herders by trade—who were "allowed" the privilege of taking an animal's life, and that applied only to large species. Buddhist philosophy reasoned that it is better to kill large animals for food as one slaughter feeds many mouths. Therefore, the consumption of small animals, birds, and fish was strictly prohibited. Furthermore, monks and priests (lamas) were forbidden to eat meat of any kind, and farmers could partake only in the event of a natural or accidental animal death. Dairy products were available to all social groups since they could be obtained without killing. Today, many Tibetans, particularly the younger generations, are beginning to overlook these religious stipulations and are now eating poultry, seafood, and other small animals.

The meats most commonly used in Tibetan cuisine come from yaks, barren female yaks (*dri*), sheep, goats, cows (*lung-pi*), and yak-cow crossbreeds (*dzo* or *dzomo*). Because the killing of animals is seen as a necessary evil, a ritual precedes each slaughtering, in which prayers, holy water, and butter lamps are offered to the animal. Consequently, no part of the animal is left unused. Fine cuts are enjoyed on special occasions, animal skins and stomachs are used in cooking or for storage, organ meats and blood are eaten in sausages, and even the dung is used to seal storage spaces and as cooking fuel. Dried meat (*sha kampo*) is particularly popular in Tibet and has been a dietary staple for hundreds of years. In the Tibetan climate foods can be dried quickly, a process that prolongs the shelf life and makes them convenient for traveling. The meat is often cut into strips and hung to dry in the sun. Sha kampo is eaten raw or cooked.

Other typical meat dishes might include meatball curry served with cream (*shabril*), blood and liver sausages (*gyuma*), spiced grilled meat with tomato sauce (*sha katsa*), and meat and noodle soup (*thugpa*), just to name a few. Meat- or vegetable-stuffed dumplings (*momo*) are the most popular of Tibetan dishes, typically served at formal meals and celebrations. The dumplings are folded into a variety of shapes, depending on the occasion, and served with chili sauce or pickled radishes and cabbages (*lakyur*). In recent years, momo have become so popular with tourists that restaurants in urban areas offer them daily.

Momo

In a typical Tibetan home, these dumplings are filled with yak meat, beef, or mutton, but in monasteries and areas where meat is not available, a vegetable mixture is substituted. The traditional and most popular cooking method is steaming, but the dumplings are sometimes fried as well.

Filling

1 lb ground beef or lamb

½ c celery, diced

¼ c green onion, finely sliced

1 tsp fresh ginger, minced

¼ tsp ground cumin

¼ tsp ground nutmeg

2–3 tbsp water, or just enough to bind

Salt to taste

Dough

3 c white flour

½ tsp baking soda

Water, just enough to bring together into a firm dough (approximately ½ c)

In a large bowl, mix together all ingredients for the filling, cover, and chill.

To make the dough, mix together all the dry ingredients in a large bowl. Add water little by little, making sure to stop just when the dough comes together into a firm ball. Chill the dough for approximately 30 minutes (dough can be prepared and chilled overnight). Then cut the dough into 4 pieces. Using a rolling pin, roll each piece out until it is ⅛ inch thick. Using a round cookie cutter, cut the dough into approximately 2–3 round disks. Be sure to roll the dough in stages to prevent it from drying out. In the center of each round put about a teaspoon of filling. Fold the disk in half and firmly pinch together the edges, creating a half-moon shape. Repeat until all the dough and filling have been used. Be sure to keep the completed dumplings covered with a damp cloth or paper towel. The dumplings can be stored overnight and cooked the next day. To cook them, use a bamboo steamer placed over a wok or pot with a little boiling water, and heat, covered, for about 30 minutes or until the filling is well cooked.

Traditional Tibetan dishes, momos (center) and bouillon (left). Momos are doughy pouches often filled with a variety of items, including meat, vegetables, or cheese. (Shutterstock)

In Tibetan cuisine, dairy products are equally significant to tsampa (toasted barley flour), forming a major portion of the diet and maintaining a prominent position at religious ceremonies. Butter (mar), above all other foods in this category, is indispensable in a Tibetan kitchen. Traditionally a high-value trade item produced by nomads, butter is used in everyday cooking and beverages, or as cooking and lighting fuel (butter lamps). In religious rituals, it is shaped into elaborate carvings and used as offerings. The milk of dri (female yaks) is believed to deliver the finest-quality butter with a pleasant golden hue, but sheep, goat, and dzomo (female yak-cow crossbreeds) milk are used as well. Ordinarily, it is made by hand and stored in wet animal skins that shrink as they dry, creating an airtight container that preserves the butter for long periods of time. Butter is the key ingredient in Tibet's most important beverage—butter tea (*boeja*)—a warm, salty concoction that is consumed at every meal and throughout the day. It is not unusual for a Tibetan to drink up to 40 cups a day. Imported Chinese brick tea is steeped in salted water until it is very strong, then is poured into a tall churn and whipped heavily with butter and salt, resulting in a thick consistency very much akin to broth. Boeja is served as a token of hospitality in any household, and the cups are refilled after every sip.

Milk, cheese, and yogurt are common food staples as well, appearing regularly at meals and in numerous recipes. Most of the milk comes from the dri, but sheep, goat, and dzomo milk may be used as well. Two kinds of cheese are typical: a hard variety (*chura*) that is dried in the sun and a softer type (*chura loenpa*) reminiscent of cottage cheese. Chura has always been a popular snack because of its durability on long journeys. It is so hard that it is best when added to soups or stews. Yogurt (*sho*) is mostly used for making butter, but it is also enjoyed in cooking or as a snack. It is believed that sheep milk makes the best cheese and that dri (female yak) milk makes the best butter.

Cooking

The functionality and layout of traditional Tibetan kitchens varies depending on the lifestyle of the domestic unit. However, every household is equipped with a stove, a stone mill for grinding flour, and a wooden butter churner. In the past, the primary fuel for cooking was wood, but animal dung was used by nomads or in areas where wood was scarce. Today, charcoal and gas are becoming popular sources for fuel. Modern Tibetan homes in villages and towns are beginning to have access to running tap water and electricity, giving rise to more convenient cooking equipment such as electric butter churners, solar-powered stoves, and refrigerators.

It is most common for women to do all the cooking and food preparation in a Tibetan family home, but it is not unusual for men to participate in household duties as well. Children begin learning to cook as early as three years of age and are expected to regularly assist in meal preparation by the age of six. In religious houses, every inhabitant shares in domestic duties including cooking and purchasing food.

A typical kitchen for a nomadic household is placed in the center of the tent, where tables and portable stoves made of metal tripods are placed. Food is stored in animal-skin bags and kept near the stove for everyday use. Surplus food is placed in cellars dug out of the ground. Because the soil is so cold, these storage pits are excellent natural freezers, preserving foods for long periods of time. They are usually lined with animal dung, which acts as a seal when closed, creating an airtight environment for the food.

As inhabitants of permanent homes, farmers have individual rooms that are used for both cooking and eating. These kitchens are equipped with large stoves made of stone, allowing for several foods to be cooked at once. Most households have additional rooms that are used as storage pantries and for drying meat.

Tibetan monasteries tend to have large, well-equipped kitchens because of the great number of inhabitants (sometimes more than 1,000 people). It is not uncommon to find teapots the size of rooms that require the attention of multiple cooks for churning tea and cleaning.

Professional cooks are highly regarded in Tibetan society and may be hired for special occasions and religious ceremonies. Wealthy families tend to employ them as full-time household cooks. Traditionally, all professional cooks were men and were expected to learn the trade as apprentices of master cooks (*gyal se machem*).

Cooking vessels and serving dishes fluctuate depending on the region, occasion, or social status of the household. Pots for cooking are made from earthenware, brass, copper, iron, and bronze. Storage containers might also be made of wood. Serving dishes and utensils are usually made of wood or silver. Tibet has its own deposits of jade, so it is normal to find special containers and bowls for barley beer (chang), barley liquor (arag), or toasted barley flour (tsampa).

Typical Meals

Location and social status play a key role in determining the kind of meals that are consumed in Tibetan households. Nomads tend to eat dishes heavy in animal protein, whereas monks and farmers eat more vegetables and grains. Most Tibetans consume three meals a day, and snacks are always nearby. Babies also eat three daily meals that usually consist of tsampa, butter (mar), milk, and yogurt (sho) or soft cheese (chura loenpa).

Breakfast might consist of a soup (tsamtuk) made with tsampa, along with dried cheese (chura), dried meat (sha kampo), dried fat (tsilu), and roasted soybeans. Butter tea is the drink of choice, with at least three or four cups consumed at breakfast alone. A little of the tea may be mixed together with some tsampa and crumbled cheese, then hand-kneaded into a dough or "cake" (pag).

Lunch and dinner usually follow a similar pattern, although the midday meal is the heaviest and dinner tends to be light. Tsampa and butter tea are always on the table, but chang (barley beer) is common, too. Vegetarian dishes served for lunch or dinner might include buckwheat leaf salad (*yaba*), baked and buttered mushrooms (*sham trak*), and spicy potato curry (*shogok katsa*). Side dishes like pickled cabbage or radishes (lakyur) and tomato-based hot sauce (*sipen mardur*) are frequently served. Meat dishes such as grilled yak served with tomato sauce (sha katsa), blood sausages fried in mustard oil (gyuma), broth (*ruetang*), dumpling soup (*boetuk*), meat and noodle soup (thugpa), and meatball curry (shabril) are popular throughout Tibet.

Desserts are not as prominent in Tibetan cuisine as in the West but might appear on special occasions and during religious festivals. The two most prevalent sweets are both made out of rice, a food item that has been scarce in Tibet until recently. *Dresil* is sweetened rice mixed with butter and dried fruits, served with yogurt. *Omdre* is a very similar recipe, except it does not call for dried fruit or butter and may have a thicker consistency, more like a pudding. On special occasions like New Year's Day (Losar) rice cookies are popular, eaten either baked or fried.

Snacks are enjoyed throughout the day and are especially handy when traveling. The demand for Chinese snacks is growing throughout Tibet these days, following the arrival of numerous Han immigrants (mostly from the Sichuan Province). Traditional options like dried meat (sha kampo), dried cheese (chura), and toasted grains (yoe) are prevalent all over Tibet, and Chinese alternatives such as ravioli-style dumplings (*shuijiao*) and steamed dumplings (*baozi*)—much like momo—are popular in urban areas.

Tibetans have an elaborate set of rules surrounding the meal that mirror social norms and religious beliefs. The order of service is crucial, as it follows a hierarchical arrangement believed to be pleasing to Buddha. Those of the highest social status must be seated at the head of the table and served first during a meal. No one else may eat until the head of the table has prayed and begins. In some areas of Tibet, it is polite for guests to lick their bowls or plates to show appreciation. Also, belching is another sign of appreciation that is practiced in some parts of the region. Avoiding bad manners during a meal is as critical as expressing gratitude and respect. Some instances of bad manners are chewing with an open mouth, talking loudly, stepping over food, pointing one's feet or stretching the legs, eating from communal dishes or utensils, and passing one's plate or bowl over the dish of another guest.

Eating Out

Eating out in Tibet is a remarkably recent phenomenon, and the majority of restaurant patrons are tourists and urban dwellers (young people). As an isolated territory for much of its history and a region closed to foreign visitors between the 1960s and the 1980s, this comes as no surprise. Traditional society was not conducive to restaurant development because so much of the population lived as nomads or in remote areas. Some monasteries did offer food and accommodations to travelers, but this practice never became a point of focus.

Following Chinese occupation in 1950, Sichuan restaurants began to appear in cities and towns throughout Tibet. Today, they outnumber any other type of eating establishment. Menus feature specialties such as stir-fried meats and vegetables, noodles, dumplings, rice noodles cooked in a clay pot (*shaguo mixian*), fried noodles (*chaomian*), and egg-fried rice (*dan chao fan*). Even the smallest villages in Tibet will have a Sichuan restaurant, but the prices are much higher than what can be found in the capital city of Lhasa. These eating establishments, and the growing numbers of Han Chinese immigrants, have been responsible for introducing foods into the Tibetan diet that hitherto were forbidden by Buddhist law. Prawns, crabs, chicken, duck, pork, and fish appear on many restaurant menus and are easily found in supermarkets.

Cities and towns are beginning to have a variety of restaurants that serve Nepalese, Indian, Muslim, and Western-style foods, in addition to those that serve traditional Tibetan dishes. Western foods like sandwiches, burgers, pizzas, cookies, and snack foods are easy to find in supermarkets and hotel restaurants. Nepalese and Indian curries are popular as well.

Restaurants in urban parts of Tibet now offer a variety of beverages in addition to butter tea and barley beer (chang). Sodas, mineral water, Chinese green tea, and Pakistani sweet tea (*cha ngamo*) are widely available. Bottled beers are gaining popularity as well, including the Tibetan Snow and Lhasa brands, as well as Budweiser. Chinese red wine can be found on some restaurant menus and in supermarkets.

Special Occasions

The Tibetan people love to celebrate, which has given rise to many special holidays and festivals. Many of these events originated as religious ceremonies and have become part of the popular culture today. Food staples like barley flour (tsampa) and butter

Typical dishes one might find in a feast in Tibet. This one was prepared for a wedding. (StockPhotoPro)

(mar) are commonly used as offerings and made into elaborate carvings. No matter what the occasion, feasting is always part of the agenda.

The Tibetan New Year is considered the most important annual festival, as it is a time for cleansing and new beginnings. It is celebrated over a period of several days and involves a series of monastic and popular rituals. It begins on the 29th day of the 12th month (following a lunar calendar) with monastic prayers and the burning of a giant sculpture called *Goutor*. On the same day, families clean their homes and enjoy a meal of dumpling soup (*gouthouk*) and dough made from tsampa (barley flour). From the dough and the remaining soup a human sculpture is created and taken out of the house to ward off any negative elements. On the first day of the New Year, all monasteries are cleaned, and offerings of scarves, butter lamps, and luxury foods—rock sugar, candies, nuts, and dried fruits—are brought. The monks hold a ceremony where they burn incense and distribute small amounts of barley flour (tsampa) to all the people, who eventually throw the grains into the air as a symbol of luck and the passing into a new year. During the ceremony there is plenty of chanting, music, and dancing. Inside family homes, everyone wears new clothes and celebrates the upcoming year with a feast that includes the finest meat and vegetable dishes, tsampa mixed with butter and sugar (*chemar*), rice dishes, yogurt (sho), rice cookies, and barley beer (chang). The chemar is meant to symbolize a plentiful barley

Decorative food prepared in anticipation of the New Year celebration, Tibet. (Jeeraphat Jantarat | Dreamstime.com)

harvest for the upcoming year, and the sho, plentiful animal products. Prior to the arrival of Buddhism, a sheep was sacrificed as an offering during this festival, and the head (*luggo*) was served during the meal. Although sacrificing sheep is not part of the celebration today, an image of a sheep's head carved out of tsampa is served as a substitute. Meatball curry (shabril) is an example of the kind of dish enjoyed on New Year's Day and other festive occasions.

Shabril

Ingredients

2 lb ground lamb or beef, or 1 lb each combined

4 tsp vegetable oil

½ c onions, diced

2 tsp fresh ginger, minced

2 cloves garlic, minced

½ tsp turmeric

1 tbsp soy sauce

1 c mushrooms, sliced

½ c daikon radish, finely sliced

8 oz sour cream or plain yogurt

Salt to taste

½ c green onions, sliced

Season the meat with salt, and shape into ½-inch balls. Set aside. In a large saucepan, sauté onions in the oil over medium heat until golden brown. Add the ginger and garlic, and cook for 2–3 minutes more. Add the meatballs, and cook on one side for 2–3 minutes, or until lightly brown on one side, and then flip. Repeat. Add the turmeric and soy sauce and cook for 2 more minutes. Reduce the heat to low, cover, and simmer for 4–5 minutes. Add the mushrooms and radishes, and cook for an additional 10–15 minutes. Remove the pan from the heat, and add sour cream in small batches, stirring constantly. Once the sour cream is well incorporated, return pan to the heat and bring to a gentle simmer. Then turn off the heat, season with salt to taste, and add green onions. Serve with rice and hot sauce or pickled cabbage.

The Great Butter Festival is a traditional Buddhist ceremony held in Lhasa that falls on the 15th day of the first month, when butter lamps are burned and a variety of sculptures are created out of butter including birds, animals, figurines, and flowers. It is the last day of the festival of prayer and a celebration of Buddhist enlightenment.

Diet and Health

Known as the "science of healing" (*gsowa rigpa*), Tibetan medicine is an ancient practice with strong links to Buddhist philosophy, Ayurvedic traditions from India, Chinese medicine, and various forms of astrology. It involves a series of complicated diagnoses and treatments including acupuncture, pulse and urine analysis, herbal remedies, diet and lifestyle modifications, heat therapy, and the like. Tibetan medicine upholds the belief that the health of the body depends on the health of the mind. All illnesses, therefore, come from the three poisons of desire, hatred, and ignorance. The ignorant state of consciousness is the root of all disease because it gives rise to desire, which in turn breeds hatred.

Tibetan medical theory asserts that the body is composed of three humors—wind, bile, and phlegm—that control all bodily functions and correspond to the five elements found in nature—earth, water, fire, wind, and space. There are numerous subcategories for each humor as well. The key to good health is to maintain a balance of these humors in the body, in the mind, and in relationship to nature. It is believed that individuals have a tendency toward a predominant humor, or a distinct combination thereof, determining a physical disposition and temperament. That is, a person with a bile temperament is prone to bile-related illnesses.

Furthermore, this system classifies all matter as either hot or cold, both in the environment and in the body. The wind humor is associated with air and thus has a cold quality; bile is linked with fire, producing a hot disposition; and phlegm is associated with earth and water and has a cold quality. Since bile is connected to the element of fire, for example, its function in the body might include producing internal body heat and strength and promoting digestion. And a person with a bile humor, or bile-related illness, has a hot disposition.

Foods are either hot or cold as well, playing an important role in overall health. To promote equilibrium of the body, all foods must be consumed in moderation and should correspond to an individual's predisposition. That is, persons with cool temperaments should consume mostly warm foods, and vice versa. Not only is diet a preventative measure for health, it can be used in healing treatments as well. Many Tibetan doctors prescribe diet modifications to improve internal balance. All the major food groups in Tibetan cuisine are categorized in this manner, and the staples of the local diet are considered some of the healthiest foods. Fresh barley flour (tsampa) is considered a cool food and is believed to cure headaches, stomachaches, and fevers (all hot) if cooked as a porridge with milk. Fresh meat is cool, whereas aged meat is warm and thought to strengthen digestion. These classifications do not correspond with the temperature of the foods but rather their constituents. Broadly speaking, Tibetans believe that cooked foods are superior to anything raw.

In the same manner that a proper diet can restore health, poor food habits are believed to destroy it. An improper diet involves the consumption of anything in excess and the combination of foods that do not belong together. Some examples might include hot milk and fruit, hot milk and sour foods, or drinking cold water with heavy, greasy foods.

Jennifer Hostetter

Further Reading

Cramer, Marc. "Tibet: Crossroads of Cookery and Culture." *Flavor and Fortune.* http://www.flavorandfortune.com/dataaccess/article.php?ID=332.

Dorje, Rinjing. *Food in Tibetan Life.* London: Prospect Books, 1985.

Jacob, Jeanne, and Michael Ashkenazi. "Tibet." In *The World Cookbook for Students.* Volume 5, *Sri Lanka to Zimbabwe,* edited by Jeanne Jacob and Michael Ashkenazi, 77–83. Westport, CT: Greenwood Press, 2007.

Kelly, Elizabeth. "Elizabeth Kelly's Tibetan Recipes." YouTube. http://www.youtube.com/user/elizamas#p/u.

Kelly, Elizabeth. *Tibetan Cooking: Recipes for Daily Living, Celebration, and Ceremony.* Ithaca, NY: Snow Lion, 2007.

Wangmo, Tsering, and Zara Houshmand. *The Lhasa Moon Tibetan Cookbook.* Ithaca, NY: Snow Lion, 2007.

Vietnam

Overview

The Socialist Republic of Vietnam curves along the western edge of the Indo-Chinese peninsula of mainland Southeast Asia. After nearly 20 centuries of war, colonization, and foreign occupation, the country is now undergoing rapid economic and social development.

Vietnam is bordered by China to its north and Laos and Cambodia to its west. Tropical lowlands and densely forested highlands cover nearly 80 percent of the country, leaving most of its agricultural and urban development concentrated into two main areas, the Red River Delta of the north and the Mekong Delta of the south. Hanoi and Ho Chi Minh City (once known as Saigon) are located, respectively, in these deltas. The two burgeoning cities contribute to Vietnam's standing as the 14th most densely populated country in the world. Its population reached 86 million in 2008 and continues to increase by 1 million every year.

Vietnam's geography, culture, climate, and cuisine can be divided into three distinct regions: the cool north, the central highlands, and the hot south. Neighboring China, which ruled the area as a tributary state for 2,000 years, heavily influenced the food of northern Vietnam. In the 16th century, the Nguyen dynasty established Hue, located at the narrow fulcrum of the country, for its imperial capital and created an elaborate cuisine for the central region. The hot, fertile lowlands of southern Vietnam, once a part of the Funan Empire that reached from northeastern India, have long boasted an abundance of fresh fruit, vegetables, and fish.

After its arrival in Vietnam in the second century A.D. Buddhism blended easily with Confucianism, Taoism, ancestor worship, and indigenous animism. After decades of Communism, the country has become strongly secular, yet a majority of Vietnamese still consider themselves Buddhists. The most devout Buddhists are vegetarian, while others may simply abstain from eating eggs or the flesh of any animals on the 1st and 15th days of each lunar month. Strict Catholics, who make up about 7 percent of the population, observe the Lenten fast. Followers of Cao Dai, a syncretic religion unique to South Vietnam, must eat a vegetarian diet for at least 10 days during each month. All food served in Buddhist and Cao Dai temples is vegetarian, though Cao Dai allows the use of garlic and onions, which are typically prohibited by Buddhist strictures.

🍽 Food Culture Snapshot

The Nguyen family resides in Long Xuyen, a prosperous town with a population of nearly 300,000 in the Mekong Delta region. Dung Cong is a swimming coach at the local university, while his wife, Dung Phuong, takes care of their household. Their daughter, Thao, 21, works as an administrative assistant in a downtown office. Their son, Duc, 19, is a full-time student of engineering. As is typical for unmarried children, both Thao and Duc live with their parents and return home to eat most of their lunches and nearly all their dinners there.

Dung Phuong, who cooks for the family, shops for ingredients every day at 9 A.M. Most days, she walks about 300 feet to the neighborhood open-air market. There, she chats briefly with the vendors while she typically selects freshwater fish such as eel or *basa* catfish. Increasingly, she has been able to buy pork and poultry, and for special occasions, she can now choose a cut of beef. Seasonal fruit, fresh greens such as watercress or spinach, herbs, spices, eggs, and tofu will also make their way into her basket. Once or twice a week, she rides one of the family's scooters to a large, newly built supermarket. Frozen foods, dry staples, soft drinks, beer, ocean fish, and packaged snacks are all items the family prefers to obtain from the supermarket.

Two or three times a month, each family member enjoys eating at a favorite street vendor, especially for *pho bo* or *bun rieu,* noodle soup specialties that require too many ingredients and too much time to prepare easily at home. During especially hot days, Dung Cong, Thao, and Duc might purchase a small snack, such as sticky rice pudding or fresh fruit skewers sprinkled with salt and chili, to carry them over to a late cooked dinner.

During the past decade, as Vietnam prospered and distanced itself from the difficult postwar years, Dung Phuong has noticed food becoming more affordable for her family. Many ingredients, especially meats and vegetables, are abundant year-round, and her family now has access to products from other countries. Ingredients such as Italian pasta, American apples, French mustard, Chinese noodles, and Japanese pickles are available at the large supermarkets. Thao has been learning to cook from her mother and is beginning to shop for meals during the weekends when she is not working at the office. Though food tends to be more expensive at the new supermarket, Thao values the hygienic packaging and the convenience of the fixed prices she finds there. Dung Phuong enjoys experimenting with unfamiliar foods. Still, most of the meals she prepares for her family revolve around the local region's freshwater fish, vegetables, and rice.

Major Foodstuffs

Rice in some form appears at the center of nearly every meal in Vietnam. Of the arable land in Vietnam, 60 percent is dedicated to growing rice. The Red River Delta and the Mekong Delta have long symbolized the country's rice baskets, and recent economic growth is especially evident in their increased supply of rice. Vietnam now ranks fifth in the world in consumption of rice and is the third-largest exporter of the grain after Thailand and the United States.

Jasmine rice, or long-grain *gao thom,* literally "fragrant rice," is the preferred variety for its flowery aroma. Its long and narrow grains are typically polished to a white color during milling and are then rinsed well before cooking to remove excess starch, as Vietnamese diners tend to like less starchy grains that retain a firmer bite while fluffing to a lighter texture. While there is some awareness of eating whole-grain rice with its healthful bran layer, polished white rice is still very much widely preferred.

A batter made from ground rice also becomes the base for distinctive *banh trang,* or rice paper. As a cottage industry throughout the countryside, women spread rice batter into paper-thin rounds onto fabric stretched tightly over simmering water. After steaming briefly, the rounds are then transferred to woven mats to dry in the sun. They become thin, translucent, parchment-like rounds that can be stored indefinitely. Later, after a quick dip in warm water at the table, they transform in seconds into delicate wrappers that are used for wrapping thinly sliced meat, seafood, fresh vegetables, and herbs. These rolls, called *banh cuon,* are one of the classic dishes of the Vietnamese table.

In the cooler highlands of the west and north, hill tribes terrace their mountain slopes with curving fields of glutinous rice. Also known as sticky rice or sweet rice, it contains much higher amounts of amylopectin, a branching molecule that results in a stickier, starchier texture upon cooking. There are different varieties of glutinous rice, from short, white, pearly grains to long, thin, purple-black rice. All are eaten as an accompaniment to savory dishes as well as being added to sweet desserts and snacks. Also distinctive to highland cooking is the use of *thinh,* a powder made from raw rice grains that have been roasted until golden brown and then ground fine. The powder lends a sweet, nutty flavor to savory dishes, helps bind minced-meat preparations, and adds a delicate, powdery texture to salads.

Vietnamese cooks have developed a variety of noodles based on rice, from threads as fine as hair for serving with delicate fish to wide, silken ribbons for hearty stews. Each type of noodle has a different name. *Banh pho* are the flat, square-cut strands that appear in the popular beef soup. *Banh canh* are thick, chewy, round noodles that have both heft and resilience for soups with rich, spicy broths. *Bun,* also known as rice vermicelli, lend their name to the cold noodle salads that are commonly eaten for lunch. *Banh hoi* are extremely thin strands that are delicately steamed, pressed into a veil of noodles, and then cut into small squares for rolling inside lettuce leaves with slices of grilled meat.

Wheat and egg noodles reveal Chinese influence. Known as *mi* in Vietnamese, the golden, toothsome noodles typically marry with heartier flavors. *Mi vit* features a rich broth and duck flavored with five-spice powder and orange peel. When deep-fried, egg noodles become a crunchy, fluffy pillow that serves as the base for a variety of stir-fried dishes such as sweet and sour shrimp or mushrooms with yellow chives.

Mien noodles, made from the starch of mung beans, turn transparent once boiled. Also known as cellophane or glass noodles, the chewy noodles hold up well to stir-frying and braising. They star in *mien ga,* a popular, comforting soup with a clear broth and shredded chicken. Chopped finely, mung bean noodles also help bind the filling for fried spring rolls, steamed pork cakes, and other minced-meat preparations.

Fish and shellfish play an important role in Vietnam's cuisine. The country's long coastline, defined by the Gulf of Thailand, the South China Sea, and the Gulf of Tonkin, stretches 1,860 miles (3,440 kilometers). Further inland, Vietnam's navigable waterways total nearly 9,700 miles (18,000 kilometers), placing it eighth in the world, significant for a country of its small size. Vietnam's many rivers and lakes, along with its flooded rice paddies and irrigation canals, teem with freshwater life. Catfish, eel, and shrimp—along with frogs and snails—all figure heavily in the day-to-day meals of rural communities.

Mud crabs thrive among the roots of coastal mangrove trees. Meaty and sweet, they are cracked and coated with a sweet-sour tamarind glaze or dry-fried with butter and black pepper. A delicate crab and asparagus soup served at formal banquets reveals the influence of French cooks.

One of the most popular ways to serve shellfish of all kinds is simply steamed or grilled and then dipped in a mixture of fresh lime juice, salt, and coarsely ground black pepper. Bream, grouper, and trevally (giant kingfish) are highly sought, expensive fish reserved for special meals. Squid, octopus, clams, mussels, lobster, and other seafood are not widely available locally, as the majority of the catch is destined for fine restaurants, luxury hotels, or the export trade. Freshwater channel fish, perch, and carp appear more frequently in local markets.

Fish and shellfish are often dried for easy, inexpensive transport and storage. Shrimp, crab, and small fish such as anchovies and sardines are also preserved in salt and fermented to make *mam,* a pungent paste that adds depth of flavor to many traditional dishes. *Nuoc mam,* or fish sauce, is an amber-colored liquid that seasons nearly every Vietnamese dish. It is pressed from anchovies that have been salted and fermented. Fish sauce serves as a seasoning in the kitchen, a condiment at the table, and a base for numerous dipping sauces. Dried shrimp is another very common and versatile ingredient. It can be cooked whole with glutinous rice, shredded for garnishing steamed noodles, or ground into a fine powder to make a convenient base for quick stocks.

Vietnam's fishing industry, concentrated in the Mekong Delta, is still dominated by small boats, though many are mechanized. Fish-sauce makers are also based in the south, especially on and near Phu Quoc Island, where the same families have been pressing high-quality fish sauce in small batches and aging it in wooden casks for generations.

Vietnamese cooks prefer to purchase their meat and poultry live from wet markets. Pork is the predominant meat in Vietnam. More than 98 percent of households consume pork, and it comprises about 75 percent of the meat eaten in the country. *Thit kho nuoc dua,* or pork stewed with fresh coconut juice, and *nem nuong,* small meatballs grilled on skewers and served over rice noodles, are two popular ways of enjoying pork. The French introduced charcuterie such as pâté and forcemeats. Adapting European techniques, Vietnamese cooks perfected *cha lua,* a smooth, pale bologna made with finely pureed pork and potato starch and then cooked inside banana leaves. Other specialties such as head-cheese and cured ham have also been incorporated into the Vietnamese kitchen.

Pork is among the most affordable of meats, as pigs can be raised on much less land than other animals and are much easier to feed. Furthermore, the country does not export pork and can thus maintain low domestic prices. As urban dwellers become more affluent, they tend to include more pork in their diets, and pork consumption remains concentrated near the large cities of the Red River and Mekong deltas. Most pigs are raised on small farms of only a few animals.

Poultry accounts for about 15 percent of meat consumption. Vietnamese cooks prefer *ga di bo* (literally, "walking chicken"), small, free-range chickens that have firm, dark, lean flesh. Younger chickens are cooked in *ga xa ot,* a highly flavored dish with lemongrass, chilies, and turmeric. Long-simmered *chao ga* combines creamy rice congee with the rich flavor of older, tougher hens.

The penchant for eating beef was introduced into Vietnam, as through much of Asia, by Mongolian horsemen. Dishes that now highlight beef were once predominantly made from the meat of water buffalo or oxen. These traditionally involved grinding, mincing, thin slicing, or long simmering to tenderize the meat of an old animal that had worked much of its life pulling a plow or cart. Hanoi is home to the country's most famous dish, pho bo. The rice noodle soup, now enjoyed all over Vietnam, highlights the meat in many forms: rare slices, well-cooked brisket, chewy meatballs, crunchy tripe, and rich tendon. Oxtail and beef shank enrich the soup's broth, while ginger and onion scorched over an open flame deepen its color and flavor.

Bo bay mon is the name of a festive meal involving seven courses of beef. Certain restaurants specialize in this traditional feast. The most famous dishes of the meal include thin slices of beef rolled

Pho, Vietnamese soup at a restaurant in Ho Chi Minh City. (Shutterstock)

with peppery *la lot* leaves and grilled, slices of beef cooked at the table in lemongrass-infused vinegar, and a soothing rice soup made from the bones that closes the meal. *Bo kho,* chunks of beef stewed with carrots, potatoes, lemongrass, and star anise, can be served with rice or with thick slices of crusty French bread. In the highlands, strips of sun-dried beef complement green papaya salad for a simple lunch.

Chuot dong, sweet-fleshed field mice that live in rice fields and feed only on the ripened grain, are eaten by nostalgic older diners who remember the more difficult war years; they have also, increasingly, become popular among young, urban food adventurers who travel to the countryside. Historically, dog meat has been a delicacy in Vietnam. Increasing exposure to Western culture, however, has imported an awareness of discomfort in serving it.

Rau song, literally, "live greens," refers to the abundance of raw vegetables that are served at the Vietnamese table. Wrapping food in lettuce or young mustard leaves is a common way of eating. Crisp *goi* salads often start formal banquets or are served as a side salad with rice soups. These salads feature crisp, finely shredded vegetables, from everyday carrots, celery, or cabbage to special ingredients such as the segmented stems of lotus plants (*bap chuoi*) or shredded strips of banana blossoms (*sen*).

Cooked greens accompany meats and fish. *Rau muong,* known as water spinach, has long, hollow stems and dark green, arrowhead-shaped leaves that

Goi Ga, a traditional Vietnamese chicken salad. (Shutterstock)

are similar in flavor to spinach. It grows at the edge of rivers and canals and is an especially important vegetable in northern Vietnam. Watercress, Chinese chives, chrysanthemum greens, and a wide array of cabbages are other leafy vegetables often served at the Vietnamese table. Chayote (*su hao*), bitter melon (*kho qua*), angle squash, long beans, taro stems, and bottle gourds are green vegetables that appear in soups and quick stir-fries.

Canh Chua Ca Loc (Sour Broth)

This colorful soup depends on tamarind's fruity tartness. *Canh chua,* literally, "sour broth," is traditionally served alongside other dishes as a palate cleanser. Ladled over rice, it becomes a comforting, filling meal. Catfish is the most common protein added, but shrimp, eel, and fried tofu are all common substitutes.

Serves 6

1 lb fish fillets, cut into 2-in. pieces

2 tbsp fish sauce

½ tsp ground black pepper

4 c fish or chicken stock

¼ c tamarind pulp, softened in 1 c boiling water and strained

6 thin slices ginger

1 red or green chili pepper, sliced thinly

1 tbsp canola oil

1 shallot, thinly sliced

2 cloves garlic, thinly sliced

2 tomatoes, seeded and cut into wedges

2 c chopped fresh pineapple

1 c mung bean sprouts

¼ c fresh cilantro leaves

2 scallions, sliced thinly

Combine the fish, fish sauce, and black pepper in a bowl, rubbing to coat the fish evenly; set aside. In a large pot, stir together the stock, tamarind, ginger, and chili pepper. Bring to a boil, then reduce heat and simmer, partially covered, for 15 minutes.

Heat oil in a large skillet over medium-high heat. Add shallots, and cook, stirring, for 30 seconds. Add garlic and cook 1 minute. Add the marinated catfish and sear 3 minutes on each side. Transfer the fish to the soup along with the flavorful oil. Add the tomato, pineapple, and bean sprouts. Increase heat to bring the soup to a boil, then reduce heat and simmer until the fish is opaque at the center, 3 to 5 minutes. Sprinkle with the cilantro and scallions; serve immediately.

Goi Ga

This savory salad is a classic example of the fresh vegetables and herbs that frequently appear on the Vietnamese table. It may be offered as a first course in a banquet or as an accompaniment to a bowl of rice congee.

1½ c cooked chicken, torn into bite-sized shreds

½ small head cabbage, cut into thin ribbons

1 carrot, coarsely grated

¼ small onion, cut into paper-thin slices

¼ c chopped mint leaves

¼ c chopped *rau ram* leaves

3 tbsp fish sauce

3 tbsp fresh lime juice

1½–2 tbsp sugar

1 red chili pepper, thinly sliced (optional)

Freshly ground black pepper

2 tbsp cilantro leaves

2 tbsp chopped, toasted peanuts

In a large bowl, combine the chicken, cabbage, carrot, onion, mint, and rau ram. In a small bowl, stir together the fish sauce, lime juice, sugar, chili, and black pepper until the sugar is completely dissolved. Drizzle the dressing over the salad, and toss to mix evenly. Set aside to let flavors meld for 15 to 30 minutes. Just before serving, toss again, transfer to a serving platter, and garnish with cilantro and peanuts.

In Vietnam, green tea was traditionally the drink of choice. A large pitcher filled with weakly brewed tea, cooled with a solid block of ice, and placed on a table in the main room of the home will provide refreshment for a family throughout the hot, dusty day. Restaurants immediately offer glasses of tea to each table to welcome diners. Tea infused with jasmine is a favorite served both hot and iced, while for special occasions, tea flavored with lotus blossoms may be poured for guests.

French colonists first planted coffee on the mist-covered slopes of Vietnam's central highlands. Since then, both arabica and robusta coffee plants have flourished, and *cafe sua da,* or iced milk coffee, has become an iconic, much-loved beverage. Preparing the coffee is as much a ritual as drinking it: A metal filter fits over each individual cup, and an intensely dark, thick, strong brew drips slowly through it. A spoonful or two of sweetened condensed milk, a tall glass of chipped ice, and a long spoon all aid in transforming the coffee into a sweet, cooling drink.

The country's hot weather prompts many sidewalk vendors to sell local fruit drinks. *Nuoc mia* is the faintly sweet juice pressed from fresh sugarcane. Limeade and orangeade sweetened with sugar and frequently dressed up with fizzy soda water are refreshing drinks offered at nearly every eatery. The country's abundant coconut trees provide a steady source of *nuoc dua,* the clear and refreshing water of young coconuts. *Chanh muoi,* a limeade flavored with salted plums, replaces valuable minerals sweated out of the body on particularly sultry days. Sodas are becoming increasingly popular among younger generations. European and Australian wines, domestic and imported beers, and special, fruit-based cocktails fill the menus of popular clubs and bars.

Many families still make their own rice wine from cooked glutinous rice. Formed into balls, sprinkled with brewer's yeast, packed into ceramic crocks, and immersed in water, the rice ferments within days to create *ruou nep,* which may have 10 to 20 percent alcohol by volume. In the highland regions, the fermented rice wine is infused with herbs and spices for serving from communal jugs at weddings, festivals, and other special occasions.

Diet and Health

Chinese medicine, called *thuoc bac,* has long been practiced alongside traditional Vietnamese folk remedies, called *thuoc nam.* Tue Tinh, considered the founder of traditional Vietnamese medicine, was a scholar and Buddhist monk of the 14th century. He wrote several books that listed hundreds of medical herbs and thousands of recipes for herbal remedies. Today, common home-based cures for colds and pains include massaging with aromatic oils, inhaling steam imbued with healing herbs, and sipping bitter teas and rich broths.

From the 1940s through the 1980s, the country endured severe shortages of food. A drop in livestock numbers after the Vietnam War, combined with devastating floods in 1978 that destroyed 20 percent of the remaining cattle herds, led to a significant decrease in meat consumption. After the United States lifted its economic embargo against the Communist government in 1994, food from around the world began entering the country. Income levels have doubled every few years since 1990, and after decades of severe food shortages, Vietnam has resumed food exports.

While increasing prosperity has improved the diet of the average Vietnamese, the nutritional status of both children and adults remains poor. The country continues to have one of the highest malnutrition rates in Asia, with 22 percent of children under age five considered low in weight for their age and 33 percent of children under age five considered low in height for their age. For adults, the average consumption is 1,850 calories, or one-fifth less than the accepted minimum daily standard of 2,300 calories.

Thy Tran

Further Reading

Nguyen, Andrea Leigh Beisch, and Bruce Cost. *Into the Vietnamese Kitchen: Treasured Foodways, Modern Flavors.* Berkeley, CA: Ten Speed Press, 2006.

Pham, Mai. *The Best of Vietnamese and Thai Cooking: Favorite Recipes from Lemon Grass Restaurant and Cafes.* Rocklin, CA: Prima, 1995.

Pham, Mai. *Pleasures of the Vietnamese Table.* New York: HarperCollins, 2001.

Trang, Corinne. *Authentic Vietnamese Cooking: Food from a Family Table.* Burlington, VT: Verve, 1999.

Other

Antarctica

Overview

Antarctica is a large continent of ice, over five million square miles in area (nearly 14 million square kilometers). It has no native population and no agriculture. While there are potential native foods on the continent—penguins and seals, for example—their hunting is restricted, and they were significant as food products only during early exploration of the continent. Still, Antarctica is a fascinating case in food culture. About 4,000 scientists and support staff live and work for months at a time on the continent (with a much smaller population over the winter). A somewhat newer tourism industry brings tens of thousands of visitors to the continent each year.

Antarctica is the highest, driest, windiest, and most remote continent. Its international contingent of researchers and staff operates out of research stations run by Great Britain, Norway, Russia, Japan, Argentina, Chile, France, Germany, Australia, New Zealand, and the United States of America.

Many explorers, beginning with Ferdinand Magellan in 1519, reported seeing a Terra Australis (southern land). Magellan's sighting, south of his eponymous strait, was actually Tierra del Fuego, South America, now divided between Chile and Argentina. Subsequent exploration, most famously by the British Captain James Cook from 1773 to 1775, revealed a number of Antarctica's outlying islands, called the Subantarctic Islands. Inspired by these early explorers, European nations dispatched numerous expeditions to discover and claim this most southerly land. The first explorer credited with seeing the continent of Antarctica proper (as opposed to outlying islands) is the Russian explorer Fabian Gottlieb von Bellingshousen in 1820.

The heyday of Antarctic exploration occurred in the decades preceding and following the "race to the [South] Pole," begun in 1902 with the attempt by Robert F. Scott, Edward Wilson, and Ernest Shackleton. The race was won (to England's dismay) by Norwegian Roald Amundsen and his team in 1911, beating another attempt by the British team of Robert F. Scott, Edward Wilson, Edgar Evans, and Lawrence Oates by about one month. These and other early explorers hunted seals for fur, perhaps the only industry besides exploration on the continent. Many nations dispatched expedition teams to survey and claim portions of the continent.

By 1959, the age of exploration of Antarctica gave way to the age of scientific discovery with the signing of the Antarctic Treaty. The treaty, effective as of 1961, designated the continent for peaceful purposes, banned mining, and later limited the use of sled dogs and the killing of local wildlife.

Major Foodstuffs

"Food assumes a role of abnormal importance in a place so deficient of so many of life's pleasures" (Wheeler 1996, 86). Since the earliest days of Antarctic exploration, food has meant survival, solace, a heavy, impractical burden, a waste of time and fuel, a tangible reminder of the good life "off the ice," and much more for the men (and more recently women) who have sought to know this inhospitable land.

Provisioning a continent with no agriculture and few native foods and cooking that food in subfreezing temperatures without vegetation that can be used for fuel are challenges going back to the earliest days of exploration. Even fresh water—abundant in millions of cubic miles of ice—was a challenge to make usable, requiring a great deal of time, effort, and fuel to melt.

Food in the early days of Antarctic exploration was largely utilitarian. Given the energy required to live and function in this harsh environment (early explorers rationed about 4,700 calories per person per day, about double the U.S. Department of Agriculture's recommended allowance for adults), and the importance of the expedition at hand, it is little wonder that early expeditioners would not have wanted to spend even more energy to make food pleasurable (Swithinbank 1997). Even today, Antarctic cooks take a certain pride in making do with what's available rather than fussing over perfect ingredients as one might do off the ice.

Pride in cooking with efficiency of fuel and time, in opposition to the waste and delicacy of the homeland, is a sentiment that can be found among the earliest Antarctic literature, such as this journal entry of Edward Wilson (1872–1912), dating to the Discovery expedition of 1901–1904: "I confess I do fancy myself as a sledge cook, which doesn't mean that I can make a good omelette, but I can manage a primus lamp and melt the snow and boil up the tea, cocoa or pemmican, and fry the bacon with little wasted time" (Savours 1966/1904, 181).

Pemmican, a food mentioned in the preceding quotation, was a staple of early Antarctica and is a good example of a food that maximizes efficiency. It is a preparation adapted from a Native American food that combines pounded dried meat with animal fat and berries into a dense cake or bars. For Douglas Mawson (Australian Antarctic explorer and geologist, 1882–1958) and other early Antarctic explorers, pemmican was ideal as it was a highly concentrated source of calories and could fulfill their goal of "reduc[ing] as far as possible the weight of food taken upon any journey . . . [such that] only highly concentrated foods are admissible" (Mawson 1998/1911, 116).

Mawson's need for efficiency on the trail was almost consuming as he recounts in his journal on Christmas Eve, 1912: "A violent blizzard, could not travel. . . . I cannot sleep, and keep thinking of all manner of things—how to improve the cooker, etc.—to while away the time. The end is always food, how to save oil, and as experiment I am going to make dog pem[mican] & put the cocoa in it" (Jacka and Jacka 1988, 165).

More efficient than pemmican for early explorers was to live off the land, which in Antarctica meant killing and eating seals, penguins, skua (another seabird), and, in times of desperation, their own sled dogs. The blubber of seals was also the primary source of cooking fuel, and the meat of all these animals was used to feed dogs as well. Mawson wrote in 1908, "We must live on seal flesh and local food cooked by local means as much as possible" (Jacka and Jacka 1988, 16).

Early into the Antarctic exploration, seal had made its place as an integral part of the explorers' diet. An entry from Edward Wilson's Discovery diary reads: "Seal meat for breakfast, jam and bread and butter and tea at 1 o'clock and seal meat for dinner at 6. . . . We eat the whole seal, heart, liver and kidneys. The liver is as good as any I have ever eaten, the kidneys are tougher in texture than sheep's even when well cooked and quite fresh. The flesh is dark indeed, but makes very excellent dishes. . . . Appetites simply immense and *how* we enjoy our food, *and* our sleeping bags, though the joy of breakfast always makes up for the necessity of turning out in the morning" (Savours 1966/1904, 218, emphasis in original).

Later, Wilson remarked, "Our food here is always either seal liver, or Adelie penguin, or skua cut up and fried in butter—simply excellent" (Savours 1966/1904, 335). Local meat became so integral to the Antarctic diet that as late as the 1950s, when the Antarctic Treaty was signed to protect the local wildlife, the United States airdropped beef tenderloins to camping expeditioners. Although the expeditioners had ample food, including non-Antarctic meat, the government considered seal and penguin a sufficiently important part of the diet to bring fresh meat at any expense (Bechervaise 1964).

Despite this recent trend toward luxury amid hardship, today's chefs emphasize the extra steps it takes to be successful on the continent:

All our produce is brought in once a year at the main re-supply so we make do with that. One thing I will say is you adapt to using aged produce. I have to make my own self-rising flour, my eggs are nearly twelve months old so need to be floated first to weed out the rotten ones (they float). The first thing that comes to mind is the age of produce and other products that are used here that you would never use under most other circumstances. For example eggs that are twelve months old (dipped in oil to help with preservation), carrots (10 months old), potatoes (10 months old). They tend to look very ratty after a while but as you're not likely to get anymore you make do and are forced to make the most of it. It's not unusual for me to rummage through a box of apples on the off chance I'll find 10–15 good ones." (Chef Michael Lunny, Casey Antarctic Station [Australian], in an interview with the author)

While floating eggs may seem a world away from Mawson's experiments with dog and cocoa pemmican, the sentiment is similar. Antarctica is a harsh place calling for a can-do attitude with little patience for the niceties of home. At the same time, while efficiency may be a noble goal for an Antarctic expedition, living on a continent with no indigenous foodways, vegetation, or even sunlight for much of the year reminds even the most diehard expeditioner that she or he is human and has food needs far beyond adequate nutrition. Even Mawson, who passionately touted the efficiency of "highly concentrated foods" for sledging, had a soft spot for an occasional treat: "Speaking generally, while living for months in an Antarctic hut, it is a splendid thing to have more than the mere necessaries of life. Luxuries are good in moderation, and mainly for their psychological effect. With due regard for variety during the monotonous winter months, there is a corresponding rise in the 'tide of life' and the ennui of the same task, in the same place, in the same *wind,* is not so noticeable" (Mawson 1998/1911, 115–16, emphasis in original).

This theme of nostalgia is poignantly shown in the diary of Wilson, who earlier preaches the wonders of seal in the rigorous Antarctic diet but cannot let it corrupt his English Sunday dinner. In July, he writes, "Sunday dinner all through this winter has been celebrated by fresh roast mutton off the sheep given us in New Zealand. They have been frozen in the rigging since December [approximately seven months], but are excellent with mint sauce and beer" (Savours 1966/1904, 161). It is not until the first of September that Wilson acknowledges that his nostalgia may have had the upper hand in their menu, when he writes, "We have finished all our mutton, having had it every Sunday all through the winter. As it was tainted, I think it's a good thing there was no more" (Savours 1996/1904, 287).

Even in contemporary Antarctica with its modern kitchens; the ability to ship, store, and cook a year's supply of fresh, canned, and frozen foods; and relative comfort, there is a need to reinforce the idea of home. When asked if he perceived a nostalgic sentiment for food back home, Chef Michael Lunney replied, "Every minute of every day. This becomes more of a topic of conversation as the year draws on." The lack of fresh produce is especially felt at certain times of year, with expeditioners saying things like, "It's strawberry season back home." While hydroponics on the continent have helped to curb some of the cravings for fresh produce, production is low as authorities are wary of introducing new microbes into the Antarctic ecosystem.

Still, the governments are cognizant of the need to provide a semblance of normalcy in Antarctic life and attempt to achieve this by making luxury items such as wine, quail, and good cheese available to chefs, installing espresso machines, and encouraging chefs to keep flexible menus to respond to special requests for traditional dishes.

Cooking

On the barren and remote continent of Antarctica, there has long been pride in cooking with efficiency, juxtaposed against another theme of nostalgia for home and for the early days of Antarctic exploration. The methods themselves are similar to those done in a typical kitchen environment—baking, roasting, sautéing, braising, simmering. Due to the extreme environment, outdoor cooking is rarely done unless camping out. Even then the food is usually prepared under some shelter as it is nearly impossible to cook in the subfreezing wind.

For early explorers, gastronomic pursuits at the campsite—specifically, adapting cooking methods to the Antarctic environment—were detailed alongside the scientific pursuits of the day. Mawson writes, "I have tried yeast bread but find there is not sufficient constancy or warmth in the Hut temperature for proving" and "Correll is now turning out fine scones" (Jacka and Jacka 1988, 85, 90). Wheeler (1996, 87) recalls that "in the early days culinary ingenuity occupied a good deal of the time. One man assured himself lifelong popularity by producing minty peas, revealing later that he had squirted toothpaste into the pot."

Cooking with a minimum expenditure of fuel has long been valued on the continent. Even after Antarctica was settled with buildings and working kitchens and the local wildlife was protected, there was evidence of a certain pride in being as efficient as possible. Charles Swithinbank, writing of his expeditions in the 1960s, recounts an innovation that reinforces the dichotomy between the efficient and the nostalgic:

> Copper-bottomed stainless steel saucepans replaced the traditional aluminum pans, and hard plastic mugs and bowls replaced enamel plates and cups. Though visitors to the tent never knew it, the result was that we went through the whole season without ever washing dishes. The high fat content of our diet and the absence of burnt food sticking to the pans meant that we could clean everything by wiping it with toilet paper. Water on the trail is expensive. Every drop has to be melted from cold snow. Wiping saved fuel. However there is residual ethic in the sledging fraternity that favors primitive and inconvenient cooking utensils. Thus our eminently successful improvements never caught on outside our little group. Burned aluminum, cracked enamel mugs, crumbling pot scourers, and dirty dishwater are evidently the order of the day for macho explorers. (1997, 72)

With a span of over 50 years of Antarctic exploration, Swithinbank straddled the end of the discovery era and the beginning of the scientific era. His unheralded dedication to efficiency was felt not only in the preceding quotation but also when he returned to Antarctica in his late sixties to follow up on some research. To his surprise, a two-pound bag of brown sugar was airdropped over their camp at the request of a research assistant who didn't like white sugar on his morning oatmeal. What would early intrepid explorers have thought of that?

Typical Meals

By 1912, Mawson's diary reveals a balance between living off the land and living off the rations. An early menu found in his diary shows the rotating entrée from the dinner menu: "Monday—Penguin, Tuesday—Seal, Wednesday—Canned Meats, Thursday—Penguin, Friday—Seal, Saturday—Variable, Sunday—Mutton" (Jacka and Jacka 1988, 59, 63). Wilson's crew incorporated the local fauna into traditional British dishes including seal steak and kidney pie.

In the 1970s the first Indian Antarctic expedition was planned. While the meat-centered European diet adapted relatively easily to the Antarctic climate, the challenge of cooking dried pulses at negative 40 degrees Fahrenheit is greater. Consequently, a line of Indian rations was developed: preserved chapatis, dehydrated pilaf, and dehydrated dal (Subramanian and Sharma 1982–1984).

Because Antarctic research stations are tied to a national government entity, the daily meals are typically reflective of the host nation's dining habits. There is typically a commissary or cafeteria in each research station staffed by government or military employees or, increasingly, by government contractors. Because there are no options for meals outside of the station (there are no real restaurants beyond a burger bar at McMurdo station), great attention is given to providing variety, nutritional balance, and food that feels like home. Increasingly, there is more effort to prepare food reflective of the diversity of the researchers themselves. In general, most researchers report that Antarctic food is quality institutional food, perhaps equivalent to food in a good college cafeteria. Monotonous and institutional, to be sure, but not as bad as is often expected.

Nearly every food item needs to be brought from home, often at an annual resupply (some limited fresh produce is grown indoors). Consequently, elaborate planning as well as culinary ingenuity is needed to maintain quality. Running out of an ingredient is no problem at home—you can run to a store or call a vendor to replace it. Not so on a continent of ice!

Eating Out

Eating out is largely a moot question on Antarctica. While McMurdo station boasts a burger bar in addition to the cafeteria, most of the continent's dining is restricted to the institutional cafeterias at research stations or aboard the tourist cruise ships.

Special Occasions

Feelings of nostalgia, contrasted with a lack of practical resources, spur a unique improvisation that would hardly be appropriate anywhere else in the world. Sara Wheeler tells about a visit to Scott Base, a New Zealand Antarctic base: "They put on an Italian night and even produced ciabatta [bread]. An Andres Segovia tape was unearthed; they admitted he was Spanish, but Antarctica taught you to improvise. . . . In the evening we drank the wine the winterers [those relative few who stay over the Antarctic winter] had made from raisins and sultanas. It tasted of cooking sherry, but they had decanted it into Chateau Lafite bottles" (1996, 215). An earlier example dates to 1957, when John Behrendt tells of an improvised cocktail party where "Clint and Mac mixed up some martinis using ethanol (190 proof) for gin and Chilean white wine for vermouth. . . . They must [have been] quite sick of beer" (1957, 138).

Such improvisation is no recent phenomenon. On Christmas Day in 1902, Edward Wilson recounts the menu, which concludes: "Then a very small plum pudding, the size of a cricket ball, with biscuit, and the remains of the blackberry jam and two pannikins [small cups] of cocoa with plasmon [dried milk]. We meant to have had some brandy alight on the plum pudding, but all our brandy has turned black in its tin for some reason, so we left it alone" (Savours 1966/1904, 228).

While a plum pudding sans plum seems a strange improvisation in 1902, Wilson's compatriot on this side of the century, Sara Wheeler, has made numerous "Bread and Butter Puddings (Antarctic Version)" on the ice, whether or not there was actually any butter, milk, eggs, or sugar available. For special occasions in Antarctica it is very much the thought that counts (Wheeler 1996, 301). Because there is no native population on Antarctica, every holiday is necessarily a time of homesickness and nostalgia. Cooks make efforts to reproduce the foods and feelings of home.

Diet and Health

Because of the extreme Antarctic climate, early rations were more than double the recommended daily dietary intake: about 4,700 calories (Swithinbank 1997). Now that many researchers spend the majority of their time indoors, efforts are made to provide lower-calorie, healthy meals as well as ample opportunities for physical exercise, especially in the dark winter when it is nearly impossible to venture outdoors.

Early explorers suffered from scurvy and vitamin A toxicity (hypervitaminosis A) due to a diet based on seal and penguin (high in vitamin A, especially the liver) with few or no fruits or vegetables. This caused a loss of hair and teeth and skin lesions. Starvation and extreme hunger were constant concerns—and the unfortunate end—of many early Antarctic explorers.

While many tend to view gastronomic variety as a luxury, there seems to be evidence that in times of scarcity, thought of food can be psychologically debilitating if left untended. Mawson and his colleagues wrote extensive menus while subsisting on dog through an Antarctic trek. "Young duck with apple sauce, *petit pois,* new potatoes and American sweet corn," are some of the 11 courses they devise for their return home to Sydney, Australia (Jacka and Jacka 1988, 39).

Similarly elaborate food dreams abound in the early Antarctic literature, characterized by an abundance of food and a rude awakening when the dreamer discovers it is unattainable. Mawson dreamed of buying an elaborate cake in a confectioner's shop and accidentally leaving the store without the cake. When he returned, the shop had a sign in the door that read "early closing" (Jacka and Jacka 1988, 175–76).

Wilson writes of dreams with unnerving similarity to Mawson's:

> Nearly every night we dream of eating and food. Very hungry always, our allowance being a bare one. Dreams as a rule of splendid food, ball suppers, sirloins of beef, cauldrons full of steaming vegetables. But one spends all one's time shouting at waiters who won't bring one a plate of anything, or else one finds the beef is only ashes when one gets it, or a pot full of honey has been poured out on a sawdusty floor. One very rarely gets a feed in one's sleep, though occasionally one does. For one night I dreamed that I eat the whole of a large cake in the hall at Westal without thinking and was horribly ashamed when I realized it had been put there for a drawing room tea, and everyone was asking where the cake was gone. These dreams are very vivid, I remember them now, though it is two months since I dreamed them. (Savours 1966/1904, 221)

Because of the diversity of the research station personnel and the international treaty managing the continent, all of the world's major religions are represented on the continent at one time or another. There are particular challenges for researchers who require a vegetarian, halal, or kosher diet, and extensive arrangements need to be made in advance since food deliveries to the stations are infrequent and other options for dining do not exist.

In considering the food of Antarctica, past and present, two themes emerge. The first is the idea that food is a necessary burden that needs to be handled deftly and efficiently in order to make for a successful expedition, be it one of early exploration or present-day research. The second theme is that despite the inhospitable climate and geography of the continent, there is a need to occasionally eschew efficiency and practicality to feed the nostalgic, impractical impulses of the resident. These two themes synthesize to form a contemporary Antarctic food culture that is neither wanton nor ascetic and that prides itself on improvisation, making the most of that which is available. In the words of Sir Douglas Mawson, it is "a subject . . . which requires particular consideration and study" (1998/1911, 115).

Jonathan Deutsch

Further Reading

Bechervaise, John. *Blizzard and Fire: A Year at Mawson, Antarctica.* London: Angus & Robertson, 1964.

Behrendt, John C. *Innocents on the Ice: A Memoir of Antarctic Exploration.* Boulder: University Press of Colorado, 1957.

Jacka, Fred, and Eleanor Jacka, eds. *Mawson's Antarctic Diaries.* Winchester, MA: Unwin Hyman, 1988.

Mawson, Douglas. *The Home of the Blizzard.* 1911. New York: St. Martin's Press, 1998.

Savours, Ann, ed. *Edward Wilson: Diary of the Discovery Expedition to the Antarctic Regions, 1901–1904.* 1904. London: Blandford, 1966.

Subramanian, V., and T. R. Sharma. "Processed Food on Antarctica." *Indian Food Industry* 3, No. 3 (1982–1984): 99–100.

Swithinbank, Charles. *An Alien in Antarctica.* Blacksburg, VA: McDonald & Woodward, 1997.

Wheeler, Sara. *Terra Incognita: Travels in Antarctica.* London: Jonathan Cape, 1996.

Space

Overview

Food is an essential component in human space exploration. If it had not proved possible to eat and digest in space, none of the longer-term space missions since the 1960s would have been achievable. Space travel has such a significant impact on the body that good nutrition is critical. Bone density decreases; muscles waste; cardiovascular deconditioning occurs; red blood cells are lost. Space sickness affects more than half of all astronauts, regardless of experience; and exposure to high levels of radiation can increase susceptibility to other problems such as cataracts and cancer later in life. Space conditions—in particular, the shift of fluid to the head and a low intake of zinc—impact the senses of smell and taste, both of which are reduced, making stimulation of the appetite more difficult. At the same time, the cramped, stuffy, smelly, and noisy conditions on board the spacecraft conspire to dampen the appetite further. Early on, the astronauts would return to Earth thinner and weaker—and with a large proportion of their allotted food uneaten.

Major Foodstuffs

Every aspect of eating in space must be planned months ahead of any meal being eaten. Minimal quantities of fresh food can be taken into space, so seasonality is not a consideration. Rather, an approved list of pre-prepared foods are tasted by the astronauts, their selections are made, and menus for the complete mission are constructed for each one of them. Nutritional balance is an important consideration in the design of each menu, as is the need to ensure that favorite foods—including snacks like M&Ms—are included in sufficient quantities to keep morale boosted throughout the trip.

Exactly what the foods on the menu are depends largely on the space program. The Chinese *yuhangyuan* don't eat with chopsticks, but they do eat a recognizable Chinese cuisine with rice, meats, and vegetables in classic sauces of bean, chili and Sichuan pepper (kung pao chicken), or garlic, and fruit dishes; the Soviet Union's space program supplied Russian favorites like borscht (beet soup), pickled herring, and porridge; and the United States' food teams made sure they developed classic meat and vegetable dishes like chicken à la king and mashed potatoes, as well as hamburgers, hot dogs, and Thanksgiving dinners. The impact of space conditions seems to make most travelers crave strong flavors, so sauces are popular with every visitor—fresh onions and garlic for the Russians and chili sauce for the Americans.

Cooking

Astronauts open cans and packets and rehydrate and reheat fully pre-prepared meals. Storage problems and lack of refrigeration mean that there is little or no fresh food except at the very beginning of a mission or immediately after a resupply visit, but even if ingredients were available, there is no kitchen and no equipment to process it with. Every space capsule is a closed environment, so the production of fumes, steam, or, worst of all, smoke, is best avoided. Historically, there was barely enough room to move, and even now interior space is limited to a fairly tight 1,438 cubic yards (1,100 cubic meters) for six astronauts in the International Space Station. Making room for kitchen equipment would be an expensive undertaking, and it has never been a priority. The astronauts have a demanding work schedule, often cited as another important reason for freeing them from kitchen drudgery and providing ready-to-go convenience foods.

Everything that is consumed in space is prepared in advance—several months in advance—having been tested and tasted by the astronauts, who choose their menus as part of the preflight planning. The food is packaged carefully to minimize its weight and bulk and to reduce spoilage in the extreme and fluctuating conditions of space. The packaging often doubles as the serving dish, and a number of foods can be eaten straight from the package without the need for any utensils other than the scissors to open the bag.

The cooking techniques used on the ground vary according to the type of food being prepared. Historically, pureed foods in aluminum tubes, originally developed in the 1940s and 1950s for air force pilots who had to use pressurized headgear, were the archetypal space food for both the United States and the Soviet Union. Almost anything could be put into these containers, both savory and sweet. In the early 1960s, U.S. scientists put a lot of effort into developing bite-sized compressed foods, which were tested on some of the early Mercury missions. These foods were small, dehydrated cubes (coated in gelatins, starches, or oils to stop them from disintegrating) that would rehydrate in the mouth as they were chewed. They came in a number of flavors—bacon, cheese and crackers, toast, peanut butter, fruitcake—but it was hard to tell them apart without looking at the label. The astronauts found them unpleasant in the mouth and to the taste, and some of the coatings caused stomach upset, so they were discontinued.

Given the concerns about the weight and bulk of everything that is launched into space, dehydration has remained an important technique for preserving and preparing food for space travel. A wide range of freeze-dried meat- and vegetable-based meals were developed during the 1960s, first for the Gemini and then the Apollo missions. These foods were packed into plastic packages that would then have water injected into them before being massaged by hand to ensure even distribution of the water. The water used was a by-product of the fuel cells that operated the generators on board, but the Gemini capsule produced only cold water, which did little to increase the appeal of items like mashed potatoes. Apollo had warm water, which helped, although the need to knead the food probably did little for its texture and appearance. These types of foods continued to be developed and remain an important source of food on the Space Shuttle, and the range has increased to include fish dishes and breakfast foods as well as soups and casseroles and a variety of drinks provided in powdered form.

By the end of the 1960s there was another advance: thermostabilized wet meat products in plastic pouches or cans. These foods are heat-treated to destroy bacteria, in the same process as is used in normal canning. The Soviet Union used many canned foods on its missions from the earliest stages of the space race. It seems that the weight of the cans discouraged the United States from doing the same, so the development of the pouches was an important step forward in providing better and more familiar food for the astronauts. Thermostabilized foods are commonly warmed on board before being eaten with a spoon or fork. This type of packaging has become particularly used for fish, fruit, and puddings. More recently, irradiated food has been provided on the Space Shuttle. This technique helps to prolong the shelf life of smoked and fresh-cooked meats, fruit, and vegetables.

Bread has been variously provided in cans, pouches, and vacuum packs, all in an effort to reduce crumb production. Crumbs floating in a weightless cabin would, of course, be impossible to sweep up. The provision of tortillas instead of more traditional breads has helped overcome the crumb issue. The tortillas are preserved for up to 12 months by being packaged in a nitrogen atmosphere with an oxygen scavenger packet to ensure no mold can grow.

Everything prepared for space flight is given a technical name. "Intermediate-moisture" foods have long been a staple of the space larder and would simply be described as dried fruit or jerky by a non-astronaut. "Natural-form" foods like M&Ms, nuts, or granola bars would, equally, simply be called by their own name anywhere but in space. The preparation required on the ground is limited to putting them into appropriate secure and portion-controlled packaging. Condiments like ketchup and chili sauce are provided in individual pouches, requiring no special preparation before launch; but pepper and salt must be liquefied (pepper in oil and salt in water) and put into dropper bottles.

Typical Meals

The meals devised for space fit into to a typical Western pattern of three meals (breakfast, lunch, and dinner) with snacks. However, it is not clear that every mission conforms to this pattern in the timing of its meals. The workload is extensive, and the impact of being in space can reduce the appetite. Many meals are eaten on the move, alone, and without really taking a break.

Gemini Mashed Potatoes

Most of the processing of space food demands industrial techniques that are impossible to replicate domestically. The keen experimenter is limited to using common foods available in the local supermarket and attempting to replicate the space experience by improvising appropriate packaging.

1 package dehydrated mashed potatoes

1 ziplock bag with label

1 syringe

Cold water (quantity according to instructions on original package)

Carefully tip the dehydrated potatoes into the ziplock bag. Seal the bag. Measure the water into the syringe. Inject water into the bag, as close to the seal as possible. Gently massage the bag until the water is evenly distributed and the potato is hydrated. Open one corner of the package and eat with a teaspoon.

For Apollo mashed potatoes, follow the same procedure, but rehydrate with warm water instead of cold.

Eating Out

Every meal in space is a meal eaten in—although every meal in some sense lies far beyond the ordinary. Astronaut Michael Collins apparently devised his own Michelin-style grading system for space food, awarding helmets rather than stars for the items he most enjoyed, although it is not clear that any of the items on the menu would have been award winning back on Earth.

The best way to get a space meal that might come close to eating in a restaurant seems to be to invite a French *spationaut* to join one. From their earliest collaboration with the Russian program to the present day, French chefs have devised delicious meals for spationauts to share with their colleagues on special occasions. Richard Filippi, a chef and cookery school teacher, worked on the first of these dishes in the mid- to late 1990s, developing magnificent delicacies for Mir. In 1996 Claudie Haigneré treated her fellow cosmonauts to beef daube, confit of duck with capers, pigeons in wine, and a rich tomato sauce, all washed down with wine from the Alsace. Filippi's other dishes were sent to Mir with French spationauts throughout the 1990s: squid in lobster sauce, toffee rice pudding, and, most spectacular, whole quail cooked in wine sauce, then deboned, sliced, and reassembled (including its wings) into a 3.5-ounce can.

More recently, space tourism has given a boost to the idea of restaurant-quality food in space, with chefs like Emeril Lagasse and television cooks like Martha Stewart and Rachel Ray contributing ideas and recipes to the development teams. Bringing a feast to share with the crew has become a component of the experience for the visitor.

Looking further to the future, Michelin-starred chef Alain Ducasse has turned his attention to fine dining for a possible mission to Mars, devising exquisite vegetarian recipes from the foods that could be grown on board or at a base on Mars: Martian bread with green tomato jam, spirulina gnocchi, tomato and potato mille-feuille. He's even said he would open a restaurant there, so perhaps there is hope for a future of eating very far out indeed.

Special Occasions

Creating an environment that can feel as much like home as possible is a tremendously important consideration for the crews, which means that providing familiar foods is the priority in food provisioning. Of course, occasional treats are part of fostering team spirit and boosting morale. The Soviet Union used to send caviar to the cosmonauts for New Year and birthday celebrations, and the United States developed Thanksgiving and Christmas meals for its astronauts in the Apollo program. Individual teams on long-term missions in space have developed their own traditional treat foods, like Shannon Lucid's Sunday night Jell-O parties with her colleagues on Mir in the mid-1990s.

Diet and Health

Health is a primary concern on all space missions, and every facet of the astronaut's physiology and metabolism is scrupulously monitored, especially given the unique circumstances of weightlessness and the tendency to lose muscle mass and experience other forms of fatigue. The dietary composition of space food is likewise carefully analyzed by nutritionists and naturally changes with the development of nutritional science over the decades since humans were first sent into space.

Jane Levi

Further Reading

Bourland, Charles T., and Gregory L. Vogt. *The Astronaut's Cookbook: Tales, Recipes and More.* New York: Springer, 2009.

"Space Food." National Aeronautics and Space Administration. http://spaceflight.nasa.gov/living/spacefood/index.html.

About the Editor and Contributors

Ken Albala, Editor, is professor of history at the University of the Pacific in Stockton, California. He also teaches in the gastronomy program at Boston University. Albala is the author of many books, including *Eating Right in the Renaissance* (University of California Press, 2002), *Food in Early Modern Europe* (Greenwood Press, 2003), *Cooking in Europe 1250–1650* (Greenwood Press, 2005), *The Banquet: Dining in the Great Courts of Late Renaissance Europe* (University of Illinois Press, 2007), *Beans: A History* (Berg Publishers, 2007; winner of the 2008 International Association of Culinary Professionals Jane Grigson Award), and *Pancake* (Reaktion Press, 2008). He has co-edited two works, *The Business of Food* and *Human Cuisine.* He is also editor of three food series with 29 volumes in print, including the Food Cultures Around the World series for Greenwood Press. Albala is also co-editor of the journal *Food Culture and Society.* He is currently researching a history of theological controversies surrounding fasting in the Reformation Era and is editing two collected volumes of essays, one on the Renaissance and the other entitled *The Lord's Supper.* He has also coauthored a cookbook for Penguin/Perigee entitled *The Lost Art of Real Cooking,* which was released in July 2010.

Julia Abramson has visited France on a regular basis for more than 25 years to study, research, travel, and eat. She has published essays on aspects of food culture from vegetable carving to gastronomic writing and is the author of the book *Food Culture in France.* Abramson teaches French literature and culture and food studies at the University of Oklahoma, Norman.

M. Shahrim Al-Karim is a senior lecturer of food service and hospitality management at the Universiti Putra Malaysia. His research interests include food and culture, culinary tourism, food habits, and consumer behavior. He received a BS in hotel and restaurant management from New York University; an MBA from Universiti Teknologi MARA, Malaysia; and a PhD in hospitality and tourism from Oklahoma State University, United States.

E. N. Anderson is professor emeritus of the Department of Anthropology, University of California, Riverside.

Laura P. Appell-Warren holds a doctorate in psychological anthropology from Harvard University. Her primary focus of research has been the study of personhood; however, she has also studied the effects of social change on children's play. She has done research among the Bulusu' of East Kalimantan, Indonesia, and among the Rungus Momogon, a Dusunic-speaking peoples, of Sabah, Malyasia. In addition, she has traveled widely throughout Arctic Canada. She is the editor of *The Iban Diaries of Monica Freeman 1949–1951: Including Ethnographic Drawings, Sketches, Paintings, Photographs and Letters* and is author of the forthcoming volume entitled *Personhood: An Examination of the History and Use of an Anthropological Concept.* In addition to her current research on cradleboard use among Native North Americans, she is a teacher of anthropology at St. Mark's School in Southborough, Massachusetts.

Heather Arndt-Anderson is a Portland, Oregon, native who draws culinary inspiration from many world cuisines but prefers cooking from her own backyard. She is a part-time natural resources consultant and a full-time radical homemaker; in her (rare) spare time she writes the food blog *Voodoo & Sauce.*

Michael Ashkenazi is a scholar, writer, and consultant who has been researching and writing about Japanese food since 1990. In addition to books and articles on Japanese society, including its food culture, he has written numerous scholarly and professional articles and papers on various subjects including theoretical and methodological issues in anthropology, organized violence, space exploration, migration, religion and ritual, resettling ex-combatants, and small arms. He has taught at higher-education institutions in Japan, Canada, Israel, and the United Kingdom, directing graduate and undergraduate students. He is currently senior researcher and project leader at the Bonn International Center for Conversion in Germany, with responsibility for the areas of small arms and reintegration of ex-combatants. He has conducted field research in East and Southeast Asia, East and West Africa, the Middle East, and Latin America.

Babette Audant went to Prague after college, where she quickly gave up teaching English in order to cook at a classical French restaurant. After graduating from the Culinary Institute of America, she worked as a chef in New York City for eight years, working at Rainbow Room, Beacon Bar & Grill, and other top-rated restaurants. She is a lecturer at City University of New York Kingsborough's Department of Tourism and Hospitality, and a doctoral candidate in geography at the City University of New York Graduate Center. Her research focuses on public markets and food policy in New York City.

Gabriela Villagran Backman, MA (English and Hispanic literature), was born in Sweden and raised in Mexico and the United States; she currently lives in Stockholm, Sweden. She is an independent researcher, interested in food studies, cultural heritage, writing cookbooks, red wine, and the Internet.

Carolyn Bánfalvi is a writer based in Budapest. She is the author of *Food Wine Budapest* (Little Bookroom) and *The Food and Wine Lover's Guide to Hungary: With Budapest Restaurants and Trips to the Wine Country* (Park Kiado). She contributes to numerous international food and travel publications and leads food and wine tours through Taste Hungary, her culinary tour company.

Peter Barrett is a painter who writes a food blog and is also the Food & Drink writer for *Chronogram Magazine* in New York's Hudson Valley.

Cynthia D. Bertelsen is an independent culinary scholar, nutritionist, freelance food writer, and food columnist. She lived in Haiti for three years and worked on a food-consumption study for a farming-systems project in Jacmel, Haiti. She writes a food history blog, *Gherkins & Tomatoes,* found at http://gherkinstoma toes.com.

Megan K. Blake is a senior lecturer in geography at the University of Sheffield. She has published research that examines the intersections between place and social practices. While her previous work focused on entrepreneurship and innovation, her recent work has examined food practices and family life.

Janet Boileau is a culinary historian who holds a master of arts degree in gastronomy from Le Cordon Bleu Paris and a doctorate in history from the University of Adelaide.

Andrea Broomfield is associate professor of English at Johnson County Community College in Overland Park, Kansas, and author of *Food and Cooking in Victorian England: A History.*

Cynthia Clampitt is a culinary historian, world traveler, and award-winning author. In 2010, she was elected to the Society of Women Geographers.

Neil L. Coletta is assistant director of food, wine, and the arts and lecturer in the MLA in gastronomy program at Boston University. His current research includes food and aesthetics and experimental pedagogy in the field of food studies.

Paul Crask is a travel writer and the author of two travel guides: *Dominica* (2008) and *Grenada, Carriacou and Petite Martinique* (2009).

Christine Crawford-Oppenheimer is the information services librarian and archivist at the Culinary Institute of America. She grew up in Ras Tanura, Saudi Arabia.

Anita Verna Crofts is on the faculty at the University of Washington's Department of Communication, where she serves as an associate director of the master of communication in digital media program. In addition, she holds an appointment at the University of Washington's Department of Global Health, where she collaborates with partner institutions in Sudan, Namibia, and India on trainings that address leadership, management, and policy development, with her contributions targeted at the concept of storytelling as a leadership and evidence tool. Anita is an intrepid chowhound and publishes on gastroethnographic topics related to the intersection of food and identity. She hosts the blog *Sneeze!* at her Web site www.pepperforthebeast.com.

Liza Debevec is a research fellow at the Scientific Research Centre of the Slovene Academy of sciences and arts in Ljubljana, Slovenia. She has a PhD in social anthropology from the University of St. Andrews, United Kingdom. Her research interests are West Africa and Burkina Faso, food studies, Islam, gender, identity, and practice of everyday life.

Jonathan Deutsch is associate professor of culinary arts at Kingsborough Community College, City University of New York, and Public Health, City University of New York Graduate Center. He is the author or editor of five books including, with Sarah Billingsley, *Culinary Improvisation* (Pearson, 2010) and, with Annie Hauck-Lawson, *Gastropolis: Food and New York City* (Columbia University Press, 2009).

Deborah Duchon is a nutritional anthropologist in Atlanta, Georgia.

Nathalie Dupree is the author of 10 cookbooks, many of which are about the American South, for which she has won two James Beard Awards. She has hosted over 300 television shows on the Public Broadcasting Service, The Food Network, and TLC. She lives with her husband, Jack Bass, who has authored 9 books about the American South and helped with her contribution to *Food Cultures of the World.*

Pamela Elder has worked in food public relations and online culinary education and is a freelance writer in the San Francisco Bay area.

Rachel Finn is a freelance writer whose work has appeared in various print and online publications. She is the founder and director of Roots Cuisine, a non-profit organization dedicated to promoting the foodways of the African diaspora around the globe.

Richard Foss has been a food writer and culinary historian since 1986, when he started as a restaurant critic for the *Los Angeles Reader*. His book on the history of rum is slated for publication in 2011, to be followed by a book on the history of beachside dining in Los Angeles. He is also a science fiction and fantasy author, an instructor in culinary history and Elizabethan theater at the University of California, Los Angeles, Extension, and is on the board of the Culinary Historians of Southern California.

Nancy G. Freeman is a food writer and art historian living in Berkeley, California, with a passion for food history. She has written about cuisines ranging from Ethiopia to the Philippines to the American South.

Ramin Ganeshram is a veteran journalist and professional chef trained at the Institute of Culinary Education in New York City, where she has also worked as a recreational chef instructor. Ganeshram also holds a master's degree in journalism from Columbia University. For eight years she worked as a feature writer/ stringer for the *New York Times* regional sections, and she spent another eight years as a food columnist and feature writer for *Newsday*. She is the author of *Sweet Hands: Island Cooking from Trinidad and Tobago* (Hippocrene NY, 2006; 2nd expanded edition, 2010) and *Stir It Up* (Scholastic, 2011). In addition to contributing to a variety of food publications including *Saveur, Gourmet, Bon Appetit,* and epicurious.com, Ganeshram has written articles on food, culture, and travel for *Islands* (as contributing editor), *National Geographic Traveler,*

Forbes Traveler, Forbes Four Seasons, and many others. Currently, Ganeshram teaches food writing for New York University's School of Continuing Professional Studies.

Hanna Garth is a doctoral candidate in the Department of Anthropology at the University of California, Los Angeles. She is currently working on a dissertation on household food practices in Santiago de Cuba. Previously, she has conducted research on food culture, health, and nutrition in Cuba, Chile, and the Philippines.

Mary Gee is a medical sociology doctoral student at the University of California, San Francisco. Her current research interests include herbalism and Asian and Asian American foodways, especially with regards to multigenerational differences. Since 1995, she has actively worked with local and national eating disorders research and policy and advocacy organizations as well as for a program evaluation research consulting firm.

Che Ann Abdul Ghani holds a bachelor's degree in English and a master's degree in linguistics. She has a keen interest in studying language and language use in gastronomy. She is currently attached to the English Department at Universiti Putra Malaysia. Her research interests range from the use of language in context (pragmatics) to language use in multidisciplinary areas, namely, disciplines related to the social sciences. She also carries out work in translation and editing.

Maja Godina-Golija is research adviser at the Institute of Slovenian Ethnology, Scientific Research Centre of Slovenian Academy of Science and Arts, Ljubljana, Slovenia.

Annie Goldberg is a graduate student studying gastronomy at Boston University.

Darra Goldstein is Frances Christopher Oakley Third Century Professor of Russian at Williams College and the founding editor-in-chief of *Gastronomica: The Journal of Food and Culture.*

Keiko Goto, PhD, is associate professor at the Department of Nutrition and Food Sciences, California State University, Chico. Dr. Goto has more than 15 years of work experience in the field of nutrition and has worked as a practitioner and researcher in various developing countries. Dr. Goto's current research areas include food and culture, child and adolescent nutrition, sustainable food systems, and international nutrition.

Carla Guerrón Montero is a cultural and applied anthropologist trained in Latin America and the United States. She is currently associate professor of anthropology in the Department of Anthropology at the University of Delaware. Dr. Guerrón Montero's areas of expertise include gender, ethnicity, and identity; processes of globalization/nationalism, and particularly tourism; and social justice and human rights.

Mary Gunderson calls her practice paleocuisineology, where food and cooking bring cultures alive. Through many media, including the sites HistoryCooks.com and MaryGunderson.com, she writes and speaks about South and North American food history and contemporary creative living and wellness. She wrote and published the award-winning book *The Food Journal of Lewis and Clark: Recipes for an Expedition* (History Cooks, 2003) and has authored six food-history books for kids.

Liora Gvion is a senior lecturer at the Kibbutzim College of Education and also teaches at the Faculty of Agriculture, Food and Environment at the Institute of Biochemistry, Food Science and Nutrition Hebrew University of Jerusalem.

Cherie Y. Hamilton is a cookbook author and specialist on the food cultures and cuisines of the Portuguese-speaking countries in Europe, South America, Africa, and Asia.

Jessica B. Harris teaches English at Queens College/City University of New York and is director of the Institute for the Study of Culinary Cultures at Dillard University.

Melanie Haupt is a doctoral candidate in English at the University of Texas at Austin. Her dissertation, "Starting from Scratch: Reading Women's Cooking Communities," explores women's use of cookbooks and recipes in the formation and reification of real and virtual communities.

Ursula Heinzelmann is an independent scholar and culinary historian, twice awarded the prestigious Sophie Coe Prize. A trained chef, sommelier, and ex-restaurateur, she now works as a freelance wine and food writer and journalist based in Berlin, Germany.

Jennifer Hostetter is an independent food consultant specializing in writing, research, and editing. She has degrees in history and culinary arts and holds a master's degree in food culture and communications from the University of Gastronomic Sciences in Italy. She also served as editorial assistant for this encyclopedia.

Kelila Jaffe is a doctoral candidate in the Food Studies Program at New York University. Originally from Sonoma, California, and the daughter of a professional chef, she has pursued anthropological and archaeological foodways research since her entry into academia. She received a BA with distinction in anthropology from the University of Pennsylvania, before attending the University of Auckland, where she earned an MA with honors in anthropology, concentrating in archaeology. Her research interests include past foodways, domestication, and zooarchaeology, and she has conducted fieldwork in Fiji, New Zealand, and Hawaii.

Zilkia Janer is associate professor of global studies at Hofstra University in New York. She is the author of *Puerto Rican Nation-Building Literature: Impossible Romance* (2005) and *Latino Food Culture* (2008).

Brelyn Johnson is a graduate of the master's program in food studies at New York University.

Kate Johnston is currently based in Italy, where she is an independent cultural food researcher and writer and a daily ethnographer of people's food habits. She has a degree in anthropology from Macquarie University in Sydney, Australia, and a recent master's degree in food culture and communication from the University of Gastronomic Sciences, Italy. She was also editorial assistant for this encyclopedia.

Desiree Koh was born and raised in Singapore. A writer focusing on travel, hospitality, sports, fitness, business, and, of course, food, Koh's explorations across the globe always begin at the market, as she believes that the sight, scent, and savoring of native produce and cuisine are the key to the city's heart. The first and only female in Major League Eating's Asia debut, Koh retired from competition to better focus on each nibble and sip of fine, hopefully slow food.

Bruce Kraig is emeritus professor of history at Roosevelt University in Chicago and adjunct faculty at the Culinary School of Kendall College, Chicago. He has published and edited widely in the field of American and world food history. Kraig is also the founding president of the Culinary Historians of Chicago and the Greater Midwest Foodways Alliance.

R. J. Krajewski is the research services librarian at Simmons College, where among other things he facilitates discovery of food-culture research, especially through the lens of race, class, and gender. His own engagement with food is seasonally and locally rooted, starting in his own small, urban homestead, much like his Polish and German ancestors.

Erin Laverty is a freelance food writer and researcher based in Brooklyn, New York. She holds a master's degree in food studies from New York University.

Robert A. Leonard has a PhD in theoretical linguistics from Columbia. He studies the way people create and communicate meaning, including through food. He was born in Brooklyn and trained as a cook and *panaderia-reposteria* manager in the Caribbean; his doctoral studies led him to eight years of fieldwork in language, culture, and food in Africa and Southeast Asia. In the arts, as an undergraduate he cofounded and led the rock group Sha Na Na and with them opened for their friend Jimi Hendrix at the Woodstock Festival. Leonard is probably one of a very few people who have worked with both the Grateful Dead and the Federal Bureau of Investigation, which in recent years recruited him to teach the emerging science of forensic linguistics at Quantico.

Jane Levi is an independent consultant and writer based in London, England. She is currently working on her PhD at the London Consortium, examining food in utopias, funded by her work on post-trade financial policy in the City of London.

Yrsa Lindqvist is a European ethnologist working as the leading archivist at the Folk Culture Archive in Helsinki. Her research about food and eating habits in the late 1990s, combined with earlier collections at the archive, resulted in 2009 in the publication *Mat, Måltid, Minne. Hundraår av finlandssvensk matkulur.* The book analyzes the changes in housekeeping and attitudes toward food. She has also contributed to other publications focusing on identity questions and has worked as a junior researcher at the Academy of Finland.

William G. Lockwood is professor emeritus of cultural anthropology at the University of Michigan. His central interest is ethnicity and interethnic relations. He has conducted long-term field research in Bosnia-Herzegovina and the Croatian community in Austria and also among Roma and with a variety of ethnic groups in America, including Arabs, Finns, and Bosnians. He has long held a special interest in how food functions in ethnic group maintenance and in reflecting intra- and intergroup relations.

Yvonne R. Lockwood is curator emeritus of folklife at the Michigan State University Museum. Her formal training is in folklore, history, and Slavic languages and literatures. Research in Bosnia, Austria, and the United States, especially the Great Lakes region, has resulted in numerous publications, exhibitions, festival presentations, and workshops focused on her primary interests of foodways and ethnic traditions.

Janet Long-Solís, an anthropologist and archaeologist, is a research associate at the Institute of Historical Research at the National University of Mexico. She has published several books and articles on the chili pepper, the history of Mexican food, and the exchange of food products between Europe and the Americas in the 16th century.

Kristina Lupp has a background in professional cooking and has worked in Toronto and Florence. She is currently pursuing a master of arts in gastronomy at the University of Adelaide.

Máirtín Mac Con Iomaire is a lecturer in culinary arts in the Dublin Institute of Technology. Máirtín is well known as a chef, culinary historian, food writer, broadcaster, and ballad singer. He lives in Dublin with his wife and two daughters. He was the first Irish chef to be awarded a PhD, for his oral history of Dublin restaurants.

Glenn R. Mack is a food historian with extensive culinary training in Uzbekistan, Russia, Italy, and the United States. He cofounded the Culinary Academy of Austin and the Historic Foodways Group of Austin and currently serves as president of Le Cordon Bleu College of Culinary Arts Atlanta.

Andrea MacRae is a lecturer in the Le Cordon Bleu Graduate Program in Gastronomy at the University of Adelaide, Australia.

Giorgos Maltezakis earned his PhD in anthropology with research in cooperation with the Institute Studiorium Humanitatis of the Ljubljana Graduate School of the Humanities. His dissertation was on consumerism, the global market, and food, which was an ethnographic approach to the perception of food in Greece and Slovenia.

Bertie Mandelblatt is assistant professor at the University of Toronto, cross-appointed to the departments of Historical Studies and Geography. Her research concerns the early-modern French Atlantic, with a focus on commodity exchanges at the local and global scales: Her two current projects are the history of food provisioning in the Franco-Caribbean and the transatlantic circulation of French rum and molasses, both in the 17th and 18th centuries.

Marty Martindale is a freelance writer living in Largo, Florida.

Laura Mason is a writer and food historian with a special interest in local, regional, and traditional foods in the United Kingdom and elsewhere. Her career has explored many dimensions of food and food production, including cooking for a living, unraveling the history of sugar confectionery, and trying to work out how many traditional and typically British foods relate to culture and landscape. Her publications include *Taste of Britain* (with Catherine Brown; HarperCollins, 2006), *The Food Culture of Great Britain* (Greenwood, 2004), and *The National Trust Farmhouse Cookbook* (National Trust, 2009).

Anton Masterovoy is a PhD candidate at the Graduate Center, City University of New York. He is working on his dissertation, titled "Eating Soviet: Food and Culture in USSR, 1917–1991."

Anne Engammare McBride, a Swiss native, food writer, and editor, is the director of the Experimental Cuisine Collective and a food studies PhD candidate at New York University. Her most recent book is *Culinary Careers: How to Get Your Dream Job in Food,* coauthored with Rick Smilow.

Michael R. McDonald is associate professor of anthropology at Florida Gulf Coast University. He is the author of *Food Culture in Central America.*

Naomi M. McPherson is associate professor of cultural anthropology and graduate program coordinator at the University of British Columbia, Okanagan Campus. Since 1981, she has accumulated over three years of field research with the Bariai of West New Britain, Papua New Guinea.

Katrina Meynink is an Australia-based freelance food writer and researcher. She has a master's degree in gastronomy through Le Cordon Bleu and the University of Adelaide under a scholarship from the James Beard Foundation. She is currently completing her first cookbook.

Barbara J. Michael is a sociocultural anthropologist whose research focuses on social organization, economics, decision making, and gender. Her geographic focus is on the Middle East and East Africa, where she has done research with the pastoral nomadic Hawazma Baggara and on traditional medicine in Yemen and is working on a video about men's cafes as a social institution. She teaches anthropology at the University of North Carolina Wilmington and has also worked as a consultant for several United Nations agencies.

Diana Mincyte is a fellow at the Rachel Carson Center at the Ludwig Maximilian University-Munich and visiting assistant professor in the Department of Advertising at the University of Illinois, Urbana-Champaign. Mincyte examines topics at the interface of food, the environment, risk society, and global inequalities. Her book investigates raw-milk politics in the European Union to consider the production risk society and its institutions in post-Socialist states.

Rebecca Moore is a doctoral student studying the history of biotechnology at the University of Toronto in Ontario, Canada.

Nawal Nasrallah, a native of Iraq, was a professor of English and comparative literature at the universities of Baghdad and Mosul until 1990. As an independent scholar, she wrote the award-winning *Delights from the Garden of Eden: A Cookbook and a History of the Iraqi Cuisine* and *Annals of the Caliphs' Kitchens* (an English translation of Ibn Sayyar al-Warraq's 10th-century Baghdadi cookbook).

Henry Notaker graduated from the University of Oslo with a degree in literature and worked for many years as a foreign correspondent and host of arts and letters shows on Norwegian national television. He has written several books about food history, and with *Food Culture in Scandinavia* he won the Gourmand World Cookbook Award for best culinary history in 2009. His last book is a bibliography of early-modern culinary literature, *Printed Cookbooks in Europe 1470–1700.* He is a member of the editorial board of the journal *Food and History.*

Kelly O'Leary is a graduate student at Boston University in gastronomy and food studies and executive chef at the Bayridge University Residence and Cultural Center.

Fabio Parasecoli is associate professor and coordinator of food studies at the New School in New York City. He is author of *Food Culture in Italy* (2004) and *Bite Me: Food and Popular Culture* (2008).

Susan Ji-Young Park is the program director and head of curriculum development at École de Cuisine Pasadena (www.ecolecuisine.com); project leader for Green Algeria, a national environmental initiative; and a writer for LAWEEKLY'S Squid Ink. She has written curriculum for cooking classes at Los Angeles Unified School District, Sur La Table, Whole Foods Market, Central Market, and Le Cordon Bleu North America. She and her husband, Chef Farid Zadi, have co-written recipes for *Gourmet Magazine* and the *Los Angeles Times.* The couple are currently writing several cookbooks on North African, French, and Korean cuisines.

Rosemary Parkinson is author of *Culinaria: The Caribbean, Nyam Jamaica,* and *Barbados Bu'n-Bu'n,* and she contributes culinary travel stories to Caribbean magazines.

Charles Perry majored in Middle East languages at Princeton University, the University of California, Berkeley, and the Middle East Centre for Arab Studies, Shimlan, Lebanon. From 1968 to 1976 he was a copy editor and staff writer at *Rolling Stone* magazine in San Francisco, before leaving to work as a freelance writer specializing in food. From 1990 to 2008, he was a staff writer in the food section of the *Los Angeles Times.* He has published widely on the history of Middle Eastern food and was a major contributor to the *Oxford Companion to Food* (1999).

Irina Petrosian is a native of Armenia and a professional journalist who has written for Russian, Armenian, and U.S.-based newspapers. She is the coauthor of

Armenian Food: Fact, Fiction, and Folklore and holds degrees in journalism from Moscow State University and Indiana University.

Suzanne Piscopo is a nutrition, family, and consumer studies lecturer at the University of Malta in Malta. She is mainly involved in the training of home economics and primary-level teachers, as well as in nutrition and consumer-education projects in different settings. Suzanne is a registered public health nutritionist, and her research interests focus on socioecological determinants of food intake, nutrition interventions, and health promotion. She has also written a series of short stories for children about food. Suzanne enjoys teaching and learning about the history and culture of food and is known to creatively experiment with the ingredients at hand when cooking the evening meal together with her husband, Michael.

Theresa Preston-Werner is an advanced graduate student in anthropology at Northwestern University.

Meg Ragland is a culinary history researcher and librarian. She lives in Boston, Massachusetts.

Carol Selva Rajah is an award-winning chef and food writer currently based in Sydney, Australia. She has written 10 cookbooks on Malaysian and Southeast Asian cuisine. Her book *The Food of India* won the gold award for the Best Hardcover Recipe Book at the prestigious Jacob's Creek World Food Media Awards.

Birgit Ricquier is pursuing a PhD in linguistics at the Université Libre de Bruxelles and the Royal Museum for Central Africa, Tervuren, Belgium, with a fellowship from the Fonds de la Recherche Scientifique (FNRS). The topic of her PhD project is "A Comparative Linguistic Approach to the History of Culinary Practice in Bantu-Speaking Africa." She has spent several months in central Africa, including one month in the Democratic Republic of the Congo as a member of the Boyekoli Ebale Congo 2010 Expedition and two months of research focused on food cultures in Congo.

Amy Riolo is an award-winning author, lecturer, cooking instructor, and consultant. She is the author of *Arabian Delights: Recipes and Princely Entertaining Ideas from the Arabian Peninsula, Nile Style: Egyptian Cuisine and Culture,* and *The Mediterranean Diabetes Cookbook.* Amy has lived, worked, and traveled extensively through Egypt and enjoys fusing cuisine, culture, and history into all aspects of her work. Please see www.amyriolo.com, www.baltimoreegypt.org, and diningwithdiplomats.blogspot.com for more information and further reading.

Owen Roberts is a journalist, communications instructor, and director of research communications for the University of Guelph in Guelph, Ontario, Canada. He holds a doctorate of education from Texas Tech University and Texas A&M University.

Fiona Ross is a gastrodetective whose headquarters is the Bodleian Library in Oxford, United Kingdom. She spends her time there investigating the eating foibles of the famous and infamous. Her cookery book *Dining with Destiny* is the result: When you want to know what Lenin lunched on or what JFK ate by the poolside, *Dining with Destiny* has the answer.

Signe Rousseau (née Hansen) is Danish by birth but a long-term resident of southern Africa and is a researcher and part-time lecturer at the University of Cape Town. Following an MA in the Department of English and a PhD (on food media and celebrity chefs) in the Centre for Film and Media Studies, she now teaches critical literacy and professional communication in the School of Management Studies (Faculty of Commerce).

Kathleen Ryan is a consulting scholar in the African Section of the University of Pennsylvania Museum of Archaeology and Anthropology, Philadelphia. She has carried out research in Kenya since 1990, when she began a study of Maasai cattle herders in Kajiado District.

Helen Saberi was Alan Davidson's principal assistant in the completion of the *Oxford Companion to Food*. She is the author of *Noshe Djan: Afghan Food and Cookery;* coauthor of *Trifle* with Alan Davidson; and coauthor of *The Road to Vindaloo* with David Burnett; her latest book is *Tea: A Global History.*

Cari Sánchez holds a master of arts in gastronomy from the University of Adelaide/Le Cordon Bleu in South Australia. Her dissertation explores the global spread of the Argentine *asado*. She currently lives in Jacksonville, Florida, where she writes the food and travel blog *viCARIous* and is the marketing manager for a craft brewery.

Peter Scholliers teaches history at the Vrije Universiteit Brussel and is currently head of the research group "Social and Cultural Food Studies" (FOST). He studies the history of food in Europe in the 19th and 20th centuries. He co-edits the journal *Food and History* and is involved in various ways in the Institut Européen d'Histoire et des Cultures de l'Alimentation (Tours, France). Recently, he published *Food Culture in Belgium* (Greenwood, 2008). More information can be found at http://www.vub.ac.be/FOST/fost_in_english/.

Colleen Taylor Sen is the author of *Food Culture in India; Curry: A Global History; Pakoras, Paneer, Pappadums: A Guide to Indian Restaurant Menus,* and many articles on the food of the Indian Subcontinent. She is a regular participant in the Oxford Food Symposium.

Roger Serunyigo was born and lives in Kampala, Uganda. He graduated from Makerere University with a degree in urban and regional planning, has worked in telecommunications, and is now a professional basketball player for the Uganda National Team. He also coaches a women's basketball team (The Magic Stormers).

Dorette Snover is a chef and author. Influenced by French heritage and the food traditions of the Pennsylvania Dutch country, Chef Snover teaches exploration of the world via a culinary map at her school, C'est si Bon! in Chapel Hill. While the stock simmers, she is writing a novel about a French bread apprentice.

Celia Sorhaindo is a freelance photographer and writer. She was the editor of the 2008 and 2009 *Dominica Food and Drink Guide* magazine and content manager for the Dominica section of the magazine *Caribbean Homes & Lifestyle.*

Lyra Spang is a PhD candidate in the Department of Anthropology and the Food Studies Program at Indiana University. She has written about food, sex, and symbolism; the role of place in defining organic; and the importance of social relationships in small-scale food business in Belize. She grew up on a farm in southern Belize and is a proud promoter of that country's unique and diverse culinary heritage.

Lois Stanford is an agricultural anthropologist in the Department of Anthropology at New Mexico State University. In her research, she has examined the globalization of food systems both in Mexico and in the U.S. Southwest. Her current research focuses on the critical role of food heritage and plant conservation in constructing and maintaining traditional foodways and cultural identity in New Mexico. In collaboration with local food groups, she is currently developing a community food assessment project in the Mesilla Valley in southern New Mexico.

Aliza Stark is a senior faculty member at the Agriculture, Food, and Environment Institute of Biochemistry, Food Science, and Nutrition at the Hebrew University of Jerusalem.

Maria "Ging" Gutierrez Steinberg is a marketing manager for a New York City–based specialty food company and a food writer. She has a master's degree in food studies from New York University and is a graduate of Le Cordon Bleu. Her articles have appeared in various publications in Asia and the United States.

Anita Stewart is a cookbook author and Canadian culinary activist from Elora, Ontario, Canada.

Emily Stone has written about Guatemalan cuisine in the *Radcliffe Culinary Times,* and she is at work on a nonfiction book about chocolate in Central America. She currently teaches journalism and creative writing at Sun Yat-sen University in Guangzhou, China.

Asele Surina is a Russian native and former journalist who now works as a translator and interpreter. Since 1999 she has worked at the Institute of Classical Archaeology at the University of Texas on joint projects with an archaeological museum in Crimea, Ukraine.

Aylin Öney Tan is an architect by training and studied conservation of historic structures in Turkey, Italy, and the United Kingdom. Eventually, her passion for food and travel led her to write on food. Since 2003, she has had a weekly food column in *Cumhuriyet,* a prestigious national daily, and contributes to various food magazines. She was a jury member of the Slow Food Award 2000–2003, with her nominees receiving awards. She contributes to the Terra Madre and Presidia projects as the leader of the Ankara Convivium. She won the Sophie Coe Award on food history in 2008 for her article "Poppy: Potent yet Frail," presented previously at the Oxford Symposium on Food and Cookery where she's become a regular presenter. Currently, she is the curator of the Culinary Culture Section of Princess Islands' City Museum. She is happy to unite her expertise in archaeology and art history from her previous career with her unbounded interest in food culture.

Nicole Tarulevicz teaches at the School of Asian Languages and Studies at the University of Tasmania.

Karen Lau Taylor is a freelance food writer and consultant whose food curriculum vitae includes a master's degree in food studies from New York University, an advanced certificate from the Wine and Spirits Education Trust, and a gig as pastry cook at a five-star hotel after completing L'Academie de Cuisine's pastry arts program. She is working toward a master's degree in public health while she continues to write, teach, test recipes, eat, and drink from her home in Alexandria, Virginia.

Thy Tran is trained as a professional chef. She established Wandering Spoon to provide cooking classes, culinary consultation, and educational programming for culinary academies and nonprofit organizations throughout Northern California. Currently, she is a chef instructor at the International Culinary Schools at the Art Institute of California–San Francisco and Tante Marie's. She is also the founder and director of the Asian Culinary Forum. She co-authored *The Essentials of Asian Cooking, Taste of the World,* and the award-winning guide, *Kitchen Companion.*

Leena Trivedi-Grenier is a Bay-area food writer, cooking teacher, and social media consultant. Her writings have appeared in *The Business of Food: Encyclopedia of the Food and Drink Industry, Culinary Trends* magazine, and the *Cultural Arts Resources for Teachers and Students* newsletter and will be featured in several upcoming titles by Greenwood Press. She also runs a food/travel/gastronomy blog called *Leena Eats This Blog* (www.leenaeats.com).

Karin Vaneker graduated from the AKI Academy of Visual Arts in Enschede, the Netherlands. She later attended Sint-Lukas Hoger Instituut voor Schone Kunsten in Brussels, Belgium. She has written for numerous Dutch newspapers and magazines, specializing in trends and the cultural and other histories of ingredients and cuisines, and has published several books. Furthermore, Vaneker has worked for museums and curated an exhibition about New World taro (L. *Xanthosoma* spp.). At present she is researching its potential in domestic cuisines and gastronomy.

Penny Van Esterik is professor of anthropology at York University, Toronto, where she teaches nutritional anthropology, advocacy anthropology, and feminist theory. She does fieldwork in Southeast Asia and has developed materials on breast-feeding and women's work and infant and young child feeding.

Richard Wilk is professor of anthropology and gender studies at Indiana University, where he directs the Food Studies Program. With a PhD in anthropology from the University of Arizona, he has taught at the University of California,

Berkeley; University of California, Santa Cruz; New Mexico State University; and University College London and has held fellowships at Gothenburg University and the University of London. His publications include more than 125 papers and book chapters, a textbook in economic anthropology, and several edited volumes. His most recent books are *Home Cooking in the Global Village* (Berg Publishers), *Off the Edge: Experiments in Cultural Analysis* (with Orvar Lofgren; Museum Tusculanum Press), *Fast Food/Slow Food* (Altamira Press), and *Time, Consumption, and Everyday Life* (with Elizabeth Shove and Frank Trentmann; Berg Publishers).

Chelsie Yount is a PhD student of anthropology at Northwestern University in Evanston, Illinois. She lived in Senegal in 2005 and again in 2008, when performing ethnographic research for her master's thesis at the École des Hautes Études en Sciences Sociales in Paris, on the topic of Senegalese food and eating habits.

Marcia Zoladz is a cook, food writer, and food-history researcher with her own Web site, Cozinha da Marcia (Marcia's Kitchen; www.cozinhadamarcia.com.br). She is a regular participant and contributor at the Oxford Symposium on Food and History and has published three books in Brazil, Germany, and Holland— *Cozinha Portuguesa* (Portuguese cooking), *Muito Prazer* (Easy recipes), and *Brigadeiros e Bolinhas* (Sweet and savory Brazilian finger foods).

Index

Boldface numbers refer to volume numbers. A key appears on all verso pages.